ASTROLOGICAL

POCKET

PLANNER

Copyright © 2015 Llewellyn Worldwide Ltd. All rights reserved.
ISBN-13: 978-0-7387-3408-8

Cover design by Adrienne Zimiga
Zodiac Circle: © 2009 Classix/iStockphoto.com
Designed by Susan Van Sant
Edited by Ed Day

A special thanks to Phoebe Aina Allen for astrological proofreading.

Astrological calculations compiled and programmed by Rique Pottenger based on
the earlier work of Neil F. Michelsen. Re-use is prohibited.

Published by
LLEWELLYN WORLDWIDE LTD.
2143 Wooddale Drive
Woodbury, MN 55125-2989

Printed in the United States of America
Typography property of Llewellyn Worldwide Ltd.
Llewellyn is a registered trademark of Llewellyn Worldwide Ltd.

Table of Contents

Mercury Retrograde 2016

	DATE	ET	PT			DATE	ET	PT
Mercury Retrograde	1/5	**8:06 am**	5:06 am	—	Mercury Direct	1/25	**4:50 pm**	1:50 pm
Mercury Retrograde	4/28	**1:20 pm**	10:20 am	—	Mercury Direct	5/22	**9:20 am**	6:20 am
Mercury Retrograde	8/30		6:04 am	—	Mercury Direct	9/21		10:31 pm
Mercury Retrograde	8/30	**9:04 am**		—	Mercury Direct	9/22	**1:31 am**	
Mercury Retrograde	12/19	**5:55 am**	2:55 am	—	Mercury Direct	1/8/17	**4:43 am**	1:43 am

Moon Void-of-Course 2016

Times are listed in Eastern time in this table only. All other information in the *Pocket Planner* is listed in both Eastern time and Pacific time. Refer to "Time Zone Conversions" on page 7 for changing to other time zones. Note: All times are corrected for Daylight Saving Time.

Last Aspect		Moon Enters New Sign			Last Aspect		Moon Enters New Sign			Last Aspect		Moon Enters New Sign		
Date	Time	Date	Sign	Time	Date	Time	Date	Sign	Time	Date	Time	Date	Sign	Time
JANUARY					**FEBRUARY**					**MARCH**				
1	12:33 am	1	♎	1:41 am	1	7:35 pm	2	♐	10:50 am	2	9:55 pm	3	♈	5:01 am
2	11:23 am	3	♏	2:36 pm	4	5:04 am	4	♑	7:44 pm	5	11:05 am	5	♒	11:22 am
5	12:47 pm	6	♐	1:56 am	6	10:54 am	7	♒	12:59 am	7	3:46 am	7	♓	2:08 pm
7	9:44 pm	8	♑	10:07 am	8	9:39 am	9	♓	3:31 am	8	8:54 pm	9	♈	2:40 pm
10	12:39 pm	10	♒	3:23 pm	10	11:25 pm	11	♈	4:55 am	11	1:24 pm	11	♉	2:44 pm
11	8:09 pm	12	♓	6:53 pm	13	5:32 am	13	♉	6:36 am	13	5:46 am	13	♊	5:03 pm
14	11:31 am	14	♈	9:48 pm	15	5:54 am	15	♊	9:35 am	15	1:03 pm	15	♋	8:57 pm
16	6:26 pm	17	♉	12:48 am	17	11:37 am	17	♋	2:24 pm	18	12:09 am	18	♌	3:54 am
19	1:50 am	19	♊	4:13 am	19	9:36 am	19	♌	9:17 pm	19	4:43 pm	20	♍	1:39 pm
21	3:01 am	21	♋	8:28 am	21	8:17 pm	22	♍	6:24 am	21	11:55 pm	23	♎	1:23 am
23	1:21 am	23	♌	2:21 pm	24	9:22 am	24	♎	5:41 pm	24	4:55 pm	25	♏	2:09 pm
24	9:51 pm	25	♍	10:46 pm	26	6:18 am	27	♏	6:26 am	27	3:25 am	28	♐	2:46 am
27	7:11 pm	28	♎	9:59 am	29	2:55 pm	29	♐	6:56 pm	29	9:55 pm	30	♑	1:45 pm
29	8:34 pm	30	♏	10:50 pm										

Moon Void-of-Course 2016 (cont.)

APRIL

Last Aspect		Moon Enters New Sign		
Date	Time	Date	Sign	Time
1	12:39 pm	1	≈	9:37 pm
3	7:16 pm	4	♓	1:45 am
5	6:33 am	6	♈	2:46 am
7	10:56 am	8	♉	2:10 am
9	5:49 am	10	♊	1:59 am
11	2:57 pm	12	♋	4:07 am
13	11:59 pm	14	♌	9:53 am
16	1:48 pm	16	♍	7:23 pm
18	8:29 am	19	♎	7:24 am
21	2:13 am	21	♏	8:17 pm
23	5:46 pm	24	♐	8:46 am
26	11:51 am	26	♑	7:54 pm
29	3:07 am	29	≈	4:47 am
30	10:56 pm	5/1	♓	10:33 am

MAY

Last Aspect		Moon Enters New Sign		
Date	Time	Date	Sign	Time
4/30	10:56 pm	1	♓	10:33 am
3	1:08 am	3	♈	1:04 pm
5	12:17 am	5	♉	1:10 pm
6	10:10 pm	7	♊	12:35 pm
9	12:15 am	9	♋	1:24 pm
11	3:34 am	11	♌	5:32 pm
13	1:02 pm	14	♍	1:52 am
16	5:20 am	16	♎	1:33 pm
18	11:23 am	19	♏	2:29 am
21	7:40 am	21	♐	2:48 pm
23	11:37 am	24	♑	1:34 am
25	9:11 pm	26	≈	10:27 am
28	4:19 pm	28	♓	5:06 pm
30	7:10 pm	30	♈	9:09 pm

JUNE

Last Aspect		Moon Enters New Sign		
Date	Time	Date	Sign	Time
1	11:42 am	1	♉	10:46 pm
3	7:02 pm	3	♊	11:01 pm
5	12:47 pm	5	♋	11:41 pm
7	8:18 pm	8	♌	2:47 am
10	3:14 am	10	♍	9:46 am
12	10:47 am	12	♎	8:33 pm
15	3:00 am	15	♏	9:18 am
17	9:52 am	17	♐	9:34 pm
20	7:02 am	20	♑	7:55 am
22	4:57 am	22	≈	4:08 pm
24	11:48 am	24	♓	10:30 pm
26	3:55 pm	27	♈	3:08 am
29	3:46 am	29	♉	6:03 am
30	8:19 pm	7/1	♊	7:44 am

JULY

Last Aspect		Moon Enters New Sign		
Date	Time	Date	Sign	Time
6/30	8:19 pm	1	♊	7:44 am
2	11:43 pm	3	♋	9:20 am
5	2:29 am	5	♌	12:28 pm
7	8:07 am	7	♍	6:41 pm
9	11:28 pm	10	♎	4:32 am
12	11:01 am	12	♏	4:52 pm
14	6:22 pm	15	♐	5:14 am
17	4:57 am	17	♑	3:33 pm
19	6:57 pm	19	≈	11:10 pm
21	9:56 pm	22	♓	4:35 am
24	3:06 am	24	♈	8:33 am
26	2:19 am	26	♉	11:37 am
28	11:13 am	28	♊	2:17 pm
30	7:46 am	30	♋	5:09 pm

AUGUST

Last Aspect		Moon Enters New Sign		
Date	Time	Date	Sign	Time
1	8:44 pm	1	♌	9:12 pm
4	12:13 am	4	♍	3:34 am
5	11:20 pm	6	♎	12:57 pm
8	1:41 pm	9	♏	12:51 am
11	1:22 am	11	♐	1:24 pm
13	1:37 pm	14	♑	12:11 am
15	10:45 pm	16	≈	7:52 am
18	5:27 am	18	♓	12:34 pm
20	8:21 am	20	♈	3:18 pm
22	7:48 am	22	♉	5:19 pm
24	3:38 pm	24	♊	7:40 pm
26	8:30 pm	26	♋	11:06 pm
29	2:23 am	29	♌	4:11 am
31	12:20 am	31	♍	11:22 am

SEPTEMBER

Last Aspect		Moon Enters New Sign		
Date	Time	Date	Sign	Time
2	6:13 pm	2	♎	8:55 pm
4	8:30 pm	5	♏	8:38 am
7	8:43 pm	7	♐	9:20 pm
9	8:51 pm	10	♑	8:55 am
12	6:00 am	12	≈	5:28 pm
14	11:31 am	14	♓	10:23 pm
16	3:05 pm	17	♈	12:22 am
18	4:11 pm	19	♉	12:58 am
20	11:32 pm	21	♊	1:53 am
23	3:57 am	23	♋	4:33 am
24	9:42 pm	25	♌	9:48 am
27	4:52 am	27	♍	5:43 pm
29	6:05 am	30	♎	3:52 am

OCTOBER

Last Aspect		Moon Enters New Sign		
Date	Time	Date	Sign	Time
2	1:43 am	2	♏	3:43 pm
4	9:04 pm	5	♐	4:26 am
7	2:26 am	7	♑	4:40 pm
9	12:51 pm	10	≈	2:33 am
11	7:49 pm	12	♓	8:43 am
14	3:13 am	14	♈	11:08 am
16	12:23 am	16	♉	11:04 am
17	10:47 am	18	♊	10:30 am
20	7:17 am	20	♋	11:28 am
22	3:14 pm	22	♌	3:34 pm
24	8:21 am	24	♍	11:16 pm
26	2:33 pm	27	♎	9:51 am
29	6:09 am	29	♏	10:01 pm
31	10:44 pm	11/1	♐	10:43 am

NOVEMBER

Last Aspect		Moon Enters New Sign		
Date	Time	Date	Sign	Time
10/31	10:44 pm	1	♐	10:43 am
3	6:35 am	3	♑	11:05 pm
6	4:56 am	6	≈	8:55 am
8	8:54 am	8	♓	4:45 pm
10	6:16 pm	10	♈	8:45 pm
12	7:45 am	12	♉	9:24 pm
14	8:52 am	14	♊	8:23 pm
16	5:58 am	16	♋	7:57 pm
18	5:02 pm	18	♌	10:14 pm
21	3:33 am	21	♍	4:34 am
22	12:41 pm	23	♎	2:42 pm
25	8:52 am	26	♏	3:01 am
27	4:48 pm	28	♐	3:46 pm
30	11:08 pm	12/1	♑	3:52 am

DECEMBER

Last Aspect		Moon Enters New Sign		
Date	Time	Date	Sign	Time
11/30	11:08 pm	1	♑	3:52 am
3	5:16 am	3	≈	2:44 pm
5	6:23 am	5	♓	11:31 pm
7	9:05 am	8	♈	5:15 am
9	8:06 pm	10	♉	7:41 am
11	11:04 pm	12	♊	7:41 am
14	12:58 am	14	♋	7:09 am
15	4:37 pm	16	♌	8:15 am
18	11:55 am	18	♍	12:52 pm
20	8:56 pm	20	♎	9:40 pm
22	2:31 pm	23	♏	9:32 am
25	2:22 am	25	♐	10:19 pm
27	8:45 pm	28	♑	10:12 am
30	3:07 am	30	≈	8:29 pm

How to Use the *Pocket Planner*

by Leslie Nielsen

This handy guide contains information that can be most valuable to you as you plan your daily activities. As you read through the first few pages, you can start to get a feel for how well organized this guide is.

Read the Symbol Key on the next page, which is rather like astrological shorthand. The characteristics of the planets can give you direction in planning your strategies. Much like traffic signs that signal "go," "stop," or even "caution," you can determine for yourself the most propitious time to get things done.

You'll find tables that show the dates when Mercury is retrograde (Rx) or direct (D). Because Mercury deals with the exchange of information, a retrograde Mercury makes miscommunication more noticeable.

There's also a section dedicated to the times when the Moon is void-of-course (V/C). These are generally poor times to conduct business because activities begun during these times usually end badly or fail to get started. If you make an appointment during a void-of-course, you might save yourself a lot of aggravation by confirming the time and date later. The Moon is only void-of-course for 7 percent of the time when business is usually conducted during a normal workday (that is, 8:00 am to 5:00 pm). Sometimes, by waiting a matter of minutes or a few hours until the Moon has left the void-of-course phase, you have a much better chance to make action move more smoothly. Moon voids can also be used successfully to do routine activities or inner work, such as dream therapy or personal contemplation.

You'll find Moon phases, as well as each of the Moon's entries into a new sign. Times are expressed in Eastern time (in bold type) and Pacific time (in medium type). The New Moon time is generally best for beginning new activities, as the Moon is increasing in light and can offer the element of growth to our endeavors. When the Moon is Full, its illumination is greatest and we can see the results of our efforts. When it moves from the Full stage back to the New stage, it can best be used to reflect on our projects. If necessary, we can make corrections at the New Moon.

The section of "Planetary Stations" will give you the times when the planets are changing signs or direction, thereby affording us opportunities for new starts.

The ephemeris in the back of your *Pocket Planner* can be very helpful to you. As you start to work with the ephemeris, you may notice that not all planets seem to be comfortable in every sign. Think of the planets as actors, and the signs as the costumes they wear. Sometimes, costumes just itch. If you find this to be so for a certain time period, you may choose to delay your plans for a time or be more creative with the energies at hand.

As you turn to the daily pages, you'll find information about the Moon's sign, phase, and the time it changes phase. You'll find icons indicating the best days to plant and fish. Also, you will find times and dates when the planets and asteroids change sign and go either retrograde or direct, major holidays, a three-month calendar, and room to record your appointments.

This guide is a powerful tool. Make the most of it!

Symbol Key

Planets:	☉	Sun	⚳	Ceres	♄	Saturn
	☽	Moon	⚴	Pallas	⚷	Chiron
	☿	Mercury	⚵	Juno	♅	Uranus
	♀	Venus	⚶	Vesta	♆	Neptune
	♂	Mars	♃	Jupiter	♇	Pluto
Signs:	♈	Aries	♌	Leo	♐	Sagittarius
	♉	Taurus	♍	Virgo	♑	Capricorn
	♊	Gemini	♎	Libra	♒	Aquarius
	♋	Cancer	♏	Scorpio	♓	Pisces
Aspects:	☌	Conjunction (0°)	⚺	Semisextile (30°)	⚹	Sextile (60°)
	□	Square (90°)	△	Trine (120°)		
	⚻	Quincunx (150°)	☍	Opposition (180°)		
Motion:	℞	Retrograde	D	Direct		

Best Days for Planting: 🌱   Best Days for Fishing: 🐟

5

World Map of Time Zones

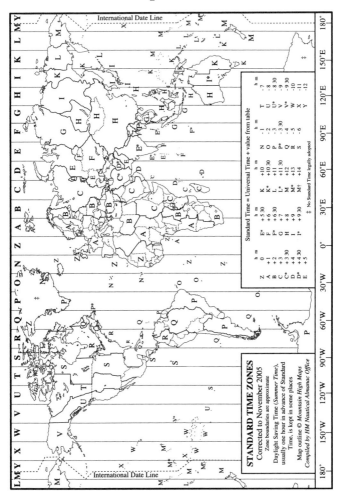

International Date Line

Standard Time = Universal Time + value from table

	h m			h m
Z	0	N	-1	T	-7
A	+1	O	-2	U	-8
B	+2	P	-3	U*	-8.30
C	+3	P*	-3.30	V	-9
C*	+3.30	Q	-4	V*	-9.30
D	+4	R	-5	W	-10
D*	+4.30	S	-6	X	-11
E	+5			Y	-12
E*	+5.30	K	+10		
F	+6	K*	+10.30		
F*	+6.30	L	+11		
G	+7	L*	+11.30		
H	+8	M	+12		
I	+9	M*	+13		
I*	+9.30	M†	+14		

‡ No Standard Time legally adopted

STANDARD TIME ZONES
Corrected to November 2005

Zone boundaries are approximate

Daylight Saving Time (Summer Time),
usually one hour in advance of Standard
Time, is kept in some places

Map outline © Mountain High Maps
Compiled by HM Nautical Almanac Office

International Date Line

Time Zone Conversions

World Time Zones
Compared to Eastern Standard Time

( ) From Map	(Y) Subtract 7 hours	(C*) Add 8.5 hours
(S) CST/Subtract 1 hour	(A) Add 6 hours	(D*) Add 9.5 hours
(R) EST	(B) Add 7 hours	(E*) Add 10.5 hours
(Q) Add 1 hour	(C) Add 8 hours	(F*) Add 11.5 hours
(P) Add 2 hours	(D) Add 9 hours	(I*) Add 14.5 hours
(O) Add 3 hours	(E) Add 10 hours	(K*) Add 15.5 hours
(N) Add 4 hours	(F) Add 11 hours	(L*) Add 16.5 hours
(Z) Add 5 hours	(G) Add 12 hours	(M*) Add 18 hours
(T) MST/Subtract 2 hours	(H) Add 13 hours	(P*) Add 2.5 hours
(U) PST/Subtract 3 hours	(I) Add 14 hours	(U*) Subtract 3.5 hours
(V) Subtract 4 hours	(K) Add 15 hours	(V*) Subtract 4.5 hours
(W) Subtract 5 hours	(L) Add 16 hours	
(X) Subtract 6 hours	(M) Add 17 hours	

World Map of Time Zones is supplied by HM Nautical Almanac Office, © Center for the Central Laboratory of the Research Councils. Note: This is not an official map. Countries change their time zones as they wish.

Planetary Stations for 2016

	JAN	FEB	MAR	APR	MAY	JUN	JUL	AUG	SEP	OCT	NOV	DEC
☿	1/5–1/25				4/28–5/22				8/30–9/22			12/19–1/8
♀												
♂					4/17–6/29							
♃			1/7–5/9									
♄						3/25–8/13						
♅										7/29–12/29		
♆								6/13–11/19				
♇							4/18–9/26					
⚷									6/27–12/1			
♈										8/31–12/9		
◇								6/21–10/17				
✳				3/2–6/22								
⚹												12/1–3/7/17

8

1 Friday

3rd ♍
☽ V/C   **12:33 am**
☽ enters ♎ **1:41 am**
☿ enters ♒ **9:20 pm** 6:20 pm
4th quarter   9:30 pm

New Year's Day • Kwanzaa ends

2 Saturday

3rd ♎
4th quarter **12:30 am**
☽ V/C   **11:23 am** 8:23 am

3 Sunday

4th ♎
♂ enters ♏ **9:32 am** 6:32 am
☽ enters ♏ **2:36 pm** 11:36 am

December 2015						
S	M	T	W	T	F	S
		1	2	3	4	5
6	7	8	9	10	11	12
13	14	15	16	17	18	19
20	21	22	23	24	25	26
27	28	29	30	31		

January 2016						
S	M	T	W	T	F	S
					1	2
3	4	5	6	7	8	9
10	11	12	13	14	15	16
17	18	19	20	21	22	23
24	25	26	27	28	29	30
31						

February 2016						
S	M	T	W	T	F	S
	1	2	3	4	5	6
7	8	9	10	11	12	13
14	15	16	17	18	19	20
21	22	23	24	25	26	27
28	29					

Eastern time in bold type
Pacific time in medium type

4 Monday
4th ♏

5 Tuesday
4th ♏
☿ R	**8:06 am**	5:06 am
☽ V/C	**12:47 pm**	9:47 am
☽ enters ♐		10:56 pm

Mercury retrograde until 1/25

6 Wednesday
4th ♏
| ☽ enters ♐ | **1:56 am** | |

7 Thursday
4th ♐
| ☽ V/C | **9:44 pm** | 6:44 pm |
| ♃ R | **11:40 pm** | 8:40 pm |

8 Friday
4th ♐

☽ enters ♑ **10:07 am** 7:07 am
☿ enters ♑ **2:36 pm** 11:36 am

9 Saturday
4th ♑
New Moon **8:31 pm** 5:31 pm

10 Sunday
1st ♑

☽ V/C **12:39 pm** 9:39 am
☽ enters ♒ **3:23 pm** 12:23 pm

December 2015						
S	M	T	W	T	F	S
		1	2	3	4	5
6	7	8	9	10	11	12
13	14	15	16	17	18	19
20	21	22	23	24	25	26
27	28	29	30	31		

January 2016						
S	M	T	W	T	F	S
					1	2
3	4	5	6	7	8	9
10	11	12	13	14	15	16
17	18	19	20	21	22	23
24	25	26	27	28	29	30
31						

February 2016						
S	M	T	W	T	F	S
	1	2	3	4	5	6
7	8	9	10	11	12	13
14	15	16	17	18	19	20
21	22	23	24	25	26	27
28	29					

11 Monday

1st ≈

☽ V/C   **8:09 pm**   5:09 pm

12 Tuesday

1st ≈

☽ enters ♓   **6:53 pm**   3:53 pm

13 Wednesday

1st ♓

14 Thursday

1st ♓

☽ V/C   **11:31 am**   8:31 am

☽ enters ♈   **9:48 pm**   6:48 pm

Eastern time in bold type
Pacific time in medium type

15 Friday
1st ♈

16 Saturday

1st ♈
☽ V/C   **6:26 pm**   3:26 pm
2nd quarter   **6:26 pm**   3:26 pm
☽ enters ♉   9:48 pm

17 Sunday

2nd ♈
☽ enters ♉   **12:48 am**

December 2015						
S	M	T	W	T	F	S
		1	2	3	4	5
6	7	8	9	10	11	12
13	14	15	16	17	18	19
20	21	22	23	24	25	26
27	28	29	30	31		

January 2016						
S	M	T	W	T	F	S
					1	2
3	4	5	6	7	8	9
10	11	12	13	14	15	16
17	18	19	20	21	22	23
24	25	26	27	28	29	30
31						

February 2016						
S	M	T	W	T	F	S
	1	2	3	4	5	6
7	8	9	10	11	12	13
14	15	16	17	18	19	20
21	22	23	24	25	26	27
28	29					

18 Monday

2nd ♉

☽ V/C   10:50 pm

Birthday of Martin Luther King, Jr. (observed)

19 Tuesday

2nd ♉
☽ V/C   **1:50 am**
☽ enters ♊   **4:13 am**   1:13 am

20 Wednesday

2nd ♊
☉ enters ♒ **10:27 am**   7:27 am

Sun enters Aquarius

21 Thursday

2nd ♊

☽ V/C   **3:01 am** 12:01 am

☽ enters ♋   **8:28 am**   5:28 am

Eastern time in bold type
Pacific time in medium type

22 Friday

2nd ⊗
♀ enters ≈   **2:03 pm** 11:03 am
☽ V/C   10:21 pm

23 Saturday

2nd ⊗
☽ V/C   **1:21 am**
☽ enters ♌   **2:21 pm** 11:21 am
♀ enters ♑   **3:31 pm** 12:31 pm
Full Moon   **8:46 pm** 5:46 pm

24 Sunday

3rd ♌
☽ V/C   **9:51 pm** 6:51 pm

December 2015						
S	M	T	W	T	F	S
		1	2	3	4	5
6	7	8	9	10	11	12
13	14	15	16	17	18	19
20	21	22	23	24	25	26
27	28	29	30	31		

January 2016						
S	M	T	W	T	F	S
					1	2
3	4	5	6	7	8	9
10	11	12	13	14	15	16
17	18	19	20	21	22	23
24	25	26	27	28	29	30
31						

February 2016						
S	M	T	W	T	F	S
	1	2	3	4	5	6
7	8	9	10	11	12	13
14	15	16	17	18	19	20
21	22	23	24	25	26	27
28	29					

Eastern time in bold type
Pacific time in medium type

25 Monday
3rd ♌
| ☿ D | **4:50 pm** | 1:50 pm |
| ☽ enters ♍ | **10:46 pm** | 7:46 pm |

26 Tuesday
3rd ♍

27 Wednesday
3rd ♍
| ☽ V/C | **7:11 pm** | 4:11 pm |

28 Thursday
3rd ♍
| ☽ enters ♎ | **9:59 am** | 6:59 am |
| ♀ enters ♓ | **1:42 pm** | 10:42 am |

Eastern time in bold type
Pacific time in medium type

29 Friday
3rd ♎
☽ V/C   **8:34 pm**   5:34 pm

30 Saturday
3rd ♎
☽ enters ♏, **10:50 pm**   7:50 pm

31 Sunday
3rd ♏
4th quarter   **10:28 pm**   7:28 pm

December 2015						
S	M	T	W	T	F	S
		1	2	3	4	5
6	7	8	9	10	11	12
13	14	15	16	17	18	19
20	21	22	23	24	25	26
27	28	29	30	31		

January 2016						
S	M	T	W	T	F	S
					1	2
3	4	5	6	7	8	9
10	11	12	13	14	15	16
17	18	19	20	21	22	23
24	25	26	27	28	29	30
31						

February 2016						
S	M	T	W	T	F	S
	1	2	3	4	5	6
7	8	9	10	11	12	13
14	15	16	17	18	19	20
21	22	23	24	25	26	27
28	29					

1 Monday
4th ♏
☽ V/C   **7:35 pm**   4:35 pm

2 Tuesday
4th ♏
☽ enters ♐ **10:50 am**   7:50 am

Groundhog Day • Imbolc

3 Wednesday
4th ♐

4 Thursday
4th ♐
☽ V/C   **5:04 am**   2:04 am
☽ enters ♑ **7:44 pm**   4:44 pm

5 Friday
4th ♑

6 Saturday
4th ♑
☽ V/C **10:54 am** 7:54 am
☽ enters ♒ 9:59 pm

7 Sunday
4th ♑
☽ enters ♒ **12:59 am**

January 2016						
S	M	T	W	T	F	S
					1	2
3	4	5	6	7	8	9
10	11	12	13	14	15	16
17	18	19	20	21	22	23
24	25	26	27	28	29	30
31						

February 2016						
S	M	T	W	T	F	S
	1	2	3	4	5	6
7	8	9	10	11	12	13
14	15	16	17	18	19	20
21	22	23	24	25	26	27
28	29					

March 2016						
S	M	T	W	T	F	S
		1	2	3	4	5
6	7	8	9	10	11	12
13	14	15	16	17	18	19
20	21	22	23	24	25	26
27	28	29	30	31		

8 Monday
4th ≈
☽ V/C   **9:39 am**   6:39 am
New Moon   **9:39 am**   6:39 am

Chinese New Year (monkey)

9 Tuesday
1st ≈
☽ enters ♓   **3:31 am** 12:31 am

Mardi Gras (Fat Tuesday)

10 Wednesday
1st ♓
☽ V/C   **11:25 pm**   8:25 pm

Ash Wednesday

11 Thursday
1st ♓
☽ enters ♈   **4:55 am**   1:55 am

12 Friday
1st ♈

13 Saturday
1st ♈
☽ V/C   **5:32 am**   2:32 am
☽ enters ♉   **6:36 am**   3:36 am
☿ enters ≈   **5:43 pm**   2:43 pm

14 Sunday
1st ♉
2nd quarter   11:46 pm

Valentine's Day

January 2016						
S	M	T	W	T	F	S
					1	2
3	4	5	6	7	8	9
10	11	12	13	14	15	16
17	18	19	20	21	22	23
24	25	26	27	28	29	30
31						

February 2016						
S	M	T	W	T	F	S
	1	2	3	4	5	6
7	8	9	10	11	12	13
14	15	16	17	18	19	20
21	22	23	24	25	26	27
28	29					

March 2016						
S	M	T	W	T	F	S
		1	2	3	4	5
6	7	8	9	10	11	12
13	14	15	16	17	18	19
20	21	22	23	24	25	26
27	28	29	30	31		

Eastern time in bold type
Pacific time in medium type

15 Monday

1st ♉
2nd quarter **2:46 am**
☽ V/C **5:54 am** 2:54 am
☽ enters ♊ **9:35 am** 6:35 am

Presidents' Day

16 Tuesday

2nd ♊
♀ enters ≈ **11:17 pm** 8:17 pm

17 Wednesday

2nd ♊
☽ V/C **11:37 am** 8:37 am
☽ enters ♋ **2:24 pm** 11:24 am

18 Thursday

2nd ♋
☉ enters ♓ 9:34 pm

Sun enters Pisces

Eastern time in bold type
Pacific time in medium type

19 Friday
2nd ⚋

☉ enters ♓ **12:34 am**
☽ V/C   **9:36 am** 6:36 am
☽ enters ♌ **9:17 pm** 6:17 pm

Sun enters Pisces

20 Saturday
2nd ♌

21 Sunday
2nd ♌

☽ V/C   **8:17 pm** 5:17 pm

January 2016						
S	M	T	W	T	F	S
					1	2
3	4	5	6	7	8	9
10	11	12	13	14	15	16
17	18	19	20	21	22	23
24	25	26	27	28	29	30
31						

February 2016						
S	M	T	W	T	F	S
	1	2	3	4	5	6
7	8	9	10	11	12	13
14	15	16	17	18	19	20
21	22	23	24	25	26	27
28	29					

March 2016						
S	M	T	W	T	F	S
		1	2	3	4	5
6	7	8	9	10	11	12
13	14	15	16	17	18	19
20	21	22	23	24	25	26
27	28	29	30	31		

22 Monday

2nd ♌
☽ enters ♍ **6:24 am** 3:24 am
Full Moon **1:20 pm** 10:20 am

23 Tuesday

3rd ♍

24 Wednesday

3rd ♍
☽ V/C **9:22 am** 6:22 am
☽ enters ♎ **5:41 pm** 2:41 pm

25 Thursday

3rd ♎

Eastern time in bold type
Pacific time in medium type

26 Friday
3rd ♎︎
☽ V/C   **6:18 am**   3:18 am

27 Saturday
3rd ♎︎
☽ enters ♏︎ **6:26 am**   3:26 am

28 Sunday
3rd ♏︎

January 2016						
S	M	T	W	T	F	S
					1	2
3	4	5	6	7	8	9
10	11	12	13	14	15	16
17	18	19	20	21	22	23
24	25	26	27	28	29	30
31						

February 2016						
S	M	T	W	T	F	S
	1	2	3	4	5	6
7	8	9	10	11	12	13
14	15	16	17	18	19	20
21	22	23	24	25	26	27
28	29					

March 2016						
S	M	T	W	T	F	S
		1	2	3	4	5
6	7	8	9	10	11	12
13	14	15	16	17	18	19
20	21	22	23	24	25	26
27	28	29	30	31		

29 Monday
3rd ♏

☽ V/C	**2:55 pm**	11:55 am
☽ enters ♐	**6:56 pm**	3:56 pm

1 Tuesday
3rd ♐

4th quarter	**6:11 pm**	3:11 pm

2 Wednesday
4th ♐

☿ R	**5:40 am**	2:40 am
☽ V/C	**9:55 pm**	6:55 pm

3 Thursday
4th ♐

☽ enters ♑	**5:01 am**	2:01 am

Eastern time in bold type
Pacific time in medium type

4 Friday
4th ♑

5 Saturday
4th ♑
☿ enters ♓ **5:23 am** 2:23 am
☽ V/C **11:05 am** 8:05 am
☽ enters ♒ **11:22 am** 8:22 am
♂ enters ♐ **9:29 pm** 6:29 pm

6 Sunday
4th ♒

February 2016						
S	M	T	W	T	F	S
	1	2	3	4	5	6
7	8	9	10	11	12	13
14	15	16	17	18	19	20
21	22	23	24	25	26	27
28	29					

March 2016						
S	M	T	W	T	F	S
		1	2	3	4	5
6	7	8	9	10	11	12
13	14	15	16	17	18	19
20	21	22	23	24	25	26
27	28	29	30	31		

April 2016						
S	M	T	W	T	F	S
					1	2
3	4	5	6	7	8	9
10	11	12	13	14	15	16
17	18	19	20	21	22	23
24	25	26	27	28	29	30

7 Monday
4th ≈
☽ V/C   **3:46 am** 12:46 am
☽ enters ♓   **2:08 pm** 11:08 am
⚸ enters ♉   **7:53 pm** 4:53 pm

8 Tuesday
4th ♓
☽ V/C   **8:54 pm** 5:54 pm
New Moon   **8:54 pm** 5:54 pm

Total solar eclipse 18° ♓ 57' • 8:57 pm EST/5:57 pm PST

9 Wednesday
1st ♓
☽ enters ♈   **2:40 pm** 11:40 am

10 Thursday
1st ♈

Eastern time in bold type
Pacific time in medium type

11 Friday

1st ♈
☽ V/C   **1:24 pm** 10:24 am
☽ enters ♉   **2:44 pm** 11:44 am

12 Saturday

1st ♉
♀ enters ♓   **5:24 am** 2:24 am

13 Sunday

1st ♉
☽ V/C   **5:46 am** 2:46 am
☽ enters ♊   **5:03 pm** 2:03 pm

Daylight Saving Time begins at 2 am

February 2016						
S	M	T	W	T	F	S
	1	2	3	4	5	6
7	8	9	10	11	12	13
14	15	16	17	18	19	20
21	22	23	24	25	26	27
28	29					

March 2016						
S	M	T	W	T	F	S
		1	2	3	4	5
6	7	8	9	10	11	12
13	14	15	16	17	18	19
20	21	22	23	24	25	26
27	28	29	30	31		

April 2016						
S	M	T	W	T	F	S
					1	2
3	4	5	6	7	8	9
10	11	12	13	14	15	16
17	18	19	20	21	22	23
24	25	26	27	28	29	30

Eastern time in bold type
Pacific time in medium type

14 Monday
1st ♊

15 Tuesday
1st ♊
☽ V/C	**1:03 pm** 10:03 am
2nd quarter	**1:03 pm** 10:03 am
☽ enters ♋	**8:57 pm** 5:57 pm

16 Wednesday
2nd ♋

17 Thursday
2nd ♋
| ☽ V/C | 9:09 pm |

St. Patrick's Day

Eastern time in bold type
Pacific time in medium type

18 Friday
2nd ⊗
☽ V/C · **12:09 am**
☽ enters ♌ · **3:54 am** 12:54 am

19 Saturday
2nd ♌
☽ V/C · **4:43 pm** 1:43 pm
☉ enters ♈ · 9:30 pm

Sun enters Aries • Ostara • Spring Equinox • 9:30 pm PDT

20 Sunday
2nd ♌
☉ enters ♈ **12:30 am**
☽ enters ♍ · **1:39 pm** 10:39 am

Palm Sunday
International Astrology Day
Sun enters Aries • Ostara • Spring Equinox • 12:30 am EDT

February 2016						
S	M	T	W	T	F	S
	1	2	3	4	5	6
7	8	9	10	11	12	13
14	15	16	17	18	19	20
21	22	23	24	25	26	27
28	29					

March 2016						
S	M	T	W	T	F	S
		1	2	3	4	5
6	7	8	9	10	11	12
13	14	15	16	17	18	19
20	21	22	23	24	25	26
27	28	29	30	31		

April 2016						
S	M	T	W	T	F	S
					1	2
3	4	5	6	7	8	9
10	11	12	13	14	15	16
17	18	19	20	21	22	23
24	25	26	27	28	29	30

21 Monday
2nd ♍
☿ enters ♈   **8:19 pm** 5:19 pm
☽ V/C   **11:55 pm** 8:55 pm

22 Tuesday

2nd ♍
☽ enters ♎   10:23 pm

23 Wednesday

2nd ♍
☽ enters ♎   **1:23 am**
Full Moon   **8:01 am** 5:01 am

Lunar eclipse 3° ♎ 10' • 7:47 am EDT/4:47 am PDT

24 Thursday

3rd ♎
☽ V/C   **4:55 pm** 1:55 pm

Purim

25 Friday
3rd ♎︎
♄ ℞   **6:01 am** 3:01 am
☽ enters ♏︎ **2:09 pm** 11:09 am

Good Friday

26 Saturday
3rd ♏︎

27 Sunday
3rd ♏︎
☽ V/C   **3:25 am** 12:25 am
☽ enters ♐︎   11:46 pm

Easter

February 2016						
S	M	T	W	T	F	S
	1	2	3	4	5	6
7	8	9	10	11	12	13
14	15	16	17	18	19	20
21	22	23	24	25	26	27
28	29					

March 2016						
S	M	T	W	T	F	S
		1	2	3	4	5
6	7	8	9	10	11	12
13	14	15	16	17	18	19
20	21	22	23	24	25	26
27	28	29	30	31		

April 2016						
S	M	T	W	T	F	S
					1	2
3	4	5	6	7	8	9
10	11	12	13	14	15	16
17	18	19	20	21	22	23
24	25	26	27	28	29	30

28 Monday
3rd ♏
☽ enters ♐ **2:46 am**

29 Tuesday
3rd ♐
☽ V/C **9:55 pm** 6:55 pm

30 Wednesday
3rd ♐
☽ enters ♑ **1:45 pm** 10:45 am

31 Thursday
3rd ♑
4th quarter **11:17 am** 8:17 am

1 Friday
4th ♑
☽ V/C **12:39 pm** 9:39 am
☽ enters ♒ **9:37 pm** 6:37 pm

April Fools' Day (All Fools' Day—Pagan)

2 Saturday
4th ♒

3 Sunday
4th ♒
☽ V/C **7:16 pm** 4:16 pm
☽ enters ♓ 10:45 pm

March 2016						
S	M	T	W	T	F	S
		1	2	3	4	5
6	7	8	9	10	11	12
13	14	15	16	17	18	19
20	21	22	23	24	25	26
27	28	29	30	31		

April 2016						
S	M	T	W	T	F	S
					1	2
3	4	5	6	7	8	9
10	11	12	13	14	15	16
17	18	19	20	21	22	23
24	25	26	27	28	29	30

May 2016						
S	M	T	W	T	F	S
1	2	3	4	5	6	7
8	9	10	11	12	13	14
15	16	17	18	19	20	21
22	23	24	25	26	27	28
29	30	31				

4 Monday
4th ≈
☽ enters ♓   **1:45 am**

5 Tuesday
4th ♓
☽ V/C   **6:33 am**   3:33 am
♀ enters ♈ **12:50 pm**   9:50 am
☿ enters ♉   **7:09 pm**   4:09 pm
☽ enters ♈   11:46 pm

6 Wednesday
4th ♓
☽ enters ♈   **2:46 am**

7 Thursday
4th ♈
New Moon   **7:24 am**   4:24 am
☽ V/C   **10:56 am**   7:56 am
☽ enters ♉   11:10 pm

Eastern time in bold type
Pacific time in medium type

8 Friday
1st ♈
☽ enters ♉   **2:10 am**

9 Saturday
1st ♉
☽ V/C   **5:49 am**   2:49 am
☽ enters ♊   10:59 pm

10 Sunday
1st ♉
☽ enters ♊   **1:59 am**

March 2016						
S	M	T	W	T	F	S
		1	2	3	4	5
6	7	8	9	10	11	12
13	14	15	16	17	18	19
20	21	22	23	24	25	26
27	28	29	30	31		

April 2016						
S	M	T	W	T	F	S
					1	2
3	4	5	6	7	8	9
10	11	12	13	14	15	16
17	18	19	20	21	22	23
24	25	26	27	28	29	30

May 2016						
S	M	T	W	T	F	S
1	2	3	4	5	6	7
8	9	10	11	12	13	14
15	16	17	18	19	20	21
22	23	24	25	26	27	28
29	30	31				

11 Monday

1st ♊
☽ V/C   **2:57 pm** 11:57 am

12 Tuesday

1st ♊
☽ enters ♋   **4:07 am**   1:07 am

13 Wednesday

1st ♋
☽ V/C   **11:59 pm** 8:59 pm
2nd quarter **11:59 pm** 8:59 pm

14 Thursday

2nd ♋
☽ enters ♌   **9:53 am**   6:53 am
♀ enters ♈   **10:52 am** 7:52 am

15 Friday
2nd ♌

16 Saturday
2nd ♌
☽ V/C   **1:48 pm** 10:48 am
☽ enters ♍   **7:23 pm** 4:23 pm

17 Sunday
2nd ♍
♂ ℞   **8:14 am** 5:14 am

		March 2016				
S	M	T	W	T	F	S
			1	2	3	4	5

March 2016
S M T W T F S
1 2 3 4 5
6 7 8 9 10 11 12
13 14 15 16 17 18 19
20 21 22 23 24 25 26
27 28 29 30 31

April 2016
S M T W T F S
1 2
3 4 5 6 7 8 9
10 11 12 13 14 15 16
17 18 19 20 21 22 23
24 25 26 27 28 29 30

May 2016
S M T W T F S
1 2 3 4 5 6 7
8 9 10 11 12 13 14
15 16 17 18 19 20 21
22 23 24 25 26 27 28
29 30 31

18 Monday
2nd ♍
ℙ R⃰   **3:26 am** 12:26 am
☽ V/C   **8:29 am** 5:29 am

19 Tuesday
2nd ♍
☽ enters ♎ **7:24 am** 4:24 am
☉ enters ♉ **11:29 am** 8:29 am

Sun enters Taurus

20 Wednesday
2nd ♎
☽ V/C   11:13 pm

21 Thursday
2nd ♎
☽ V/C   **2:13 am**
☽ enters ♏ **8:17 pm** 5:17 pm
Full Moon   10:24 pm

22 Friday
2nd ♏
Full Moon **1:24 am**

Earth Day

23 Saturday
3rd ♏
☽ V/C **5:46 pm** 2:46 pm

Passover begins

24 Sunday
3rd ♏
☽ enters ♐ **8:46 am** 5:46 am

March 2016						
S	M	T	W	T	F	S
		1	2	3	4	5
6	7	8	9	10	11	12
13	14	15	16	17	18	19
20	21	22	23	24	25	26
27	28	29	30	31		

April 2016						
S	M	T	W	T	F	S
					1	2
3	4	5	6	7	8	9
10	11	12	13	14	15	16
17	18	19	20	21	22	23
24	25	26	27	28	29	30

May 2016						
S	M	T	W	T	F	S
1	2	3	4	5	6	7
8	9	10	11	12	13	14
15	16	17	18	19	20	21
22	23	24	25	26	27	28
29	30	31				

25 Monday
3rd ♐

26 Tuesday
3rd ♐
☿ enters ♓   **3:54 am** 12:54 am
☽ V/C   **11:51 am** 8:51 am
☽ enters ♑ **7:54 pm** 4:54 pm

27 Wednesday
3rd ♑

28 Thursday
3rd ♑
☿ ℞   **1:20 pm** 10:20 am

Mercury retrograde until 5/22

29 Friday

3rd ♍
☽ V/C	**3:07 am**	12:07 am
☽ enters ♒	**4:47 am**	1:47 am
♀ enters ♉	**8:36 pm**	5:36 pm
4th quarter	**11:29 pm**	8:29 pm

Orthodox Good Friday

30 Saturday

4th ♒
☽ V/C	**10:56 pm**	7:56 pm

Passover ends

1 Sunday

4th ♒
☽ enters ♓	**10:33 am**	7:33 am

Orthodox Easter • Beltane

March 2016	April 2016	May 2016
S M T W T F S	S M T W T F S	S M T W T F S
1 2 3 4 5	1 2	1 2 3 4 5 6 7
6 7 8 9 10 11 12	3 4 5 6 7 8 9	8 9 10 11 12 13 14
13 14 15 16 17 18 19	10 11 12 13 14 15 16	15 16 17 18 19 20 21
20 21 22 23 24 25 26	17 18 19 20 21 22 23	22 23 24 25 26 27 28
27 28 29 30 31	24 25 26 27 28 29 30	29 30 31

2 Monday

4th ♓
☽ V/C   10:08 pm

3 Tuesday

4th ♓
☽ V/C   **1:08 am**
☽ enters ♈   **1:04 pm** 10:04 am

4 Wednesday

4th ♈
☽ V/C   9:17 pm

5 Thursday

4th ♈
☽ V/C   **12:17 am**
☽ enters ♉   **1:10 pm** 10:10 am

Cinco de Mayo

Eastern time in bold type
Pacific time in medium type

6 Friday
4th ♉
New Moon **3:30 pm** 12:30 pm
☽ V/C **10:10 pm** 7:10 pm

7 Saturday
1st ♉
☽ enters ♊ **12:35 pm** 9:35 am

8 Sunday
1st ♊
☽ V/C 9:15 pm

Mother's Day

April 2016
S M T W T F S
1 2
3 4 5 6 7 8 9
10 11 12 13 14 15 16
17 18 19 20 21 22 23
24 25 26 27 28 29 30

May 2016
S M T W T F S
1 2 3 4 5 6 7
8 9 10 11 12 13 14
15 16 17 18 19 20 21
22 23 24 25 26 27 28
29 30 31

June 2016
S M T W T F S
1 2 3 4
5 6 7 8 9 10 11
12 13 14 15 16 17 18
19 20 21 22 23 24 25
26 27 28 29 30

Eastern time in bold type
Pacific time in medium type

9 Monday

1st ♊
D V/C   **12:15 am**
♃ D   **8:14 am** 5:14 am
D enters ♋ **1:24 pm** 10:24 am

10 Tuesday

1st ♋

11 Wednesday

1st ♋
D V/C   **3:34 am** 12:34 am
D enters ♌ **5:32 pm** 2:32 pm

12 Thursday

1st ♌

Eastern time in bold type
Pacific time in medium type

13 Friday

1st ♌
☽ V/C   **1:02 pm** 10:02 am
2nd quarter   **1:02 pm** 10:02 am
☽ enters ♍   10:52 pm

14 Saturday

2nd ♌
☽ enters ♍   **1:52 am**

15 Sunday

2nd ♍

April 2016						
S	M	T	W	T	F	S
					1	2
3	4	5	6	7	8	9
10	11	12	13	14	15	16
17	18	19	20	21	22	23
24	25	26	27	28	29	30

May 2016						
S	M	T	W	T	F	S
1	2	3	4	5	6	7
8	9	10	11	12	13	14
15	16	17	18	19	20	21
22	23	24	25	26	27	28
29	30	31				

June 2016						
S	M	T	W	T	F	S
			1	2	3	4
5	6	7	8	9	10	11
12	13	14	15	16	17	18
19	20	21	22	23	24	25
26	27	28	29	30		

16 Monday
2nd ♍
☽ V/C   **5:20 am** 2:20 am
☽ enters ♎   **1:33 pm** 10:33 am
⚸ enters ♊   **2:29 pm** 11:29 am

17 Tuesday
2nd ♎

18 Wednesday
2nd ♎
☽ V/C   **11:23 am** 8:23 am
☽ enters ♏   11:29 pm

19 Thursday
2nd ♎
☽ enters ♏ **2:29 am**

Eastern time in bold type
Pacific time in medium type

20 Friday

2nd ♏
☉ enters ♊ **10:36 am** 7:36 am

Sun enters Gemini

21 Saturday

2nd ♏
☽ V/C **7:40 am** 4:40 am
☽ enters ♐ **2:48 pm** 11:48 am
Full Moon **5:14 pm** 2:14 pm

22 Sunday

3rd ♐
☿ D **9:20 am** 6:20 am

April 2016						
S	M	T	W	T	F	S
					1	2
3	4	5	6	7	8	9
10	11	12	13	14	15	16
17	18	19	20	21	22	23
24	25	26	27	28	29	30

May 2016						
S	M	T	W	T	F	S
1	2	3	4	5	6	7
8	9	10	11	12	13	14
15	16	17	18	19	20	21
22	23	24	25	26	27	28
29	30	31				

June 2016						
S	M	T	W	T	F	S
			1	2	3	4
5	6	7	8	9	10	11
12	13	14	15	16	17	18
19	20	21	22	23	24	25
26	27	28	29	30		

Eastern time in bold type
Pacific time in medium type

23 Monday
3rd ♐
☽ V/C	**11:37 am**	8:37 am
☽ enters ♑		10:34 pm

24 Tuesday
3rd ♐

☽ enters ♑	**1:34 am**	
♀ enters ♊	**5:45 am**	2:45 am

25 Wednesday
3rd ♑

☽ V/C	**9:11 pm**	6:11 pm

26 Thursday
3rd ♑
☽ enters ≈	**10:27 am**	7:27 am

27 Friday
3rd ≈
♂ enters ♏, **9:51 am** 6:51 am

28 Saturday
3rd ≈
☽ V/C **4:19 pm** 1:19 pm
☽ enters ♓ **5:06 pm** 2:06 pm

29 Sunday
3rd ♓
4th quarter **8:12 am** 5:12 am

April 2016						
S	M	T	W	T	F	S
					1	2
3	4	5	6	7	8	9
10	11	12	13	14	15	16
17	18	19	20	21	22	23
24	25	26	27	28	29	30

May 2016						
S	M	T	W	T	F	S
1	2	3	4	5	6	7
8	9	10	11	12	13	14
15	16	17	18	19	20	21
22	23	24	25	26	27	28
29	30	31				

June 2016						
S	M	T	W	T	F	S
			1	2	3	4
5	6	7	8	9	10	11
12	13	14	15	16	17	18
19	20	21	22	23	24	25
26	27	28	29	30		

30 Monday
4th ♓

| ☽ V/C | **7:10 pm** | 4:10 pm |
| ☽ enters ♈ | **9:09 pm** | 6:09 pm |

Memorial Day (observed)

31 Tuesday
4th ♈

1 Wednesday
4th ♈

| ☽ V/C | **11:42 am** | 8:42 am |
| ☽ enters ♉ | **10:46 pm** | 7:46 pm |

2 Thursday
4th ♉

Eastern time in bold type
Pacific time in medium type

3 Friday

4th ♉

☽ V/C	**7:02 pm**	4:02 pm
☽ enters ♊	**11:01 pm**	8:01 pm

4 Saturday

4th ♊

New Moon	**11:00 pm**	8:00 pm

5 Sunday

1st ♊

☽ V/C	**12:47 pm**	9:47 am
☽ enters ♋	**11:41 pm**	8:41 pm

May 2016

S	M	T	W	T	F	S
1	2	3	4	5	6	7
8	9	10	11	12	13	14
15	16	17	18	19	20	21
22	23	24	25	26	27	28
29	30	31				

June 2016

S	M	T	W	T	F	S
			1	2	3	4
5	6	7	8	9	10	11
12	13	14	15	16	17	18
19	20	21	22	23	24	25
26	27	28	29	30		

July 2016

S	M	T	W	T	F	S
					1	2
3	4	5	6	7	8	9
10	11	12	13	14	15	16
17	18	19	20	21	22	23
24	25	26	27	28	29	30
31						

Eastern time in bold type
Pacific time in medium type

6 Monday
1st ♋

Ramadan begins

7 Tuesday
1st ♋
☿ enters ♎ **7:03 pm** 4:03 pm
☽ V/C   **8:18 pm** 5:18 pm
☽ enters ♌   11:47 pm

8 Wednesday
1st ♋
☽ enters ♌ **2:47 am**

9 Thursday
1st ♌

10 Friday

1st ♌
☽ V/C   **3:14 am** 12:14 am
☽ enters ♍ **9:46 am** 6:46 am

11 Saturday

1st ♍

12 Sunday

1st ♍
2nd quarter   **4:10 am** 1:10 am
☽ V/C   **10:47 am** 7:47 am
☿ enters ♊   **7:22 pm** 4:22 pm
☽ enters ♎   **8:33 pm** 5:33 pm

Shavuot

May 2016						
S	M	T	W	T	F	S
1	2	3	4	5	6	7
8	9	10	11	12	13	14
15	16	17	18	19	20	21
22	23	24	25	26	27	28
29	30	31				

June 2016						
S	M	T	W	T	F	S
			1	2	3	4
5	6	7	8	9	10	11
12	13	14	15	16	17	18
19	20	21	22	23	24	25
26	27	28	29	30		

July 2016						
S	M	T	W	T	F	S
					1	2
3	4	5	6	7	8	9
10	11	12	13	14	15	16
17	18	19	20	21	22	23
24	25	26	27	28	29	30
31						

Eastern time in bold type
Pacific time in medium type

13 Monday
2nd ♎︎

♆ ℞   **4:43 pm** 1:43 pm

14 Tuesday
2nd ♎︎

Flag Day

15 Wednesday
2nd ♎︎

☽ V/C   **3:00 am** 12:00 am

☽ enters ♏︎ **9:18 am** 6:18 am

16 Thursday
2nd ♏︎

17 Friday

2nd ♏

☽ V/C	**9:52 am**	6:52 am
♀ enters ⊗	**3:39 pm**	12:39 pm
☽ enters ♐	**9:34 pm**	6:34 pm

18 Saturday

2nd ♐

19 Sunday

2nd ♐

Father's Day

			May 2016								June 2016								July 2016			
S	M	T	W	T	F	S		S	M	T	W	T	F	S		S	M	T	W	T	F	S
1	2	3	4	5	6	7					1	2	3	4							1	2
8	9	10	11	12	13	14		5	6	7	8	9	10	11		3	4	5	6	7	8	9
15	16	17	18	19	20	21		12	13	14	15	16	17	18		10	11	12	13	14	15	16
22	23	24	25	26	27	28		19	20	21	22	23	24	25		17	18	19	20	21	22	23
29	30	31						26	27	28	29	30				24	25	26	27	28	29	30
																31						

Eastern time in bold type
Pacific time in medium type

20 Monday

2nd ✗

☽ V/C	**7:02 am**	4:02 am
Full Moon	**7:02 am**	4:02 am
☽ enters ♈	**7:55 am**	4:55 am
☉ enters ♋	**6:34 pm**	3:34 pm

Sun enters Cancer • Litha • Summer Solstice • 6:34 pm EDT/3:34 am PDT

21 Tuesday

3rd ♑

♀ ℞	**9:21 am**	6:21 am

22 Wednesday

3rd ♑

☽ V/C	**4:57 am**	1:57 am
✳ D	**4:01 pm**	1:01 pm
☽ enters ♒	**4:08 pm**	1:08 pm

23 Thursday

3rd ♒

Eastern time in bold type
Pacific time in medium type

24 Friday
3rd ≈≈
☽ V/C   **11:48 am** 8:48 am
☽ enters ♓ **10:30 pm** 7:30 pm

25 Saturday
3rd ♓

26 Sunday
3rd ♓
☽ V/C   **3:55 pm** 12:55 pm

		May 2016				
S	M	T	W	T	F	S
1	2	3	4	5	6	7
8	9	10	11	12	13	14
15	16	17	18	19	20	21
22	23	24	25	26	27	28
29	30	31				

		June 2016				
S	M	T	W	T	F	S
			1	2	3	4
5	6	7	8	9	10	11
12	13	14	15	16	17	18
19	20	21	22	23	24	25
26	27	28	29	30		

		July 2016				
S	M	T	W	T	F	S
					1	2
3	4	5	6	7	8	9
10	11	12	13	14	15	16
17	18	19	20	21	22	23
24	25	26	27	28	29	30
31						

27 Monday

3rd ♓
☽ enters ♈ **3:08 am** 12:08 am
☿ ℞ **7:10 am** 4:10 am
4th quarter **2:19 pm** 11:19 am

28 Tuesday

4th ♈

29 Wednesday

4th ♈
☽ V/C **3:46 am** 12:46 am
☽ enters ♉ **6:03 am** 3:03 am
☿ enters ♋ **7:24 pm** 4:24 pm
♂ D **7:38 pm** 4:38 pm

30 Thursday

4th ♉
☽ V/C **8:19 pm** 5:19 pm

1 Friday
4th ♉
☽ enters ♊   **7:44 am**   4:44 am

2 Saturday
4th ♊
☽ V/C   **11:43 pm**   8:43 pm

3 Sunday
4th ♊
☽ enters ♋   **9:20 am**   6:20 am

June 2016						
S	M	T	W	T	F	S
			1	2	3	4
5	6	7	8	9	10	11
12	13	14	15	16	17	18
19	20	21	22	23	24	25
26	27	28	29	30		

July 2016						
S	M	T	W	T	F	S
					1	2
3	4	5	6	7	8	9
10	11	12	13	14	15	16
17	18	19	20	21	22	23
24	25	26	27	28	29	30
31						

August 2016						
S	M	T	W	T	F	S
	1	2	3	4	5	6
7	8	9	10	11	12	13
14	15	16	17	18	19	20
21	22	23	24	25	26	27
28	29	30	31			

4 Monday
4th ⊙
New Moon **7:01 am** 4:01 am
☽ V/C 11:29 pm

Independence Day

5 Tuesday
1st ⊙
☽ V/C **2:29 am**
☽ enters ♌ **12:28 pm** 9:28 am

Ramadan ends

6 Wednesday
1st ♌

7 Thursday
1st ♌
☽ V/C **8:07 am** 5:07 am
☽ enters ♍ **6:41 pm** 3:41 pm
☿ enters ♏ **11:45 pm** 8:45 pm

Eastern time in bold type
Pacific time in medium type

8 Friday
1st ♍

9 Saturday
1st ♍
☽ V/C   **11:28 pm** 8:28 pm

10 Sunday
1st ♍
☽ enters ♎ **4:32 am** 1:32 am

June 2016						
S	M	T	W	T	F	S
			1	2	3	4
5	6	7	8	9	10	11
12	13	14	15	16	17	18
19	20	21	22	23	24	25
26	27	28	29	30		

July 2016						
S	M	T	W	T	F	S
					1	2
3	4	5	6	7	8	9
10	11	12	13	14	15	16
17	18	19	20	21	22	23
24	25	26	27	28	29	30
31						

August 2016						
S	M	T	W	T	F	S
	1	2	3	4	5	6
7	8	9	10	11	12	13
14	15	16	17	18	19	20
21	22	23	24	25	26	27
28	29	30	31			

11 Monday

1st ♎
2nd quarter **8:52 pm** 5:52 pm
♀ enters ♌ 10:34 pm

12 Tuesday

2nd ♎
♀ enters ♌ **1:34 am**
☽ V/C **11:01 am** 8:01 am
☽ enters ♏ **4:52 pm** 1:52 pm

13 Wednesday

2nd ♏
☿ enters ♌ **8:47 pm** 5:47 pm

14 Thursday

2nd ♏
☽ V/C **6:22 pm** 3:22 pm

Eastern time in bold type
Pacific time in medium type

15 Friday
2nd ♏
☽ enters ♐ **5:14 am** 2:14 am

16 Saturday
2nd ♐
♀ enters ♉ 9:10 pm

17 Sunday
2nd ♐
♀ enters ♉ **12:10 am**
☽ V/C **4:57 am** 1:57 am
☽ enters ♑ **3:33 pm** 12:33 pm

June 2016						
S	M	T	W	T	F	S
			1	2	3	4
5	6	7	8	9	10	11
12	13	14	15	16	17	18
19	20	21	22	23	24	25
26	27	28	29	30		

July 2016						
S	M	T	W	T	F	S
					1	2
3	4	5	6	7	8	9
10	11	12	13	14	15	16
17	18	19	20	21	22	23
24	25	26	27	28	29	30
31						

August 2016						
S	M	T	W	T	F	S
	1	2	3	4	5	6
7	8	9	10	11	12	13
14	15	16	17	18	19	20
21	22	23	24	25	26	27
28	29	30	31			

Eastern time in bold type
Pacific time in medium type

18 Monday
2nd \VS

19 Tuesday
2nd \VS
☽ V/C	**6:57 pm**	3:57 pm
Full Moon	**6:57 pm**	3:57 pm
☽ enters ≈	**11:10 pm**	8:10 pm

20 Wednesday
3rd ≈

21 Thursday
3rd ≈
☽ V/C	**9:56 pm**	6:56 pm

Eastern time in bold type
Pacific time in medium type

22 Friday

3rd ≈

D enters ♓ **4:35 am** 1:35 am
☉ enters ♌ **5:30 am** 2:30 am

Sun enters Leo

23 Saturday

3rd ♓

24 Sunday

3rd ♓
D V/C **3:06 am** 12:06 am
D enters ♈ **8:33 am** 5:33 am

June 2016						
S	M	T	W	T	F	S
				1	2	3	4
5	6	7	8	9	10	11
12	13	14	15	16	17	18
19	20	21	22	23	24	25
26	27	28	29	30		

July 2016						
S	M	T	W	T	F	S
					1	2
3	4	5	6	7	8	9
10	11	12	13	14	15	16
17	18	19	20	21	22	23
24	25	26	27	28	29	30
31						

August 2016						
S	M	T	W	T	F	S
	1	2	3	4	5	6
7	8	9	10	11	12	13
14	15	16	17	18	19	20
21	22	23	24	25	26	27
28	29	30	31			

Eastern time in bold type
Pacific time in medium type

25 Monday

3rd ♈
⚸ enters ⊗ **5:21 pm** 2:21 pm
☽ V/C   11:19 pm

26 Tuesday

3rd ♈
☽ V/C   **2:19 am**
☽ enters ♉ **11:37 am** 8:37 am
4th quarter **7:00 pm** 4:00 pm

27 Wednesday

4th ♉

28 Thursday

4th ♉
☽ V/C   **11:13 am** 8:13 am
☽ enters ♊ **2:17 pm** 11:17 am

29 Friday
4th ♊
♅ R℞ **5:06 pm** 2:06 pm

30 Saturday
4th ♊
☽ V/C **7:46 am** 4:46 am
☿ enters ♍ **2:18 pm** 11:18 am
☽ enters ♋ **5:09 pm** 2:09 pm

31 Sunday
4th ♋

June 2016						
S	M	T	W	T	F	S
			1	2	3	4
5	6	7	8	9	10	11
12	13	14	15	16	17	18
19	20	21	22	23	24	25
26	27	28	29	30		

July 2016						
S	M	T	W	T	F	S
					1	2
3	4	5	6	7	8	9
10	11	12	13	14	15	16
17	18	19	20	21	22	23
24	25	26	27	28	29	30
31						

August 2016						
S	M	T	W	T	F	S
	1	2	3	4	5	6
7	8	9	10	11	12	13
14	15	16	17	18	19	20
21	22	23	24	25	26	27
28	29	30	31			

1 Monday

4th ♋
☽ V/C **8:44 pm** 5:44 pm
☽ enters ♌ **9:12 pm** 6:12 pm

Lammas

2 Tuesday

4th ♌
♂ enters ♐ **1:49 pm** 10:49 am
New Moon **4:45 pm** 1:45 pm

3 Wednesday

1st ♌
☽ V/C 9:13 pm

4 Thursday

1st ♌
☽ V/C **12:13 am**
☽ enters ♍ **3:34 am** 12:34 am

5 Friday
1st ♍
♀ enters ♍ **11:27 am** 8:27 am
☽ V/C   **11:20 pm** 8:20 pm

6 Saturday
1st ♍
☽ enters ♎ **12:57 pm** 9:57 am

7 Sunday
1st ♎

July 2016						
S	M	T	W	T	F	S
					1	2
3	4	5	6	7	8	9
10	11	12	13	14	15	16
17	18	19	20	21	22	23
24	25	26	27	28	29	30
31						

August 2016						
S	M	T	W	T	F	S
	1	2	3	4	5	6
7	8	9	10	11	12	13
14	15	16	17	18	19	20
21	22	23	24	25	26	27
28	29	30	31			

September 2016						
S	M	T	W	T	F	S
				1	2	3
4	5	6	7	8	9	10
11	12	13	14	15	16	17
18	19	20	21	22	23	24
25	26	27	28	29	30	

8 Monday
1st ♎
☽ V/C   **1:41 pm** 10:41 am
☽ enters ♏   9:51 pm

9 Tuesday
1st ♎
☽ enters ♏ **12:51 am**

10 Wednesday
1st ♏
2nd quarter **2:21 pm** 11:21 am
☽ V/C   10:22 pm

11 Thursday
2nd ♏
☽ V/C   **1:22 am**
☽ enters ♐   **1:24 pm** 10:24 am

12 Friday

2nd ♐
♀ enters ≈ **3:03 am** 12:03 am

13 Saturday

2nd ♐
♄ D **5:50 am** 2:50 am
☽ V/C **1:37 pm** 10:37 am
☽ enters ♑ 9:11 pm

14 Sunday

2nd ♐
☽ enters ♑ **12:11 am**

		July 2016				
S	M	T	W	T	F	S
					1	2
3	4	5	6	7	8	9
10	11	12	13	14	15	16
17	18	19	20	21	22	23
24	25	26	27	28	29	30
31						

		August 2016				
S	M	T	W	T	F	S
	1	2	3	4	5	6
7	8	9	10	11	12	13
14	15	16	17	18	19	20
21	22	23	24	25	26	27
28	29	30	31			

		September 2016				
S	M	T	W	T	F	S
				1	2	3
4	5	6	7	8	9	10
11	12	13	14	15	16	17
18	19	20	21	22	23	24
25	26	27	28	29	30	

Eastern time in bold type
Pacific time in medium type

15 Monday

2nd ♑
☽ V/C   **10:45 pm** 7:45 pm

16 Tuesday

2nd ♑
☽ enters ♒   **7:52 am** 4:52 am

17 Wednesday

2nd ♒

18 Thursday

2nd ♒
☽ V/C   **5:27 am** 2:27 am
Full Moon   **5:27 am** 2:27 am
☽ enters ♓ **12:34 pm** 9:34 am

19 Friday
3rd ♓

20 Saturday
3rd ♓
☽ V/C   **8:21 am** 5:21 am
☽ enters ♈ **3:18 pm** 12:18 pm

21 Sunday
3rd ♈

July 2016						
S	M	T	W	T	F	S
					1	2
3	4	5	6	7	8	9
10	11	12	13	14	15	16
17	18	19	20	21	22	23
24	25	26	27	28	29	30
31						

August 2016						
S	M	T	W	T	F	S
	1	2	3	4	5	6
7	8	9	10	11	12	13
14	15	16	17	18	19	20
21	22	23	24	25	26	27
28	29	30	31			

September 2016						
S	M	T	W	T	F	S
				1	2	3
4	5	6	7	8	9	10
11	12	13	14	15	16	17
18	19	20	21	22	23	24
25	26	27	28	29	30	

Eastern time in bold type
Pacific time in medium type

22 Monday
3rd ♈
☽ V/C   **7:48 am**   4:48 am
☉ enters ♍ **12:38 pm** 9:38 am
☽ enters ♉ **5:19 pm**   2:19 pm

Sun enters Virgo

23 Tuesday
3rd ♉

24 Wednesday
3rd ♉
☽ V/C   **3:38 pm** 12:38 pm
☽ enters ♊   **7:40 pm** 4:40 pm
4th quarter **11:41 pm** 8:41 pm

25 Thursday
4th ♊

Eastern time in bold type
Pacific time in medium type

26 Friday

4th ♊
☽ V/C   **8:30 pm**   5:30 pm
☽ enters ♋ **11:06 pm**   8:06 pm

27 Saturday

4th ♋

28 Sunday

4th ♋
☽ V/C   11:23 pm

July 2016						
S	M	T	W	T	F	S
					1	2
3	4	5	6	7	8	9
10	11	12	13	14	15	16
17	18	19	20	21	22	23
24	25	26	27	28	29	30
31						

August 2016						
S	M	T	W	T	F	S
	1	2	3	4	5	6
7	8	9	10	11	12	13
14	15	16	17	18	19	20
21	22	23	24	25	26	27
28	29	30	31			

September 2016						
S	M	T	W	T	F	S
				1	2	3
4	5	6	7	8	9	10
11	12	13	14	15	16	17
18	19	20	21	22	23	24
25	26	27	28	29	30	

29 Monday

4th ♋
☽ V/C   **2:23 am**
☽ enters ♌   **4:11 am** 1:11 am
♀ enters ♎ **10:07 pm** 7:07 pm

30 Tuesday

4th ♌
☿ ℞   **9:04 am** 6:04 am
☽ V/C   9:20 pm

Mercury retrograde until 9/22

31 Wednesday

4th ♌
☽ V/C   **12:20 am**
♇ ℞   **3:09 am** 12:09 am
☽ enters ♍ **11:22 am** 8:22 am

1 Thursday

4th ♍
New Moon   **5:03 am** 2:03 am

Solar eclipse 9° ♍ 20' • 5:07 am EDT/2:07 am PDT

Eastern time in bold type
Pacific time in medium type

2 Friday

1st ♍

☽ V/C   **6:13 pm** 3:13 pm
☽ enters ♎ **8:55 pm** 5:55 pm

3 Saturday

1st ♎

4 Sunday

1st ♎
☽ V/C   **8:30 pm** 5:30 pm

		August 2016				
S	M	T	W	T	F	S
	1	2	3	4	5	6
7	8	9	10	11	12	13
14	15	16	17	18	19	20
21	22	23	24	25	26	27
28	29	30	31			

		September 2016				
S	M	T	W	T	F	S
				1	2	3
4	5	6	7	8	9	10
11	12	13	14	15	16	17
18	19	20	21	22	23	24
25	26	27	28	29	30	

		October 2016				
S	M	T	W	T	F	S
						1
2	3	4	5	6	7	8
9	10	11	12	13	14	15
16	17	18	19	20	21	22
23	24	25	26	27	28	29
30	31					

Eastern time in bold type
Pacific time in medium type

5 Monday

1st ♎︎
☽ enters ♏︎ **8:38 am** 5:38 am

Labor Day

6 Tuesday

1st ♏︎

7 Wednesday

1st ♏︎
☽ V/C **8:43 pm** 5:43 pm
☽ enters ♐︎ **9:20 pm** 6:20 pm

8 Thursday

1st ♐︎

Eastern time in bold type
Pacific time in medium type

9 Friday

1st ♐
♃ enters ♎	**7:18 am**	4:18 am
2nd quarter	**7:49 am**	4:49 am
☽ V/C	**8:51 pm**	5:51 pm

10 Saturday

2nd ♐
☽ enters ♑	**8:55 am**	5:55 am

11 Sunday

2nd ♑

August 2016						
S	M	T	W	T	F	S
	1	2	3	4	5	6
7	8	9	10	11	12	13
14	15	16	17	18	19	20
21	22	23	24	25	26	27
28	29	30	31			

September 2016						
S	M	T	W	T	F	S
				1	2	3
4	5	6	7	8	9	10
11	12	13	14	15	16	17
18	19	20	21	22	23	24
25	26	27	28	29	30	

October 2016						
S	M	T	W	T	F	S
						1
2	3	4	5	6	7	8
9	10	11	12	13	14	15
16	17	18	19	20	21	22
23	24	25	26	27	28	29
30	31					

12 Monday

2nd ♑
| ☽ V/C | **6:00 am** | 3:00 am |
| ☽ enters ♒ | **5:28 pm** | 2:28 pm |

13 Tuesday

2nd ♒

14 Wednesday

2nd ♒
| ☽ V/C | **11:31 am** | 8:31 am |
| ☽ enters ♓ | **10:23 pm** | 7:23 pm |

15 Thursday

2nd ♓

Eastern time in bold type
Pacific time in medium type

16 Friday

2nd ♓

☽ V/C	**3:05 pm** 12:05 pm
Full Moon	**3:05 pm** 12:05 pm
☽ enters ♈	9:22 pm

Lunar eclipse 24° ♓ 12' • 2:54 pm EDT/11:54 am PDT

17 Saturday

3rd ♓
☽ enters ♈ **12:22 am**

18 Sunday

3rd ♈

☽ V/C	**4:11 pm** 1:11 pm
☽ enters ♉	9:58 pm

August 2016						
S	M	T	W	T	F	S
	1	2	3	4	5	6
7	8	9	10	11	12	13
14	15	16	17	18	19	20
21	22	23	24	25	26	27
28	29	30	31			

September 2016						
S	M	T	W	T	F	S
				1	2	3
4	5	6	7	8	9	10
11	12	13	14	15	16	17
18	19	20	21	22	23	24
25	26	27	28	29	30	

October 2016						
S	M	T	W	T	F	S
						1
2	3	4	5	6	7	8
9	10	11	12	13	14	15
16	17	18	19	20	21	22
23	24	25	26	27	28	29
30	31					

Eastern time in bold type
Pacific time in medium type

19 Monday
3rd ♈
☽ enters ♉ **12:58 am**

20 Tuesday
3rd ♉
☽ V/C   **11:32 pm** 8:32 pm
☽ enters ♊   10:53 pm

21 Wednesday
3rd ♉
☽ enters ♊   **1:53 am**
☿ D   10:31 pm

UN International Day of Peace

22 Thursday
3rd ♊
☿ D   **1:31 am**
☉ enters ♎ **10:21 am** 7:21 am

Sun enters Libra • Mabon • Fall Equinox • 10:21 am EDT/7:21 am PDT

Eastern time in bold type
Pacific time in medium type

23 Friday

3rd ♊

D V/C   **3:57 am** 12:57 am
D enters ♋ **4:33 am** 1:33 am
4th quarter   **5:56 am** 2:56 am
♀ enters ♏ **10:51 am** 7:51 am

24 Saturday

4th ♋
D V/C   **9:42 pm** 6:42 pm

25 Sunday

4th ♋
D enters ♌ **9:48 am** 6:48 am

August 2016						
S	M	T	W	T	F	S
	1	2	3	4	5	6
7	8	9	10	11	12	13
14	15	16	17	18	19	20
21	22	23	24	25	26	27
28	29	30	31			

September 2016						
S	M	T	W	T	F	S
				1	2	3
4	5	6	7	8	9	10
11	12	13	14	15	16	17
18	19	20	21	22	23	24
25	26	27	28	29	30	

October 2016						
S	M	T	W	T	F	S
						1
2	3	4	5	6	7	8
9	10	11	12	13	14	15
16	17	18	19	20	21	22
23	24	25	26	27	28	29
30	31					

26 Monday
4th ♌
♇ D   **11:01 am** 8:01 am

27 Tuesday
4th ♌
♂ enters ♑ **4:07 am** 1:07 am
☽ V/C   **4:52 am** 1:52 am
☽ enters ♍ **5:43 pm** 2:43 pm

28 Wednesday
4th ♍

29 Thursday
4th ♍
☽ V/C   **6:05 am** 3:05 am

30 Friday
4th ♍
☽ enters ♎ **3:52 am** 12:52 am
New Moon **8:11 pm** 5:11 pm

1 Saturday
1st ♎
☽ V/C 10:43 pm

2 Sunday
1st ♎
☽ V/C **1:43 am**
☽ enters ♏ **3:43 pm** 12:43 pm

Islamic New Year

August 2016						
S	M	T	W	T	F	S
	1	2	3	4	5	6
7	8	9	10	11	12	13
14	15	16	17	18	19	20
21	22	23	24	25	26	27
28	29	30	31			

September 2016						
S	M	T	W	T	F	S
				1	2	3
4	5	6	7	8	9	10
11	12	13	14	15	16	17
18	19	20	21	22	23	24
25	26	27	28	29	30	

October 2016						
S	M	T	W	T	F	S
						1
2	3	4	5	6	7	8
9	10	11	12	13	14	15
16	17	18	19	20	21	22
23	24	25	26	27	28	29
30	31					

3 Monday
1st ♏

Rosh Hashanah

4 Tuesday
1st ♏
☽ V/C   **9:04 pm** 6:04 pm

5 Wednesday
1st ♏
☽ enters ♐   **4:26 am** 1:26 am

6 Thursday
1st ♐
☽ V/C   11:26 pm

7 Friday

1st ♐

☽ V/C	**2:26 am**	
☿ enters ♎	**3:56 am**	12:56 am
☽ enters ♑	**4:40 pm**	1:40 pm

8 Saturday

1st ♑

2nd quarter	9:33 pm

9 Sunday

1st ♑

2nd quarter	**12:33 am**	
☽ V/C	**12:51 pm**	9:51 am
☽ enters ♒		11:33 pm

September 2016	October 2016	November 2016
S M T W T F S	S M T W T F S	S M T W T F S
1 2 3	1	1 2 3 4 5
4 5 6 7 8 9 10	2 3 4 5 6 7 8	6 7 8 9 10 11 12
11 12 13 14 15 16 17	9 10 11 12 13 14 15	13 14 15 16 17 18 19
18 19 20 21 22 23 24	16 17 18 19 20 21 22	20 21 22 23 24 25 26
25 26 27 28 29 30	23 24 25 26 27 28 29	27 28 29 30
	30 31	

Eastern time in bold type
Pacific time in medium type

10 Monday

2nd ♑
☽ enters ♒ **2:33 am**

Columbus Day (observed)

11 Tuesday

2nd ♒
☽ V/C **7:49 pm** 4:49 pm

12 Wednesday

2nd ♒
☽ enters ♓ **8:43 am** 5:43 am

Yom Kippur

13 Thursday

2nd ♓
♀ enters ♈ **6:41 am** 3:41 am

14 Friday
2nd ♓
☽ V/C   **3:13 am** 12:13 am
☽ enters ♈ **11:08 am** 8:08 am

15 Saturday
2nd ♈
☽ V/C   9:23 pm
Full Moon   9:23 pm

16 Sunday
2nd ♈
☽ V/C   **12:23 am**
Full Moon   **12:23 am**
☽ enters ♉ **11:04 am** 8:04 am

September 2016						
S	M	T	W	T	F	S
					1	2	3
4	5	6	7	8	9	10
11	12	13	14	15	16	17
18	19	20	21	22	23	24
25	26	27	28	29	30	

October 2016						
S	M	T	W	T	F	S
						1
2	3	4	5	6	7	8
9	10	11	12	13	14	15
16	17	18	19	20	21	22
23	24	25	26	27	28	29
30	31					

November 2016						
S	M	T	W	T	F	S
		1	2	3	4	5
6	7	8	9	10	11	12
13	14	15	16	17	18	19
20	21	22	23	24	25	26
27	28	29	30			

17 Monday

3rd ♉

| ☽ V/C | **10:47 am** | 7:47 am |
| ☿ D | **3:31 pm** | 12:31 pm |

Sukkot begins

18 Tuesday

3rd ♉
| ♀ enters ♐ | **3:01 am** | 12:01 am |
| ☽ enters ♊ | **10:30 am** | 7:30 am |

19 Wednesday

3rd ♊
| ⚷ enters ♌ | **9:06 pm** | 6:06 pm |

20 Thursday

3rd ♊

| ☽ V/C | **7:17 am** | 4:17 am |
| ☽ enters ♋ | **11:28 am** | 8:28 am |

Eastern time in bold type
Pacific time in medium type

21 Friday
3rd ♋

22 Saturday
3rd ♋
☽ V/C	**3:14 pm** 12:14 pm
4th quarter	**3:14 pm** 12:14 pm
☽ enters ♌	**3:34 pm** 12:34 pm
☉ enters ♏	**7:46 pm** 4:46 pm

Sun enters Scorpio

23 Sunday
4th ♌

Sukkot ends

September 2016	October 2016	November 2016
S M T W T F S	S M T W T F S	S M T W T F S
1 2 3	1	1 2 3 4 5
4 5 6 7 8 9 10	2 3 4 5 6 7 8	6 7 8 9 10 11 12
11 12 13 14 15 16 17	9 10 11 12 13 14 15	13 14 15 16 17 18 19
18 19 20 21 22 23 24	16 17 18 19 20 21 22	20 21 22 23 24 25 26
25 26 27 28 29 30	23 24 25 26 27 28 29	27 28 29 30
	30 31	

24 Monday
4th ♌
☽ V/C	**8:21 am**	5:21 am
☿ enters ♏	**4:46 pm**	1:46 pm
☽ enters ♍	**11:16 pm**	8:16 pm

25 Tuesday
4th ♍

26 Wednesday
4th ♍
☽ V/C	**2:33 pm**	11:33 am

27 Thursday
4th ♍
☽ enters ♎	**9:51 am**	6:51 am

Eastern time in bold type
Pacific time in medium type

28 Friday
4th ♎

29 Saturday
4th ♎
☽ V/C **6:09 am** 3:09 am
☽ enters ♏ **10:01 pm** 7:01 pm

30 Sunday
4th ♏
New Moon **1:38 pm** 10:38 am

September 2016						
S	M	T	W	T	F	S
				1	2	3
4	5	6	7	8	9	10
11	12	13	14	15	16	17
18	19	20	21	22	23	24
25	26	27	28	29	30	

October 2016						
S	M	T	W	T	F	S
						1
2	3	4	5	6	7	8
9	10	11	12	13	14	15
16	17	18	19	20	21	22
23	24	25	26	27	28	29
30	31					

November 2016						
S	M	T	W	T	F	S
		1	2	3	4	5
6	7	8	9	10	11	12
13	14	15	16	17	18	19
20	21	22	23	24	25	26
27	28	29	30			

Eastern time in bold type
Pacific time in medium type

31 Monday
1st ♏
☽ V/C   **10:44 pm**   7:44 pm

Halloween/Samhain

1 Tuesday
1st ♏
☽ enters ♐ **10:43 am**   7:43 am

All Saints' Day

2 Wednesday
1st ♐

3 Thursday
1st ♐
☽ V/C   **6:35 am**   3:35 am
☽ enters ♑ **11:05 pm**   8:05 pm

Eastern time in bold type
Pacific time in medium type

4 Friday
1st ♑

5 Saturday
1st ♑

6 Sunday
1st ♑

⚹ enters ♐	**4:40 am**	1:40 am
☽ V/C	**4:56 am**	1:56 am
☽ enters ♒	**8:55 am**	5:55 am

Daylight Saving Time ends at 2 am

October 2016	November 2016	December 2016
S M T W T F S	S M T W T F S	S M T W T F S
1	1 2 3 4 5	1 2 3
2 3 4 5 6 7 8	6 7 8 9 10 11 12	4 5 6 7 8 9 10
9 10 11 12 13 14 15	13 14 15 16 17 18 19	11 12 13 14 15 16 17
16 17 18 19 20 21 22	20 21 22 23 24 25 26	18 19 20 21 22 23 24
23 24 25 26 27 28 29	27 28 29 30	25 26 27 28 29 30 31
30 31		

7 Monday

1st ≈
2nd quarter **2:51 pm** 11:51 am

8 Tuesday

2nd ≈
☽ V/C **8:54 am** 5:54 am
☽ enters ♓ **4:45 pm** 1:45 pm
♂ enters ≈ 9:51 pm

Election Day

9 Wednesday

2nd ♓
♂ enters ≈ **12:51 am**

10 Thursday

2nd ♓
☽ V/C **6:16 pm** 3:16 pm
☽ enters ♈ **8:45 pm** 5:45 pm

Eastern time in bold type
Pacific time in medium type

11 Friday

2nd ♈
♀ enters ♑ **11:54 pm** 8:54 pm

Veterans Day

12 Saturday

2nd ♈
☽ V/C **7:45 am** 4:45 am
☿ enters ♐ **9:40 am** 6:40 am
☽ enters ♉ **9:24 pm** 6:24 pm

13 Sunday

2nd ♉

October 2016								November 2016								December 2016					
S	M	T	W	T	F	S		S	M	T	W	T	F	S		S	M	T	W	T	F	S
						1				1	2	3	4	5							1	2	3
2	3	4	5	6	7	8		6	7	8	9	10	11	12		4	5	6	7	8	9	10
9	10	11	12	13	14	15		13	14	15	16	17	18	19		11	12	13	14	15	16	17
16	17	18	19	20	21	22		20	21	22	23	24	25	26		18	19	20	21	22	23	24
23	24	25	26	27	28	29		27	28	29	30					25	26	27	28	29	30	31
30	31																				

14 Monday

2nd ♉
☽ V/C	**8:52 am**	5:52 am
Full Moon	**8:52 am**	5:52 am
☽ enters ♊	**8:23 pm**	5:23 pm

15 Tuesday

3rd ♊

16 Wednesday

3rd ♊
| ☽ V/C | **5:58 am** | 2:58 am |
| ☽ enters ♋ | **7:57 pm** | 4:57 pm |

17 Thursday

3rd ♋

Eastern time in bold type
Pacific time in medium type

18 Friday
3rd ⊗
☽ V/C   **5:02 pm**   2:02 pm
☽ enters ♌ **10:14 pm** 7:14 pm

19 Saturday
3rd ♌
♆ D   **11:38 pm** 8:38 pm

20 Sunday
3rd ♌

October 2016						
S	M	T	W	T	F	S
						1
2	3	4	5	6	7	8
9	10	11	12	13	14	15
16	17	18	19	20	21	22
23	24	25	26	27	28	29
30	31					

November 2016						
S	M	T	W	T	F	S
		1	2	3	4	5
6	7	8	9	10	11	12
13	14	15	16	17	18	19
20	21	22	23	24	25	26
27	28	29	30			

December 2016						
S	M	T	W	T	F	S
				1	2	3
4	5	6	7	8	9	10
11	12	13	14	15	16	17
18	19	20	21	22	23	24
25	26	27	28	29	30	31

21 Monday

3rd ♌
☽ V/C	**3:33 am**	12:33 am
4th quarter	**3:33 am**	12:33 am
☽ enters ♍	**4:34 am**	1:34 am
☉ enters ♐	**4:22 pm**	1:22 pm

Sun enters Sagittarius

22 Tuesday

4th ♍
☽ V/C	**12:41 pm**	9:41 am

23 Wednesday

4th ♍
☽ enters ♎	**2:42 pm**	11:42 am

24 Thursday

4th ♎

Thanksgiving Day

Eastern time in bold type
Pacific time in medium type

25 Friday
4th ♎
☽ V/C   **8:52 am**   5:52 am

26 Saturday
4th ♎
☽ enters ♏   **3:01 am** 12:01 am

27 Sunday
4th ♏
☽ V/C   **4:48 pm**   1:48 pm

October 2016						
S	M	T	W	T	F	S
						1
2	3	4	5	6	7	8
9	10	11	12	13	14	15
16	17	18	19	20	21	22
23	24	25	26	27	28	29
30	31					

November 2016						
S	M	T	W	T	F	S
		1	2	3	4	5
6	7	8	9	10	11	12
13	14	15	16	17	18	19
20	21	22	23	24	25	26
27	28	29	30			

December 2016						
S	M	T	W	T	F	S
				1	2	3
4	5	6	7	8	9	10
11	12	13	14	15	16	17
18	19	20	21	22	23	24
25	26	27	28	29	30	31

28 Monday
4th ♏
☽ enters ♐ **3:46 pm** 12:46 pm

29 Tuesday
4th ♐
New Moon **7:18 am** 4:18 am

30 Wednesday
1st ♐
☽ V/C **11:08 pm** 8:08 pm

1 Thursday
1st ♐
☽ enters ♑ **3:52 am** 12:52 am
⚷ D **4:53 am** 1:53 am
♆ Rₓ **10:38 am** 7:38 am

Eastern time in bold type
Pacific time in medium type

2 Friday
1st ♑
☿ enters ♑   **4:18 pm**   1:18 pm

3 Saturday
1st ♑
☽ V/C   **5:16 am**   2:16 am
☽ enters ≈ **2:44 pm**   11:44 am

4 Sunday
1st ≈

November 2016						
S	M	T	W	T	F	S
		1	2	3	4	5
6	7	8	9	10	11	12
13	14	15	16	17	18	19
20	21	22	23	24	25	26
27	28	29	30			

December 2016						
S	M	T	W	T	F	S
				1	2	3
4	5	6	7	8	9	10
11	12	13	14	15	16	17
18	19	20	21	22	23	24
25	26	27	28	29	30	31

January 2017						
S	M	T	W	T	F	S
1	2	3	4	5	6	7
8	9	10	11	12	13	14
15	16	17	18	19	20	21
22	23	24	25	26	27	28
29	30	31				

5 Monday
1st ≈
☽ V/C · **6:23 am** · 3:23 am
☽ enters ♓ · **11:31 pm** · 8:31 pm

6 Tuesday
1st ♓

7 Wednesday
1st ♓
2nd quarter · **4:03 am** · 1:03 am
☽ V/C · **9:05 am** · 6:05 am
♀ enters ≈ · **9:51 am** · 6:51 am

8 Thursday
2nd ♓
☽ enters ♈ · **5:15 am** · 2:15 am

9 Friday
2nd ♈
♀ D   **7:26 pm**   4:26 pm
☽ V/C   **8:06 pm**   5:06 pm

10 Saturday

2nd ♈
☽ enters ♉   **7:41 am**   4:41 am

11 Sunday

2nd ♉
☽ V/C   **11:04 pm**   8:04 pm

November 2016						
S	M	T	W	T	F	S
		1	2	3	4	5
6	7	8	9	10	11	12
13	14	15	16	17	18	19
20	21	22	23	24	25	26
27	28	29	30			

December 2016						
S	M	T	W	T	F	S
				1	2	3
4	5	6	7	8	9	10
11	12	13	14	15	16	17
18	19	20	21	22	23	24
25	26	27	28	29	30	31

January 2017						
S	M	T	W	T	F	S
1	2	3	4	5	6	7
8	9	10	11	12	13	14
15	16	17	18	19	20	21
22	23	24	25	26	27	28
29	30	31				

12 Monday

2nd ♉
☽ enters ♊   **7:41 am**   4:41 am

13 Tuesday

2nd ♊
Full Moon   **7:06 pm**   4:06 pm
☽ V/C   9:58 pm

14 Wednesday

3rd ♊
☽ V/C   **12:58 am**
☽ enters ♋   **7:09 am**   4:09 am

15 Thursday

3rd ♋
☽ V/C   **4:37 pm**   1:37 pm

Eastern time in bold type
Pacific time in medium type

16 Friday
3rd ♋
☽ enters ♌   **8:15 am**   5:15 am

17 Saturday
3rd ♌

18 Sunday
3rd ♌
☽ V/C   **11:55 am**   8:55 am
☽ enters ♍ **12:52 pm**   9:52 am

November 2016						
S	M	T	W	T	F	S
		1	2	3	4	5
6	7	8	9	10	11	12
13	14	15	16	17	18	19
20	21	22	23	24	25	26
27	28	29	30			

December 2016						
S	M	T	W	T	F	S
				1	2	3
4	5	6	7	8	9	10
11	12	13	14	15	16	17
18	19	20	21	22	23	24
25	26	27	28	29	30	31

January 2017						
S	M	T	W	T	F	S
1	2	3	4	5	6	7
8	9	10	11	12	13	14
15	16	17	18	19	20	21
22	23	24	25	26	27	28
29	30	31				

Eastern time in bold type
Pacific time in medium type

19 Monday
3rd ♍
♂ enters ♓ **4:23 am** 1:23 am
☿ R **5:55 am** 2:55 am

Mercury retrograde until 1/8/17

20 Tuesday
3rd ♍
☽ V/C **8:56 pm** 5:56 pm
4th quarter **8:56 pm** 5:56 pm
☽ enters ♎ **9:40 pm** 6:40 pm

21 Wednesday
4th ♎
☉ enters ♑ **5:44 am** 2:44 am

Sun enters Capricorn • Yule • Winter Solstice • 5:44 am EST/2:44 am PST

22 Thursday
4th ♎
☽ V/C **2:31 pm** 11:31 am

Eastern time in bold type
Pacific time in medium type

23 Friday
4th ♎︎
☽ enters ♏︎ **9:32 am** 6:32 am

24 Saturday
4th ♏︎
☽ V/C   11:22 pm

Christmas Eve

25 Sunday
4th ♏︎
☽ V/C   **2:22 am**
☽ enters ♐︎ **10:19 pm** 7:19 pm

Christmas Day • Hanukkah begins

November 2016						
S	M	T	W	T	F	S
		1	2	3	4	5
6	7	8	9	10	11	12
13	14	15	16	17	18	19
20	21	22	23	24	25	26
27	28	29	30			

December 2016						
S	M	T	W	T	F	S
				1	2	3
4	5	6	7	8	9	10
11	12	13	14	15	16	17
18	19	20	21	22	23	24
25	26	27	28	29	30	31

January 2017						
S	M	T	W	T	F	S
1	2	3	4	5	6	7
8	9	10	11	12	13	14
15	16	17	18	19	20	21
22	23	24	25	26	27	28
29	30	31				

26 Monday
4th ♐

Kwanzaa begins

---

27 Tuesday
4th ♐
☿ enters ♓   **7:23 pm**   4:23 pm
☽ V/C   **8:45 pm**   5:45 pm

---

28 Wednesday
4th ♐
☽ enters ♑ **10:12 am**   7:12 am
New Moon   10:53 pm

---

29 Thursday
4th ♑
New Moon   **1:53 am**
♅ D   **4:29 am**   1:29 am

Eastern time in bold type
Pacific time in medium type

30 Friday
1st ♑
☽ V/C   **3:07 am** 12:07 am
☽ enters ♒   **8:29 pm** 5:29 pm

31 Saturday
1st ♒

New Year's Eve

1 Sunday
1st ♒
☽ V/C   11:59 pm

New Year's Day • Kwanzaa ends • Hanukkah ends

November 2016						
S	M	T	W	T	F	S
		1	2	3	4	5
6	7	8	9	10	11	12
13	14	15	16	17	18	19
20	21	22	23	24	25	26
27	28	29	30			

December 2016						
S	M	T	W	T	F	S
				1	2	3
4	5	6	7	8	9	10
11	12	13	14	15	16	17
18	19	20	21	22	23	24
25	26	27	28	29	30	31

January 2017						
S	M	T	W	T	F	S
1	2	3	4	5	6	7
8	9	10	11	12	13	14
15	16	17	18	19	20	21
22	23	24	25	26	27	28
29	30	31				

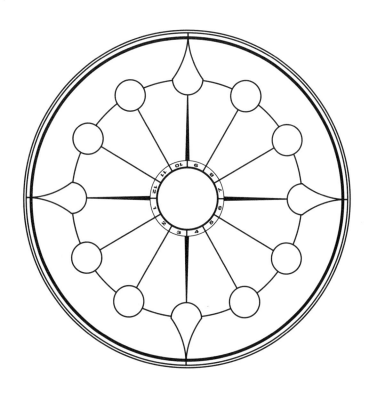

The Year 2017

January
S	M	T	W	T	F	S
1	2	3	4	5	6	7
8	9	10	11	12	13	14
15	16	17	18	19	20	21
22	23	24	25	26	27	28
29	30	31				

February
S	M	T	W	T	F	S
			1	2	3	4
5	6	7	8	9	10	11
12	13	14	15	16	17	18
19	20	21	22	23	24	25
26	27	28				

March
S	M	T	W	T	F	S
			1	2	3	4
5	6	7	8	9	10	11
12	13	14	15	16	17	18
19	20	21	22	23	24	25
26	27	28	29	30	31	

April
S	M	T	W	T	F	S
						1
2	3	4	5	6	7	8
9	10	11	12	13	14	15
16	17	18	19	20	21	22
23	24	25	26	27	28	29
30						

May
S	M	T	W	T	F	S
	1	2	3	4	5	6
7	8	9	10	11	12	13
14	15	16	17	18	19	20
21	22	23	24	25	26	27
28	29	30	31			

June
S	M	T	W	T	F	S
				1	2	3
4	5	6	7	8	9	10
11	12	13	14	15	16	17
18	19	20	21	22	23	24
25	26	27	28	29	30	

July
S	M	T	W	T	F	S
						1
2	3	4	5	6	7	8
9	10	11	12	13	14	15
16	17	18	19	20	21	22
23	24	25	26	27	28	29
30	31					

August
S	M	T	W	T	F	S
		1	2	3	4	5
6	7	8	9	10	11	12
13	14	15	16	17	18	19
20	21	22	23	24	25	26
27	28	29	30	31		

September
S	M	T	W	T	F	S
					1	2
3	4	5	6	7	8	9
10	11	12	13	14	15	16
17	18	19	20	21	22	23
24	25	26	27	28	29	30

October
S	M	T	W	T	F	S
1	2	3	4	5	6	7
8	9	10	11	12	13	14
15	16	17	18	19	20	21
22	23	24	25	26	27	28
29	30	31				

November
S	M	T	W	T	F	S
			1	2	3	4
5	6	7	8	9	10	11
12	13	14	15	16	17	18
19	20	21	22	23	24	25
26	27	28	29	30		

December
S	M	T	W	T	F	S
					1	2
3	4	5	6	7	8	9
10	11	12	13	14	15	16
17	18	19	20	21	22	23
24	25	26	27	28	29	30
31						

JANUARY 2015

☽ Last Aspect day	ET / hr:mn / PT		asp	☽ Ingress sign	day	ET / hr:mn / PT	
1	**7:19 am**	4:19 am	△♀	♊	1	**12:09 pm**	9:09 am
3	**6:55 am**	3:55 am	△♂	♋	3	**8:08 pm**	5:08 pm
4	**11:53 pm**	8:53 pm	☍☉	♌	6	**6:03 am**	3:03 am
8	**12:05 pm**	9:05 am	☍♂	♍	8	**5:58 pm**	2:58 pm
10	**10:46 am**	7:46 am	△☉	♎	11	**6:57 am**	3:57 am
13	**4:46 am**	1:46 am	□☉	♏	13	**6:44 pm**	3:44 pm
15	**6:52 pm**	3:52 pm	⚹☉	♐	16	**3:01 am**	12:01 am
17	**2:25 pm**	11:25 am	△♃	♑	18	**7:04 am**	4:04 am
19	**5:51 am**	2:51 am	☌♇	♒	20	**7:59 am**	4:59 am
21	**8:45 pm**	5:45 pm	☌♀	♓	22	**7:48 am**	4:48 am
23	**6:13 am**	3:13 am	⚹♇	♈	24	**8:31 am**	5:31 am
26	**9:23 am**	6:23 am	⚹♀	♉	26	**11:37 am**	8:37 am
27	**9:18 pm**	6:18 pm	□♃	♊	28	**5:36 pm**	2:36 pm
30	**4:24 am**	1:24 am	⚹♃	♉	30		11:09 pm
30	**4:24 am**	1:24 am	⚹♃	♉	31	**2:09 am**	

☽ Phases & Eclipses phase	day	ET / hr:mn / PT	
Full Moon	4	**11:53 pm**	8:53 pm
4th Quarter	13	**4:46 am**	1:46 am
New Moon	20	**8:14 am**	5:14 am
2nd Quarter	26	**11:48 pm**	8:48 pm

Planet Ingress		day	ET / hr:mn / PT	
♀	♒	3	**9:48 am**	6:48 am
☿	♒	4	**8:08 pm**	5:08 pm
⚳	♑	8	**10:24 am**	7:24 am
♂	♓	12	**5:20 am**	2:20 am
☉	♒	20	**4:43 am**	1:43 am
♀	♓	27	**10:00 am**	7:00 am
⚶	♒	28	**2:43 pm**	11:43 am

Planetary Motion		day	ET / hr:mn / PT	
☿	℞	21	**10:54 am**	7:54 am

1 THURSDAY
☽ △ ☿ **1:18 am**
☽ △ ♀ **7:19 am** 4:19 am
☽ ☍ ♄ **1:53 pm** 10:53 am
♂ ☍ ♃ **2:49 pm** 11:49 am
☽ □ ♆ **10:07 pm** 7:07 pm

2 FRIDAY
☽ ⚻ ☉ **10:07 am** 7:07 am
☽ ⚹ ♅ **11:30 am** 8:30 am
☽ ⚻ ♇ **12:36 pm** 9:36 am

3 SATURDAY
☉ □ ♅ **3:40 am** 12:40 am
☽ ⚹ ♃ **4:13 am** 1:13 am
☽ △ ♂ **6:55 am** 3:55 am
☽ ⚻ ☿ **4:47 pm** 1:47 pm
☉ ☌ ♇ **6:34 pm** 3:34 pm
☽ ⚻ ♀ **9:16 pm** 6:16 pm
☽ ⚻ ♄ **10:22 pm** 7:22 pm

4 SUNDAY
☽ △ ♆ **6:32 am** 3:32 am
♀ ⚹ ♄ **9:15 am** 6:15 am
☽ □ ♅ **8:18 pm** 5:18 pm
☽ ☍ ♇ **9:34 pm** 6:34 pm
☽ ☍ ☉ **11:53 pm** 8:53 pm

5 MONDAY
☽ ⚺ ♃ **1:11 pm** 10:11 am
☿ ⚹ ♄ **5:21 pm** 2:21 pm
☽ ⚻ ♂ **8:16 pm** 5:16 pm

6 TUESDAY
☽ △ ♄ **8:50 am** 5:50 am
☽ ☍ ☿ **10:53 am** 7:53 am
☽ ☍ ♀ **1:52 pm** 10:52 am
☽ ⚻ ♆ **4:58 pm** 1:58 pm

7 WEDNESDAY
☽ △ ♅ **7:10 am** 4:10 am
☽ ⚻ ♇ **8:34 am** 5:34 am
☽ ⚻ ☉ **4:17 pm** 1:17 pm
♀ ⚺ ♆ **8:34 pm** 5:34 pm
☽ ☌ ♃ 9:07 pm

8 THURSDAY
☽ ☌ ♃ **12:07 am**
☽ ☍ ♂ **12:05 pm** 9:05 am
☿ ⚺ ♆ **1:56 pm** 10:56 am
☽ □ ♄ **9:19 pm** 6:19 pm

9 FRIDAY
☽ ☍ ♆ **5:20 am** 2:20 am
☽ ⚻ ☿ **7:24 am** 4:24 am
☽ ⚻ ♀ **9:08 am** 6:08 am
☽ ⚻ ♅ **7:49 pm** 4:49 pm
☽ △ ♇ **9:21 pm** 6:21 pm

10 SATURDAY
☽ △ ☉ **10:46 am** 7:46 am
☽ ⚺ ♃ **12:29 pm** 9:29 am

11 SUNDAY
☉ ⚻ ♃ **5:05 am** 2:05 am
☽ ⚻ ♂ **5:21 am** 2:21 am
☽ ⚹ ♄ **10:46 am** 7:46 am
☽ ⚻ ♆ **6:26 pm** 3:26 pm

12 MONDAY
☽ △ ☿ **3:59 am** 12:59 am
☽ △ ♀ **5:12 am** 2:12 am
☽ ☍ ♅ **8:42 am** 5:42 am
☽ □ ♇ **10:18 am** 7:18 am
☽ ⚹ ♃ 9:25 pm

13 TUESDAY
☽ ⚹ ♃ **12:25 am**
☽ □ ☉ **4:46 am** 1:46 am
♀ ⚹ ♅ **3:12 pm** 12:12 pm
☽ △ ♂ **9:16 pm** 6:16 pm
☽ ⚺ ♄ **10:50 pm** 7:50 pm

14 WEDNESDAY
☿ ⚹ ♅ **5:25 am** 2:25 am
☽ △ ♆ **5:51 am** 2:51 am
♀ ⚺ ♇ **7:20 am** 4:20 am
☽ ⚻ ♅ **7:18 pm** 4:18 pm
☽ □ ☿ **8:30 pm** 5:30 pm
☽ ⚹ ♇ **8:53 pm** 5:53 pm
☽ □ ♀ **10:18 pm** 7:18 pm
♂ □ ♄ 10:10 pm
☿ ⚺ ♇ 10:25 pm

15 THURSDAY
♂ □ ♄ **1:10 am**
☿ ⚺ ♇ **1:25 am**
☽ □ ♃ **9:29 am** 6:29 am
☽ ⚹ ☉ **6:52 pm** 3:52 pm

16 FRIDAY
☽ ☌ ♄ **7:11 am** 4:11 am
☽ □ ♂ **8:50 am** 5:50 am
☽ □ ♆ **1:26 pm** 10:26 am
☽ △ ♅ 10:50 pm

17 SATURDAY
☽ △ ♅ **1:50 am**
☽ ⚺ ♇ **3:20 am** 12:20 am
☽ ⚹ ☿ **6:28 am** 3:28 am
☽ ⚹ ♀ **9:53 am** 6:53 am
☽ △ ♃ **2:25 pm** 11:25 am

18 SUNDAY
☽ ⚺ ☉ **3:34 am** 12:34 am
☽ ⚺ ♄ **11:15 am** 8:15 am
☽ ⚹ ♂ **3:26 pm** 12:26 pm
☽ ⚹ ♆ **4:52 pm** 1:52 pm

19 MONDAY
☽ □ ♅ **4:24 am** 1:24 am
☽ ☌ ♇ **5:51 am** 2:51 am
♀ ☍ ♃ **8:44 am** 5:44 am
☽ ⚺ ☿ **10:35 am** 7:35 am
☽ ⚻ ♃ **3:47 pm** 12:47 pm
☽ ⚺ ♀ **4:30 pm** 1:30 pm
♂ ☌ ♆ **7:08 pm** 4:08 pm

20 TUESDAY
☽ ☌ ☉ **8:14 am** 5:14 am
☽ ⚹ ♄ **12:16 pm** 9:16 am
☽ ⚺ ♆ **5:30 pm** 2:30 pm
☽ ⚺ ♂ **6:41 pm** 3:41 pm

21 WEDNESDAY
☽ ⚹ ♅ **4:40 am** 1:40 am
☽ ⚺ ♇ **6:06 am** 3:06 am
☽ ☌ ☿ **11:13 am** 8:13 am
☽ ☍ ♃ **3:21 pm** 12:21 pm
☽ ☌ ♀ **8:45 pm** 5:45 pm

22 THURSDAY
☽ ⚺ ☉ **11:31 am** 8:31 am
☽ □ ♄ **12:20 pm** 9:20 am
☽ ☌ ♆ **5:27 pm** 2:27 pm
☽ ☌ ♂ **9:10 pm** 6:10 pm
☉ ⚹ ♄ 9:23 pm

23 FRIDAY
☉ ⚹ ♄ **12:23 am**
☽ ⚺ ♅ **4:43 am** 1:43 am
☽ ⚹ ♇ **6:13 am** 3:13 am
☽ ⚺ ☿ **10:42 am** 7:42 am
☽ ⚻ ♃ **3:10 pm** 12:10 pm
☽ ⚺ ♀ 10:38 pm

24 SATURDAY
☽ ⚺ ♀ **1:38 am**
☽ △ ♄ **1:29 pm** 10:29 am
☽ ⚹ ☉ **4:06 pm** 1:06 pm
☽ ⚺ ♆ **6:40 pm** 3:40 pm
☽ ⚺ ♂ 10:18 pm

25 SUNDAY
☽ ⚺ ♂ **1:18 am**
☽ ☌ ♅ **6:27 am** 3:27 am
☽ □ ♇ **8:02 am** 5:02 am
☽ ⚹ ☿ **10:41 am** 7:41 am
☽ △ ♃ **4:52 pm** 1:52 pm

26 MONDAY
☉ ⚺ ♆ **5:30 am** 2:30 am
☽ ⚹ ♀ **9:23 am** 6:23 am
☽ ⚻ ♄ **5:09 pm** 2:09 pm
☽ ⚹ ♆ **10:29 pm** 7:29 pm
☽ □ ☉ **11:48 pm** 8:48 pm

27 TUESDAY
☿ ⚺ ♇ **3:23 am** 12:23 am
☽ ⚹ ♂ **8:34 am** 5:34 am
☽ ⚺ ♅ **10:55 am** 7:55 am
☽ □ ☿ **11:55 am** 8:55 am
☽ △ ♇ **12:36 pm** 9:36 am
☽ □ ♃ **9:18 pm** 6:18 pm
☿ ⚹ ♅ 9:02 pm

28 WEDNESDAY
☿ ⚹ ♅ **12:02 am**
☿ ⚺ ♂ **10:26 am** 7:26 am
☽ □ ♀ **8:57 pm** 5:57 pm
☽ ☍ ♄ **11:44 pm** 8:44 pm
♂ ⚺ ♅ 11:30 pm

29 THURSDAY
♂ ⚺ ♅ **2:30 am**
☽ □ ♆ **5:10 am** 2:10 am
☽ △ ☉ **11:07 am** 8:07 am
☽ △ ☿ **2:35 pm** 11:35 am
☽ ⚹ ♅ **6:13 pm** 3:13 pm
☽ □ ♂ **7:12 pm** 4:12 pm
☽ ⚻ ♇ **8:00 pm** 5:00 pm

30 FRIDAY
♀ □ ♄ **3:23 am** 12:23 am
☽ ⚹ ♃ **4:24 am** 1:24 am
♂ ⚹ ♇ **8:40 am** 5:40 am
☉ ☌ ☿ **8:45 am** 5:45 am

31 SATURDAY
☽ ⚻ ♄ **8:50 am** 5:50 am
☽ △ ♀ **11:56 am** 8:56 am
☽ △ ♆ **2:20 pm** 11:20 am
☽ ⚻ ☿ **6:42 pm** 3:42 pm
☽ ⚻ ☉ 10:28 pm

Eastern time in bold type
Pacific time in medium type

JANUARY 2015

DATE	SID.TIME	SUN	MOON	NODE	MERCURY	VENUS	MARS	JUPITER	SATURN	URANUS	NEPTUNE	PLUTO	CERES	PALLAS	JUNO	VESTA	CHIRON
1 Th	6 41 19	10♑13 50	20♉37	15♎26	23♑23	26≈39	21≈03	21♌32	0♐52	12♈37	5♓23	13♑10	26♐54	1♐47	16♌08	15♑13	13♓46
2 F	6 45 16	11 14 58	3♊44	15 20℞	25 14	27 58	21 50	21 41℞	0 58	12 37	5 25	13 12	27 18	2 12	16 00℞	15 45	13 49
3 Sa	6 49 12	12 16 06	16 39	15 10	26 49	29 14	22 37	21 36	1 04	12 38	5 26	13 14	27 43	2 36	15 51	16 17	13 51
4 Su	6 53 09	13 17 14	29 24	14 57	28 23	0♓29	23 24	21 32	1 10	12 39	5 28	13 16	28 07	3 00	15 41	16 49	13 53
5 M	6 57 06	14 18 22	11♋59	14 43	29 56	1 44	24 11	21 27	1 16	12 39	5 29	13 18	28 31	3 25	15 31	17 21	13 55
6 T	7 01 02	15 19 30	24 22	14 29	1≈28	2 59	24 58	21 21	1 22	12 40	5 31	13 20	28 56	3 49	15 21	17 53	13 57
7 W	7 04 59	16 20 38	6♌34	14 15	2 58	4 14	25 45	21 16	1 27	12 41	5 32	13 22	29 20	4 13	15 10	18 25	14 00
8 Th	7 08 55	17 21 46	18 36	14 03	4 27	5 29	26 32	21 11	1 33	12 42	5 34	13 25	29 44	4 37	14 58	18 57	14 02
9 F	7 12 52	18 22 54	0♍31	13 53	5 54	6 44	27 19	21 05	1 39	12 43	5 36	13 27	0♑09	5 01	14 47	19 29	14 04
10 Sa	7 16 48	19 24 02	12 20	13 47	7 18	7 59	28 06	20 59	1 44	12 44	5 37	13 29	0 33	5 24	14 34	20 01	14 07
11 Su	7 20 45	20 25 10	24 07	13 43	8 39	9 14	28 53	20 53	1 50	12 45	5 39	13 31	0 57	5 48	14 22	20 33	14 09
12 M	7 24 41	21 26 17	5♎58	13 42	9 57	10 30	29 40	20 47	1 55	12 46	5 41	13 33	1 21	6 12	14 09	21 05	14 12
13 T	7 28 38	22 27 25	17 56	13 42℞	11 11	11 45	0♓27	20 41	2 01	12 47	5 43	13 35	1 45	6 35	13 56	21 37	14 15
14 W	7 32 35	23 28 33	0♏08	13 42	12 20	13 00	1 14	20 35	2 06	12 48	5 44	13 37	2 09	6 59	13 42	22 09	14 17
15 Th	7 36 31	24 29 40	12 40	13 41	13 24	14 15	2 01	20 28	2 11	12 49	5 46	13 39	2 33	7 22	13 29	22 41	14 20
16 F	7 40 28	25 30 48	25 35	13 37	14 21	15 30	2 48	20 22	2 17	12 50	5 48	13 41	2 57	7 45	13 15	23 13	14 23
17 Sa	7 44 24	26 31 55	8♐58	13 31	15 11	16 45	3 35	20 15	2 22	12 52	5 50	13 43	3 21	8 08	13 00	23 45	14 25
18 Su	7 48 21	27 33 02	22 51	13 23	15 53	18 00	4 21	20 08	2 27	12 53	5 52	13 45	3 45	8 32	12 46	24 16	14 28
19 M	7 52 17	28 34 09	7♑17	13 12	16 26	19 14	5 08	20 01	2 32	12 54	5 54	13 47	4 09	8 55	12 31	24 48	14 31
20 T	7 56 14	29 35 15	22 00	13 01	16 50	20 29	5 55	19 54	2 37	12 56	5 56	13 49	4 33	9 17	12 16	25 20	14 34
21 W	8 00 10	0≈36 21	7♒00	12 49	17 05℞	21 44	6 42	19 47	2 42	12 57	5 58	13 51	4 57	9 40	12 01	25 52	14 37
22 Th	8 04 07	1 37 26	22 01	12 40	17 05	22 59	7 29	19 40	2 46	12 59	5 59	13 53	5 20	10 03	11 46	26 24	14 40
23 F	8 08 04	2 38 30	6♓56	12 33	16 55	24 14	8 16	19 33	2 51	13 00	6 01	13 55	5 44	10 25	11 30	26 55	14 43
24 Sa	8 12 00	3 39 33	21 47	12 29	16 34	25 29	9 03	19 25	2 56	13 02	6 03	13 57	6 08	10 48	11 15	27 27	14 46
25 Su	8 15 57	4 40 36	6♈17	12 27 D	16 01	26 44	9 50	19 18	3 00	13 04	6 05	13 59	6 31	11 10	10 59	27 59	14 49
26 M	8 19 53	5 41 37	20 25	12 27	15 18	27 59	10 37	19 10	3 05	13 06	6 07	14 01	6 55	11 32	10 44	28 31	14 52
27 T	8 23 50	6 42 37	4♉12	12 26℞	14 25	29 13	11 23	19 03	3 09	13 07	6 09	14 03	7 18	11 54	10 28	29 02	14 55
28 W	8 27 46	7 43 36	17 38	12 27	13 23	0♈28	12 10	18 55	3 14	13 09	6 12	14 05	7 41	12 16	10 13	29 34	14 58
29 Th	8 31 43	8 44 33	0♊45	12 25	12 15	1 43	12 57	18 47	3 18	13 11	6 14	14 07	8 05	12 38	9 57	0≈06	15 01
30 F	8 35 39	9 45 30	13 38	12 20	11 03	2 57	13 44	18 39	3 22	13 13	6 16	14 09	8 28	13 00	9 41	0 37	15 04
31 Sa	8 39 36	10 46 26	26 16	12 12	9 48	4 12	14 30	18 32	3 26	13 15	6 18	14 11	8 51	13 21	9 26	1 09	15 07

EPHEMERIS CALCULATED FOR 12 MIDNIGHT GREENWICH MEAN TIME. ALL OTHER DATA AND FACING ASPECTARIAN PAGE IN **EASTERN TIME (BOLD)** AND PACIFIC TIME (REGULAR).

FEBRUARY 2015

☽ Last Aspect				☽ Ingress			
day	ET / hr:mn / PT		asp	sign	day	ET / hr:mn / PT	
1	**8:37 am**	5:37 am	△♂	♌	2	**12:41 pm**	9:41 am
3		9:31 pm	☌♃	♍	4		9:46 pm
4	**12:31 am**		☌♃	♍	5	**12:46 am**	
6	**5:09 pm**	2:09 pm	☍♂	♎	7	**1:44 pm**	10:44 am
9	**6:58 am**	3:58 am	△☉	♏	9		11:05 pm
9	**6:58 am**	3:58 am	△☉	♏	10	**2:05 am**	
11		9:32 pm	△♂	♐	12	**11:46 am**	8:46 am
12	**12:32 am**		△♂	♐	12	**11:46 am**	8:46 am
14	**10:15 am**	7:15 am	☐♂	♑	14	**5:24 pm**	2:24 pm
16	**3:17 pm**	12:17 pm	⚹♂	♒	16	**7:13 pm**	4:13 pm

☽ Last Aspect				☽ Ingress			
day	ET / hr:mn / PT		asp	sign	day	ET / hr:mn / PT	
18	**6:47 pm**	3:47 pm	☌☉	♓	18	**6:47 pm**	3:47 pm
19	**6:02 pm**	3:02 pm	⚹♇	♈	20	**6:13 pm**	3:13 pm
21	**7:36 pm**	4:36 pm	△♃	♉	22	**7:28 pm**	4:28 pm
23	**9:57 pm**	6:57 pm	☐♃	♊	24	**11:54 pm**	8:54 pm
26	**3:43 am**	12:43 am	⚹♃	♋	27	**7:50 am**	4:50 am
28	**12:53 pm**	9:53 am	☍♇	♌	3/1	**6:34 pm**	3:34 pm

☽ Phases & Eclipses			
phase	day	ET / hr:mn / PT	
Full Moon	3	**6:09 pm**	3:09 pm
4th Quarter	11	**10:50 pm**	7:50 pm
New Moon	18	**6:47 pm**	3:47 pm
2nd Quarter	25	**12:14 pm**	9:14 am

Planet Ingress				
		day	ET / hr:mn / PT	
☉	♓	18	**6:50 pm**	3:50 pm
♂	♈	19	**7:11 pm**	4:11 pm
♀	♈	20	**3:05 pm**	12:05 pm

Planetary Motion				
		day	ET / hr:mn / PT	
☿	D	11	**9:57 am**	6:57 am

1 SUNDAY
☽⚻☉ **1:28 am**
☽☐♅ **3:52 am** 12:52 am
☽☍♇ **5:42 am** 2:42 am
☽△♂ **8:37 am** 5:37 am
♀☌♆ **12:36 pm** 9:36 am
☽⚺♃ **1:38 pm** 10:38 am
☿⚺♀ 10:35 pm

2 MONDAY
☿⚺♀ **1:35 am**
☉⚹♅ **7:30 am** 4:30 am
☿⚺♆ **2:52 pm** 11:52 am
☽△♄ **7:53 pm** 4:53 pm
☽☍☿ 9:30 pm
☽⚻♆ 10:24 pm

3 TUESDAY
☽☍☿ **12:30 am**
☽⚻♆ **1:24 am**
☽⚻♀ **5:31 am** 2:31 am
☉⚺♇ **6:17 am** 3:17 am
☽△♅ **3:19 pm** 12:19 pm
☽⚻♇ **5:10 pm** 2:10 pm
☽☍☉ **6:09 pm** 3:09 pm
☽⚻♂ 9:09 pm
☽☌♃ 9:31 pm

4 WEDNESDAY
☽⚻♂ **12:09 am**
☽☌♃ **12:31 am**
♂⚻♃ **5:04 am** 2:04 am

5 THURSDAY
☿⚹♄ **6:39 am** 3:39 am
☽⚻☿ **8:19 am** 5:19 am
☽☐♄ **8:26 am** 5:26 am
☽☍♆ **1:56 pm** 10:56 am
☽☍♀ 10:02 pm

6 FRIDAY
☽☍♀ **1:02 am**
☽⚻♅ **4:06 am** 1:06 am
☽△♇ **5:58 am** 2:58 am
☽⚻☉ **12:29 pm** 9:29 am
☽⚺♃ **12:34 pm** 9:34 am
☉☍♃ **1:20 pm** 10:20 am
☽☍♂ **5:09 pm** 2:09 pm

7 SATURDAY
♀⚺♅ **6:55 am** 3:55 am
☽△☿ **6:07 pm** 3:07 pm
☽⚹♄ **9:44 pm** 6:44 pm
♀⚹♇ 9:53 pm

8 SUNDAY
♀⚹♇ **12:53 am**
☽⚻♆ **3:07 am** 12:07 am
☽☍♅ **5:13 pm** 2:13 pm
☽☐♇ **7:02 pm** 4:02 pm
☽⚻♀ **9:05 pm** 6:05 pm
☽⚹♃ 9:45 pm

9 MONDAY
☽⚹♃ **12:45 am**
☽△☉ **6:58 am** 3:58 am
☽⚻♂ **10:09 am** 7:09 am

10 TUESDAY
☽☐☿ **4:50 am** 1:50 am
♀⚻♃ **5:19 am** 2:19 am
☽⚺♄ **10:08 am** 7:08 am
☽△♆ **3:15 pm** 12:15 pm

11 WEDNESDAY
☽⚻♅ **4:49 am** 1:49 am
☽⚹♇ **6:29 am** 3:29 am
☽☐♃ **11:12 am** 8:12 am
☽△♀ **2:49 pm** 11:49 am
☽☐☉ **10:50 pm** 7:50 pm
☽△♂ 9:32 pm

12 THURSDAY
☽△♂ **12:32 am**
☽⚹☿ **2:20 pm** 11:20 am
☽☌♄ **7:32 pm** 4:32 pm
☽☐♆ 9:15 pm

13 FRIDAY
☽☐♆ **12:15 am**
☽△♅ **12:54 pm** 9:54 am
☽⚺♇ **2:25 pm** 11:25 am
☽△♃ **6:07 pm** 3:07 pm

14 SATURDAY
☽☐♀ **3:31 am** 12:31 am
☽⚹☉ **9:46 am** 6:46 am
☽☐♂ **10:15 am** 7:15 am
☽⚺☿ **8:47 pm** 5:47 pm
☽⚺♄ 9:45 pm

15 SUNDAY
☽⚺♄ **12:45 am**
☽⚹♆ **5:05 am** 2:05 am
☉⚺♂ **12:19 pm** 9:19 am
☽☐♅ **4:48 pm** 1:48 pm
☽☌♇ **6:09 pm** 3:09 pm
☽⚻♃ **9:02 pm** 6:02 pm

16 MONDAY
☽⚹♀ **10:53 am** 7:53 am
☽⚹♂ **3:17 pm** 12:17 pm
☽⚺☉ **3:45 pm** 12:45 pm
☽☌☿ 9:00 pm
☽⚹♄ 11:16 pm

17 TUESDAY
☽☌☿ **12:00 am**
☽⚹♄ **2:16 am**
☽⚺♆ **6:20 am** 3:20 am
☽⚹♅ **5:29 pm** 2:29 pm
☽⚺♇ **6:43 pm** 3:43 pm
☽☍♃ **8:59 pm** 5:59 pm

18 WEDNESDAY
☽⚺♀ **2:54 pm** 11:54 am
☽⚺♂ **5:30 pm** 2:30 pm
☽☌☉ **6:47 pm** 3:47 pm
☽⚺☿ 10:31 pm
☽☐♄ 10:49 pm

19 THURSDAY
☽⚺☿ **1:31 am**
☽☐♄ **1:49 am**
☽☌♆ **5:48 am** 2:48 am
☿⚹♄ **8:06 am** 5:06 am
☽⚺♅ **4:51 pm** 1:51 pm
☽⚹♇ **6:02 pm** 3:02 pm
☽⚻♃ **7:49 pm** 4:49 pm

20 FRIDAY
☽☌♀ **6:30 pm** 3:30 pm
☽☌♂ **7:28 pm** 4:28 pm
☽⚺☉ **9:39 pm** 6:39 pm
☽△♄ 10:31 pm

21 SATURDAY
☽△♄ **1:31 am**
☽⚹☿ **3:43 am** 12:43 am
☽⚺♆ **5:37 am** 2:37 am
☽☌♅ **5:04 pm** 2:04 pm
☽☐♇ **6:13 pm** 3:13 pm
☽△♃ **7:36 pm** 4:36 pm
♀☌♂ 9:13 pm

22 SUNDAY
♀☌♂ **12:13 am**
☿⚺♆ **1:08 pm** 10:08 am
☽⚺♂ **11:37 pm** 8:37 pm
☽⚺♀ 9:27 pm
☽⚹☉ 11:53 pm

23 MONDAY
☽⚺♀ **12:27 am**
☽⚹☉ **2:53 am**
☽⚻♄ **3:19 am** 12:19 am
☽⚹♆ **7:40 am** 4:40 am
☉☐♄ **8:56 am** 5:56 am
☽☐☿ **8:57 am** 5:57 am
☽⚺♅ **7:52 pm** 4:52 pm
☽△♇ **9:01 pm** 6:01 pm
☽☐♃ **9:57 pm** 6:57 pm

24 TUESDAY
♀△♄ **9:58 am** 6:58 am

25 WEDNESDAY
☽⚹♂ **7:35 am** 4:35 am
☽☍♄ **8:24 am** 5:24 am
☽⚹♀ **10:40 am** 7:40 am
☽☐☉ **12:14 pm** 9:14 am
☽☐♆ **1:06 pm** 10:06 am
☽△☿ **6:48 pm** 3:48 pm
♂△♄ **10:08 pm** 7:08 pm
☉☌♆ **11:55 pm** 8:55 pm
☽⚹♅ 11:11 pm

26 THURSDAY
☽⚹♅ **2:11 am**
☽⚻♇ **3:19 am** 12:19 am
☽⚹♃ **3:43 am** 12:43 am
♀⚺♆ **1:22 pm** 10:22 am

27 FRIDAY
☽⚻♄ **4:58 pm** 1:58 pm
♃⚻♇ **6:11 pm** 3:11 pm
☽☐♂ **7:41 pm** 4:41 pm
☽△♆ **9:59 pm** 6:59 pm
☽☐♀ 10:27 pm
☽△☉ 10:54 pm

28 SATURDAY
☽☐♀ **1:27 am**
☽△☉ **1:54 am**
☽⚻☿ **9:29 am** 6:29 am
☽☐♅ **11:50 am** 8:50 am
☽⚺♃ **12:41 pm** 9:41 am
☽☍♇ **12:53 pm** 9:53 am
☉⚺♀ 9:20 pm

Eastern time in bold type
Pacific time in medium type

FEBRUARY 2015

DATE	SID.TIME	SUN	MOON	NODE	MERCURY	VENUS	MARS	JUPITER	SATURN	URANUS	NEPTUNE	PLUTO	CERES	PALLAS	JUNO	VESTA	CHIRON
1 Su	8 43 33	11 ≈ 47 20	8 ♋ 44	12 ≏ 03	8 ≈ 03	5 ✶ 34	15 ✶ 27	18 ♌ 24 R	3 ✗ 30	13 ♈ 17	6 ✶ 20	14 ♑ 13	9 ♑ 14	13 ✗ 43	9 ♌ 11	1 ≈ 40	15 ✶ 11
2 M	8 47 29	12 48 13	21 02	11 51 R	7 21 R	6 41	16 04	18 16 R	3 34	13 19	6 22	14 15	9 37	14 04	8 55 R	2 12	15 14
3 T	8 51 26	13 49 05	3 ♌ 11	11 40	6 12	7 56	16 50	18 08	3 38	13 21	6 24	14 17	10 00	14 25	8 40	2 43	15 17
4 W	8 55 22	14 49 56	15 13	11 29	5 09	9 10	17 37	18 00	3 42	13 23	6 26	14 19	10 23	14 46	8 25	3 15	15 20
5 Th	8 59 19	15 50 45	27 09	11 19	4 12	10 25	18 24	17 52	3 45	13 25	6 28	14 21	10 46	15 07	8 11	3 46	15 24
6 F	9 03 15	16 51 34	9 ♍ 00	11 12	3 23	11 39	19 10	17 44	3 49	13 27	6 31	14 22	11 09	15 28	7 56	4 18	15 27
7 Sa	9 07 12	17 52 21	20 48	11 07	2 42	12 54	19 57	17 36	3 53	13 30	6 33	14 24	11 32	15 49	7 42	4 49	15 31
8 Su	9 11 08	18 53 07	2 ♎ 36	11 04 D	2 09	14 08	20 43	17 28	3 56	13 32	6 35	14 26	11 54	16 09	7 27	5 21	15 34
9 M	9 15 05	19 53 53	14 27	11 04	1 44	15 23	21 30	17 20	3 59	13 34	6 37	14 28	12 17	16 30	7 14	5 52	15 37
10 T	9 19 02	20 54 37	26 26	11 05	1 28	16 37	22 16	17 12	4 03	13 36	6 39	14 30	12 40	16 50	7 00	6 23	15 41
11 W	9 22 58	21 55 20	8 ♏ 36	11 06 R	1 19 D	17 51	23 03	17 04	4 06	13 39	6 41	14 31	13 02	17 10	6 47	6 55	15 44
12 Th	9 26 55	22 56 02	21 04	11 06	1 19	19 05	23 49	16 56	4 09	13 41	6 44	14 33	13 24	17 30	6 34	7 26	15 48
13 F	9 30 51	23 56 43	3 ✗ 54	11 06	1 25	20 20	24 36	16 48	4 12	13 44	6 46	14 35	13 47	17 49	6 21	7 57	15 51
14 Sa	9 34 48	24 57 24	17 11	11 04	1 38	21 34	25 22	16 41	4 15	13 46	6 48	14 36	14 09	18 09	6 09	8 28	15 55
15 Su	9 38 44	25 58 02	0 ♑ 56	11 00	1 57	22 48	26 08	16 33	4 17	13 49	6 50	14 38	14 31	18 28	5 57	8 59	15 58
16 M	9 42 41	26 58 40	15 10	10 54	2 21	24 02	26 55	16 25	4 20	13 51	6 53	14 40	14 53	18 48	5 45	9 31	16 02
17 T	9 46 37	27 59 17	29 52	10 47	2 51	25 16	27 41	16 17	4 23	13 54	6 55	14 41	15 15	19 07	5 34	10 02	16 06
18 W	9 50 34	28 59 52	14 ≈ 54	10 40	3 26	26 30	28 27	16 10	4 25	13 57	6 57	14 43	15 37	19 26	5 23	10 33	16 09
19 Th	9 54 31	0 ✶ 00 26	0 ✶ 08	10 35	4 06	27 44	29 13	16 02	4 28	13 59	7 00	14 45	15 59	19 44	5 12	11 04	16 13
20 F	9 58 27	1 00 58	15 23	10 30	4 49	28 58	0 ♈ 00	15 55	4 30	14 02	7 02	14 46	16 20	20 03	5 02	11 35	16 16
21 Sa	10 02 24	2 01 28	0 ♈ 29	10 28 R	5 37	0 ♈ 12	0 46	15 47	4 32	14 05	7 04	14 48	16 42	20 21	4 52	12 06	16 20
22 Su	10 06 20	3 01 57	15 18	10 28	6 27	1 26	1 32	15 40	4 34	14 07	7 06	14 49	17 04	20 39	4 43	12 37	16 24
23 M	10 10 17	4 02 24	29 43	10 29	7 22	2 40	2 18	15 33	4 36	14 10	7 09	14 51	17 25	20 57	4 34	13 07	16 27
24 T	10 14 13	5 02 49	13 ♉ 48	10 32 R	8 19	3 53	3 04	15 26	4 38	14 13	7 11	14 52	17 47	21 15	4 26	13 38	16 31
25 W	10 18 10	6 03 12	27 17	10 32	9 19	5 07	3 50	15 18	4 40	14 16	7 13	14 54	18 08	21 32	4 18	14 09	16 35
26 Th	10 22 06	7 03 33	10 ♊ 21	10 32	10 21	6 21	4 36	15 11	4 42	14 19	7 15	14 55	18 29	21 50	4 11	14 40	16 38
27 F	10 26 03	8 03 52	23 16	10 31	11 26	7 34	5 22	15 05	4 43	14 22	7 18	14 57	18 50	22 07	4 03	15 10	16 42
28 Sa	10 30 00	9 04 10	5 ♋ 48	10 28	12 33	8 48	6 08	14 58	4 45	14 25	7 20	14 58	19 11	22 24	3 57	15 41	16 46

EPHEMERIS CALCULATED FOR 12 MIDNIGHT GREENWICH MEAN TIME. ALL OTHER DATA AND FACING ASPECTARIAN PAGE IN **EASTERN TIME (BOLD)** AND PACIFIC TIME (REGULAR).

☽ Last Aspect day	ET / hr:mn / PT	asp	☽ Ingress sign day	ET / hr:mn / PT
2/28	**12:53 pm** 9:53 am	☍ ♇	♌ 1	**6:34 pm** 3:34 pm
3	**3:48 am** 12:48 am	☍ ☿	♍ 4	**6:58 am** 3:58 am
5	**1:36 pm** 10:36 am	△ ♇	♎ 6	**7:52 pm** 4:52 pm
8	**9:24 pm** 6:24 pm	△ ☿	♏ 9	**9:10 am** 6:10 am
11	**3:46 pm** 12:46 pm	□ ☿	♐ 11	**7:30 pm** 4:30 pm
13	**7:11 pm** 4:11 pm	△ ♀	♑ 13	11:40 pm
13	**7:11 pm** 4:11 pm	△ ♀	♑ 14	**2:40 am**
16	**4:02 am** 1:02 am	□ ♀	♒ 16	**6:14 am** 3:14 am
17	**2:18 pm** 11:18 am	⚹ ♂	♓ 18	**6:58 am** 3:58 am
20	**5:36 am** 2:36 am	☌ ☉	♈ 20	**6:28 am** 3:28 am

☽ Last Aspect day	ET / hr:mn / PT	asp	☽ Ingress sign day	ET / hr:mn / PT
21	**6:51 pm** 3:51 pm	☌ ♂	♉ 22	**6:40 am** 3:40 am
23	**10:25 am** 7:25 am	⚹ ☿	♊ 24	**9:23 am** 6:23 am
26	**8:35 am** 5:35 am	⚹ ♀	♋ 26	**3:45 pm** 12:45 pm
28	**9:58 pm** 6:58 pm	□ ♂	♌ 28	10:48 pm
28	**9:58 pm** 6:58 pm	□ ♂	♌ 29	**1:48 am**
30	**9:57 am** 6:57 am	△ ♅	♍ 31	**2:12 pm** 11:12 pm

☽ Phases & Eclipses phase	day	ET / hr:mn / PT
Full Moon	5	**1:05 pm** 10:05 am
4th Quarter	13	**1:48 pm** 10:48 am
New Moon	20	**5:36 am** 2:36 am
●	20	29° ♓ 29'
2nd Quarter	27	**3:43 am** 12:43 am

Planet Ingress		day	ET / hr:mn / PT
☿	♓	12	**11:52 pm** 8:52 pm
♀	♉	17	**6:15 am** 3:15 am
☉	♈	20	**6:45 pm** 3:45 pm
⚶	♓	28	**1:53 pm** 10:53 am
☿	♈	30	**9:44 pm** 6:44 pm
♂	♉	31	**12:26 pm** 9:26 am

Planetary Motion		day	ET / hr:mn / PT
⚵	D	13	**3:42 pm** 12:42 pm
♄	℞	14	**11:02 am** 8:02 am

1 SUNDAY
☉ ⚺ ♀ **12:20 am**
♂ ⚺ ♆ **10:44 am** 7:44 am
☿ ⚹ ♅ **10:55 am** 7:55 am
☿ ☍ ♃ **4:15 pm** 1:15 pm
☿ ⚺ ♇ **9:25 pm** 6:25 pm

2 MONDAY
☽ △ ♄ **4:10 am** 1:10 am
☽ ⚻ ♆ **9:25 am** 6:25 am
☽ △ ♂ **10:53 am** 7:53 am
☽ ⚻ ☉ **6:44 pm** 3:44 pm
☽ △ ♀ **7:36 pm** 4:36 pm
☽ △ ♅ **11:46 pm** 8:46 pm
☽ ☌ ♃ **11:52 pm** 8:52 pm
☽ ⚻ ♇ 9:43 pm

3 TUESDAY
☽ ⚻ ♇ **12:43 am**
☽ ☍ ☿ **3:48 am** 12:48 am
♃ △ ♅ **7:25 am** 4:25 am

4 WEDNESDAY
♀ △ ♃ **10:14 am** 7:14 am
♀ ☌ ♅ **1:46 pm** 10:46 am
☽ □ ♄ **4:48 pm** 1:48 pm
☽ ☍ ♆ **10:14 pm** 7:14 pm
♀ □ ♇ **10:17 pm** 7:17 pm
☉ ⚻ ♃ 11:33 pm

5 THURSDAY
☉ ⚻ ♃ **2:33 am**
☽ ⚻ ♂ **3:42 am** 12:42 am
☉ ⚺ ♅ **9:30 am** 6:30 am
☽ ⚺ ♃ **12:07 pm** 9:07 am
☽ ⚻ ♅ **12:48 pm** 9:48 am
☽ ☍ ☉ **1:05 pm** 10:05 am
☽ △ ♇ **1:36 pm** 10:36 am
☽ ⚻ ♀ **3:21 pm** 12:21 pm
☉ ⚹ ♇ **7:19 pm** 4:19 pm
☽ ⚻ ☿ 9:01 pm

6 FRIDAY
☽ ⚻ ☿ **12:01 am**

7 SATURDAY
☽ ⚹ ♄ **5:46 am** 2:46 am
☽ ⚻ ♆ **11:18 am** 8:18 am
☽ ☍ ♂ **8:41 pm** 5:41 pm
☽ ⚹ ♃ 9:24 pm
☽ ☍ ♅ 10:50 pm
☽ □ ♇ 11:28 pm

8 SUNDAY
☽ ⚹ ♃ **12:24 am**
☽ ☍ ♅ **1:50 am**
☽ □ ♇ **3:28 am**
☽ ⚻ ☉ **8:24 am** 5:24 am
☽ ☍ ♀ **11:58 am** 8:58 am
☽ △ ☿ **9:24 pm** 6:24 pm

9 MONDAY
☽ ⚺ ♄ **6:53 pm** 3:53 pm
☽ △ ♆ 9:25 pm
♂ △ ♃ 11:04 pm

10 TUESDAY
☽ △ ♆ **12:25 am**
♂ △ ♃ **2:04 am**
☽ □ ♃ **12:31 pm** 9:31 am
☽ ⚻ ♂ **1:17 pm** 10:17 am
☽ ⚻ ♅ **2:35 pm** 11:35 am
☽ ⚹ ♇ **3:03 pm** 12:03 pm
☽ △ ☉ 9:55 pm

11 WEDNESDAY
☽ △ ☉ **12:55 am**
☽ ⚻ ♀ **5:34 am** 2:34 am
♂ ☌ ♅ **12:06 pm** 9:06 am
☽ □ ☿ **3:46 pm** 12:46 pm
♂ □ ♇ **6:41 pm** 3:41 pm

12 THURSDAY
☽ ☌ ♄ **4:48 am** 1:48 am
☽ □ ♆ **10:12 am** 7:12 am
☽ △ ♃ **9:08 pm** 6:08 pm
☽ △ ♅ **11:42 pm** 8:42 pm
☽ ⚺ ♇ **11:58 pm** 8:58 pm
☽ △ ♂ 10:43 pm

13 FRIDAY
☽ △ ♂ **1:43 am**
☽ □ ☉ **1:48 pm** 10:48 am
☽ △ ♀ **7:11 pm** 4:11 pm

14 SATURDAY
☽ ⚹ ☿ **6:00 am** 3:00 am
☽ ⚺ ♄ **11:23 am** 8:23 am
☽ ⚹ ♆ **4:34 pm** 1:34 pm
☽ ⚻ ♃ 11:20 pm

15 SUNDAY
☽ ⚻ ♃ **2:20 am**
☽ □ ♅ **5:14 am** 2:14 am
☽ ☌ ♇ **5:20 am** 2:20 am
☽ □ ♂ **9:56 am** 6:56 am
☽ ⚹ ☉ **10:08 pm** 7:08 pm

16 MONDAY
☽ □ ♀ **4:02 am** 1:02 am
☿ □ ♄ **5:41 am** 2:41 am
☽ ⚹ ♄ **2:23 pm** 11:23 am
☽ ⚺ ☿ **3:26 pm** 12:26 pm
☽ ⚺ ♆ **7:24 pm** 4:24 pm
♅ □ ♇ **10:54 pm** 7:54 pm

17 TUESDAY
☽ ☍ ♃ **4:13 am** 1:13 am
☽ ⚺ ♇ **7:22 am** 4:22 am
☽ ⚹ ♅ **7:23 am** 4:23 am
☽ ⚹ ♂ **2:18 pm** 11:18 am
☽ ⚺ ☉ 11:44 pm

18 WEDNESDAY
☽ ⚺ ☉ **2:44 am**
☿ ☌ ♆ **4:49 am** 1:49 am
☽ ⚹ ♀ **9:07 am** 6:07 am
☽ □ ♄ **2:47 pm** 11:47 am
☽ ☌ ♆ **7:44 pm** 4:44 pm
☽ ☌ ☿ **9:28 pm** 6:28 pm

19 THURSDAY
☽ ⚻ ♃ **3:58 am** 12:58 am
☽ ⚹ ♇ **7:17 am** 4:17 am
☽ ⚺ ♅ **7:26 am** 4:26 am
☽ ⚺ ♂ **4:30 pm** 1:30 pm

20 FRIDAY
☽ ☌ ☉ **5:36 am** 2:36 am
☽ ⚺ ♀ **12:43 pm** 9:43 am
☽ △ ♄ **2:14 pm** 11:14 am
☽ ⚺ ♆ **7:21 pm** 4:21 pm
☽ ⚺ ☿ 11:46 pm

21 SATURDAY
☽ ⚺ ☿ **2:46 am**
☽ △ ♃ **3:21 am** 12:21 am
☽ □ ♇ **6:57 am** 3:57 am
☽ ☌ ♅ **7:14 am** 4:14 am
♀ ⚻ ♄ **7:39 am** 4:39 am
☿ ⚻ ♃ **7:54 am** 4:54 am
☽ ☌ ♂ **6:51 pm** 3:51 pm

22 SUNDAY
☽ ⚺ ☉ **9:17 am** 6:17 am
☽ ⚻ ♄ **2:42 pm** 11:42 am
☿ ⚹ ♇ **4:27 pm** 1:27 pm
☽ ☌ ♀ **5:32 pm** 2:32 pm
☿ ⚺ ♅ **7:55 pm** 4:55 pm
☽ ⚹ ♆ **8:11 pm** 5:11 pm

23 MONDAY
☽ □ ♃ **4:16 am** 1:16 am
☽ △ ♇ **8:17 am** 5:17 am
☽ ⚺ ♅ **8:43 am** 5:43 am
☽ ⚹ ☿ **10:25 am** 7:25 am
☽ ⚺ ♂ **11:38 pm** 8:38 pm
♀ ⚹ ♆ 11:25 pm

24 TUESDAY
♀ ⚹ ♆ **2:25 am**
☽ ⚹ ☉ **4:10 pm** 1:10 pm
☽ ☍ ♄ **5:53 pm** 2:53 pm
☽ □ ♆ **11:58 pm** 8:58 pm
☽ ⚺ ♀ 11:00 pm

25 WEDNESDAY
☽ ⚺ ♀ **2:00 am**
☽ ⚹ ♃ **8:17 am** 5:17 am
☽ ⚻ ♇ **12:50 pm** 9:50 am
☽ ⚹ ♅ **1:29 pm** 10:29 am
☉ △ ♄ **3:25 pm** 12:25 pm
☽ □ ☿ **11:05 pm** 8:05 pm

26 THURSDAY
☽ ⚹ ♂ **8:35 am** 5:35 am
☽ ⚻ ♄ 9:49 pm

27 FRIDAY
☽ ⚻ ♄ **12:49 am**
☽ □ ☉ **3:43 am** 12:43 am
☽ △ ♆ **7:34 am** 4:34 am
☽ ⚹ ♀ **3:29 pm** 12:29 pm
☽ ⚺ ♃ **4:09 pm** 1:09 pm
☽ ☍ ♇ **9:14 pm** 6:14 pm
☽ □ ♅ **10:09 pm** 7:09 pm
♀ □ ♃ **10:11 pm** 7:11 pm

28 SATURDAY
☽ △ ☿ **5:55 pm** 2:55 pm
☽ □ ♂ **9:58 pm** 6:58 pm

29 SUNDAY
☉ ⚺ ♆ **6:19 am** 3:19 am
☽ △ ♄ **11:14 am** 8:14 am
☽ ⚻ ♆ **6:36 pm** 3:36 pm
☽ △ ☉ **7:40 pm** 4:40 pm

30 MONDAY
☽ ☌ ♃ **3:15 am** 12:15 am
♀ △ ♇ **3:47 am** 12:47 am
☽ ⚻ ♇ **8:46 am** 5:46 am
☽ □ ♀ **9:19 am** 6:19 am
☽ △ ♅ **9:57 am** 6:57 am
☿ ⚺ ♂ **12:01 pm** 9:01 am
♀ ⚺ ♅ **3:59 pm** 12:59 pm

31 TUESDAY
☽ △ ♂ **2:19 pm** 11:19 am
☽ ⚻ ☿ **5:19 pm** 2:19 pm
☽ □ ♄ **11:42 pm** 8:42 pm

Eastern time in bold type
Pacific time in medium type

MARCH 2015

DATE	SID.TIME	SUN	MOON	NODE	MERCURY	VENUS	MARS	JUPITER	SATURN	URANUS	NEPTUNE	PLUTO	CERES	PALLAS	JUNO	VESTA	CHIRON
1 Su	10 33 56	10♓04 25	18 ♋ 06	10 ♎ 24	13 ≈ 42	10 ♈ 01	6 ♈ 54	14 ♌ 51	4 ♐ 46	14 ♈ 27	7 ♓ 22	14 ♑ 59	19 ♑ 32	22 ♐ 40	3 ♌ 51	16 ≈ 12	16 ♓ 49
2 M	10 37 53	11 04 38	0 ♌ 13	10 19 R	14 54	11 15	7 40	14 45 R	4 48	14 30	7 25	15 00	19 53	22 57	3 45 R	16 42	16 53
3 T	10 41 49	12 04 49	12 12	10 14	16 07	12 28	8 25	14 38	4 49	14 33	7 27	15 02	20 13	23 13	3 40	17 13	16 57
4 W	10 45 46	13 04 58	24 06	10 09	17 22	13 42	9 11	14 32	4 50	14 36	7 29	15 03	20 34	23 29	3 35	17 43	17 01
5 Th	10 49 42	14 05 06	5 ♍ 56	10 05	18 38	14 55	9 57	14 26	4 51	14 40	7 31	15 05	20 54	23 45	3 31	18 14	17 04
6 F	10 53 39	15 05 11	17 45	10 02	19 57	16 08	10 42	14 20	4 52	14 43	7 34	15 06	21 15	24 01	3 27	18 44	17 08
7 Sa	10 57 35	16 05 15	29 34	10 00 D	21 17	17 21	11 28	14 14	4 53	14 46	7 36	15 07	21 35	24 16	3 24	19 14	17 12
8 Su	11 01 32	17 05 17	11 ♎ 26	10 00	22 38	18 34	12 14	14 08	4 54	14 49	7 38	15 08	21 55	24 31	3 21	19 45	17 15
9 M	11 05 28	18 05 17	23 24	10 00	24 01	19 47	12 59	14 03	4 54	14 52	7 40	15 10	22 15	24 46	3 19	20 15	17 19
10 T	11 09 25	19 05 15	5 ♏ 29	10 02	25 25	21 00	13 45	13 57	4 55	14 55	7 43	15 11	22 35	25 00	3 17	20 45	17 23
11 W	11 13 22	20 05 12	17 45	10 03	26 50	22 13	14 30	13 52	4 55	14 58	7 45	15 12	22 55	25 15	3 15	21 15	17 27
12 Th	11 17 18	21 05 07	0 ♐ 16	10 05	28 17	23 26	15 15	13 47	4 55	15 01	7 47	15 13	23 14	25 29	3 14	21 45	17 30
13 F	11 21 15	22 05 00	13 05	10 06 R	29 46	24 39	16 01	13 42	4 56	15 05	7 49	15 14	23 34	25 43	3 14 D	22 15	17 34
14 Sa	11 25 11	23 04 52	26 16	10 06	1 ♓ 17	25 51	16 46	13 37	4 56 R	15 08	7 52	15 15	23 53	25 56	3 13	22 45	17 38
15 Su	11 29 08	24 04 42	9 ♑ 52	10 05	2 46	27 04	17 31	13 33	4 56	15 11	7 54	15 16	24 12	26 10	3 14	23 15	17 42
16 M	11 33 04	25 04 31	23 54	10 04	4 18	28 17	18 17	13 28	4 56	15 14	7 56	15 17	24 32	26 23	3 14	23 45	17 45
17 T	11 37 01	26 04 17	8 ♒ 20	10 01	5 52	29 29	19 02	13 24	4 56	15 18	7 58	15 18	24 51	26 35	3 16	24 14	17 49
18 W	11 40 57	27 04 02	23 09	9 59	7 26	0 ♉ 42	19 47	13 20	4 55	15 21	8 00	15 19	25 10	26 48	3 17	24 44	17 53
19 Th	11 44 54	28 03 46	8 ♓ 12	9 59	9 02	1 54	20 32	13 16	4 55	15 24	8 03	15 20	25 28	27 00	3 19	25 14	17 56
20 F	11 48 51	29 03 27	23 23	9 58	10 39	3 06	21 17	13 12	4 55	15 28	8 05	15 21	25 47	27 12	3 22	25 44	18 00
21 Sa	11 52 47	0 ♈03 06	8 ♈ 31	9 58 D	12 17	4 18	22 02	13 08	4 54	15 31	8 07	15 21	26 05	27 23	3 25	26 13	18 04
22 Su	11 56 44	1 02 43	23 27	9 58	13 57	5 31	22 47	13 05	4 53	15 34	8 09	15 22	26 24	27 35	3 28	26 43	18 07
23 M	12 00 40	2 02 18	8 ♉ 04	9 59	15 38	6 43	23 32	13 02	4 52	15 38	8 11	15 23	26 42	27 46	3 32	27 12	18 11
24 T	12 04 37	3 01 51	22 17	9 59	17 20	7 55	24 17	12 59	4 51	15 41	8 13	15 24	27 00	27 56	3 36	27 42	18 15
25 W	12 08 33	4 01 22	6 ♊ 02	10 00	19 04	9 06	25 02	12 56	4 50	15 44	8 15	15 25	27 18	28 07	3 40	28 11	18 18
26 Th	12 12 30	5 00 50	19 21	10 00	20 48	10 18	25 46	12 53	4 49	15 48	8 17	15 25	27 35	28 17	3 45	28 40	18 22
27 F	12 16 26	6 00 16	2 ♋ 15	10 01 R	22 34	11 30	26 31	12 51	4 48	15 51	8 20	15 26	27 53	28 26	3 51	29 09	18 25
28 Sa	12 20 23	6 59 40	14 48	10 01	24 22	12 42	27 16	12 48	4 47	15 55	8 22	15 27	28 10	28 36	3 56	29 38	18 29
29 Su	12 24 20	7 59 02	27 04	10 00	26 10	13 53	28 00	12 46	4 45	15 58	8 24	15 27	28 28	28 44	4 02	0 ♓ 07	18 33
30 M	12 28 16	8 58 21	9 ♌ 07	10 00 D	28 01	15 05	28 45	12 44	4 44	16 01	8 26	15 28	28 45	28 53	4 09	0 36	18 36
31 T	12 32 13	9 57 37	21 02	10 00	29 52	16 16	29 30	12 43	4 42	16 05	8 28	15 28	29 02	29 01	4 16	1 05	18 40

EPHEMERIS CALCULATED FOR 12 MIDNIGHT GREENWICH MEAN TIME. ALL OTHER DATA AND FACING ASPECTARIAN PAGE IN EASTERN TIME (BOLD) AND PACIFIC TIME (REGULAR).

APRIL 2015

☽ Last Aspect				☽ Ingress			
day	ET / hr:mn / PT		asp	sign	day	ET / hr:mn / PT	
2	**5:01 am**	2:01 am	△♀	♎	3	**3:07 am**	12:07 am
4	**11:59 am**	8:59 am	☍♅	♏	5	**3:04 pm**	12:04 pm
7	**4:42 pm**	1:42 pm	☍♀	♐	7		10:08 pm
7	**4:42 pm**	1:42 pm	☍♀	♐	8	**1:08 am**	
9	**1:42 pm**	10:42 am	△☉	♑	10	**8:47 am**	5:47 am
12	**4:15 am**	1:15 am	□☿	♒	12	**1:44 pm**	10:44 am
14	**3:45 pm**	12:45 pm	⚹☿	♓	14	**4:12 pm**	1:12 pm
15	**5:37 pm**	2:37 pm	⚹♇	♈	16	**5:00 pm**	2:00 pm
18	**2:57 pm**	11:57 am	☌☉	♉	18	**5:31 pm**	2:31 pm
19	**7:07 pm**	4:07 pm	△♇	♊	20	**7:28 pm**	4:28 pm

☽ Last Aspect				☽ Ingress			
day	ET / hr:mn / PT		asp	sign	day	ET / hr:mn / PT	
21		10:38 pm	⚹♅	♋	22		9:25 pm
22	**1:38 am**		⚹♅	♋	23	**12:25 am**	
24	**1:04 pm**	10:04 am	⚹☿	♌	25	**9:13 am**	6:13 am
27	**10:12 am**	7:12 am	□☿	♍	27	**9:07 pm**	6:07 pm
30	**8:23 am**	5:23 am	△☿	♎	30	**10:03 am**	7:03 am

☽ Phases & Eclipses			
phase	day	ET / hr:mn / PT	
Full Moon	4	**8:06 am**	5:06 am
●	4	14° ♎ 21'	
4th Quarter	11	**11:44 pm**	8:44 pm
New Moon	18	**2:57 pm**	11:57 am
2nd Quarter	25	**7:55 pm**	4:55 pm

Planet Ingress				
		day	ET / hr:mn / PT	
⚳	♒	3	**8:21 am**	5:21 am
⚵	♑	8	**10:48 pm**	7:48 pm
♀	♊	11	**11:28 am**	8:28 am
☿	♉	14	**6:51 pm**	3:51 pm
☉	♉	20	**5:42 am**	2:42 am
⚵	♐	30	**1:59 pm**	10:59 am
☿	♊	30	**10:00 pm**	7:00 pm

Planetary Motion				
		day	ET / hr:mn / PT	
♃	D	8	**12:57 pm**	9:57 am
♇	℞	16	**11:56 pm**	8:56 pm
⚵	℞	19	**9:29 pm**	6:29 pm

1 WEDNESDAY
☽☍♆ **7:31 am** 4:31 am
☽⚻☉ **1:58 pm** 10:58 am
☽⚺♃ **3:58 pm** 12:58 pm
☽△♇ **9:42 pm** 6:42 pm
☽⚻♅ **11:09 pm** 8:09 pm

2 THURSDAY
☽△♀ **5:01 am** 2:01 am
☿△♄ **8:20 am** 5:20 am
☉△♃ **1:20 pm** 10:20 am

3 FRIDAY
☽⚻♂ **7:17 am** 4:17 am
☽⚹♄ **12:24 pm** 9:24 am
☽☍☿ **5:57 pm** 2:57 pm
☽⚻♆ **8:27 pm** 5:27 pm

4 SATURDAY
☽⚹♃ **4:31 am** 1:31 am
☽☍☉ **8:06 am** 5:06 am
☿⚺♆ **9:22 am** 6:22 am
☽□♇ **10:18 am** 7:18 am
☽☍♅ **11:59 am** 8:59 am
☽⚻♀ 9:01 pm

5 SUNDAY
☽⚻♀ **12:01 am**
☉□♇ **11:08 am** 8:08 am
☽☍♂ **10:58 pm** 7:58 pm
☽⚺♄ **11:56 pm** 8:56 pm

6 MONDAY
☽△♆ **8:05 am** 5:05 am
☿△♃ **9:26 am** 6:26 am
☉☌♅ **10:08 am** 7:08 am
♂⚻♄ **2:17 pm** 11:17 am
☽□♃ **3:43 pm** 12:43 pm
☽⚻☿ **4:57 pm** 1:57 pm
☽⚹♇ **9:23 pm** 6:23 pm
☽⚻♅ **11:15 pm** 8:15 pm
☽⚻☉ 9:19 pm

7 TUESDAY
☽⚻☉ **12:19 am**
☽☍♀ **4:42 pm** 1:42 pm
☿□♇ **8:07 pm** 5:07 pm

8 WEDNESDAY
☿☌♅ **8:20 am** 5:20 am
☽☌♄ **9:30 am** 6:30 am
☽⚻♂ **12:17 pm** 9:17 am
☽□♆ **5:38 pm** 2:38 pm
☽△♃ 9:48 pm

9 THURSDAY
☽△♃ **12:48 am**
☽⚺♇ **6:16 am** 3:16 am
☽△♅ **8:17 am** 5:17 am
☽△☿ **12:40 pm** 9:40 am
☽△☉ **1:42 pm** 10:42 am
☉☌☿ 9:00 pm

10 FRIDAY
☉☌☿ **12:00 am**
☽⚻♀ **6:11 am** 3:11 am
☽⚺♄ **4:35 pm** 1:35 pm
☽△♂ **10:36 pm** 7:36 pm
☽⚹♆ 9:37 pm

11 SATURDAY
☽⚹♆ **12:37 am**
☽⚻♃ **7:21 am** 4:21 am
☽☌♇ **12:32 pm** 9:32 am
☽□♅ **2:41 pm** 11:41 am
☽□☉ **11:44 pm** 8:44 pm

12 SUNDAY
☽□☿ **4:15 am** 1:15 am
♂⚹♆ **1:22 pm** 10:22 am
☽△♀ **4:08 pm** 1:08 pm
☽⚹♄ **8:59 pm** 5:59 pm

13 MONDAY
☽⚺♆ **4:54 am** 1:54 am
☽□♂ **5:43 am** 2:43 am
☽☍♃ **11:15 am** 8:15 am
☽⚺♇ **4:09 pm** 1:09 pm
☽⚹♅ **6:23 pm** 3:23 pm

14 TUESDAY
☽⚹☉ **6:32 am** 3:32 am
☽⚹☿ **3:45 pm** 12:45 pm
☽□♀ **10:51 pm** 7:51 pm
☽□♄ **10:59 pm** 7:59 pm
♀☍♄ 9:25 pm

15 WEDNESDAY
♀☍♄ **12:25 am**
☽☌♆ **6:52 am** 3:52 am
☽⚹♂ **10:09 am** 7:09 am
☽⚻♃ **12:56 pm** 9:56 am
☽⚹♇ **5:37 pm** 2:37 pm
☽⚺♅ **7:58 pm** 4:58 pm

16 THURSDAY
☽⚺☉ **11:02 am** 8:02 am
☿⚻♄ **5:06 pm** 2:06 pm
☽△♄ **11:30 pm** 8:30 pm
☽⚺☿ 9:34 pm

17 FRIDAY
☽⚺☿ **12:34 am**
☽⚹♀ **3:39 am** 12:39 am
☽⚺♆ **7:30 am** 4:30 am
☽⚺♂ **1:10 pm** 10:10 am
☽△♃ **1:30 pm** 10:30 am
☽□♇ **6:04 pm** 3:04 pm
♂□♃ **8:29 pm** 5:29 pm
☽☌♅ **8:36 pm** 5:36 pm

18 SATURDAY
☽☌☉ **2:57 pm** 11:57 am
☿⚺♀ **11:03 pm** 8:03 pm
☽⚻♄ **11:56 pm** 8:56 pm

19 SUNDAY
☿⚹♆ **3:12 am** 12:12 am
♀□♆ **6:29 am** 3:29 am
☽⚹♆ **8:22 am** 5:22 am
☽⚺♀ **8:32 am** 5:32 am
☽☌☿ **9:12 am** 6:12 am
☽□♃ **2:31 pm** 11:31 am
☽☌♂ **4:39 pm** 1:39 pm
☽△♇ **7:07 pm** 4:07 pm
☽⚺♅ **9:54 pm** 6:54 pm

20 MONDAY
☽⚺☉ **8:30 pm** 5:30 pm
☿□♃ 9:15 pm
☽☍♄ 11:00 pm

21 TUESDAY
☿□♃ **12:15 am**
☽☍♄ **2:00 am**
☽□♆ **11:10 am** 8:10 am
☽☌♀ **3:53 pm** 12:53 pm
♂△♇ **5:35 pm** 2:35 pm
☽⚹♃ **5:43 pm** 2:43 pm
☽⚺☿ **8:37 pm** 5:37 pm
☽⚻♇ **10:27 pm** 7:27 pm
☽⚺♂ **10:43 pm** 7:43 pm
☽⚹♅ 10:38 pm

22 WEDNESDAY
☽⚹♅ **1:38 am**
☿△♇ **9:26 am** 6:26 am
♀⚹♃ **2:41 pm** 11:41 am
☿☌♂ **7:03 pm** 4:03 pm

23 THURSDAY
☽⚹☉ **5:48 am** 2:48 am
☽⚻♄ **7:11 am** 4:11 am
☿⚺♅ **9:03 am** 6:03 am
☽△♆ **5:22 pm** 2:22 pm
☉⚻♄ **11:17 pm** 8:17 pm
☽⚺♃ 9:29 pm

24 FRIDAY
☽⚺♃ **12:29 am**
☽⚺♀ **3:42 am** 12:42 am
☽☍♇ **5:21 am** 2:21 am
☽⚹♂ **9:00 am** 6:00 am
☽□♅ **9:02 am** 6:02 am
♂⚺♅ **9:44 am** 6:44 am
☽⚹☿ **1:04 pm** 10:04 am
♀⚻♇ **9:54 pm** 6:54 pm

25 SATURDAY
☽△♄ **4:09 pm** 1:09 pm
☽□☉ **7:55 pm** 4:55 pm

26 SUNDAY
☽⚻♆ **3:23 am** 12:23 am
☽☌♃ **11:04 am** 8:04 am
☽⚻♇ **3:56 pm** 12:56 pm
♀⚹♅ **5:31 pm** 2:31 pm
☽△♅ **8:06 pm** 5:06 pm
☽⚹♀ **8:22 pm** 5:22 pm
☽□♂ **11:34 pm** 8:34 pm

27 MONDAY
☽□☿ **10:12 am** 7:12 am

28 TUESDAY
☽□♄ **4:00 am** 1:00 am
☽△☉ **1:37 pm** 10:37 am
☽☍♆ **4:00 pm** 1:00 pm
☽⚺♃ 9:01 pm

29 WEDNESDAY
☽⚺♃ **12:01 am**
☽△♇ **4:39 am** 1:39 am
☽⚻♅ **9:12 am** 6:12 am
☽□♀ **3:38 pm** 12:38 pm
☽△♂ **4:21 pm** 1:21 pm
☉⚹♆ **7:11 pm** 4:11 pm

30 THURSDAY
☽△☿ **8:23 am** 5:23 am
♀⚺♂ **11:14 am** 8:14 am
☽⚹♄ **4:33 pm** 1:33 pm

Eastern time in bold type
Pacific time in medium type

APRIL 2015

DATE	SID.TIME	SUN	MOON	NODE	MERCURY	VENUS	MARS	JUPITER	SATURN	URANUS	NEPTUNE	PLUTO	CERES	PALLAS	JUNO	VESTA	CHIRON
1 W	12 36 09	10 ♈ 56 52	25 ♌ 29	10 ♎ 00	1 ♈ 45	17 ♉ 27	0 ♉ 14	12 ♌ 41	4 ♐ 41	16 ♈ 08	8 ♓ 30	15 ♑ 29	29 ♑ 19	29 ♐ 09	4 ♌ 23	1 ♓ 34	18 ♓ 43
2 Th	12 40 06	11 56 04	8 ♍ 11	10 00	3 39	18 39	0 58	12 40 R	4 39 R	16 11	8 32	15 30	29 35	29 17	4 30	2 03	18 47
3 F	12 44 02	12 55 14	21 09	10 01	5 34	19 50	1 43	12 39	4 37	16 15	8 34	15 31	29 52	29 24	4 38	2 32	18 50
4 Sa	12 47 59	13 54 22	5 ♎ 47	10 01 R	7 31	21 01	2 27	12 38	4 35	16 18	8 36	15 30	0 ♒ 08	29 31	4 46	3 00	18 53
5 Su	12 51 55	14 53 28	18 21	10 00	9 29	22 12	3 11	12 37	4 33	16 22	8 38	15 30	0 24	29 37	4 55	3 29	18 57
6 M	12 55 52	15 52 32	2 ♏ 30	10 00	11 29	23 22	3 56	12 36	4 31	16 25	8 39	15 31	0 40	29 44	5 04	3 57	19 00
7 T	12 59 48	16 51 34	14 48	9 59	13 29	24 33	4 40	12 36	4 29	16 29	8 41	15 31	0 56	29 49	5 13	4 26	19 04
8 W	13 03 45	17 50 34	27 18	9 57	15 31	25 44	5 24	12 35 D	4 26	16 32	8 43	15 31	1 11	29 55	5 22	4 54	19 07
9 Th	13 07 42	18 49 33	10 ♐ 01	9 56	17 34	26 54	6 08	12 35	4 24	16 36	8 45	15 32	1 27	29 59	5 32	5 22	19 10
10 F	13 11 38	19 48 29	22 59	9 56	19 38	28 04	6 52	12 36	4 22	16 39	8 47	15 32	1 42	0 ♑ 04	5 42	5 50	19 14
11 Sa	13 15 35	20 47 24	6 ♑ 14	9 55	21 42	29 15	7 36	12 36	4 16	16 42	8 49	15 32	1 57	0 08	5 53	6 18	19 17
12 Su	13 19 31	21 46 17	19 47	9 55	23 48	0 ♊ 25	8 20	12 36	4 14	16 46	8 51	15 32	2 12	0 12	6 03	6 46	19 20
13 M	13 23 28	22 45 09	3 ♒ 39	9 56	25 54	1 35	9 04	12 37	4 11	16 49	8 52	15 33	2 26	0 15	6 14	7 14	19 24
14 T	13 27 24	23 43 58	17 50	9 56	28 00	2 45	9 48	12 38	4 08	16 53	8 54	15 33	2 41	0 18	6 26	7 42	19 27
15 W	13 31 21	24 42 46	2 ♓ 19	9 57	0 ♉ 08	3 55	10 32	12 39	4 05	16 56	8 56	15 33	2 55	0 20	6 37	8 10	19 30
16 Th	13 35 17	25 41 32	17 01	9 58	2 12	5 04	11 15	12 40	4 02	16 59	8 57	15 33 R	3 09	0 22	6 49	8 38	19 33
17 F	13 39 14	26 40 17	1 ♈ 52	9 59 R	4 18	6 14	11 59	12 42	3 59	17 03	8 59	15 33	3 23	0 24	7 01	9 05	19 36
18 Sa	13 43 11	27 38 59	16 44	9 59	6 22	7 24	12 43	12 44	3 56	17 06	9 01	15 33	3 36	0 25	7 13	9 33	19 39
19 Su	13 47 07	28 37 40	1 ♉ 31	9 57	8 26	8 33	13 26	12 45	3 53	17 10	9 02	15 33	3 49	0 26	7 26	10 00	19 42
20 M	13 51 04	29 36 19	16 05	9 55	10 28	9 42	14 10	12 47	3 49	17 13	9 04	15 33	4 03	0 26 R	7 39	10 27	19 46
21 T	13 55 00	0 ♉ 34 56	0 ♊ 19	9 52	12 29	10 51	14 53	12 50	3 46	17 16	9 06	15 33	4 15	0 26	7 52	10 55	19 49
22 W	13 58 57	1 33 30	14 09	9 49	14 27	12 00	15 37	12 52	3 43	17 20	9 07	15 32	4 28	0 25	8 05	11 22	19 52
23 Th	14 02 53	2 32 03	27 34	9 46	16 23	13 09	16 20	12 54	3 39	17 23	9 09	15 32	4 41	0 24	8 19	11 49	19 54
24 F	14 06 50	3 30 34	10 ♋ 34	9 44 D	18 16	14 18	17 04	12 57	3 35	17 26	9 10	15 32	4 53	0 23	8 33	12 16	19 57
25 Sa	14 10 46	4 29 02	23 12	9 43	20 06	15 26	17 47	13 00	3 32	17 30	9 12	15 32	5 05	0 21	8 47	12 43	20 00
26 Su	14 14 43	5 27 28	5 ♌ 30	9 43	21 53	16 35	18 30	13 03	3 28	17 33	9 13	15 32	5 17	0 18	9 01	13 09	20 03
27 M	14 18 40	6 25 52	17 33	9 44	23 37	17 43	19 13	13 06	3 24	17 36	9 15	15 31	5 28	0 15	9 15	13 36	20 06
28 T	14 22 36	7 24 14	29 27	9 46	25 17	18 51	19 56	13 10	3 21	17 40	9 16	15 31	5 39	0 12	9 30	14 03	20 09
29 W	14 26 33	8 22 34	11 ♍ 16	9 47	26 53	19 59	20 40	13 13	3 17	17 43	9 18	15 31	5 50	0 08	9 45	14 29	20 11
30 Th	14 30 29	9 20 52	23 04	9 48	28 25	21 07	21 23	13 17	3 14	17 46	9 20	15 30	6 01	0 04	10 00	14 55	20 14

EPHEMERIS CALCULATED FOR 12 MIDNIGHT GREENWICH MEAN TIME. ALL OTHER DATA AND FACING ASPECTARIAN PAGE IN **EASTERN TIME (BOLD)** AND PACIFIC TIME (REGULAR).

MAY 2015

☽ Last Aspect day	ET / hr:mn / PT	asp	☽ Ingress sign	day	ET / hr:mn / PT
2	**10:03 am** 7:03 am	△♀	♏	2	**9:47 pm** 6:47 pm
4	**9:49 pm** 6:49 pm	☍♂	♐	5	**7:13 am** 4:13 am
7	**1:51 pm** 10:51 am	☍♀	♑	7	**2:16 pm** 11:16 am
9	**4:35 pm** 1:35 pm	△♂	♒	9	**7:22 pm** 4:22 pm
11	**6:36 am** 3:36 am	□☉	♓	11	**10:53 pm** 7:53 pm
13	**12:55 pm** 9:55 am	✶☉	♈	13	10:13 pm
13	**12:55 pm** 9:55 am	✶☉	♈	14	**1:13 am**
15	**8:04 am** 5:04 am	☌♅	♉	16	**3:02 am** 12:02 am
17	9:13 pm	☌☉	♊	18	**5:27 am** 2:27 am
18	**12:13 am**	☌☉	♊	18	**5:27 am** 2:27 am
19	**1:57 pm** 10:57 am	✶♅	♋	20	**9:56 am** 6:56 am
21	**8:36 pm** 5:36 pm	□♅	♌	22	**5:42 pm** 2:42 pm
24	**6:50 am** 3:50 am	△♅	♍	25	**4:52 am** 1:52 am
26	**10:21 pm** 7:21 pm	✶♀	♎	27	**5:42 pm** 2:42 pm
29	**4:20 pm** 1:20 pm	□♀	♏	30	**5:34 am** 2:34 am

☽ Phases & Eclipses phase	day	ET / hr:mn / PT
Full Moon	3	**11:42 pm** 8:42 pm
4th Quarter	11	**6:36 am** 3:36 am
New Moon	17	9:13 pm
New Moon	18	**12:13 am**
2nd Quarter	25	**1:19 pm** 10:19 am

Planet Ingress		day	ET / hr:mn / PT
♀	♋	7	**6:52 pm** 3:52 pm
♂	♊	11	**10:40 pm** 7:40 pm
☉	♊	21	**4:45 am** 1:45 am

Planetary Motion		day	ET / hr:mn / PT
☿	℞	18	**9:49 pm** 6:49 pm

1 FRIDAY
☽ ⚻ ♆ **4:52 am** 1:52 am
☽ ⚻ ☉ **7:46 am** 4:46 am
☽ ✶ ♃ **12:59 pm** 9:59 am
☽ □ ♇ **5:09 pm** 2:09 pm
☽ ☍ ♅ **9:54 pm** 6:54 pm

2 SATURDAY
☽ ⚻ ♂ **8:23 am** 5:23 am
☽ △ ♀ **10:03 am** 7:03 am

3 SUNDAY
☽ ⚻ ☿ **3:39 am** 12:39 am
☽ ⚺ ♄ **3:45 am** 12:45 am
☿ ☍ ♄ **4:35 am** 1:35 am
☽ △ ♆ **4:03 pm** 1:03 pm
☽ ☍ ☉ **11:42 pm** 8:42 pm
☽ □ ♃ 9:05 pm

4 MONDAY
☽ □ ♃ **12:05 am**
☽ ✶ ♇ **3:43 am** 12:43 am
☉ □ ♃ **5:02 am** 2:02 am
☽ ⚻ ♅ **8:34 am** 5:34 am
☽ ☍ ♂ **9:49 pm** 6:49 pm
☽ ⚻ ♀ 10:33 pm

5 TUESDAY
☽ ⚻ ♀ **1:33 am**
☽ ☌ ♄ **12:38 pm** 9:38 am
☽ ☍ ☿ **6:32 pm** 3:32 pm
☽ □ ♆ 9:47 pm

6 WEDNESDAY
☽ □ ♆ **12:47 am**
☉ △ ♇ **3:11 am** 12:11 am
☽ △ ♃ **8:45 am** 5:45 am
☽ ⚺ ♇ **11:51 am** 8:51 am
☽ ⚻ ☉ **12:33 pm** 9:33 am
☽ △ ♅ **4:45 pm** 1:45 pm

7 THURSDAY
☽ ⚻ ♂ **8:24 am** 5:24 am
☽ ☍ ♀ **1:51 pm** 10:51 am
☽ ⚺ ♄ **7:12 pm** 4:12 pm

8 FRIDAY
☽ ⚻ ☿ **5:25 am** 2:25 am
☽ ✶ ♆ **7:15 am** 4:15 am
☽ ⚻ ♃ **3:11 pm** 12:11 pm
☽ ☌ ♇ **5:48 pm** 2:48 pm
☽ △ ☉ **10:39 pm** 7:39 pm
☽ □ ♅ **10:47 pm** 7:47 pm
☉ ⚺ ♅ 9:35 pm

9 SATURDAY
☉ ⚺ ♅ **12:35 am**
☿ □ ♆ **12:08 pm** 9:08 am
☽ △ ♂ **4:35 pm** 1:35 pm
☽ ⚻ ♀ **11:34 pm** 8:34 pm
☽ ✶ ♄ **11:52 pm** 8:52 pm

10 SUNDAY
♀ ⚻ ♄ **3:01 am** 12:01 am
☽ ⚺ ♆ **11:53 am** 8:53 am
☽ △ ☿ **1:10 pm** 10:10 am
☽ ☍ ♃ **7:51 pm** 4:51 pm
☽ ⚺ ♇ **10:00 pm** 7:00 pm

11 MONDAY
☽ ✶ ♅ **3:04 am** 12:04 am
☽ □ ☉ **6:36 am** 3:36 am
☽ □ ♂ **10:54 pm** 7:54 pm

12 TUESDAY
☽ □ ♄ **3:00 am** 12:00 am
☽ △ ♀ **7:16 am** 4:16 am
☽ ☌ ♆ **3:02 pm** 12:02 pm
☽ □ ☿ **6:28 pm** 3:28 pm
☽ ⚻ ♃ **11:06 pm** 8:06 pm
☽ ✶ ♇ 9:49 pm

13 WEDNESDAY
☽ ✶ ♇ **12:49 am**
☽ ⚺ ♅ **5:59 am** 2:59 am
☽ ✶ ☉ **12:55 pm** 9:55 am

14 THURSDAY
☽ ✶ ♂ **3:50 am** 12:50 am
☽ △ ♄ **5:01 am** 2:01 am
☽ □ ♀ **1:33 pm** 10:33 am
☽ ⚺ ♆ **5:10 pm** 2:10 pm
☽ ✶ ☿ **9:59 pm** 6:59 pm
☽ △ ♃ 10:25 pm
♂ ☍ ♄ 11:03 pm
☽ □ ♇ 11:44 pm

15 FRIDAY
☽ △ ♃ **1:25 am**
♂ ☍ ♄ **2:03 am**
☽ □ ♇ **2:44 am**
☽ ☌ ♅ **8:04 am** 5:04 am
☽ ⚺ ☉ **6:20 pm** 3:20 pm

16 SATURDAY
☽ ⚻ ♄ **6:35 am** 3:35 am
☽ ⚺ ♂ **8:12 am** 5:12 am
♀ △ ♆ **2:49 pm** 11:49 am
☽ ✶ ♆ **7:05 pm** 4:05 pm
☽ ✶ ♀ **7:25 pm** 4:25 pm
☽ ⚺ ☿ 9:44 pm

17 SUNDAY
☽ ⚺ ☿ **12:44 am**
☽ □ ♃ **3:44 am** 12:44 am
☽ △ ♇ **4:38 am** 1:38 am
☽ ⚺ ♅ **10:15 am** 7:15 am
☽ ☌ ☉ 9:13 pm

18 MONDAY
☽ ☌ ☉ **12:13 am**
☽ ☍ ♄ **8:50 am** 5:50 am
☽ ☌ ♂ **1:26 pm** 10:26 am
☽ □ ♆ **10:03 pm** 7:03 pm
☽ ⚺ ♀ 11:37 pm

19 TUESDAY
☽ ⚺ ♀ 2:37 am
☽ ☌ ☿ **4:06 am** 1:06 am
☽ ✶ ♃ **7:24 am** 4:24 am
☽ ⚻ ♇ **7:51 am** 4:51 am
☽ ✶ ♅ **1:57 pm** 10:57 am
☿ ⚺ ♀ **9:11 pm** 6:11 pm

20 WEDNESDAY
☽ ⚺ ☉ **8:28 am** 5:28 am
☽ ⚻ ♄ **1:12 pm** 10:12 am
☽ ⚺ ♂ **9:20 pm** 6:20 pm

21 THURSDAY
☽ △ ♆ **3:32 am** 12:32 am
♃ ⚻ ♇ **7:39 am** 4:39 am
☽ ⚺ ☿ **9:29 am** 6:29 am
☽ ☌ ♀ **1:07 pm** 10:07 am
☽ ☍ ♇ **1:51 pm** 10:51 am
☽ ⚺ ♃ **1:55 pm** 10:55 am
☽ □ ♅ **8:36 pm** 5:36 pm
♀ ☍ ♇ **9:57 pm** 6:57 pm
♀ ⚺ ♃ 9:00 pm

22 FRIDAY
♀ ⚺ ♃ **12:00 am**
☽ ✶ ☉ **8:47 pm** 5:47 pm
☽ △ ♄ **8:51 pm** 5:51 pm
☉ ☍ ♄ **9:35 pm** 6:35 pm

23 SATURDAY
☽ ✶ ♂ **9:16 am** 6:16 am
☽ ⚻ ♆ **12:32 pm** 9:32 am
☽ ✶ ☿ **5:34 pm** 2:34 pm
☽ ⚻ ♇ **11:22 pm** 8:22 pm
☽ ☌ ♃ 9:05 pm

24 SUNDAY
☽ ☌ ♃ **12:05 am**
☽ ⚺ ♀ **4:06 am** 1:06 am
☽ △ ♅ **6:50 am** 3:50 am

25 MONDAY
☽ □ ♄ **7:48 am** 4:48 am
♀ □ ♅ **1:09 pm** 10:09 am
☽ □ ☉ **1:19 pm** 10:19 am
♂ □ ♆ **7:38 pm** 4:38 pm
☽ ☍ ♆ 9:33 pm
☽ □ ♂ 9:51 pm

26 TUESDAY
☽ ☍ ♆ **12:33 am**
☽ □ ♂ **12:51 am**
☽ □ ☿ **3:43 am** 12:43 am
☽ △ ♇ **11:36 am** 8:36 am
☽ ⚺ ♃ **1:05 pm** 10:05 am
☽ ⚻ ♅ **7:34 pm** 4:34 pm
☽ ✶ ♀ **10:21 pm** 7:21 pm

27 WEDNESDAY
☿ ☌ ♂ **6:37 am** 3:37 am
☽ ✶ ♄ **8:16 pm** 5:16 pm

28 THURSDAY
☽ △ ☉ **7:31 am** 4:31 am
☽ ⚻ ♆ **1:24 pm** 10:24 am
☽ △ ☿ **2:00 pm** 11:00 am
☽ △ ♂ **5:25 pm** 2:25 pm
☽ □ ♇ 9:10 pm
☽ ✶ ♃ 11:24 pm

29 FRIDAY
☽ □ ♇ **12:10 am**
☽ ✶ ♃ **2:24 am**
☿ □ ♆ **3:00 am** 12:00 am
☽ ☍ ♅ **8:17 am** 5:17 am
☽ □ ♀ **4:20 pm** 1:20 pm

30 SATURDAY
☽ ⚺ ♄ **7:41 am** 4:41 am
☉ ☌ ☿ **12:56 pm** 9:56 am
☽ ⚻ ☿ **10:32 pm** 7:32 pm
☽ ⚻ ☉ **11:48 pm** 8:48 pm
☽ △ ♆ 9:31 pm

31 SUNDAY
☽ △ ♆ **12:31 am**
☽ ⚻ ♂ **7:45 am** 4:45 am
☉ □ ♆ **9:08 am** 6:08 am
☽ ✶ ♇ **10:40 am** 7:40 am
☽ □ ♃ **1:31 pm** 10:31 am
☽ ⚻ ♅ **6:40 pm** 3:40 pm

Eastern time in bold type
Pacific time in medium type

MAY 2015

DATE	SID.TIME	SUN	MOON	NODE	MERCURY	VENUS	MARS	JUPITER	SATURN	URANUS	NEPTUNE	PLUTO	CERES	PALLAS	JUNO	VESTA	CHIRON
1 F	14 34 26	10♉19 07	4♎56	9♎49Rx	29♊53	22♊15	22♉06	13♌21	3♐13Rx	17♈49	9♓20	15♑30Rx	6≈12	29♐59Rx	10♌15	15♓21	20♓17
2 Sa	14 38 22	11 17 21	16 56	9 49	1♊17	23 22	22 49	13 25	3 09Rx	17 53	9 22	15 29Rx	6 22	29 53Rx	10 31	15 48	20 19
3 Su	14 42 19	12 15 33	29 05	9 48	2 36	24 29	23 31	13 29	3 05	17 56	9 23	15 29	6 32	29 48	10 47	16 14	20 22
4 M	14 46 15	13 13 44	11♏,27	9 44	3 51	25 36	24 14	13 34	3 01	17 59	9 24	15 28	6 41	29 42	11 03	16 40	20 25
5 T	14 50 12	14 11 52	24 02	9 40	5 02	26 43	24 57	13 38	2 57	18 02	9 25	15 28	6 51	29 35	11 19	17 05	20 27
6 W	14 54 09	15 09 59	6♐52	9 34	6 08	27 50	25 40	13 43	2 53	18 05	9 27	15 27	7 00	29 28	11 35	17 31	20 30
7 Th	14 58 05	16 08 04	19 55	9 28	7 09	28 57	26 23	13 48	2 49	18 08	9 28	15 26	7 09	29 20	11 51	17 57	20 32
8 F	15 02 02	17 06 08	3♑03	9 22	8 06	0♋03	27 05	13 53	2 44	18 12	9 29	15 26	7 18	29 12	12 08	18 22	20 34
9 Sa	15 05 58	18 04 11	16 41	9 18	8 58	1 09	27 48	13 58	2 40	18 15	9 30	15 25	7 26	29 04	12 25	18 47	20 37
10 Su	15 09 55	19 02 12	0≈22	9 14	9 46	2 15	28 30	14 04	2 36	18 18	9 31	15 25	7 34	28 55	12 42	19 13	20 39
11 M	15 13 51	20 00 12	14 15	9 D 13	10 28	3 21	29 13	14 09	2 32	18 21	9 32	15 24	7 42	28 45	12 59	19 38	20 41
12 T	15 17 48	20 58 10	28 18	9 13	11 06	4 27	29 55	14 15	2 27	18 24	9 33	15 24	7 49	28 36	13 16	20 03	20 44
13 W	15 21 44	21 56 07	12♓31	9 14	11 38	5 32	0♊38	14 21	2 23	18 27	9 34	15 23	7 56	28 25	13 33	20 28	20 46
14 Th	15 25 41	22 54 03	26 52	9 R15	12 06	6 37	1 20	14 27	2 19	18 30	9 35	15 22	8 03	28 15	13 51	20 52	20 48
15 F	15 29 38	23 51 57	11♈18	9 16	12 28	7 42	2 02	14 33	2 14	18 33	9 36	15 22	8 10	28 03	14 09	21 17	20 50
16 Sa	15 33 34	24 49 51	25 46	9 14	12 46	8 47	2 45	14 39	2 10	18 36	9 37	15 21	8 16	27 52	14 26	21 41	20 52
17 Su	15 37 31	25 47 43	10♉11	9 11	12 58	9 51	3 27	14 46	2 05	18 39	9 38	15 20	8 22	27 40	14 44	22 06	20 54
18 M	15 41 27	26 45 33	24 27	9 06	13 06	10 56	4 09	14 52	2 01	18 41	9 39	15 19	8 28	27 28	15 03	22 30	20 56
19 T	15 45 24	27 43 23	8♊28	8 59	13 09Rx	12 00	4 51	14 59	1 56	18 44	9 39	15 18	8 33	27 15	15 21	22 54	20 58
20 W	15 49 20	28 41 11	22 12	8 51	13 07	13 04	5 33	15 06	1 52	18 47	9 40	15 17	8 38	27 02	15 39	23 18	21 00
21 Th	15 53 17	29 38 57	5♋59	8 42	13 00	14 07	6 15	15 13	1 47	18 50	9 41	15 16	8 43	26 48	15 57	23 42	21 02
22 F	15 57 13	0♊36 42	18 34	8 35	12 49	15 10	6 57	15 20	1 43	18 53	9 42	15 16	8 47	26 34	16 16	24 05	21 03
23 Sa	16 01 10	1 34 25	1♌12	8 29	12 34	16 13	7 39	15 27	1 39	18 55	9 42	15 15	8 51	26 20	16 35	24 29	21 05
24 Su	16 05 07	2 32 07	13 31	8 25	12 15	17 16	8 21	15 34	1 34	18 58	9 43	15 14	8 55	26 06	16 54	24 52	21 07
25 M	16 09 03	3 29 47	25 35	8 23 D	11 52	18 18	9 03	15 42	1 30	19 01	9 44	15 13	8 58	25 51	17 13	25 15	21 08
26 T	16 13 00	4 27 26	7♍30	8 23	11 27	19 20	9 45	15 49	1 25	19 03	9 44	15 11	9 01	25 36	17 32	25 39	21 10
27 W	16 16 56	5 25 03	19 19	8 23	10 58	20 22	10 26	15 57	1 21	19 06	9 45	15 10	9 04	25 20	17 52	26 01	21 12
28 Th	16 20 53	6 22 39	1♎08	8 24 Rx	10 28	21 24	11 08	16 05	1 16	19 09	9 45	15 09	9 06	25 05	18 11	26 24	21 13
29 F	16 24 49	7 20 13	13 03	8 24	9 55	22 25	11 50	16 13	1 12	19 11	9 46	15 08	9 08	24 49	18 30	26 47	21 14
30 Sa	16 28 46	8 17 46	25 08	8 23	9 22	23 26	12 31	16 21	1 07	19 14	9 46	15 07	9 10	24 32	18 50	27 09	21 16
31 Su	16 32 42	9 15 17	7♏,26	8 19	8 48	24 26	13 13	16 29	1 03	19 16	9 47	15 06	9 11	24 16	19 10	27 31	21 17

EPHEMERIS CALCULATED FOR 12 MIDNIGHT GREENWICH MEAN TIME. ALL OTHER DATA AND FACING ASPECTARIAN PAGE IN **EASTERN TIME (BOLD)** AND PACIFIC TIME (REGULAR).

JUNE 2015

☽ Last Aspect day	ET / hr:mn	PT	asp	☽ Ingress sign	day	ET / hr:mn	PT
1	**7:01 am**	4:01 am	△♀	♐	1	**2:39 pm**	11:39 am
2		10:59 pm	△♅	♑	3	**8:50 pm**	5:50 pm
3	**1:59 am**		△♅	♑	3	**8:50 pm**	5:50 pm
5	**6:54 am**	3:54 am	□♅	♒	5		10:02 pm
5	**6:54 am**	3:54 am	□♅	♒	6	**1:02 am**	
7	**10:30 am**	7:30 am	✶♅	♓	8	**4:16 am**	1:16 am
9	**2:08 pm**	11:08 am	□♂	♈	10	**7:14 am**	4:14 am
11	**7:43 pm**	4:43 pm	✶♂	♉	12	**10:16 am**	7:16 am
13	**6:06 pm**	3:06 pm	□♃	♊	14	**1:51 pm**	10:51 am
16	**10:05 am**	7:05 am	☌☉	♋	16	**6:51 pm**	3:51 pm
18		10:52 pm	△♄	♌	18		11:23 pm
19	**1:52 am**		△♄	♌	19	**2:23 am**	
21	**12:09 pm**	9:09 am	□♄	♍	21	**12:59 pm**	9:59 am
23		10:12 pm	□♂	♎	23		10:41 pm
24	**1:12 am**		□♂	♎	24	**1:41 am**	
25	**7:22 pm**	4:22 pm	✶♃	♏	26	**1:57 pm**	10:57 am
28	**9:50 pm**	6:50 pm	☌♄	♐	28	**11:21 pm**	8:21 pm
30	**2:18 pm**	11:18 am	△♃	♑	7/1	**5:11 am**	2:11 am

☽ Phases & Eclipses phase	day	ET / hr:mn	PT
Full Moon	2	**12:19 pm**	9:19 am
4th Quarter	9	**11:42 am**	8:42 am
New Moon	16	**10:05 am**	7:05 am
2nd Quarter	24	**7:03 am**	4:03 am

Planet Ingress		day	ET / hr:mn	PT
♀	♌	5	**11:33 am**	8:33 am
⚴	♈	6	**5:05 pm**	2:05 pm
♄	♏	14	**8:36 pm**	5:36 pm
☉	♋	21	**12:38 pm**	9:38 am
♂	♋	24	**9:33 am**	6:33 am
⚵	♍	30	**6:59 pm**	3:59 pm

Planetary Motion		day	ET / hr:mn	PT
⚳	R	3	**12:20 am**	9:20 pm
☿	D	11	**6:33 pm**	3:33 pm
♆	R	12	**5:09 am**	2:09 am
⚷	R	24	**7:36 am**	4:36 am

1 MONDAY
☽△♀ **7:01 am** 4:01 am
☽☌♄ **4:21 pm** 1:21 pm

2 TUESDAY
☽☍☿ **4:27 am** 1:27 am
☽□♆ **8:37 am** 5:37 am
♂⚻♇ **11:40 am** 8:40 am
☽☍☉ **12:19 pm** 9:19 am
☽⚺♇ **6:09 pm** 3:09 pm
☽☍♂ **6:31 pm** 3:31 pm
☽△♃ **9:31 pm** 6:31 pm
☽△♅ 10:59 pm

3 WEDNESDAY
☽△♅ **1:59 am**
☽⚻♀ **5:51 pm** 2:51 pm
☽⚺♄ **10:10 pm** 7:10 pm

4 THURSDAY
☽⚻☿ **8:09 am** 5:09 am
☽✶♆ **2:03 pm** 11:03 am
☽⚻☉ **9:34 pm** 6:34 pm
☽☌♇ **11:07 pm** 8:07 pm
☽⚻♂ 11:20 pm

5 FRIDAY
☽⚻♂ **2:20 am**
☽⚻♃ **3:00 am** 12:00 am
☽□♅ **6:54 am** 3:54 am

☉⚻♇ **7:32 pm** 4:32 pm
♂✶♃ **7:38 pm** 4:38 pm
☽☍♀ 11:02 pm
☽✶♄ 11:03 pm
♀△♄ 11:23 pm

6 SATURDAY
☽☍♀ **2:02 am**
☽✶♄ **2:03 am**
♀△♄ **2:23 am**
☽△☿ **10:34 am** 7:34 am
☽⚺♆ **5:51 pm** 2:51 pm
☽⚺♇ 11:38 pm

7 SUNDAY
☽⚺♇ **2:38 am**
☽△☉ **4:58 am** 1:58 am
☽☍♃ **7:06 am** 4:06 am
☽△♂ **8:31 am** 5:31 am
☽✶♅ **10:30 am** 7:30 am

8 MONDAY
☽□♄ **5:02 am** 2:02 am
☽⚻♀ **8:58 am** 5:58 am
☽□☿ **12:40 pm** 9:40 am
☉✶♃ **5:56 pm** 2:56 pm
☽☌♆ **8:57 pm** 5:57 pm

9 TUESDAY
♂✶♅ **3:30 am** 12:30 am
☽✶♇ **5:36 am** 2:36 am

☽⚻♃ **10:41 am** 7:41 am
☽□☉ **11:42 am** 8:42 am
☽⚺♅ **1:39 pm** 10:39 am
☽□♂ **2:08 pm** 11:08 am

10 WEDNESDAY
☽△♄ **7:45 am** 4:45 am
☿✶♀ **8:52 am** 5:52 am
☽✶☿ **3:04 pm** 12:04 pm
☽△♀ **3:32 pm** 12:32 pm
☉✶♅ **5:30 pm** 2:30 pm
☽⚺♆ **11:54 pm** 8:54 pm

11 THURSDAY
☽□♇ **8:29 am** 5:29 am
☽△♃ **2:13 pm** 11:13 am
☽☌♅ **4:45 pm** 1:45 pm
☽✶☉ **6:22 pm** 3:22 pm
☽✶♂ **7:43 pm** 4:43 pm

12 FRIDAY
☽⚻♄ **10:32 am** 7:32 am
☽⚺☿ **6:07 pm** 3:07 pm
☽□♀ **10:12 pm** 7:12 pm

13 SATURDAY
☽✶♆ **3:03 am** 12:03 am
☽△♇ **11:38 am** 8:38 am
☽□♃ **6:06 pm** 3:06 pm
☽⚺♅ **8:11 pm** 5:11 pm
☽⚺☉ 10:30 pm
☽⚺♂ 10:43 pm

14 SUNDAY
☽⚺☉ **1:30 am**
☽⚺♂ **1:43 am**
☉☌♂ **11:56 am** 8:56 am
☽☍♄ **1:53 pm** 10:53 am
☽☌☿ **10:27 pm** 7:27 pm

15 MONDAY
☽✶♀ **5:38 am** 2:38 am
☽□♆ **6:59 am** 3:59 am
☽⚻♇ **3:41 pm** 12:41 pm
☽✶♃ **11:05 pm** 8:05 pm
☽✶♅ 9:42 pm
♀⚻♆ 11:21 pm

16 TUESDAY
☽✶♅ **12:42 am**
♀⚻♆ **2:21 am**
☽☌♂ **9:06 am** 6:06 am
☽☌☉ **10:05 am** 7:05 am
☽⚻♄ **6:38 pm** 3:38 pm

17 WEDNESDAY
☽⚺☿ **5:08 am** 2:08 am
☽△♆ **12:41 pm** 9:41 am
☽⚺♀ **3:08 pm** 12:08 pm
☽☍♇ **9:43 pm** 6:43 pm

18 THURSDAY
☽⚺♃ **6:17 am** 3:17 am
☽□♅ **7:24 am** 4:24 am
☽⚺♂ **7:12 pm** 4:12 pm

☽⚺☉ **9:37 pm** 6:37 pm
☽△♄ 10:52 pm

19 FRIDAY
☽△♄ **1:52 am**
☽✶☿ **3:36 pm** 12:36 pm
☽⚻♆ **9:12 pm** 6:12 pm

20 SATURDAY
☽☌♀ **3:59 am** 12:59 am
☽⚻♇ **6:39 am** 3:39 am
☽☌♃ **4:37 pm** 1:37 pm
☽△♅ **5:07 pm** 2:07 pm
☉⚻♄ 11:51 pm

21 SUNDAY
☉⚻♄ **2:51 am**
☽✶♂ **8:54 am** 5:54 am
☽□♄ **12:09 pm** 9:09 am
☽✶☉ **1:01 pm** 10:01 am
♀⚻♇ **6:48 pm** 3:48 pm

22 MONDAY
☽□☿ **6:27 am** 3:27 am
☽☍♆ **8:40 am** 5:40 am
♃△♅ **9:46 am** 6:46 am
☽△♇ **6:23 pm** 3:23 pm
☽⚺♀ **8:10 pm** 5:10 pm

23 TUESDAY
☽⚻♅ **5:29 am** 2:29 am
☽⚺♃ **5:44 am** 2:44 am
⊕☿□♆ **2:08 pm** 11:08 am

♂⚻♄ **2:36 pm** 11:36 am
⊕☽✶♄ 9:33 pm
☽□♂ 10:12 pm

24 WEDNESDAY
☽✶♄ **12:33 am**
☽□♂ **1:12 am**
☽□☉ **7:03 am** 4:03 am
☽⚻♆ **9:30 pm** 6:30 pm
☽△☿ 9:08 pm

25 THURSDAY
☽△☿ **12:08 am**
☽□♇ **7:07 am** 4:07 am
☽✶♀ **1:16 pm** 10:16 am
☽☍♅ **6:20 pm** 3:20 pm
☽✶♃ **7:22 pm** 4:22 pm

26 FRIDAY
☽⚺♄ **12:35 pm** 9:35 am
☽△♂ **5:01 pm** 2:01 pm
☽△☉ 9:12 pm

27 SATURDAY
☽△☉ **12:12 am**
☽△♆ **9:00 am** 6:00 am
☽⚻☿ **5:02 pm** 2:02 pm
☽✶♇ **6:06 pm** 3:06 pm

28 SUNDAY
☽□♀ **3:43 am** 12:43 am
☿⚻♇ **4:20 am** 1:20 am
☽⚻♅ **4:58 am** 1:58 am

☽□♃ **6:41 am** 3:41 am
☽☌♄ **9:50 pm** 6:50 pm
♀△♅ 11:26 pm

29 MONDAY
♀△♅ **2:26 am**
☽⚻♂ **5:21 am** 2:21 am
☽⚻☉ **1:25 pm** 10:25 am
☽□♆ **5:12 pm** 2:12 pm
☽⚺♇ 10:39 pm

30 TUESDAY
☽⚺♇ **1:39 am**
☽☍☿ **6:20 am** 3:20 am
☽△♅ **12:01 pm** 9:01 am
☽△♀ **1:47 pm** 10:47 am
☽△♃ **2:18 pm** 11:18 am

Eastern time in bold type
Pacific time in medium type

JUNE 2015

DATE	SID.TIME	SUN	MOON	NODE	MERCURY	VENUS	MARS	JUPITER	SATURN	URANUS	NEPTUNE	PLUTO	CERES	PALLAS	JUNO	VESTA	CHIRON
1 M	16 36 39	10 ♊ 12 48	20 ♏ 01	8 ♎ 13	8 ♊ 15	25 ♋ 26	13 ♊ 54	16 ♌ 37	0 ♐ 59	19 ♈ 19	9 ♓ 47	15 ♑ 05	9 ♒ 12	23 ♈ 59	19 ♌ 30	27 ♓ 54	21 ♓ 18
2 T	16 40 36	11 10 17	2 ♐ 54	8 05 R	7 42 R	26 26	14 36	16 46	0 ♐ 54 R	19 21	9 48	15 04 R	9 13	23 43 R	19 49	28 15	21 20
3 W	16 44 32	12 07 45	16 04	7 55	7 10	27 25	15 17	16 54	0 50	19 24	9 48	15 03	9 13 R	23 26	20 09	28 37	21 21
4 Th	16 48 29	13 05 12	29 31	7 44	6 40	28 24	15 59	17 03	0 45	19 26	9 48	15 01	9 12	23 08	20 29	28 59	21 22
5 F	16 52 25	14 02 39	13 ♑ 13	7 34	6 12	29 22	16 40	17 12	0 41	19 28	9 48	15 00	9 11	22 51	20 50	29 20	21 23
6 Sa	16 56 22	15 00 04	27 05	7 25	5 47	0 ♌ 20	17 21	17 21	0 37	19 30	9 48	14 59	9 11	22 34	21 10	29 41	21 24
7 Su	17 00 18	15 57 29	11 ♒ 04	7 19	5 25	1 18	18 03	17 30	0 33	19 33	9 49	14 58	9 10	22 16	21 30	0 ♈ 03	21 25
8 M	17 04 15	16 54 53	25 08	7 10	5 07	2 15	18 44	17 39	0 28	19 35	9 49	14 56	9 09	22 01	21 51	0 23	21 26
9 T	17 08 11	17 52 17	9 ♓ 15	7 13 D	4 53	3 12	19 25	17 48	0 24	19 37	9 49	14 55	9 07	21 41	22 11	0 44	21 27
10 W	17 12 08	18 49 40	23 23	7 15	4 42	4 08	20 06	17 57	0 20	19 39	9 49	14 54	9 05	21 24	22 32	1 05	21 28
11 Th	17 16 05	19 47 02	7 ♈ 31	7 13 R	4 36 D	5 04	20 47	18 07	0 16	19 41	9 49	14 53	9 02	21 06	22 53	1 25	21 28
12 F	17 20 01	20 44 24	21 38	7 12	4 34	5 59	21 28	18 16	0 12	19 43	9 49 R	14 51	8 59	20 48	23 13	1 45	21 29
13 Sa	17 23 58	21 41 46	5 ♉ 42	7 10	4 36	6 54	22 09	18 26	0 08	19 45	9 49	14 50	8 56	20 30	23 34	2 05	21 30
14 Su	17 27 54	22 39 07	19 41	7 05	4 43	7 48	22 50	18 36	0 04	19 47	9 49	14 49	8 52	20 13	23 55	2 25	21 30
15 M	17 31 51	23 36 28	3 ♊ 32	6 57	4 55	8 42	23 31	18 45	0 00	19 49	9 49	14 47	8 48	19 55	24 16	2 44	21 31
16 T	17 35 47	24 33 48	17 12	6 46	5 11	9 35	24 12	18 55	29 ♏ 56	19 51	9 49	14 46	8 43	19 38	24 37	3 04	21 31
17 W	17 39 44	25 31 07	0 ♋ 38	6 35	5 32	10 27	24 53	19 05	29 52	19 53	9 49	14 44	8 39	19 20	24 58	3 23	21 32
18 Th	17 43 40	26 28 26	13 47	6 22	5 57	11 19	25 33	19 15	29 49	19 55	9 49	14 43	8 33	19 03	25 20	3 42	21 32
19 F	17 47 37	27 25 44	26 38	6 11	6 27	12 10	26 14	19 26	29 45	19 57	9 48	14 42	8 28	18 46	25 41	4 00	21 33
20 Sa	17 51 34	28 23 02	9 ♌ 11	6 01	7 01	13 01	26 55	19 36	29 41	19 58	9 48	14 40	8 22	18 29	26 02	4 19	21 33
21 Su	17 55 30	29 20 19	21 27	5 54	7 39	13 51	27 35	19 46	29 38	20 00	9 48	14 39	8 16	18 12	26 24	4 37	21 33
22 M	17 59 27	0 ♋ 17 35	3 ♍ 30	5 50	8 22	14 40	28 16	19 57	29 34	20 02	9 48	14 37	8 09	17 56	26 45	4 55	21 33
23 T	18 03 23	1 14 50	15 24	5 47	9 09	15 28	28 57	20 07	29 31	20 03	9 47	14 36	8 02	17 39	27 07	5 12	21 33
24 W	18 07 20	2 12 05	27 12	5 47	10 00	16 16	29 37	20 17	29 27	20 05	9 47	14 34	7 55	17 23	27 28	5 30	21 33 R
25 Th	18 11 16	3 09 19	9 ♎ 02	5 47	10 55	17 03	0 ♋ 18	20 28	29 24	20 06	9 46	14 33	7 48	17 07	27 50	5 47	21 33
26 F	18 15 13	4 06 33	20 58	5 46	11 54	17 48	0 58	20 39	29 21	20 08	9 46	14 32	7 40	16 52	28 12	6 04	21 33
27 Sa	18 19 09	5 03 46	3 ♏ 05	5 44	12 57	18 34	1 38	20 50	29 17	20 09	9 46	14 30	7 32	16 37	28 33	6 21	21 33
28 Su	18 23 06	6 00 58	15 28	5 40	14 04	19 18	2 19	21 01	29 14	20 11	9 45	14 29	7 23	16 21	28 55	6 37	21 33
29 M	18 27 03	6 58 10	28 12	5 33	15 15	20 01	2 59	21 12	29 11	20 12	9 45	14 27	7 14	16 07	29 17	6 54	21 33
30 T	18 30 59	7 55 22	11 ♐ 17	5 24	16 29	20 43	3 39	21 23	29 08	20 13	9 44	14 26	7 05	15 52	29 39	7 10	21 33

EPHEMERIS CALCULATED FOR 12 MIDNIGHT GREENWICH MEAN TIME. ALL OTHER DATA AND FACING ASPECTARIAN PAGE IN **EASTERN TIME (BOLD)** AND PACIFIC TIME (REGULAR).

JULY 2015

☽ Last Aspect day	ET / hr:mn / PT	asp	☽ Ingress sign day	ET / hr:mn / PT
6/30	**2:18 pm** 11:18 am	△ ♃	♑ 1	**5:11 am** 2:11 am
3	**6:38 am** 3:38 am	✶ ♄	♒ 3	**8:21 am** 5:21 am
5	**8:32 am** 5:32 am	□ ♄	♓ 5	**10:23 am** 7:23 am
7	**10:36 am** 7:36 am	△ ♄	♈ 7	**12:38 pm** 9:38 am
9	**9:47 am** 6:47 am	△ ♀	♉ 9	**3:49 pm** 12:49 pm
11	**5:52 pm** 2:52 pm	☍ ♄	♊ 11	**8:16 pm** 5:16 pm
13	**11:31 pm** 8:31 pm	✶ ♀	♋ 13	11:14 pm
13	**11:31 pm** 8:31 pm	✶ ♀	♋ 14	**2:14 am**
16	**7:24 am** 4:24 am	△ ♄	♌ 16	**10:15 am** 7:15 am
18	**5:41 pm** 2:41 pm	□ ♄	♍ 18	**8:47 pm** 5:47 pm
21	**6:07 am** 3:07 am	✶ ♄	♎ 21	**9:23 am** 6:23 am
23	**2:12 pm** 11:12 am	✶ ♃	♏ 23	**10:07 pm** 7:07 pm
26	**5:14 am** 2:14 am	☌ ♄	♐ 26	**8:24 am** 5:24 am
28	**9:36 am** 6:36 am	△ ♃	♑ 28	**2:47 pm** 11:47 am
30	**2:50 pm** 11:50 am	✶ ♄	♒ 30	**5:40 pm** 2:40 pm

☽ Phases & Eclipses phase	day	ET / hr:mn / PT
Full Moon	1	**10:20 pm** 7:20 pm
4th Quarter	8	**4:24 pm** 1:24 pm
New Moon	15	**9:24 pm** 6:24 pm
2nd Quarter	23	9:04 pm
2nd Quarter	24	**12:04 am**
Full Moon	31	**6:43 am** 3:43 am

Planet Ingress	day	ET / hr:mn / PT
☿ ♋	8	**2:52 pm** 11:52 am
♀ ♍	18	**6:38 pm** 3:38 pm
☉ ♌	22	**11:30 pm** 8:30 pm
☿ ♌	23	**8:14 am** 5:14 am
♀ ♌	31	**11:27 am** 8:27 am

Planetary Motion	day	ET / hr:mn / PT
♀ ℞	25	**5:29 am** 2:29 am
♅ ℞	26	**6:38 am** 3:38 am

1 WEDNESDAY
☽ ⚺ ♄ **3:34 am** 12:34 am
♀ ☌ ♃ **3:51 am** 12:51 am
☽ ☍ ♂ **1:32 pm** 10:32 am
☉ △ ♆ **5:10 pm** 2:10 pm
☽ ✶ ♆ **9:58 pm** 6:58 pm
☽ ☍ ☉ **10:20 pm** 7:20 pm

2 THURSDAY
☽ ☌ ♇ **5:56 am** 2:56 am
☿ ✶ ♅ **2:50 pm** 11:50 am
☽ □ ♅ **3:58 pm** 12:58 pm
☽ ⚻ ☿ **4:05 pm** 1:05 pm
☽ ⚻ ♃ **6:45 pm** 3:45 pm
☽ ⚻ ♀ **8:06 pm** 5:06 pm

3 FRIDAY
☽ ✶ ♄ **6:38 am** 3:38 am
☽ ⚻ ♂ **6:54 pm** 3:54 pm
☿ ✶ ♃ **8:53 pm** 5:53 pm
☽ ⚺ ♆ 9:34 pm

4 SATURDAY
☽ ⚺ ♆ **12:34 am**
☽ ⚻ ☉ **4:32 am** 1:32 am
☽ ⚺ ♇ **8:16 am** 5:16 am
☽ ✶ ♅ **6:16 pm** 3:16 pm
☽ ☍ ♃ **9:37 pm** 6:37 pm
☽ △ ☿ 9:14 pm
☽ ☍ ♀ 9:32 pm

5 SUNDAY
☽ △ ☿ **12:14 am**
☽ ☍ ♀ **12:32 am**
☿ ✶ ♀ **4:19 am** 1:19 am
☽ □ ♄ **8:32 am** 5:32 am
☽ △ ♂ **11:19 pm** 8:19 pm
☽ ☌ ♆ 11:30 pm

6 MONDAY
☽ ☌ ♆ **2:30 am**
☽ △ ☉ **10:05 am** 7:05 am
☽ ✶ ♇ **10:11 am** 7:11 am
☉ ☍ ♇ **11:38 am** 8:38 am
☽ ⚺ ♅ **8:23 pm** 5:23 pm
☽ ⚻ ♃ 9:23 pm

7 TUESDAY
☽ ⚻ ♃ **12:23 am**
☽ ⚻ ♀ **4:45 am** 1:45 am
☽ □ ☿ **8:56 am** 5:56 am
☽ △ ♄ **10:36 am** 7:36 am
☿ ⚻ ♄ **10:19 pm** 7:19 pm

8 WEDNESDAY
☽ □ ♂ **4:16 am** 1:16 am
☽ ⚺ ♆ **4:57 am** 1:57 am
☽ □ ♇ **12:44 pm** 9:44 am
☽ □ ☉ **4:24 pm** 1:24 pm
♂ △ ♆ **6:42 pm** 3:42 pm
☽ ☌ ♅ **11:17 pm** 8:17 pm

9 THURSDAY
☽ △ ♃ **4:02 am** 1:02 am
☽ △ ♀ **9:47 am** 6:47 am
☽ ⚻ ♄ **1:37 pm** 10:37 am
☽ ✶ ☿ **7:35 pm** 4:35 pm

10 FRIDAY
☽ ✶ ♆ **8:29 am** 5:29 am
☽ ✶ ♂ **10:26 am** 7:26 am
☽ △ ♇ **4:24 pm** 1:24 pm
☽ ✶ ☉ 9:08 pm

11 SATURDAY
☽ ✶ ☉ **12:08 am**
☽ ⚺ ♅ **3:21 am** 12:21 am
☽ □ ♃ **8:56 am** 5:56 am
☽ □ ♀ **3:57 pm** 12:57 pm
☽ ☍ ♄ **5:52 pm** 2:52 pm

12 SUNDAY
☽ ⚺ ☿ **8:47 am** 5:47 am
☽ □ ♆ **1:19 pm** 10:19 am
☽ ⚺ ♂ **6:08 pm** 3:08 pm
☽ ⚻ ♇ **9:25 pm** 6:25 pm
☉ □ ♅ **10:53 pm** 7:53 pm

13 MONDAY
☽ ✶ ♅ **8:50 am** 5:50 am
☽ ⚺ ☉ **9:36 am** 6:36 am
☿ △ ♆ **3:14 pm** 12:14 pm
☽ ✶ ♃ **3:21 pm** 12:21 pm
☽ ✶ ♀ **11:31 pm** 8:31 pm
☽ ⚻ ♄ **11:37 pm** 8:37 pm
♀ □ ♄ 11:48 pm

14 TUESDAY
♀ □ ♄ **2:48 am**
☽ △ ♆ **7:48 pm** 4:48 pm
☽ ☌ ☿ 10:11 pm

15 WEDNESDAY
☽ ☌ ☿ **1:11 am**
☽ ☌ ♂ **3:50 am** 12:50 am
☽ ☍ ♇ **4:10 am** 1:10 am
♂ ☍ ♇ **10:12 am** 7:12 am
☽ □ ♅ **4:10 pm** 1:10 pm
☿ ☍ ♇ **7:40 pm** 4:40 pm
☽ ☌ ☉ **9:24 pm** 6:24 pm
☽ ⚺ ♃ **11:48 pm** 8:48 pm
☿ ☌ ♂ 9:14 pm

16 THURSDAY
☿ ☌ ♂ **12:14 am**
☽ △ ♄ **7:24 am** 4:24 am
☽ ⚺ ♀ **9:00 am** 6:00 am

17 FRIDAY
☽ ⚻ ♆ **4:31 am** 1:31 am
☉ ⚺ ♃ **1:03 pm** 10:03 am
☽ ⚻ ♇ **1:13 pm** 10:13 am
☽ ⚺ ♂ **4:14 pm** 1:14 pm
☽ ⚺ ☿ **9:54 pm** 6:54 pm
☽ △ ♅ 10:55 pm

18 SATURDAY
☽ △ ♅ **1:55 am**
☽ ☌ ♃ **10:50 am** 7:50 am
☽ ⚺ ☉ **12:19 pm** 9:19 am
☽ □ ♄ **5:41 pm** 2:41 pm
☽ ☌ ♀ **8:49 pm** 5:49 pm
☿ □ ♅ **9:07 pm** 6:07 pm

19 SUNDAY
☽ ☍ ♆ **3:43 pm** 12:43 pm
☽ △ ♇ 9:45 pm

20 MONDAY
☽ △ ♇ **12:45 am**
☽ ✶ ♂ **7:30 am** 4:30 am
☽ ⚻ ♅ **2:02 pm** 11:02 am
☽ ✶ ☿ **11:02 pm** 8:02 pm
☽ ⚺ ♃ 9:15 pm

21 TUESDAY
☽ ⚺ ♃ **12:15 am**
☽ ✶ ☉ **6:01 am** 3:01 am
☽ ✶ ♄ **6:07 am** 3:07 am
☿ ⚺ ♃ **6:18 am** 3:18 am
☉ △ ♄ **7:07 am** 4:07 am
☽ ⚺ ♀ **10:24 am** 7:24 am

22 WEDNESDAY
☽ ⚻ ♆ **4:33 am** 1:33 am
☽ □ ♇ **1:36 pm** 10:36 am
☿ △ ♄ **1:51 pm** 10:51 am
☽ □ ♂ 9:04 pm

23 THURSDAY
☽ □ ♂ **12:04 am**
☽ ☍ ♅ **3:02 am** 12:02 am
☽ ✶ ♃ **2:12 pm** 11:12 am
☉ ☌ ☿ **3:24 pm** 12:24 pm
☿ ⚺ ♀ **4:28 pm** 1:28 pm
☉ ⚺ ♀ **5:53 pm** 2:53 pm
☽ ⚺ ♄ **6:49 pm** 3:49 pm
☽ ✶ ♀ **11:36 pm** 8:36 pm
☽ □ ☉ 9:04 pm
☽ □ ☿ 10:05 pm

24 FRIDAY
☽ □ ☉ **12:04 am**
☽ □ ☿ **1:05 am**
☽ △ ♆ **4:40 pm** 1:40 pm
☽ ✶ ♇ 10:23 pm

25 SATURDAY
☽ ✶ ♇ **1:23 am**
♂ □ ♅ **5:43 am** 2:43 am
☽ ⚻ ♅ **2:21 pm** 11:21 am
☽ △ ♂ **2:49 pm** 11:49 am
☽ □ ♃ 10:55 pm

26 SUNDAY
☽ □ ♃ **1:55 am**
☽ ☌ ♄ **5:14 am** 2:14 am
☽ □ ♀ **9:48 am** 6:48 am
☽ △ ☉ **2:55 pm** 11:55 am
☽ △ ☿ **10:26 pm** 7:26 pm
☽ □ ♆ 10:43 pm

27 MONDAY
☽ □ ♆ **1:43 am**
☽ ⚺ ♇ **9:50 am** 6:50 am
☿ ⚻ ♆ **7:06 pm** 4:06 pm
☽ △ ♅ **10:00 pm** 7:00 pm
☽ ⚻ ♂ 10:18 pm

28 TUESDAY
☽ ⚻ ♂ **1:18 am**
☽ △ ♃ **9:36 am** 6:36 am
☽ ⚺ ♄ **11:49 am** 8:49 am
☽ △ ♀ **3:44 pm** 12:44 pm
☽ ⚻ ☉ 9:50 pm

29 WEDNESDAY
☽ ⚻ ☉ **12:50 am**
☽ ✶ ♆ **6:49 am** 3:49 am
☽ ⚻ ☿ **12:54 pm** 9:54 am
☽ ☌ ♇ **2:23 pm** 11:23 am
☿ ⚻ ♇ **11:21 pm** 8:21 pm
☽ □ ♅ 10:51 pm

30 THURSDAY
☽ □ ♅ **1:51 am**
☽ ☍ ♂ **7:24 am** 4:24 am
☽ ⚻ ♃ **1:32 pm** 10:32 am
☽ ✶ ♄ **2:50 pm** 11:50 am
☽ ⚻ ♀ **5:57 pm** 2:57 pm

31 FRIDAY
☽ ☍ ☉ **6:43 am** 3:43 am
☽ ⚺ ♆ **8:50 am** 5:50 am
☽ ⚺ ♇ **4:05 pm** 1:05 pm
☽ ☍ ☿ **10:26 pm** 7:26 pm

Eastern time in bold type
Pacific time in medium type

JULY 2015

DATE	SID.TIME	SUN	MOON	NODE	MERCURY	VENUS	MARS	JUPITER	SATURN	URANUS	NEPTUNE	PLUTO	CERES	PALLAS	JUNO	VESTA	CHIRON
1 W	18 34 56	8 ♋ 52 34	24 ♐ 45	5 ♎ 13	17 ♊ 48	21 ♌ 24	4 ♋ 20	21 ♌ 34	29 ♏ 05	20 ♈ 14	9 ♓ 44	14 ♑ 24	6 ♒ 56	15 ♐ 38	0 ♍ 23	7 ♈ 25	21 ♓ 32
2 Th	18 38 52	9 49 45	8 ♑ 34	5 01 R	19 10	22 04	5 00	21 45	29 02 R	20 16	9 42 R	14 23 R	6 46 R	15 24 R	0 45	7 41	21 32 R
3 F	18 42 49	10 46 56	22 40	4 50	20 35	22 43	5 40	21 56	29 00	20 17	9 42	14 21	6 36	15 11	1 07	7 56	21 31
4 Sa	18 46 45	11 44 07	6 ♒ 58	4 40	22 05	23 21	6 20	22 08	28 57	20 18	9 41	14 20	6 26	14 58	1 29	8 11	21 31
5 Su	18 50 42	12 41 18	21 22	4 33	23 37	23 58	7 00	22 19	28 54	20 19	9 41	14 18	6 16	14 45	1 51	8 26	21 30
6 M	18 54 38	13 38 29	5 ♓ 46	4 28	25 14	24 34	7 40	22 30	28 52	20 20	9 40	14 17	6 05	14 33	2 14	8 40	21 30
7 T	18 58 35	14 35 41	20 07	4 26	26 54	25 08	8 20	22 42	28 49	20 21	9 39	14 15	5 54	14 21	2 36	8 54	21 29
8 W	19 02 32	15 32 53	4 ♈ 22	4 25	28 37	25 41	9 00	22 53	28 47	20 22	9 39	14 14	5 43	14 09	2 58	9 08	21 28
9 Th	19 06 28	16 30 05	18 28	4 25	0 ♋ 23	26 12	9 40	23 05	28 45	20 23	9 38	14 12	5 32	13 58	3 21	9 21	21 28
10 F	19 10 25	17 27 18	2 ♉ 25	4 25	2 12	26 42	10 20	23 17	28 43	20 24	9 37	14 11	5 20	13 47	3 43	9 34	21 27
11 Sa	19 14 21	18 24 31	16 13	4 22	4 05	27 11	11 00	23 28	28 40	20 24	9 36	14 09	5 08	13 37	4 06	9 47	21 26
12 Su	19 18 18	19 21 44	29 51	4 17	6 00	27 38	11 40	23 40	28 38	20 25	9 35	14 08	4 56	13 27	4 28	10 00	21 25
13 M	19 22 14	20 18 58	13 ♊ 19	4 10	7 58	28 04	12 19	23 52	28 36	20 26	9 34	14 06	4 44	13 18	4 51	10 12	21 24
14 T	19 26 11	21 16 13	26 35	4 00	9 58	28 28	12 59	24 04	28 35	20 27	9 33	14 05	4 32	13 09	5 13	10 24	21 23
15 W	19 30 07	22 13 28	9 ♋ 39	3 48	12 00	28 50	13 39	24 16	28 33	20 27	9 33	14 03	4 19	13 00	5 36	10 35	21 22
16 Th	19 34 04	23 10 43	22 29	3 36	14 04	29 10	14 19	24 28	28 31	20 28	9 32	14 02	4 07	12 52	5 58	10 47	21 21
17 F	19 38 01	24 07 59	5 ♌ 05	3 25	16 09	29 29	14 58	24 40	28 30	20 28	9 31	14 00	3 54	12 44	6 21	10 57	21 20
18 Sa	19 41 57	25 05 15	17 27	3 16	18 15	29 46	15 38	24 52	28 28	20 28	9 30	13 59	3 41	12 37	6 44	11 08	21 19
19 Su	19 45 54	26 02 31	29 37	3 08	20 23	0 ♍ 01	16 18	25 04	28 27	20 29	9 29	13 57	3 28	12 30	7 06	11 18	21 17
20 M	19 49 50	26 59 47	11 ♍ 35	3 04	22 31	0 14	16 57	25 17	28 25	20 29	9 28	13 56	3 15	12 23	7 29	11 28	21 16
21 T	19 53 47	27 57 04	23 26	3 02 D	24 39	0 25	17 37	25 29	28 24	20 29	9 27	13 55	3 02	12 17	7 52	11 37	21 15
22 W	19 57 43	28 54 20	5 ♎ 11	3 01	26 47	0 33	18 16	25 41	28 23	20 30	9 26	13 53	2 49	12 12	8 15	11 46	21 13
23 Th	20 01 40	29 51 38	17 01	3 02	28 55	0 40	18 55	25 53	28 22	20 30	9 25	13 52	2 36	12 07	8 38	11 55	21 12
24 F	20 05 36	0 ♌ 48 55	28 56	3 02 R	1 ♌ 02	0 46 R	19 35	26 06	28 21	20 30	9 24	13 50	2 23	12 01	9 00	12 03	21 11
25 Sa	20 09 33	1 46 13	11 ♏ 03	3 02	3 09	0 46	20 14	26 18	28 20	20 30	9 23	13 49	2 09	11 58	9 23	12 11	21 10
26 Su	20 13 30	2 43 31	23 27	3 00	5 15	0 43	20 54	26 31	28 19	20 30 R	9 22	13 47	1 56	11 54	9 46	12 19	21 08
27 M	20 17 26	3 40 50	6 ♐ 13	2 55	7 19	0 38	21 33	26 43	28 19	20 30	9 20	13 46	1 43	11 51	10 09	12 26	21 07
28 T	20 21 23	4 38 09	19 23	2 49	9 22	0 31	22 12	26 56	28 18	20 30	9 19	13 45	1 30	11 48	10 32	12 33	21 06
29 W	20 25 19	5 35 29	2 ♑ 59	2 41	11 24	0 21	22 51	27 08	28 18	20 30	9 18	13 43	1 17	11 45	10 55	12 39	21 04
30 Th	20 29 16	6 32 49	17 01	2 32	13 24	0 09	23 31	27 21	28 17	20 30	9 17	13 42	1 04	11 43	11 18	12 45	21 02
31 F	20 33 12	7 30 10	1 ♒ 25	2 24	15 24	29 ♌ 55	24 10	27 33	28 17	20 30	9 15	13 41	0 51	11 41	11 41	12 51	20 59

EPHEMERIS CALCULATED FOR 12 MIDNIGHT GREENWICH MEAN TIME. ALL OTHER DATA AND FACING ASPECTARIAN PAGE IN **EASTERN TIME (BOLD)** AND PACIFIC TIME (REGULAR).

AUGUST 2015

☽ Last Aspect day	ET / hr:mn / PT		asp	☽ Ingress sign	day	ET / hr:mn / PT	
1	**6:02 pm**	3:02 pm	☍ ♀	♓	1	**6:36 pm**	3:36 pm
3	**4:35 pm**	1:35 pm	△ ♄	♈	3	**7:24 pm**	4:24 pm
5	**7:29 pm**	4:29 pm	△ ♃	♉	5	**9:29 pm**	6:29 pm
7		9:46 pm	⚹ ♂	♊	7		10:40 pm
8	**12:46 am**		⚹ ♂	♊	8	**1:40 am**	
10	**7:45 am**	4:45 am	⚹ ♃	♋	10	**8:08 am**	5:08 am
12	**1:44 pm**	10:44 am	△ ♄	♌	12	**4:52 pm**	1:52 pm
14		9:36 pm	□ ♄	♍	15	**3:46 am**	12:46 am
15	**12:36 am**		□ ♄	♍	15	**3:46 am**	12:46 am
17	**1:16 pm**	10:16 am	⚹ ♄	♎	17	**4:23 pm**	1:23 pm

☽ Last Aspect day	ET / hr:mn / PT		asp	☽ Ingress sign	day	ET / hr:mn / PT	
19	**10:56 pm**	7:56 pm	⚹ ☉	♏	20	**5:24 am**	2:24 am
22	**3:31 pm**	12:31 pm	□ ☉	♐	22	**4:41 pm**	1:41 pm
24	**6:04 pm**	3:04 pm	□ ☿	♑	24		9:22 pm
24	**6:04 pm**	3:04 pm	□ ☿	♑	25	**12:22 am**	
27	**3:20 am**	12:20 am	△ ☿	♒	27	**4:03 am**	1:03 am
29	**3:03 am**	12:03 am	□ ♄	♓	29	**4:51 am**	1:51 am
30		11:53 pm	△ ♄	♈	31	**4:33 am**	1:33 am
31	**2:53 am**		△ ♄	♈	31	**4:33 am**	1:33 am

☽ Phases & Eclipses phase	day	ET / hr:mn / PT	
4th Quarter	6	**10:03 pm**	7:03 pm
New Moon	14	**10:53 am**	7:53 pm
2nd Quarter	22	**3:31 pm**	12:31 pm
Full Moon	29	**2:35 pm**	11:35 am

Planet Ingress		day	ET / hr:mn / PT	
⚳	♑	3	**7:08 pm**	4:08 pm
☿	♍	7	**3:15 pm**	12:15 pm
♂	♌	8	**7:32 pm**	4:32 pm
♃	♍	11	**7:11 am**	4:11 am
☉	♍	23	**6:37 am**	3:37 am
☿	♎	27	**11:44 am**	8:44 am

Planetary Motion		day	ET / hr:mn / PT	
♄	D	1		10:53 pm
♄	D	2	**1:53 am**	
♀	D	3	**7:14 am**	4:14 am
⚶	℞	11		11:02 pm
⚶	℞	12	**2:02 am**	

1 SATURDAY
☽ ⚹ ♅ **3:11 am** 12:11 am
☽ ⚻ ♂ **10:51 am** 7:51 am
☉ ⚻ ♆ **2:24 pm** 11:24 am
☽ ☍ ♃ **3:16 pm** 12:16 pm
☽ □ ♄ **3:49 pm** 12:49 pm
☽ ☍ ♀ **6:02 pm** 3:02 pm

2 SUNDAY
☽ ☌ ♆ **9:28 am** 6:28 am
☽ ⚻ ☉ **10:49 am** 7:49 am
☿ △ ♅ **10:50 am** 7:50 am
☽ ⚹ ♇ **4:40 pm** 1:40 pm

3 MONDAY
☽ ⚺ ♅ **3:50 am** 12:50 am
☽ ⚻ ☿ **6:21 am** 3:21 am
♃ □ ♄ **6:36 am** 3:36 am
☽ △ ♂ **1:50 pm** 10:50 am
☽ △ ♄ **4:35 pm** 1:35 pm
☽ ⚻ ♃ **4:44 pm** 1:44 pm
☽ ⚻ ♀ **5:44 pm** 2:44 pm

4 TUESDAY
☽ ⚺ ♆ **10:27 am** 7:27 am
☽ △ ☉ **3:23 pm** 12:23 pm
♀ ☌ ♃ **5:47 pm** 2:47 pm
☽ □ ♇ **5:50 pm** 2:50 pm

5 WEDNESDAY
☽ ☌ ♅ **5:22 am** 2:22 am
♀ □ ♄ **11:08 am** 8:08 am
☽ △ ☿ **3:25 pm** 12:25 pm
☽ □ ♂ **6:07 pm** 3:07 pm
☽ △ ♀ **6:22 pm** 3:22 pm
☽ ⚻ ♄ **6:35 pm** 3:35 pm
☽ △ ♃ **7:29 pm** 4:29 pm
♀ ⚺ ♂ **9:24 pm** 6:24 pm

6 THURSDAY
☉ ⚻ ♇ **3:30 am** 12:30 am
♂ △ ♄ **4:29 am** 1:29 am
☿ ☌ ♀ **10:25 am** 7:25 am
☽ ⚹ ♆ **1:02 pm** 10:02 am
☿ □ ♄ **4:19 pm** 1:19 pm
☽ △ ♇ **8:44 pm** 5:44 pm
☽ □ ☉ **10:03 pm** 7:03 pm
☿ ⚺ ♂ **10:59 pm** 7:59 pm

7 FRIDAY
☿ ☌ ♃ **3:08 am** 12:08 am
☽ ⚺ ♅ **8:48 am** 5:48 am
♂ ⚺ ♃ **1:59 pm** 10:59 am
☽ □ ♀ **8:38 pm** 5:38 pm
☽ ☍ ♄ **10:40 pm** 7:40 pm
☽ □ ♃ 9:25 pm
☽ ⚹ ♂ 9:46 pm

8 SATURDAY
☽ □ ♃ **12:25 am**
☽ ⚹ ♂ **12:46 am**
☽ □ ☿ **3:14 am** 12:14 am
☽ □ ♆ **5:48 pm** 2:48 pm
☽ ⚻ ♇ 10:52 pm

9 SUNDAY
☽ ⚻ ♇ **1:52 am**
☽ ⚹ ☉ **7:29 am** 4:29 am
☽ ⚹ ♅ **2:30 pm** 11:30 am
☽ ⚹ ♀ 9:46 pm

10 MONDAY
☽ ⚹ ♀ **12:46 am**
☽ ⚻ ♄ **5:03 am** 2:03 am
☽ ⚹ ♃ **7:45 am** 4:45 am
☽ ⚺ ♂ **10:04 am** 7:04 am
☽ ⚹ ☿ **6:10 pm** 3:10 pm
☽ △ ♆ 9:52 pm

11 TUESDAY
☽ △ ♆ **12:52 am**
☽ ☍ ♇ **9:16 am** 6:16 am
☽ ⚺ ☉ **7:47 pm** 4:47 pm
☽ □ ♅ **10:27 pm** 7:27 pm

12 WEDNESDAY
☽ ⚺ ♀ **6:42 am** 3:42 am
☽ △ ♄ **1:44 pm** 10:44 am
☽ ⚺ ♃ **5:28 pm** 2:28 pm
☿ ☍ ♆ **9:11 pm** 6:11 pm
☽ ☌ ♂ **10:00 pm** 7:00 pm

13 THURSDAY
☉ △ ♅ **6:27 am** 3:27 am
☽ ⚻ ♆ **10:08 am** 7:08 am
☽ ⚺ ☿ **12:08 pm** 9:08 am
☽ ⚻ ♇ **6:54 pm** 3:54 pm

14 FRIDAY
☽ △ ♅ **8:37 am** 5:37 am
☽ ☌ ☉ **10:53 am** 7:53 am
☽ ☌ ♀ **2:25 pm** 11:25 am
☽ □ ♄ 9:36 pm

15 SATURDAY
☽ □ ♄ **12:36 am**
☽ ☌ ♃ **5:27 am** 2:27 am
☽ ⚺ ♂ **12:26 pm** 9:26 am
☉ ☌ ♀ **3:22 pm** 12:22 pm
☿ △ ♇ **3:55 pm** 12:55 pm
☽ ☍ ♆ **9:29 pm** 6:29 pm

16 SUNDAY
☽ △ ♇ **6:34 am** 3:34 am
☽ ☌ ☿ **8:48 am** 5:48 am
☽ ⚻ ♅ **8:41 pm** 5:41 pm
☽ ⚺ ♀ **11:43 pm** 8:43 pm

17 MONDAY
☽ ⚺ ☉ **4:26 am** 1:26 am
☽ ⚹ ♄ **1:16 pm** 10:16 am
☽ ⚺ ♃ **7:14 pm** 4:14 pm

18 TUESDAY
☽ ⚹ ♂ **4:44 am** 1:44 am
☽ ⚻ ♆ **10:16 am** 7:16 am
☽ □ ♇ **7:30 pm** 4:30 pm

19 WEDNESDAY
☽ ⚺ ☿ **6:47 am** 3:47 am
☽ ☍ ♅ **9:41 am** 6:41 am
☽ ⚹ ♀ **9:50 am** 6:50 am
♀ △ ♅ **12:44 pm** 9:44 am
☽ ⚹ ☉ **10:56 pm** 7:56 pm
☿ ⚺ ♀ 10:11 pm
☽ ⚺ ♄ 11:28 pm

20 THURSDAY
☿ ⚺ ♀ **1:11 am**
☽ ⚺ ♄ **2:28 am**
☿ ⚻ ♅ **6:02 am** 3:02 am
☽ ⚹ ♃ **9:22 am** 6:22 am
☽ □ ♂ **9:02 pm** 6:02 pm
☽ △ ♆ **10:53 pm** 7:53 pm

21 FRIDAY
☽ ⚹ ♇ **7:58 am** 4:58 am
☽ □ ♀ **7:13 pm** 4:13 pm
☉ □ ♄ **7:40 pm** 4:40 pm
☽ ⚻ ♅ **9:41 pm** 6:41 pm
☽ ⚹ ☿ 11:57 pm

22 SATURDAY
☽ ⚹ ☿ **2:57 am**
♂ ⚻ ♆ **6:22 am** 3:22 am
☽ ☌ ♄ **2:02 pm** 11:02 am
☽ □ ☉ **3:31 pm** 12:31 pm
☽ □ ♃ **9:30 pm** 6:30 pm

23 SUNDAY
☽ □ ♆ **9:08 am** 6:08 am
☽ △ ♂ **10:37 am** 7:37 am
☽ ⚺ ♇ **5:44 pm** 2:44 pm
☽ △ ♀ 11:09 pm

24 MONDAY
☽ △ ♀ **2:09 am**
☽ △ ♅ **6:35 am** 3:35 am
☽ □ ☿ **6:04 pm** 3:04 pm
☽ ⚺ ♄ **10:02 pm** 7:02 pm

25 TUESDAY
☽ △ ☉ **3:35 am** 12:35 am
☽ △ ♃ **5:45 am** 2:45 am
☽ ⚹ ♆ **3:32 pm** 12:32 pm
☽ ⚻ ♂ **7:39 pm** 4:39 pm
☽ ☌ ♇ **11:33 pm** 8:33 pm

26 WEDNESDAY
☽ ⚻ ♀ **5:43 am** 2:43 am
☽ □ ♅ **11:26 am** 8:26 am
☿ ⚹ ♄ **12:07 pm** 9:07 am
☉ ☌ ♃ **6:02 pm** 3:02 pm
☽ ⚹ ♄ 11:02 pm

27 THURSDAY
☽ ⚹ ♄ **2:02 am**
☽ △ ☿ **3:20 am** 12:20 am
☽ ⚻ ♃ **9:51 am** 6:51 am
☽ ⚻ ☉ **10:44 am** 7:44 am
☽ ⚺ ♆ **6:08 pm** 3:08 pm
☽ ☍ ♂ 9:24 pm
☽ ⚺ ♇ 10:44 pm

28 FRIDAY
☽ ☍ ♂ **12:24 am**
☽ ⚺ ♇ **1:44 am**
☽ ☍ ♀ **6:18 am** 3:18 am
☽ ⚹ ♅ **12:55 pm** 9:55 am

29 SATURDAY
☽ □ ♄ **3:03 am** 12:03 am
♂ ⚻ ♇ **6:28 am** 3:28 am
☽ ⚻ ☿ **8:27 am** 5:27 am
☽ ☍ ♃ **11:08 am** 8:08 am
☽ ☍ ☉ **2:35 pm** 11:35 am
☽ ☌ ♆ **6:20 pm** 3:20 pm
☽ ⚹ ♇ 10:46 pm
☽ ⚻ ♂ 11:38 pm

30 SUNDAY
☽ ⚹ ♇ **1:46 am**
☽ ⚻ ♂ **2:38 am**
☽ ⚻ ♀ **5:17 am** 2:17 am
☽ ⚺ ♅ **12:41 pm** 9:41 am
☽ △ ♄ 11:53 pm
☿ ⚺ ♃ 11:59 pm

31 MONDAY
☽ △ ♄ **2:53 am**
☿ ⚺ ♃ **2:59 am**
☽ ⚻ ♃ **11:32 am** 8:32 am
☽ ☍ ☿ **12:05 pm** 9:05 am
☽ ⚻ ☉ **5:35 pm** 2:35 pm
☽ ⚺ ♆ **5:59 pm** 2:59 pm
☉ ☍ ♆ **11:38 pm** 8:38 pm
♀ ☌ ♂ 10:04 pm
☽ □ ♇ 10:33 pm

Eastern time in bold type
Pacific time in medium type

AUGUST 2015

DATE	SID.TIME	SUN	MOON	NODE	MERCURY	VENUS	MARS	JUPITER	SATURN	URANUS	NEPTUNE	PLUTO	CERES	PALLAS	JUNO	VESTA	CHIRON
1 Sa	20 37 09	8 Ω 27 31	16 ≈ 52	2 ♎ 11 ℞	17 Ω 22	29 Ω 55 ℞	24 ♌ 49	27 Ω 46	28 ♏ 17	20 Υ 29 ℞	9 ♓ 13 ℞	13 ♑ 39 ℞	0 ♑ 38	11 ♐ 40	11 ♍ 41	12 Υ 56	20 ♓ 57 ℞
2 Su	20 41 05	9 24 54	0 ♓ 52	2 08	19 18	29 ♌ 38	25 25	27 59	28 17 D	20 29	9 11	13 38	0 25 ℞	11 39 ℞	12 04	13 01	20 55
3 M	20 45 02	10 22 17	15 40	2 07 D	21 12	29 18	26 07	28 11	28 17	20 28	9 10	13 37	0 12	11 39 D	12 27	13 05	20 53
4 T	20 48 59	11 19 42	0 Υ 22	2 07	23 05	28 57	26 46	28 24	28 17	20 28	9 08	13 35	0 00	11 39	12 50	13 09	20 51
5 W	20 52 55	12 17 07	14 52	2 08	24 57	28 33	27 25	28 37	28 18	20 27	9 07	13 34	29 ♐ 47	11 40	13 13	13 13	20 49
6 Th	20 56 52	13 14 34	29 07	2 08	26 46	28 08	28 04	28 50	28 18	20 27	9 06	13 33	29 35	11 41	13 36	13 16	20 47
7 F	21 00 48	14 12 02	13 ♉ 06	2 06	28 34	27 40	28 43	29 02	28 18	20 26	9 04	13 32	29 23	11 43	13 59	13 18	20 45
8 Sa	21 04 45	15 09 32	26 48	2 01	0 ♍ 21	27 11	29 22	29 15	28 19	20 26	9 03	13 30	29 11	11 45	14 22	13 20	20 43
9 Su	21 08 41	16 07 03	10 ♊ 14	1 55	2 06	26 40	0 ♍ 01	29 28	28 19	20 26	9 01	13 29	28 59	11 47	14 46	13 22	20 41
10 M	21 12 38	17 04 35	23 25	1 48	3 49	26 07	0 40	29 41	28 20	20 25	9 00	13 28	28 47	11 50	15 09	13 23	20 39
11 T	21 16 34	18 02 08	6 ♋ 22	1 41	5 31	25 33	1 18	29 54	28 21	20 24	8 58	13 27	28 36	11 53	15 32	13 24	20 37
12 W	21 20 31	18 59 43	19 06	1 34	7 11	24 59	1 57	0 ♍ 07	28 22	20 24	8 57	13 26	28 25	11 57	15 55	13 25 ℞	20 34
13 Th	21 24 28	19 57 19	1 Ω 37	1 28	8 50	24 24	2 36	0 20	28 23	20 23	8 55	13 25	28 14	12 01	16 18	13 24	20 32
14 F	21 28 24	20 54 57	13 57	1 23	10 27	23 46	3 15	0 33	28 24	20 22	8 54	13 24	28 03	12 05	16 41	13 24	20 30
15 Sa	21 32 21	21 52 35	26 06	1 21	12 03	23 09	3 53	0 46	28 25	20 21	8 52	13 23	27 53	12 10	17 05	13 23	20 27
16 Su	21 36 17	22 50 15	8 ♍ 06	1 20	13 37	22 32	4 32	0 59	28 26	20 20	8 51	13 22	27 42	12 15	17 28	13 21	20 25
17 M	21 40 14	23 47 56	19 59	1 20	15 10	21 55	5 11	1 12	28 28	20 20	8 49	13 21	27 32	12 20	17 51	13 19	20 23
18 T	21 44 10	24 45 38	1 ♎ 47	1 22	16 41	21 18	5 49	1 25	28 29	20 18	8 47	13 20	27 23	12 26	18 14	13 17	20 21
19 W	21 48 07	25 43 21	13 33	1 22	18 11	20 41	6 28	1 38	28 31	20 17	8 46	13 19	27 13	12 32	18 37	13 14	20 18
20 Th	21 52 03	26 41 05	25 21	1 24	19 39	20 05	7 07	1 51	28 32	20 16	8 44	13 18	27 04	12 38	19 01	13 11	20 16
21 F	21 56 00	27 38 51	7 ♏ 16	1 25 ℞	21 06	19 31	7 45	2 04	28 34	20 15	8 43	13 17	26 56	12 45	19 24	13 07	20 13
22 Sa	21 59 57	28 36 37	19 22	1 26	22 31	18 57	8 24	2 17	28 36	20 13	8 41	13 16	26 47	12 52	19 47	13 02	20 10
23 Su	22 03 53	29 34 25	1 ♐ 44	1 25	23 54	18 24	9 02	2 30	28 38	20 12	8 39	13 15	26 39	12 59	20 10	12 58	20 08
24 M	22 07 50	0 ♍ 32 14	14 26	1 23	25 16	17 54	9 41	2 43	28 40	20 11	8 38	13 14	26 31	13 07	20 34	12 52	20 05
25 T	22 11 46	1 30 04	27 34	1 19	26 36	17 24	10 19	2 56	28 42	20 10	8 36	13 13	26 24	13 15	20 57	12 47	20 03
26 W	22 15 43	2 27 56	11 ♑ 09	1 16	27 54	16 57	10 57	3 09	28 44	20 08	8 34	13 12	26 16	13 23	21 20	12 41	20 00
27 Th	22 19 39	3 25 48	25 11	1 12	29 11	16 32	11 36	3 22	28 47	20 07	8 33	13 11	26 10	13 31	21 43	12 34	19 57
28 F	22 23 36	4 23 42	9 ≈ 39	1 08	0 ♎ 26	16 08	12 14	3 35	28 49	20 05	8 31	13 10	26 03	13 40	22 07	12 27	19 55
29 Sa	22 27 32	5 21 37	24 28	1 08	1 38	15 47	12 52	3 48	28 51	20 04	8 30	13 09	25 57	13 49	22 30	12 20	19 52
30 Su	22 31 29	6 19 34	9 ♓ 31	1 06	2 49	15 28	13 31	4 01	28 54	20 02	8 28	13 09	25 51	13 49	22 53	12 12	19 49
31 M	22 35 26	7 17 32	24 38	1 05 D	3 58	15 12	14 09	4 14	28 57	20 01	8 26	13 09	25 46	13 59	23 16	12 03	19 47

EPHEMERIS CALCULATED FOR 12 MIDNIGHT GREENWICH MEAN TIME. ALL OTHER DATA AND FACING ASPECTARIAN PAGE IN **EASTERN TIME (BOLD)** AND PACIFIC TIME (REGULAR).

SEPTEMBER 2015

☽ Last Aspect day	ET / hr:mn / PT		asp	☽ Ingress sign	day	ET / hr:mn / PT	
1	**12:37 pm**	9:37 am	☌ ♅	♉	2	**5:02 am**	2:02 am
4	**6:20 am**	3:20 am	☍ ♄	♊	4	**7:48 am**	4:48 am
5	**7:04 pm**	4:04 pm	⚹ ♅	♋	6	**1:40 pm**	10:40 am
8	**9:28 pm**	6:28 pm	△ ♄	♌	8	**10:36 pm**	7:36 pm
11	**9:03 am**	6:03 am	□ ♄	♍	11	**9:56 am**	6:56 am
13	**10:08 pm**	7:08 pm	⚹ ♄	♎	13	**10:41 pm**	7:41 pm
15		9:22 pm	⚹ ♂	♏	16	**11:43 am**	8:43 am
16	**12:22 am**		⚹ ♂	♏	16	**11:43 am**	8:43 am
18	**3:49 pm**	12:49 pm	□ ♂	♐	18	**11:32 pm**	8:32 pm
21	**4:59 am**	1:59 am	□ ☉	♑	21	**8:33 am**	5:33 am
22	**7:13 pm**	4:13 pm	□ ♅	♒	23	**1:51 pm**	10:51 am
24		9:02 pm	☍ ♀	♓	25	**3:43 pm**	12:43 pm
25	**12:02 am**		☍ ♀	♓	25	**3:43 pm**	12:43 pm
26	**12:32 pm**	9:32 am	⚹ ♇	♈	27	**3:29 pm**	12:29 pm
29	**3:45 am**	12:45 am	△ ♀	♉	29	**2:57 pm**	11:57 am

☽ Phases & Eclipses phase	day	ET / hr:mn / PT	
4th Quarter	5	**5:54 am**	2:54 am
New Moon	12		11:41 pm
New Moon	13	**2:41 am**	
●	13	20° ♍ 12'	
2nd Quarter	21	**4:59 am**	1:59 am
Full Moon	27	**10:51 pm**	7:51 pm
●●	27	4° ♈ 37'	

Planet Ingress		day	ET / hr:mn / PT	
⚵	♎	17	**5:58 am**	2:58 am
♄	♐	17	**10:49 pm**	7:49 pm
☉	♍	23	**4:21 am**	1:21 am
♂	♍	24	**10:18 pm**	7:18 pm

Planetary Motion		day	ET / hr:mn / PT	
♀	D	6	**4:29 am**	1:29 am
⚳	D	14	**3:14 pm**	12:14 pm
☿	℞	17	**2:09 pm**	11:09 am
♇	D	24		11:57 pm
♇	D	25	**2:57 am**	

1 TUESDAY
♀ ☌ ♂ **1:04 am**
☽ □ ♇ **1:33 am**
☽ △ ♀ **4:24 am** 1:24 am
☽ △ ♂ **4:36 am** 1:36 am
☽ ☌ ♅ **12:37 pm** 9:37 am

2 WEDNESDAY
☽ ⚻ ♄ **3:28 am** 12:28 am
☽ △ ♃ **1:01 pm** 10:01 am
☽ ⚻ ☿ **4:44 pm** 1:44 pm
☽ ⚹ ♆ **6:53 pm** 3:53 pm
☽ △ ☉ **10:06 pm** 7:06 pm
☽ △ ♇ 11:50 pm

3 THURSDAY
☽ △ ♇ **2:50 am**
☽ □ ♀ **5:19 am** 2:19 am
☽ □ ♂ **8:24 am** 5:24 am
☽ ⚺ ♅ **2:24 pm** 11:24 am
☿ ⚻ ♆ **11:02 pm** 8:02 pm

4 FRIDAY
☽ ☍ ♄ **6:20 am** 3:20 am
☽ □ ♃ **5:04 pm** 2:04 pm
☽ □ ♆ **10:22 pm** 7:22 pm
☽ △ ☿ 9:10 pm

5 SATURDAY
☽ △ ☿ **12:10 am**
☽ □ ☉ **5:54 am** 2:54 am

☽ ⚻ ♇ **6:52 am** 3:52 am
☽ ⚹ ♀ **9:15 am** 6:15 am
☽ ⚹ ♂ **3:26 pm** 12:26 pm
☽ ⚹ ♅ **7:04 pm** 4:04 pm
☉ △ ♇ **7:10 pm** 4:10 pm

6 SUNDAY
☽ ⚻ ♄ **12:20 pm** 9:20 am
☽ ⚹ ♃ 9:26 pm

7 MONDAY
☽ ⚹ ♃ **12:26 am**
☉ ⚺ ♀ **4:21 am** 1:21 am
☽ △ ♆ **5:00 am** 2:00 am
☽ □ ☿ **11:01 am** 8:01 am
☽ ☍ ♇ **2:05 pm** 11:05 am
☽ ⚺ ♀ **4:42 pm** 1:42 pm
☽ ⚹ ☉ **5:41 pm** 2:41 pm
☽ ⚺ ♂ 11:09 pm
☽ □ ♅ 11:53 pm

8 TUESDAY
☽ ⚺ ♂ **2:09 am**
☽ □ ♅ **2:53 am**
♂ △ ♅ **3:53 pm** 12:53 pm
☽ △ ♄ **9:28 pm** 6:28 pm

9 WEDNESDAY
☽ ⚺ ♃ **10:56 am** 7:56 am
☽ ⚻ ♆ **2:33 pm** 11:33 am
☿ □ ♇ **3:27 pm** 12:27 pm

☽ ⚻ ♇ 9:08 pm
☽ ⚹ ☿ 9:38 pm

10 THURSDAY
☽ ⚻ ♇ **12:08 am**
☽ ⚹ ☿ **12:38 am**
☽ ☌ ♀ **3:24 am** 12:24 am
☽ ⚺ ☉ **8:59 am** 5:59 am
☽ △ ♅ **1:20 pm** 10:20 am
☽ ☌ ♂ **3:59 pm** 12:59 pm

11 FRIDAY
☽ □ ♄ **9:03 am** 6:03 am
☽ ☌ ♃ **11:45 pm** 8:45 pm
☽ ☍ ♆ 11:14 pm

12 SATURDAY
☽ ☍ ♆ **2:14 am**
☽ △ ♇ **12:10 pm** 9:10 am
☉ ⚻ ♅ **1:18 pm** 10:18 am
☽ ⚺ ☿ **3:40 pm** 12:40 pm
☽ ⚺ ♀ **4:34 pm** 1:34 pm
☽ ⚻ ♅ 10:33 pm
☽ ☌ ☉ 11:41 pm

13 SUNDAY
☽ ⚻ ♅ **1:33 am**
☽ ☌ ☉ **2:41 am**
☽ ⚺ ♂ **7:50 am** 4:50 am
☽ ⚹ ♄ **10:08 pm** 7:08 pm

14 MONDAY
☽ ⚺ ♃ **1:49 pm** 10:49 am
☽ ⚻ ♆ **3:03 pm** 12:03 pm
☽ □ ♇ 10:11 pm

15 TUESDAY
☽ □ ♇ **1:11 am**
☽ ☌ ☿ **6:34 am** 3:34 am
☽ ⚹ ♀ **7:07 am** 4:07 am
☽ ☍ ♅ **2:27 pm** 11:27 am
☽ ⚺ ☉ **9:16 pm** 6:16 pm
☽ ⚹ ♂ 9:22 pm

16 WEDNESDAY
☽ ⚹ ♂ **12:22 am**
☽ ⚺ ♄ **11:30 am** 8:30 am
♃ ☍ ♆ 11:54 pm

17 THURSDAY
♃ ☍ ♆ **2:54 am**
☽ △ ♆ **3:47 am** 12:47 am
☽ ⚹ ♃ **3:48 am** 12:48 am
☽ ⚹ ♇ **1:51 pm** 10:51 am
☽ ⚺ ☿ **7:42 pm** 4:42 pm
☽ □ ♀ **9:35 pm** 6:35 pm
☽ ⚻ ♅ 11:42 pm

18 FRIDAY
☽ ⚻ ♅ **2:42 am**
☽ ⚹ ☉ **2:46 pm** 11:46 am
☽ □ ♂ **3:49 pm** 12:49 pm
☽ ☌ ♄ **11:40 pm** 8:40 pm

19 SATURDAY
☽ □ ♆ **2:53 pm** 11:53 am
☽ □ ♃ **4:03 pm** 1:03 pm
☽ ⚺ ♇ 9:37 pm
☉ ⚺ ♂ 10:17 pm

20 SUNDAY
☽ ⚺ ♇ **12:37 am**
☉ ⚺ ♂ **1:17 am**
☽ ⚹ ☿ **5:29 am** 2:29 am
☽ △ ♀ **10:05 am** 7:05 am
☽ △ ♅ **12:42 pm** 9:42 am

21 MONDAY
☽ △ ♂ **4:12 am** 1:12 am
☽ □ ☉ **4:59 am** 1:59 am
☽ ⚺ ♄ **9:00 am** 6:00 am
☽ ⚹ ♆ **10:51 pm** 7:51 pm
☽ △ ♃ 9:57 pm

22 TUESDAY
☽ △ ♃ **12:57 am**
☽ ☌ ♇ **8:04 am** 5:04 am
☽ □ ☿ **10:56 am** 7:56 am
☽ ⚻ ♀ **7:00 pm** 4:00 pm
☽ □ ♅ **7:13 pm** 4:13 pm
♀ △ ♅ 9:00 pm

23 WEDNESDAY
♀ △ ♅ **12:00 am**
☽ ⚻ ♂ **12:20 pm** 9:20 am
☽ △ ☉ **2:34 pm** 11:34 am

☽ ⚹ ♄ **2:34 pm** 11:34 am
☉ ⚹ ♄ **2:36 pm** 11:36 am

24 THURSDAY
☽ ⚺ ♆ **3:06 am** 12:06 am
☽ ⚻ ♃ **5:56 am** 2:56 am
☽ ⚺ ♇ **11:47 am** 8:47 am
☽ △ ☿ **12:08 pm** 9:08 am
☿ □ ♇ **6:26 pm** 3:26 pm
☽ ⚹ ♅ **10:04 pm** 7:04 pm
☽ ☍ ♀ 9:02 pm

25 FRIDAY
☽ ☍ ♀ **12:02 am**
☽ ☍ ♂ **4:30 pm** 1:30 pm
☽ □ ♄ **4:40 pm** 1:40 pm
☽ ⚻ ☉ **7:55 pm** 4:55 pm
♂ □ ♄ **9:12 pm** 6:12 pm

26 SATURDAY
☽ ☌ ♆ **4:11 am** 1:11 am
☽ ☍ ♃ **7:39 am** 4:39 am
☽ ⚻ ☿ **10:09 am** 7:09 am
☽ ⚹ ♇ **12:32 pm** 9:32 am
☽ ⚺ ♅ **10:16 pm** 7:16 pm
☽ ⚻ ♀ 11:17 pm

27 SUNDAY
☽ ⚻ ♀ **2:17 am**
☿ ⚺ ♃ **4:22 pm** 1:22 pm
☽ △ ♄ **4:39 pm** 1:39 pm
☽ ⚻ ♂ **6:16 pm** 3:16 pm
☽ ☍ ☉ **10:51 pm** 7:51 pm

28 MONDAY
☽ ⚺ ♆ **3:36 am** 12:36 am
☽ ☍ ☿ **6:32 am** 3:32 am
☽ ⚻ ♃ **7:45 am** 4:45 am
☽ □ ♇ **11:56 am** 8:56 am
☽ ☌ ♅ **9:30 pm** 6:30 pm

29 TUESDAY
☽ △ ♀ **3:45 am** 12:45 am
☽ ⚻ ♄ **4:24 pm** 1:24 pm
☽ △ ♂ **7:51 pm** 4:51 pm
☿ ⚻ ♆ **11:19 pm** 8:19 pm
☽ ⚻ ☉ 10:48 pm
☽ ⚻ ☿ 11:58 pm

30 WEDNESDAY
☽ ⚻ ☉ **1:48 am**
☽ ⚻ ☿ **2:58 am**
☽ ⚹ ♆ **3:14 am** 12:14 am
☽ △ ♃ **8:15 am** 5:15 am
☉ ☌ ☿ **10:38 am** 7:38 am
☽ △ ♇ **11:54 am** 8:54 am
☽ ⚺ ♅ **9:40 pm** 6:40 pm
☉ ⚻ ♆ **11:05 pm** 8:05 pm

Eastern time in bold type
Pacific time in medium type

SEPTEMBER 2015

DATE	SID.TIME	SUN	MOON	NODE	MERCURY	VENUS	MARS	JUPITER	SATURN	URANUS	NEPTUNE	PLUTO	CERES	PALLAS	JUNO	VESTA	CHIRON
1 T	22 39 22	8 ♍ 15 32	9 ♍ 40	1 ♎ 05	5 ♎ 05	14 ♌ 58	14 ♌ 47	4 ♍ 27	28 ♏ 59	19 ♈ 59 R	8 ♓ 25	13 ♑ 07	25 ♑ 40	14 ⟋ 08	23 ⟋ 40	11 ♈ 55	19 ♓ 44
2 W	22 43 19	9 13 34	24 30	1 06	6 10	14 46 R	14 37	15 25	16 03	4 40	29 02	19 57 R	8 23	13 06	25 38 R	14 18	24 03	11 45 R	19 41 R

DATE	SID.TIME	SUN	MOON	NODE	MERCURY	VENUS	MARS	JUPITER	SATURN	URANUS	NEPTUNE	PLUTO	CERES	PALLAS	JUNO	VESTA	CHIRON
1 T	22 39 22	8 ♍ 15 32	9 ♍ 40	1 ♎ 05	5 ♎ 05	14 ♌ 58	14 ♌ 47	4 ♍ 27	28 ♏ 59	19 ♈ 59 R	8 ♓ 25	13 ♑ 07	25 ♑ 40	14 ⟋ 08	23 ⟋ 40	11 ♈ 55	19 ♓ 44
2 W	22 43 19	9 13 34	24 30	1 06	6 10	14 46 R	15 25	16 03	4 40	29 02	19 57 R	8 23	13 06	25 38 R	14 18	24 03	11 45 R	19 41 R
3 Th	22 47 15	10 11 38	9 ♎ 01	1 07	7 12	14 37	16 03	16 03	4 53	29 05	19 56	8 21	13 06	25 31	14 28	24 26	11 36	19 38
4 F	22 51 12	11 09 44	23 11	1 08	8 12	14 31	16 42	5 06	29 08	19 54	8 20	13 05	25 27	14 39	24 49	11 26	19 36
5 Sa	22 55 08	12 07 51	6 ♏ 57	1 09 R	9 09	14 25	17 20	5 19	29 11	19 52	8 18	13 05	25 23	14 50	25 12	11 15	19 33
6 Su	22 59 05	13 06 01	20 22	1 09	10 04	14 23 D	17 58	5 32	29 15	19 51	8 16	13 04	25 20	15 01	25 36	11 05	19 30
7 M	23 03 01	14 04 13	3 ⟋ 25	1 08	10 55	14 24	18 36	5 45	29 18	19 49	8 15	13 04	25 17	15 12	25 59	10 53	19 27
8 T	23 06 58	15 02 27	16 10	1 07	11 43	14 26	19 14	5 58	29 21	19 47	8 13	13 03	25 14	15 23	26 22	10 42	19 25
9 W	23 10 55	16 00 42	28 40	1 05	12 28	14 31	19 52	6 11	29 25	19 45	8 11	13 02	25 12	15 35	26 45	10 30	19 22
10 Th	23 14 51	16 59 00	10 ♑ 56	1 02	13 10	14 39	20 30	6 24	29 28	19 43	8 10	13 02	25 10	15 47	27 08	10 18	19 19
11 F	23 18 48	17 57 20	23 03	1 00	13 47	14 48	21 08	6 37	29 32	19 41	8 08	13 02	25 09	15 59	27 32	10 05	19 16
12 Sa	23 22 44	18 55 41	5 ≈ 01	0 59	14 20	15 00	21 46	6 50	29 36	19 39	8 07	13 01	25 07	16 12	27 55	9 52	19 14
13 Su	23 26 41	19 54 05	16 53	0 58	14 49	15 13	22 24	7 03	29 39	19 37	8 05	13 01	25 07	16 24	28 18	9 39	19 11
14 M	23 30 37	20 52 30	28 41	0 57 D	15 13	15 29	23 02	7 16	29 43	19 35	8 03	13 00	25 06 D	16 37	28 41	9 26	19 08
15 T	23 34 34	21 50 57	10 ♎ 28	0 58	15 35	15 46	23 40	7 29	29 47	19 33	8 02	13 00	25 06	16 50	29 04	9 12	19 05
16 W	23 38 30	22 49 26	22 15	0 59	15 46	16 06	24 17	7 42	29 51	19 31	8 00	13 00	25 06	17 04	29 27	8 58	19 02
17 Th	23 42 27	23 47 56	4 ♓ 06	0 59	15 53 R	16 27	24 55	7 54	29 55	19 29	7 59	13 00	25 07	17 17	29 50	8 44	19 00
18 F	23 46 23	24 46 29	16 04	1 00	15 55	16 50	25 33	8 07	0 ⟋ 00	19 27	7 57	12 59	25 08	17 31	0 ♑ 14	8 30	18 57
19 Sa	23 50 20	25 45 03	28 12	1 01	15 50	17 15	26 11	8 20	0 04	19 25	7 55	12 59	25 09	17 45	0 37	8 15	18 54
20 Su	23 54 17	26 43 38	10 ⟋ 34	1 01	15 39	17 41	26 48	8 33	0 08	19 22	7 54	12 59	25 11	17 59	1 00	8 00	18 51
21 M	23 58 13	27 42 16	23 14	1 01 R	15 22	18 09	27 26	8 45	0 12	19 20	7 52	12 59	25 13	18 13	1 23	7 45	18 49
22 T	0 02 10	28 40 55	6 ♑ 16	1 01	14 54	18 39	28 04	8 58	0 17	19 18	7 51	12 59	25 15	18 28	1 46	7 30	18 46
23 W	0 06 06	29 39 36	19 43	1 01	14 22	19 10	28 41	9 11	0 22	19 16	7 49	12 59	25 18	18 42	2 09	7 15	18 43
24 Th	0 10 03	0 ≈ 38 18	3 ≈ 36	1 01 D	13 42	19 43	29 19	9 23	0 26	19 14	7 48	12 59	25 21	18 57	2 32	7 00	18 40
25 F	0 13 59	1 37 02	17 56	1 01	12 55	20 17	29 56	9 36	0 31	19 11	7 46	12 58 D	25 24	19 12	2 55	6 45	18 38
26 Sa	0 17 56	2 35 48	2 ♓ 39	1 01	12 03	20 52	0 ♍ 34	9 48	0 36	19 09	7 45	12 58	25 28	19 28	3 18	6 29	18 35
27 Su	0 21 52	3 34 36	17 40	1 01 R	11 04	21 28	1 11	10 01	0 40	19 07	7 43	12 59	25 32	19 43	3 41	6 14	18 32
28 M	0 25 49	4 33 25	2 ♈ 52	1 01	10 02	22 06	1 49	10 13	0 45	19 04	7 42	12 59	25 37	19 58	4 03	5 58	18 30
29 T	0 29 46	5 32 17	18 05	1 01	8 56	22 45	2 26	10 26	0 50	19 02	7 41	12 59	25 41	20 14	4 26	5 43	18 27
30 W	0 33 42	6 31 10	3 ♉ 09	1 00	7 48	23 25	3 04	10 38	0 55	19 00	7 39	12 59	25 46	20 30	4 49	5 27	18 24

EPHEMERIS CALCULATED FOR 12 MIDNIGHT GREENWICH MEAN TIME. ALL OTHER DATA AND FACING ASPECTARIAN PAGE IN EASTERN TIME (BOLD) AND PACIFIC TIME (REGULAR).

OCTOBER 2015

D Last Aspect / D Ingress (far left boxes)

D Last Aspect				D Ingress		
day	ET / hr:mn / PT		asp	sign day	ET / hr:mn / PT	
6	6:44 am	3:44 am	□ ♀	♊ 1	4:03 am	1:03 pm
	1:18 pm	10:18 am	★ ♀	♋ 3	8:22 am	5:22 am
	5:53 am	2:53 am	△ ♀	♌ 6	4:31 am	1:31 am
	7:04 am	4:04 am	□ ♀	♍ 8	3:50 am	12:50 am
	5:10 pm	2:10 pm	△ ♀	♎ 11	4:45 am	1:45 am
	6:12 pm	3:12 pm	△ ♂	♏ 13	5:38 am	2:38 am
	8:06 pm	5:06 pm	△ ♂	♐ 16	5:18 am	2:18 am
	8:58 pm	5:58 pm	△ ♀	♑ 18	2:52 pm	11:52 am
	4:48 am	1:48 am	★ ♀	♒ 20	9:38 pm	6:38 pm
	4:31 pm	1:31 pm	△ ☉	♓ 22		10:18 pm

D Last Aspect				D Ingress		
day	ET / hr:mn / PT		asp	sign day	ET / hr:mn / PT	
23	1:22 am		★ ♀	♈ 23	1:18 am	
24	7:18 am	4:18 am	△ ♀	♉ 24		11:22 pm
24	7:18 am	4:18 am	△ ♀	♊ 26	2:22 am	
26	8:25 am	5:25 am	□ ♀	♋ 28		11:07 pm
26	8:25 am	5:25 am	☌ ♀	♋ 28	2:07 am	
28	11:20 am	8:20 am	△ ♀	♌ 29		11:24 pm
28	11:20 am	8:20 am	△ ♀	♍ 29	2:24 am	
30	10:52 pm	7:52 pm	△ ♀	♎ 31	5:09 am	2:09 am

Planet Ingress

	day	ET / hr:mn / PT	
♀ ♍	8	1:29 am	10:29 am
☉ ♏	23	1:47 pm	10:47 am
♀ ♎	23	6:01 am	3:01 am
♂ ♍	31	11:56 am	8:56 am
☿ ♏	31	7:07 am	4:07 am

Phases & Eclipses

phase	day	ET / hr:mn / PT	
4th Quarter	4	5:06 am	2:06 am
New Moon	12	8:06 pm	5:06 pm
2nd Quarter	20	4:31 pm	1:31 pm
Full Moon	27	8:05 am	5:05 am

Planetary Motion

	day	ET / hr:mn / PT	
☿ D	9	10:57 am	7:57 am

---

1 THURSDAY
- □ ♂ ♀ 6:44 am 3:44 am
- 1:18 pm 10:18 am
- △ ♃ ♀ 5:53 am 2:53 am
- 11:30 pm 8:30 pm
- 10:08 pm

2 FRIDAY
- ☐ 1:08 am
- △ ♀ 4:58 am 1:58 am
- 7:16 am 4:16 am
- 11:06 am 8:06 am
- 2:15 pm 11:15 am
- ☐ 2:17 3:17 9:31

3 SATURDAY
- 12:31 am
- 1:18 am 10:18 am
- 10:41 pm 7:41 pm
- 11:28 pm

4 SUNDAY
- 2:28 am
- 7:00 am 4:00 am
- 10:08 am 7:08 am
- 5:06 pm 2:06 pm
- 5:41 pm 2:41 pm
- 8:14 pm 5:14 pm
- 11:40 pm

5 MONDAY
- 2:40 am
- 7:04 am 4:04 am
- 9:35 pm

6 TUESDAY
- 12:35 am
- △ ♃ 7:24 am 4:24 am
- ★ ♀ 7:56 am 4:56 am
- 10:14 am 7:14 am
- 6:53 am 3:53 am
- 6:58 am 3:58 am
- 7:06 pm 4:06 pm
- 10:53 pm 7:53 pm

7 WEDNESDAY
- 4:11 am 1:11 am
- 5:56 am 2:56 am
- 7:40 am 4:40 am
- 5:10 am 2:10 am

8 THURSDAY
- 4:01 pm 1:01 pm
- 5:45 pm 2:45 pm
- 7:18 pm 4:18 pm

9 FRIDAY
- 6:53 am 3:53 am
- 10:05 am 7:05 am
- 3:42 pm 12:42 pm
- 5:24 pm 2:24 pm
- 6:12 pm 3:12 pm
- 10:27 pm

10 SATURDAY
- 1:27 am
- 5:29 am 2:29 am
- 8:31 pm 5:31 pm

11 SUNDAY
- 7:12 am 4:12 am
- 8:45 am 5:45 am
- 9:36 am 6:36 am
- 7:50 am 4:50 am
- 7:51 am 4:51 am
- 11:49 am 8:49 am
- 11:32 pm

12 MONDAY
- 2:32 am
- 7:19 am 4:19 am
- 7:31 am 4:31 am
- 6:20 am 3:20 am
- 8:06 pm 5:06 pm

13 TUESDAY
- 5:54 am 2:54 am
- 10:05 am 7:05 am
- 10:56 am 7:56 am

14 WEDNESDAY
- 3:13 am 12:13 am
- 8:25 am 5:25 am
- 6:22 am 3:22 am
- 7:51 am 4:51 am
- 8:58 am 5:58 am

15 THURSDAY
- ☐ 6:23 am 3:23 am
- ★ ☉ 1:39 pm 10:39 am
- △ ♃ 11:36 am 8:36 am

16 FRIDAY
- 10:07 am 7:07 am
- 2:15 pm 11:15 am
- 7:17 am 4:17 am
- ★ ♀ 7:33 am 4:33 am
- 10:53 am 7:53 am

17 SATURDAY
- 6:45 am 3:45 am
- 8:20 am 5:20 am
- 4:40 am 1:40 am
- 6:40 am 3:40 am

18 SUNDAY
- ★ 4:48 am 1:48 am
- 12:11 pm 9:11 am
- 7:55 pm 4:55 pm

19 MONDAY
- ★ 4:25 am 1:25 am
- 8:37 am 5:37 am
- 3:12 pm 12:12 pm
- 5:50 pm 2:50 pm
- 7:26 pm 4:26 pm
- 9:25 pm

20 TUESDAY
- △ 12:25 am
- 4:31 am 1:31 am
- 11:49 pm

21 WEDNESDAY
- ★ 2:49 am
- 10:22 am 7:22 am
- 6:11 am 3:11 am
- 6:22 am 3:22 am
- 8:39 pm 5:39 pm
- 10:31 pm 7:31 pm
- 11:48 pm 8:48 pm

22 THURSDAY
- △ 3:02 am 12:02 am
- 5:09 am 2:09 am
- 5:22 am 2:22 am

23 FRIDAY
- ☐ 12:22 am
- 3:43 am 12:43 am
- 6:34 am 3:34 am
- 1:17 pm 10:17 am
- 11:07 pm 8:07 pm

24 SATURDAY
- 12:22 am
- 12:29 am

25 SUNDAY
- 2:34 am
- 2:41 am
- 3:51 am 12:51 am
- 7:00 am 4:00 am
- 7:18 am 4:18 am

26 MONDAY
- ★ 4:58 am 1:58 am
- 7:47 am 4:47 am
- 1:51 pm 10:51 am
- 4:03 pm 1:03 pm
- 6:59 pm 3:59 pm
- 11:28 pm 8:28 pm

27 TUESDAY
- 3:28 am 12:28 am
- 4:07 am 1:07 am
- 6:57 am 3:57 am
- 8:25 am 5:25 am
- 9:24 am 6:24 am
- 10:45 am 7:45 am

28 WEDNESDAY
- 3:58 am 12:58 am
- 7:50 am 4:50 am
- 8:05 am 5:05 am
- 1:31 pm 10:31 am
- 9:23 pm 6:23 pm
- 11:16 pm 8:16 pm

29 THURSDAY
- △ ♂ 11:20 am 8:20 am
- △ 2:10 pm 11:10 am
- 3:49 am 12:49 am
- 6:40 am 3:40 am
- 7:22 am 4:22 am

30 FRIDAY
- ☐ 8:41 am 5:41 am
- △ 12:09 pm 9:09 am
- 2:11 pm 11:11 am
- 2:49 am
- 5:04 am
- 9:49 am

31 SATURDAY
- 12:28 am
- 5:49 am 2:49 am
- 8:04 am 5:04 am
- 12:49 pm 9:49 am
- ☐ 3:24 pm 12:24 pm
- 5:06 pm 2:06 pm
- ☐ 10:52 pm 7:52 pm
- 12:17 pm 9:17 am
- 5:43 pm 2:43 pm
- 7:43 pm 4:43 pm

Eastern time in **bold type**
Pacific time in medium type

OCTOBER 2015

DATE	SID.TIME	SUN	MOON	NODE	MERCURY	VENUS	MARS	JUPITER	SATURN	URANUS	NEPTUNE	PLUTO	CERES	PALLAS	JUNO	VESTA	CHIRON
1 Th	0 37 39	7≏30 06	17♉56	1≏00	6≏41	24♌07	3♍41	10♍50	1♐00	18♈57	7♓38	12♑59	25♑52	20♏46	5≏12	5♈12	18♓22
2 F	0 41 35	8 29 04	2♊20	0 59℞	5 35℞	24 49	4 19	11 03	1 06	18 55℞	7 36℞	12 59	25 57	21 03	5 35	4 57℞	18 19℞
3 Sa	0 45 32	9 28 05	16 18	0 59	4 33	25 33	4 56	11 15	1 11	18 53	7 35	12 59	26 03	21 19	5 58	4 42	18 17
4 Su	0 49 28	10 27 07	29 48	0 58 D	3 36	26 17	5 33	11 27	1 16	18 50	7 34	13 00	26 10	21 36	6 20	4 26	18 14
5 M	0 53 25	11 26 13	12♋53	0 57	2 46	27 03	6 11	11 39	1 21	18 48	7 33	13 00	26 16	21 52	6 43	4 11	18 12
6 T	0 57 21	12 25 20	25 35	0 58	2 04	27 49	6 48	11 51	1 27	18 45	7 31	13 00	26 23	22 09	7 06	3 57	18 09
7 W	1 01 18	13 24 29	7♌58	0 58	1 31	28 36	7 25	12 03	1 32	18 43	7 30	13 01	26 30	22 26	7 28	3 42	18 07
8 Th	1 05 15	14 23 41	20 06	1 00	1 08	29 24	8 03	12 15	1 38	18 40	7 29	13 01	26 38	22 43	7 51	3 27	18 04
9 F	1 09 11	15 22 55	2♍04	1 01	0 56 D	0♍13	8 40	12 27	1 43	18 38	7 27	13 01	26 45	23 01	8 14	3 13	18 02
10 Sa	1 13 08	16 22 12	13 55	1 02	0 55	1 03	9 17	12 39	1 49	18 36	7 26	13 02	26 54	23 18	8 36	2 59	18 00
11 Su	1 17 04	17 21 30	25 42	1 03℞	1 04	1 54	9 54	12 51	1 55	18 33	7 25	13 02	27 02	23 36	8 59	2 45	17 57
12 M	1 21 01	18 20 51	7≏29	1 03	1 24	2 45	10 31	13 03	2 00	18 31	7 24	13 03	27 11	23 53	9 21	2 31	17 55
13 T	1 24 57	19 20 14	19 18	1 02	1 54	3 37	11 08	13 15	2 06	18 28	7 23	13 03	27 19	24 11	9 44	2 18	17 53
14 W	1 28 54	20 19 38	1♏10	1 00	2 33	4 30	11 45	13 26	2 12	18 26	7 22	13 04	27 29	24 29	10 06	2 05	17 50
15 Th	1 32 50	21 19 05	13 09	0 57	3 20	5 23	12 23	13 38	2 18	18 23	7 21	13 04	27 38	24 47	10 29	1 52	17 48
16 F	1 36 47	22 18 34	25 16	0 54	4 16	6 17	13 00	13 49	2 24	18 21	7 20	13 05	27 48	25 05	10 51	1 40	17 46
17 Sa	1 40 43	23 18 05	7♐32	0 50	5 18	7 12	13 37	14 01	2 30	18 19	7 19	13 06	27 58	25 24	11 13	1 28	17 44
18 Su	1 44 40	24 17 37	20 01	0 47	6 27	8 07	14 14	14 12	2 36	18 16	7 18	13 06	28 08	25 42	11 36	1 16	17 42
19 M	1 48 37	25 17 12	2♑45	0 44	7 42	9 02	14 51	14 23	2 42	18 14	7 17	13 07	28 19	26 01	11 58	1 04	17 40
20 T	1 52 33	26 16 48	15 45	0 42 D	9 01	9 59	15 27	14 35	2 48	18 11	7 16	13 08	28 29	26 19	12 20	0 53	17 38
21 W	1 56 30	27 16 25	29 05	0 42	10 24	10 56	16 04	14 46	2 54	18 09	7 15	13 09	28 40	26 38	12 42	0 42	17 36
22 Th	2 00 26	28 16 05	12≈47	0 43	11 54	11 54	16 41	14 57	3 01	18 06	7 14	13 09	28 52	26 57	13 04	0 32	17 34
23 F	2 04 23	29 15 46	26 51	0 44	13 20	12 52	17 18	15 08	3 07	18 04	7 13	13 10	29 03	27 16	13 27	0 22	17 32
24 Sa	2 08 19	0♏15 29	11♓17	0 45	14 52	13 50	17 55	15 19	3 13	18 02	7 12	13 11	29 15	27 35	13 49	0 13	17 30
25 Su	2 12 16	1 15 13	26 03	0 46℞	16 26	14 49	18 31	15 30	3 20	17 59	7 11	13 12	29 27	27 54	14 11	0♈04	17 28
26 M	2 16 12	2 15 00	11♈02	0 46	18 01	15 49	19 08	15 40	3 26	17 57	7 10	13 13	29 39	28 13	14 33	29♓55	17 27
27 T	2 20 09	3 14 48	26 09	0 44	19 38	16 48	19 45	15 51	3 33	17 55	7 10	13 14	29 52	28 33	14 55	29 47	17 25
28 W	2 24 06	4 14 38	11♉13	0 41	21 15	17 49	20 21	16 01	3 39	17 52	7 09	13 15	0≈04	28 52	15 16	29 39	17 23
29 Th	2 28 02	5 14 30	26 05	0 38	22 54	18 50	20 58	16 12	3 46	17 50	7 08	13 16	0 17	29 12	15 38	29 32	17 22
30 F	2 31 59	6 14 24	10♊37	0 30	24 33	19 51	21 35	16 23	3 52	17 48	7 08	13 17	0 30	29 31	16 00	29 25	17 20
31 Sa	2 35 55	7 14 21	24 44	0 25	26 12	20 52	22 11	16 33	3 59	17 46	7 07	13 18	0 44	29 51	16 22	29 18	17 18

EPHEMERIS CALCULATED FOR 12 MIDNIGHT GREENWICH MEAN TIME. ALL OTHER DATA AND FACING ASPECTARIAN PAGE IN **EASTERN TIME (BOLD)** AND PACIFIC TIME (REGULAR).

NOVEMBER 2015

☽ Last Aspect day	ET / hr:mn / PT		asp	☽ Ingress sign	day	ET / hr:mn / PT	
1	**10:35 pm**	7:35 pm	✶♂	♌	2	**10:48 am**	7:48 am
3	**8:46 pm**	5:46 pm	△♅	♍	4	**9:22 pm**	6:22 pm
7	**7:47 am**	4:47 am	☌♀	♎	7	**10:14 am**	7:14 am
8	**9:42 pm**	6:42 pm	☍♅	♏	9	**11:02 pm**	8:02 pm
12	**9:54 am**	6:54 am	✶♂	♐	12	**10:14 am**	7:14 am
13	**10:19 pm**	7:19 pm	□♃	♑	14	**7:21 pm**	4:21 pm
16	**3:53 pm**	12:53 pm	✶☉	♒	16		11:24 pm
16	**3:53 pm**	12:53 pm	✶☉	♒	17	**2:24 am**	
19	**3:19 am**	12:19 am	□☿	♓	19	**7:21 am**	4:21 am
21	**8:23 am**	5:23 am	△☉	♈	21	**10:12 am**	7:12 am

☽ Last Aspect day	ET / hr:mn / PT		asp	☽ Ingress sign	day	ET / hr:mn / PT	
22	**2:16 pm**	11:16 am	☌♅	♉	23	**11:26 am**	8:26 am
24	**8:26 pm**	5:26 pm	△♃	♊	25	**12:15 pm**	9:15 am
26	**10:35 pm**	7:35 pm	△♀	♋	27	**2:27 pm**	11:27 am
29	**7:46 am**	4:46 am	□♀	♌	29	**7:47 pm**	4:47 pm

☽ Phases & Eclipses phase	day	ET / hr:mn / PT	
4th Quarter	3	**7:24 am**	4:24 am
New Moon	11	**12:47 pm**	9:47 am
2nd Quarter	18		10:27 pm
2nd Quarter	19	**1:27 am**	
Full Moon	25	**5:44 pm**	2:44 pm

Planet Ingress		day	ET / hr:mn / PT	
☿	♏	1		11:06 pm
☿	♏	2	**2:06 am**	
♀	♎	8	**10:31 am**	7:31 am
♂	♎	12	**4:41 pm**	1:41 pm
☿	♐	20	**2:43 pm**	11:43 am
☉	♐	22	**10:25 am**	7:25 am

Planetary Motion		day	ET / hr:mn / PT	
⚵	D	13	**1:09 pm**	10:09 am
♆	D	18	**11:31 am**	8:31 am
⚷	D	27		10:43 pm
⚷	D	28	**1:43 am**	

1 SUNDAY
- ☽ ☍ ♇ **3:53 am** 1:53 am
- ☽ ✶ ♃ **10:17 am** 7:17 am
- ☽ □ ♅ **11:52 am** 8:52 am
- ☽ ✶ ♀ **9:47 pm** 6:47 pm
- ☽ ✶ ♂ **10:35 pm** 7:35 pm

2 MONDAY
- ☽ □ ☿ **12:06 pm** 9:06 am
- ☽ △ ♄ **6:59 pm** 3:59 pm
- ♀ ☌ ♂ **8:10 pm** 5:10 pm
- ☽ ⚻ ♆ 9:19 pm

3 TUESDAY
- ☽ ⚻ ♆ **12:19 am**
- ☽ □ ☉ **7:24 am** 4:24 am
- ☽ ⚻ ♇ **12:28 pm** 9:28 am
- ☽ ⚺ ♃ **8:02 pm** 5:02 pm
- ☽ △ ♅ **8:46 pm** 5:46 pm

4 WEDNESDAY
- ☽ ⚺ ♂ **11:27 am** 8:27 am
- ☽ ⚺ ♀ **1:03 pm** 10:03 am
- ☿ ⚺ ♄ **7:56 pm** 4:56 pm

5 THURSDAY
- ☽ □ ♄ **6:36 am** 3:36 am
- ☽ ✶ ☿ **8:12 am** 5:12 am
- ☽ ☍ ♆ **11:36 am** 8:36 am
- ♃ ⚻ ♅ **5:01 pm** 2:01 pm
- ☉ ✶ ♇ **11:01 pm** 8:01 pm
- ☽ △ ♇ 9:27 pm
- ☽ ✶ ☉ 9:35 pm

6 FRIDAY
- ☽ △ ♇ **12:27 am**
- ☽ ✶ ☉ **12:35 am**
- ☿ △ ♆ **8:39 am** 5:39 am
- ☽ ⚻ ♅ **8:48 am** 5:48 am
- ☽ ☌ ♃ **9:04 am** 6:04 am

7 SATURDAY
- ☽ ☌ ♂ **3:24 am** 12:24 am
- ☽ ☌ ♀ **7:47 am** 4:47 am
- ☽ ✶ ♄ **8:11 pm** 5:11 pm
- ☽ ⚻ ♆ 9:36 pm

8 SUNDAY
- ☽ ⚻ ♆ **12:36 am**
- ☽ ⚺ ☿ **7:05 am** 4:05 am
- ☽ □ ♇ **1:40 pm** 10:40 am
- ☽ ⚺ ☉ **7:21 pm** 4:21 pm
- ☽ ☍ ♅ **9:42 pm** 6:42 pm
- ☽ ⚺ ♃ **10:59 pm** 7:59 pm

9 MONDAY
- ☽ ⚺ ♂ **7:33 pm** 4:33 pm
- ☉ ⚻ ♅ **10:16 pm** 7:16 pm
- ☽ ⚺ ♀ 11:40 pm

10 TUESDAY
- ☽ ⚺ ♀ **2:40 am**
- ☿ ✶ ♇ **7:14 am** 4:14 am
- ☽ ⚺ ♄ **9:23 am** 6:23 am
- ☽ △ ♆ **1:06 pm** 10:06 am
- ☉ ✶ ♃ **9:17 pm** 6:17 pm
- ☽ ✶ ♇ 10:58 pm

11 WEDNESDAY
- ☽ ✶ ♇ **1:58 am**
- ☽ ☌ ☿ **4:49 am** 1:49 am
- ☽ ⚻ ♅ **9:31 am** 6:31 am
- ☽ ✶ ♃ **11:41 am** 8:41 am
- ☽ ☌ ☉ **12:47 pm** 9:47 am

12 THURSDAY
- ☽ ✶ ♂ **9:54 am** 6:54 am
- ☿ ⚻ ♅ **3:36 pm** 12:36 pm
- ☽ ✶ ♀ **7:27 pm** 4:27 pm
- ☽ ☌ ♄ **8:47 pm** 5:47 pm
- ☽ □ ♆ **11:48 pm** 8:48 pm

13 FRIDAY
- ♀ ✶ ♄ **12:12 pm** 9:12 am
- ☽ ⚺ ♇ **12:21 pm** 9:21 am
- ☿ ✶ ♃ **1:18 pm** 10:18 am
- ☽ △ ♅ **7:22 pm** 4:22 pm
- ☽ □ ♃ **10:19 pm** 7:19 pm
- ☽ ⚺ ☿ **11:30 pm** 8:30 pm

14 SATURDAY
- ☽ ⚺ ☉ **3:39 am** 12:39 am
- ♀ ⚻ ♆ **8:33 pm** 5:33 pm
- ☽ □ ♂ **9:50 pm** 6:50 pm

15 SUNDAY
- ☽ ⚺ ♄ **6:02 am** 3:02 am
- ☽ ✶ ♆ **8:25 am** 5:25 am
- ☽ □ ♀ **9:32 am** 6:32 am
- ☽ ☌ ♇ **8:38 pm** 5:38 pm

16 MONDAY
- ☽ □ ♅ **3:10 am** 12:10 am
- ☽ △ ♃ **6:45 am** 3:45 am
- ☽ ✶ ☿ **2:59 pm** 11:59 am
- ☽ ✶ ☉ **3:53 pm** 12:53 pm

17 TUESDAY
- ☽ △ ♂ **7:23 am** 4:23 am
- ☉ ☌ ☿ **9:53 am** 6:53 am
- ☽ ✶ ♄ **1:11 pm** 10:11 am
- ☽ ⚺ ♆ **2:59 pm** 11:59 am
- ☽ △ ♀ **8:59 pm** 5:59 pm
- ☽ ⚺ ♇ 11:50 pm

18 WEDNESDAY
- ☽ ⚺ ♇ **2:50 am**
- ☽ ✶ ♅ **8:55 am** 5:55 am
- ☽ ⚻ ♃ **1:02 pm** 10:02 am
- ☽ □ ☉ 10:27 pm

19 THURSDAY
- ☽ □ ☉ **1:27 am**
- ☽ □ ☿ **3:19 am** 12:19 am
- ☽ ⚻ ♂ **2:30 pm** 11:30 am
- ☽ □ ♄ **6:08 pm** 3:08 pm
- ☽ ☌ ♆ **7:26 pm** 4:26 pm

20 FRIDAY
- ☽ ⚻ ♀ **5:42 am** 2:42 am
- ☽ ✶ ♇ **6:54 am** 3:54 am
- ☽ ⚺ ♅ **12:32 pm** 9:32 am
- ☽ ☍ ♃ **5:06 pm** 2:06 pm
- ♀ □ ♇ **9:02 pm** 6:02 pm

21 SATURDAY
- ☽ △ ☉ **8:23 am** 5:23 am
- ☽ △ ☿ **12:35 pm** 9:35 am
- ☽ ☍ ♂ **7:15 pm** 4:15 pm
- ☽ △ ♄ **9:00 pm** 6:00 pm
- ☽ ⚺ ♆ **9:50 pm** 6:50 pm

22 SUNDAY
- ☽ □ ♇ **9:00 am** 6:00 am
- ☽ ☍ ♀ **11:57 am** 8:57 am
- ☽ ☌ ♅ **2:16 pm** 11:16 am
- ☽ ⚻ ♃ **7:14 pm** 4:14 pm

23 MONDAY
- ☽ ⚻ ☉ **1:16 pm** 10:16 am
- ♀ ☍ ♅ **5:13 pm** 2:13 pm
- ☽ ⚻ ☿ **7:37 pm** 4:37 pm
- ☽ ⚻ ♂ **10:20 pm** 7:20 pm
- ☽ ⚻ ♄ **10:24 pm** 7:24 pm
- ☽ ✶ ♆ **10:51 pm** 7:51 pm
- ♂ ✶ ♄ 9:19 pm

24 TUESDAY
- ♂ ✶ ♄ **12:19 am**
- ☽ △ ♇ **9:56 am** 6:56 am
- ♂ ⚻ ♆ **10:58 am** 7:58 am
- ☽ ⚺ ♅ **2:59 pm** 11:59 am
- ☽ ⚻ ♀ **4:51 pm** 1:51 pm
- ☽ △ ♃ **8:26 pm** 5:26 pm
- ☿ ☌ ♄ **11:57 pm** 8:57 pm
- ☿ □ ♆ 11:15 pm

25 WEDNESDAY
- ☿ □ ♆ **2:15 am**
- ☿ ✶ ♂ **11:32 am** 8:32 am
- ☽ ☍ ☉ **5:44 pm** 2:44 pm
- ☽ ☍ ♄ **11:46 pm** 8:46 pm
- ☽ □ ♆ **11:50 pm** 8:50 pm
- ☽ △ ♂ 10:23 pm
- ☽ ☍ ☿ 11:26 pm

26 THURSDAY
- ☽ △ ♂ **1:23 am**
- ☽ ☍ ☿ **2:26 am**
- ♄ □ ♆ **7:15 am** 4:15 am
- ☽ ⚻ ♇ **11:15 am** 8:15 am
- ☽ ✶ ♅ **4:16 pm** 1:16 pm
- ♀ ⚺ ♃ **8:01 pm** 5:01 pm
- ☽ □ ♃ **10:24 pm** 7:24 pm
- ☽ △ ♀ **10:35 pm** 7:35 pm

27 FRIDAY
- ☽ ⚻ ☉ 9:11 pm
- ☽ △ ♆ 11:38 pm

28 SATURDAY
- ☽ ⚻ ☉ **12:11 am**
- ☽ △ ♆ **2:38 am**
- ☽ ⚻ ♄ **3:00 am** 12:00 am
- ☽ □ ♂ **6:33 am** 3:33 am
- ☽ ⚻ ☿ **11:55 am** 8:55 am
- ☽ ☍ ♇ **2:49 pm** 11:49 am
- ☽ □ ♅ **7:57 pm** 4:57 pm

29 SUNDAY
- ☽ ✶ ♃ **3:04 am** 12:04 am
- ☽ □ ♀ **7:46 am** 4:46 am
- ☉ □ ♆ **9:49 am** 6:49 am
- ☿ ⚺ ♇ **1:35 pm** 10:35 am
- ☉ ☌ ♄ **7:16 pm** 4:16 pm

30 MONDAY
- ☽ ⚻ ♆ **8:56 am** 5:56 am
- ☽ △ ♄ **9:48 am** 6:48 am
- ☽ △ ☉ **10:54 am** 7:54 am
- ☽ ✶ ♂ **3:47 pm** 12:47 pm
- ☽ ⚻ ♇ **10:09 pm** 7:09 pm
- ☽ △ ☿ 11:40 pm

Eastern time in bold type
Pacific time in medium type

NOVEMBER 2015

DATE	SID. TIME	SUN	MOON	NODE	MERCURY	VENUS	MARS	JUPITER	SATURN	URANUS	NEPTUNE	PLUTO	CERES	PALLAS	JUNO	VESTA	CHIRON
1 Su	2 39 52	8 ♏ 14 19	8 ⊙ 23	0 ≏ 20 R	27 ≏ 51	21 ♍ 54	22 ♍ 48	16 ♍ 43	4 ✗ 05	17 ♈ 43 R	7 ♓ 06 R	13 ♑ 19	0 ≈ 57	0 ♑ 11	16 ≏ 43	29 ♓ 12	17 ♓ 17 R
2 M	2 43 48	9 14 20	21 34	0 17 R	29 31	22 57	23 24	16 54	4 12	17 41 R	7 06 R	13 20	1 11	0 31	17 05	29 06 R	17 15 R
3 T	2 47 45	10 14 22	4 ♌ 19	0 15 D	1 ♏ 10	23 59	24 01	17 04	4 19	17 39	7 05	13 21	1 25	0 50	17 26	29 01	17 14
4 W	2 51 41	11 14 27	16 42	0 15	2 49	25 02	24 37	17 14	4 25	17 37	7 05	13 22	1 39	1 11	17 48	28 57	17 13
5 Th	2 55 38	12 14 34	28 49	0 16	4 29	26 06	25 14	17 24	4 32	17 35	7 04	13 23	1 53	1 31	18 09	28 52	17 11
6 F	2 59 35	13 14 43	10 ♍ 44	0 18	6 07	27 10	25 50	17 33	4 39	17 32	7 04	13 25	2 08	1 51	18 31	28 48	17 10
7 Sa	3 03 31	14 14 54	22 32	0 19 R	7 46	28 14	26 26	17 43	4 46	17 30	7 03	13 26	2 23	2 11	18 52	28 45	17 09
8 Su	3 07 28	15 15 07	4 ≏ 18	0 20	9 25	29 18	27 03	17 53	4 52	17 28	7 03	13 27	2 38	2 31	19 13	28 42	17 08
9 M	3 11 24	16 15 22	16 06	0 18	11 03	0 ≏ 23	27 39	18 02	4 59	17 26	7 03	13 28	2 53	2 52	19 35	28 40	17 07
10 T	3 15 21	17 15 39	27 59	0 14	12 41	1 28	28 15	18 12	5 06	17 24	7 03	13 30	3 08	3 12	19 56	28 38	17 06
11 W	3 19 17	18 15 57	10 ♏ 00	0 08	14 18	2 33	28 51	18 21	5 13	17 22	7 02	13 31	3 23	3 33	20 17	28 36	17 05
12 Th	3 23 14	19 16 18	22 11	0 00	15 55	3 39	29 27	18 30	5 20	17 20	7 02	13 32	3 39	3 54	20 38	28 36	17 04
13 F	3 27 10	20 16 40	4 ✗ 32	29 ♍ 51	17 32	4 45	0 ≏ 03	18 39	5 27	17 18	7 02	13 34	3 55	4 14	20 59	28 35 D	17 03
14 Sa	3 31 07	21 17 04	17 05	29 41	19 09	5 51	0 40	18 48	5 34	17 16	7 02	13 35	4 11	4 35	21 20	28 35	17 02
15 Su	3 35 04	22 17 29	29 49	29 32	20 45	6 57	1 16	18 57	5 41	17 14	7 01	13 37	4 27	4 56	21 41	28 35	17 01
16 M	3 39 00	23 17 56	12 ♑ 45	29 23	22 21	8 04	1 52	19 06	5 48	17 13	7 01	13 38	4 44	5 17	22 01	28 36	17 01
17 T	3 42 57	24 18 24	25 54	29 18	23 57	9 10	2 28	19 14	5 55	17 11	7 01 D	13 39	5 00	5 38	22 22	28 37	17 00
18 W	3 46 53	25 18 54	9 ≈ 16	29 14	25 32	10 18	3 03	19 23	6 02	17 09	7 01	13 41	5 17	5 59	22 43	28 39	16 59
19 Th	3 50 50	26 19 25	22 53	29 13 D	27 07	11 25	3 39	19 31	6 09	17 07	7 01	13 43	5 34	6 20	23 03	28 41	16 59
20 F	3 54 46	27 19 57	6 ♓ 46	29 13	28 42	12 32	4 15	19 39	6 16	17 06	7 01	13 44	5 51	6 41	23 23	28 43	16 58
21 Sa	3 58 43	28 20 30	20 54	29 14 R	0 ✗ 17	13 40	4 51	19 47	6 23	17 04	7 01	13 46	6 08	7 02	23 44	28 46	16 58
22 Su	4 02 39	29 21 04	5 ♈ 18	29 14	1 51	14 48	5 27	19 55	6 30	17 02	7 01	13 47	6 25	7 23	24 04	28 50	16 57
23 M	4 06 36	0 ✗ 21 40	19 55	29 12	3 26	15 56	6 02	20 03	6 37	17 01	7 01	13 49	6 43	7 45	24 24	28 54	16 57
24 T	4 10 33	1 22 16	4 ♉ 40	29 08	5 00	17 04	6 38	20 11	6 44	16 59	7 02	13 50	7 00	8 06	24 44	28 58	16 57
25 W	4 14 29	2 22 55	19 06	29 01	6 34	18 12	7 14	20 18	6 51	16 58	7 02	13 52	7 18	8 27	25 04	29 03	16 56
26 Th	4 18 26	3 23 34	4 ♊ 06	28 52	8 07	19 22	7 49	20 26	6 59	16 56	7 02	13 54	7 36	8 49	25 24	29 08	16 56
27 F	4 22 22	4 24 15	18 33	28 41	9 41	20 30	8 25	20 33	7 06	16 55	7 02	13 55	7 54	9 10	25 44	29 13	16 56
28 Sa	4 26 19	5 24 57	2 ⊙ 39	28 30	11 14	21 39	9 00	20 40	7 13	16 53	7 03	13 57	8 12	9 32	26 04	29 19	16 56 D
29 Su	4 30 15	6 25 41	16 20	28 20	12 48	22 49	9 36	20 47	7 20	16 52	7 03	13 59	8 30	9 53	26 24	29 25	16 56
30 M	4 34 12	7 26 26	29 34	28 12	14 21	23 58	10 11	20 54	7 27	16 51	7 03	14 01	8 49	10 15	26 43	29 32	16 56

EPHEMERIS CALCULATED FOR 12 MIDNIGHT GREENWICH MEAN TIME. ALL OTHER DATA AND FACING ASPECTARIAN PAGE IN **EASTERN TIME (BOLD)** AND PACIFIC TIME (REGULAR).

DECEMBER 2015

☽ Last Aspect day	ET / hr:mn / PT		asp	☽ Ingress sign	day	ET / hr:mn / PT	
1	**10:09 pm**	7:09 pm	⚹♀	♍	2	**5:09 am**	2:09 am
3	**11:59 pm**	8:59 pm	☌♃	♎	4	**5:34 pm**	2:34 pm
6	**9:03 pm**	6:03 pm	⚹☿	♏	7	**6:26 am**	3:26 am
8		10:39 pm	⚹♃	♐	9	**5:25 pm**	2:25 pm
9	**1:39 am**		⚹♃	♐	9	**5:25 pm**	2:25 pm
11	**11:06 am**	8:06 am	□♃	♑	11		10:46 pm
11	**11:06 am**	8:06 am	□♃	♑	12	**1:46 am**	
13	**6:07 pm**	3:07 pm	△♃	♒	14	**7:59 am**	4:59 am
15		11:17 pm	⚹☉	♓	16	**12:45 pm**	9:45 am
16	**2:17 am**		⚹☉	♓	16	**12:45 pm**	9:45 am
18	**10:14 am**	7:14 am	□☉	♈	18	**4:26 pm**	1:26 pm
20	**5:01 pm**	2:01 pm	△☉	♉	20	**7:13 pm**	4:13 pm
22	**9:26 am**	6:26 am	△♃	♊	22	**9:31 pm**	6:31 pm
24	**3:04 pm**	12:04 pm	△♂	♋	24		9:27 pm
24	**3:04 pm**	12:04 pm	△♂	♋	25	**12:27 am**	
26	**10:36 pm**	7:36 pm	△♀	♌	27	**5:31 am**	2:31 am
29	**12:38 pm**	9:38 am	□♀	♍	29	**1:58 pm**	10:58 am
31		9:33 pm	△☿	♎	31		10:41 pm
1/1	**12:33 am**		△☿	♎	1/1	**1:41 am**	

☽ Phases & Eclipses phase	day	ET / hr:mn / PT	
4th Quarter	2		11:40 pm
4th Quarter	3	**2:40 am**	
New Moon	11	**5:29 am**	2:29 am
2nd Quarter	18	**10:14 am**	7:14 am
Full Moon	25	**6:12 am**	3:12 am

Planet Ingress		day	ET / hr:mn / PT	
⚴	♈	3	**12:58 pm**	9:58 am
♀	♏	4	**11:15 pm**	8:15 pm
☿	♑	9	**9:34 pm**	6:34 pm
⚵	♏	9		11:50 pm
⚵	♏	10	**2:50 am**	
☉	♑	21	**11:48 pm**	8:48 pm
♀	♐	29		11:16 pm
♀	♐	30	**2:16 am**	

Planetary Motion		day	ET / hr:mn / PT	
♅	D	25	**10:53 pm**	7:53 pm

1 TUESDAY
☽ △ ☿ **2:40 am**
☽ △ ♅ **3:28 am** 12:28 am
☿ △ ♅ **9:00 am** 6:00 am
☽ ⚺ ♃ **11:43 am** 8:43 am
☽ ⚹ ♀ **10:09 pm** 7:09 pm

2 WEDNESDAY
☽ ☍ ♆ **7:13 pm** 4:13 pm
☽ □ ♄ **8:41 pm** 5:41 pm
☽ □ ☉ 11:40 pm

3 THURSDAY
☽ □ ☉ **2:40 am**
☽ ⚺ ♂ **5:29 am** 2:29 am
☽ △ ♇ **9:20 am** 6:20 am
☽ ⚻ ♅ **2:41 pm** 11:41 am
☽ □ ☿ **10:52 pm** 7:52 pm
☽ ☌ ♃ **11:59 pm** 8:59 pm

4 FRIDAY
☿ □ ♃ **7:53 am** 4:53 am
☽ ⚺ ♀ **4:56 pm** 1:56 pm

5 SATURDAY
☽ ⚻ ♆ **8:02 am** 5:02 am
☽ ⚹ ♄ **10:06 am** 7:06 am
☽ ⚹ ☉ **9:19 pm** 6:19 pm
☽ ☌ ♂ **9:37 pm** 6:37 pm
☽ □ ♇ **10:28 pm** 7:28 pm

6 SUNDAY
☽ ☍ ♅ **3:37 am** 12:37 am
☉ ⚹ ♂ **5:14 am** 2:14 am
☉ ⚺ ♇ **11:12 am** 8:12 am
☽ ⚺ ♃ **1:32 pm** 10:32 am
♂ □ ♇ **3:52 pm** 12:52 pm
☽ ⚹ ☿ **9:03 pm** 6:03 pm

7 MONDAY
☽ ☌ ♀ **12:25 pm** 9:25 am
☽ △ ♆ **8:40 pm** 5:40 pm
☽ ⚺ ♄ **11:14 pm** 8:14 pm

8 TUESDAY
☽ ⚹ ♇ **10:49 am** 7:49 am
☽ ⚺ ♂ **12:51 pm** 9:51 am
☽ ⚺ ☉ **3:00 pm** 12:00 pm
☽ ⚻ ♅ **3:33 pm** 12:33 pm
☉ △ ♅ **9:38 pm** 6:38 pm
☽ ⚹ ♃ 10:39 pm

9 WEDNESDAY
☽ ⚹ ♃ **1:39 am**
☽ ⚺ ☿ **4:50 pm** 1:50 pm

10 THURSDAY
☽ ⚺ ♀ **5:14 am** 2:14 am
☽ □ ♆ **7:06 am** 4:06 am
☽ ☌ ♄ **10:02 am** 7:02 am
♂ ☍ ♅ **8:31 pm** 5:31 pm

☽ ⚺ ♇ **8:41 pm** 5:41 pm
☽ △ ♅ 10:01 pm
♀ △ ♆ 10:13 pm
☽ ⚹ ♂ 10:14 pm

11 FRIDAY
☽ △ ♅ **1:01 am**
♀ △ ♆ **1:13 am**
☽ ⚹ ♂ **1:14 am**
☽ ☌ ☉ **5:29 am** 2:29 am
☽ □ ♃ **11:06 am** 8:06 am

12 SATURDAY
☽ ☌ ☿ **8:43 am** 5:43 am
♀ ⚺ ♄ **1:33 pm** 10:33 am
☽ ⚹ ♆ **2:55 pm** 11:55 am
☽ ⚺ ♄ **6:12 pm** 3:12 pm
☽ ⚹ ♀ **6:36 pm** 3:36 pm

13 SUNDAY
☽ ☌ ♇ **4:03 am** 1:03 am
☽ □ ♅ **8:02 am** 5:02 am
☽ □ ♂ **10:47 am** 7:47 am
☽ ⚺ ☉ **4:55 pm** 1:55 pm
☽ △ ♃ **6:07 pm** 3:07 pm

14 MONDAY
☉ □ ♃ **10:02 am** 7:02 am
☿ ⚹ ♆ **2:40 pm** 11:40 am
☽ ⚺ ♆ **8:47 pm** 5:47 pm
☽ ⚺ ☿ **9:33 pm** 6:33 pm
☽ ⚹ ♄ 9:22 pm

15 TUESDAY
☽ ⚹ ♄ **12:22 am**
☽ □ ♀ **5:27 am** 2:27 am
☽ ⚺ ♇ **9:37 am** 6:37 am
☽ ⚹ ♅ **1:20 pm** 10:20 am
☽ △ ♂ **6:24 pm** 3:24 pm
☽ ⚻ ♃ **11:30 pm** 8:30 pm
☿ ⚺ ♄ 9:46 pm
☽ ⚹ ☉ 11:17 pm

16 WEDNESDAY
☿ ⚺ ♄ **12:46 am**
☽ ⚹ ☉ **2:17 am**
☽ ☌ ♆ 10:20 pm

17 THURSDAY
☽ ☌ ♆ **1:20 am**
☽ □ ♄ **5:14 am** 2:14 am
♀ ⚹ ♇ **6:19 am** 3:19 am
☽ ⚹ ☿ **8:24 am** 5:24 am
☽ ⚹ ♇ **1:58 pm** 10:58 am
☽ △ ♀ **2:40 pm** 11:40 am
☽ ⚺ ♅ **5:27 pm** 2:27 pm
☽ ⚻ ♂ 9:40 pm

18 FRIDAY
☽ ⚻ ♂ **12:40 am**
☽ ☍ ♃ **3:42 am** 12:42 am
☽ □ ☉ **10:14 am** 7:14 am
♀ ⚻ ♅ **10:56 pm** 7:56 pm

19 SATURDAY
☽ ⚺ ♆ **4:51 am** 1:51 am
☽ △ ♄ **9:02 am** 6:02 am
☿ ☌ ♇ **1:56 pm** 10:56 am
☽ □ ♇ **5:19 pm** 2:19 pm
☽ □ ☿ **5:41 pm** 2:41 pm
☽ ☌ ♅ **8:35 pm** 5:35 pm
☽ ⚻ ♀ **10:36 pm** 7:36 pm

20 SUNDAY
☽ ☍ ♂ **5:50 am** 2:50 am
☽ ⚻ ♃ **6:54 am** 3:54 am
☽ △ ☉ **5:01 pm** 2:01 pm
☿ □ ♅ **10:07 pm** 7:07 pm

21 MONDAY
☽ ⚹ ♆ **7:30 am** 4:30 am
♂ ⚺ ♃ **11:13 am** 8:13 am
☽ ⚻ ♄ **11:59 am** 8:59 am
☽ △ ♇ **7:53 pm** 4:53 pm
☽ ⚺ ♅ **10:59 pm** 7:59 pm
☽ △ ☿ 10:43 pm

22 TUESDAY
☽ △ ☿ **1:43 am**
☽ ☍ ♀ **5:36 am** 2:36 am
☽ △ ♃ **9:26 am** 6:26 am
☽ ⚻ ♂ **10:16 am** 7:16 am
☽ ⚻ ☉ **11:11 pm** 8:11 pm

23 WEDNESDAY
☽ □ ♆ **9:54 am** 6:54 am
☽ ☍ ♄ **2:45 pm** 11:45 am

☽ ⚻ ♇ **10:26 pm** 7:26 pm
☽ ⚹ ♅ 10:27 pm

24 THURSDAY
☽ ⚹ ♅ **1:27 am**
♀ ⚹ ♃ **5:03 am** 2:03 am
☽ ⚻ ☿ **9:38 am** 6:38 am
☽ □ ♃ **12:16 pm** 9:16 am
☽ ⚻ ♀ **12:55 pm** 9:55 am
☽ △ ♂ **3:04 pm** 12:04 pm

25 FRIDAY
☽ ☍ ☉ **6:12 am** 3:12 am
☽ △ ♆ **1:17 pm** 10:17 am
☿ △ ♃ **3:19 pm** 12:19 pm
☽ ⚻ ♄ **6:39 pm** 3:39 pm
☽ ☍ ♇ 11:21 pm

26 SATURDAY
☽ ☍ ♇ **2:21 am**
☽ □ ♅ **5:22 am** 2:22 am
♀ ⚺ ♂ **9:58 am** 6:58 am
☽ ⚹ ♃ **4:51 pm** 1:51 pm
☽ ☍ ☿ **7:21 pm** 4:21 pm
☽ □ ♂ **9:57 pm** 6:57 pm
☽ △ ♀ **10:36 pm** 7:36 pm

27 SUNDAY
☽ ⚻ ☉ **4:07 pm** 1:07 pm
☽ ⚻ ♆ **7:12 pm** 4:12 pm
☽ △ ♄ 10:17 pm

28 MONDAY
☽ △ ♄ **1:17 am**

☽ ⚻ ♇ **9:09 am** 6:09 am
☽ △ ♅ **12:14 pm** 9:14 am
☽ ⚺ ♃ 9:37 pm

29 TUESDAY
☽ ⚺ ♃ **12:37 am**
☉ ⚹ ♆ **8:18 am** 5:18 am
☽ ⚻ ☿ **8:30 am** 5:30 am
☽ ⚹ ♂ **8:33 am** 5:33 am
☿ □ ♂ **9:52 am** 6:52 am
☽ □ ♀ **12:38 pm** 9:38 am

30 WEDNESDAY
☽ ☍ ♆ **4:39 am** 1:39 am
☽ △ ☉ **6:29 am** 3:29 am
☽ □ ♄ **11:33 am** 8:33 am
☽ △ ♇ **7:32 pm** 4:32 pm
☽ ⚻ ♅ **10:38 pm** 7:38 pm

31 THURSDAY
☽ ☌ ♃ **11:50 am** 8:50 am
☽ ⚺ ♂ **10:56 pm** 7:56 pm
☽ △ ☿ 9:33 pm

Eastern time in bold type
Pacific time in medium type

DECEMBER 2015

DATE	SID.TIME	SUN	MOON	NODE	MERCURY	VENUS	MARS	JUPITER	SATURN	URANUS	NEPTUNE	PLUTO	CERES	PALLAS	JUNO	VESTA	CHIRON
1 T	4 38 08	8 ♐27 13	12 ♌ 23	28 ♍ 06	15 ♐ 23	25 ♎ 54	10 ♎ 46	21 ♍ 01	7 ♐ 34	16 ♈ 49	7 ♓ 04	14 ♑ 02	9 ♒ 07	10 ♑ 36	27 ♎ 12	29 ♓ 39	16 ♓ 56
2 W	4 42 05	9 28 01	24 50	28 03 R	17 28	26 17	11 22	21 07	7 41	16 48 R	7 05	14 04	9 26	10 58	27 22	29 46	16 57
3 Th	4 46 02	10 28 50	6 ♍ 58	28 02 R	19 01	27 27	11 57	21 14	7 48	16 47	7 05	14 06	9 45	11 20	27 42	29 54	16 57
4 F	4 49 58	11 29 41	18 54	28 02	20 34	28 37	12 32	21 20	7 55	16 46	7 05	14 08	10 04	11 41	28 01	0 ♈ 07	16 57
5 Sa	4 53 55	12 30 33	0 ♎ 42	28 02	22 07	29 48	13 07	21 26	8 03	16 45	7 06	14 09	10 23	12 03	28 20	0 11	16 58
6 Su	4 57 51	13 31 27	12 29	28 02	23 40	0 ♏ 58	13 42	21 32	8 10	16 44	7 07	14 11	10 42	12 25	28 39	0 19	16 58
7 M	5 01 48	14 32 21	24 19	27 59	25 12	2 08	14 17	21 38	8 17	16 43	7 07	14 13	11 02	12 47	28 58	0 29	16 58
8 T	5 05 44	15 33 17	6 ♏ 17	27 53	26 45	3 19	14 53	21 44	8 24	16 42	7 08	14 15	11 21	13 08	29 17	0 38	16 59
9 W	5 09 41	16 34 15	18 27	27 44	28 27	4 30	15 27	21 49	8 31	16 41	7 08	14 17	11 40	13 30	29 35	0 48	16 59
10 Th	5 13 37	17 35 13	0 ♐ 49	27 33	29 50	5 41	16 02	21 55	8 38	16 40	7 09	14 19	12 00	13 52	29 54	0 58	17 00
11 F	5 17 34	18 36 13	13 27	27 20	1 ♑ 22	6 51	16 37	22 00	8 45	16 39	7 10	14 21	12 20	14 14	0 ♏ 12	1 09	17 01
12 Sa	5 21 31	19 37 13	26 20	27 10	2 55	8 03	17 12	22 05	8 52	16 39	7 10	14 23	12 40	14 36	0 31	1 20	17 02
13 Su	5 25 27	20 38 14	9 ♑ 26	26 52	4 26	9 14	17 47	22 10	8 59	16 38	7 11	14 25	12 59	14 58	0 49	1 31	17 02
14 M	5 29 24	21 39 16	22 44	26 41	5 58	10 25	18 21	22 15	9 06	16 37	7 12	14 27	13 19	15 20	1 07	1 42	17 03
15 T	5 33 20	22 40 19	6 ♒ 13	26 32	7 29	11 36	18 56	22 19	9 13	16 37	7 13	14 28	13 40	15 42	1 25	1 54	17 04
16 W	5 37 17	23 41 22	19 50	26 26	9 00	12 48	19 30	22 24	9 20	16 36	7 14	14 30	14 00	16 04	1 43	2 06	17 05
17 Th	5 41 13	24 42 25	3 ♓ 36	26 22	10 30	14 00	20 05	22 28	9 27	16 36	7 15	14 32	14 20	16 26	2 01	2 19	17 06
18 F	5 45 10	25 43 29	17 29	26 22	12 00	15 12	20 39	22 32	9 34	16 35	7 16	14 34	14 41	16 48	2 19	2 32	17 07
19 Sa	5 49 06	26 44 33	1 ♈ 30	26 21	13 29	16 23	21 14	22 36	9 41	16 35	7 17	14 36	15 01	17 10	2 36	2 45	17 08
20 Su	5 53 03	27 45 37	15 38	26 21	14 56	17 35	21 48	22 39	9 48	16 34	7 18	14 38	15 22	17 32	2 53	2 58	17 10
21 M	5 57 00	28 46 42	29 52	26 18	16 23	18 47	22 22	22 43	9 55	16 34	7 19	14 40	15 43	17 55	3 11	3 11	17 11
22 T	6 00 56	29 47 47	14 ♉ 11	26 13	17 48	19 59	22 56	22 46	10 02	16 34	7 20	14 42	16 04	18 17	3 28	3 25	17 12
23 W	6 04 53	0 ♑48 52	28 30	26 05	19 12	21 11	23 30	22 49	10 08	16 34	7 21	14 44	16 24	18 39	3 45	3 39	17 14
24 Th	6 08 49	1 49 58	12 ♊ 45	25 54	20 33	22 23	24 04	22 52	10 15	16 34	7 22	14 46	16 45	19 01	4 02	3 54	17 15
25 F	6 12 46	2 51 04	26 50	25 42	21 52	23 35	24 38	22 55	10 22	16 34	7 24	14 48	17 06	19 23	4 18	4 08	17 17
26 Sa	6 16 42	3 52 10	10 ♋ 40	25 29	23 09	24 48	25 12	22 58	10 29	16 34 D	7 25	14 51	17 28	19 45	4 35	4 23	17 18
27 Su	6 20 39	4 53 17	24 11	25 17	24 22	26 00	25 46	23 00	10 35	16 34	7 26	14 53	17 49	20 07	4 51	4 38	17 19
28 M	6 24 35	5 54 24	7 ♌ 21	25 07	25 31	27 13	26 19	23 02	10 42	16 34	7 27	14 55	18 10	20 30	5 08	4 54	17 21
29 T	6 28 32	6 55 32	20 08	25 00	26 36	28 25	26 53	23 04	10 49	16 34	7 29	14 57	18 32	20 52	5 24	5 09	17 23
30 W	6 32 29	7 56 39	2 ♍ 35	24 55	27 36	29 38	27 27	23 06	10 55	16 34	7 30	14 59	18 53	21 14	5 40	5 25	17 24
31 Th	6 36 25	8 57 48	14 45	24 53 D	28 30	0 ♐ 51	28 00	23 08	11 02	16 34	7 31	15 01	19 15	21 36	5 56	5 41	17 26

EPHEMERIS CALCULATED FOR 12 MIDNIGHT GREENWICH MEAN TIME. ALL OTHER DATA AND FACING ASPECTARIAN PAGE IN EASTERN TIME (BOLD) AND PACIFIC TIME (REGULAR).

☽ Last Aspect				☽ Ingress			
day	ET / hr:mn / PT		asp	sign	day	ET / hr:mn / PT	
12/31		9:33 pm	△☿	♎	12/31		10:41 pm
1	**12:33 am**		△☿	♎	1	**1:41 am**	
2	**11:23 am**	8:23 am	☍♅	♏	3	**2:36 pm**	11:36 am
5	**12:47 pm**	9:47 am	⚹♃	♐	5		10:56 pm
5	**12:47 pm**	9:47 am	⚹♃	♐	6	**1:56 am**	
7	**9:44 pm**	6:44 pm	□♃	♑	8	**10:07 am**	7:07 am
10	**12:39 pm**	9:39 am	☌☿	♒	10	**3:23 pm**	12:23 pm
11	**8:09 pm**	5:09 pm	⚹♅	♓	12	**6:53 pm**	3:53 pm
14	**11:31 am**	8:31 am	⚹☉	♈	14	**9:48 pm**	6:48 pm
16	**6:26 pm**	3:26 pm	□☉	♉	16		9:48 pm

☽ Last Aspect				☽ Ingress			
day	ET / hr:mn / PT		asp	sign	day	ET / hr:mn / PT	
16	**6:26 pm**	3:26 pm	□☉	♉	17	**12:48 am**	
18		10:50 pm	△☉	♊	19	**4:13 am**	1:13 am
19	**1:50 am**		△☉	♊	19	**4:13 am**	1:13 am
21	**3:01 am**	12:01 am	☍♀	♋	21	**8:28 am**	5:28 am
22		10:21 pm	⚹♃	♌	23	**2:21 pm**	11:21 am
23	**1:21 am**		⚹♃	♌	26	**2:21 pm**	11:21 am
24	**9:51 pm**	6:51 pm	△♅	♍	25	**10:46 pm**	7:46 pm
27	**7:11 pm**	4:11 pm	☌♃	♎	28	**9:59 am**	6:59 am
29	**8:34 pm**	5:34 pm	☍♅	♏	30	**10:50 pm**	7:50 pm

☽ Phases & Eclipses			
phase	day	ET / hr:mn / PT	
4th Quarter	1		9:30 pm
4th Quarter	2	**12:30 am**	
New Moon	9	**8:31 pm**	5:31 pm
2nd Quarter	16	**6:26 pm**	3:26 pm
Full Moon	23	**8:46 pm**	5:46 pm
4th Quarter	31	**10:28 pm**	7:28 pm

Planet Ingress				
		day	ET / hr:mn / PT	
☿	♒	1	**9:20 pm**	6:20 pm
♂	♏	3	**9:32 am**	6:32 am
☿	♑	8	**2:36 pm**	11:36 am
☉	♒	20	**10:27 am**	7:27 am
♀	♒	22	**2:03 pm**	11:03 am
♀	♑	23	**3:31 pm**	12:31 pm
⚳	♓	28	**1:42 pm**	10:42 am

Planetary Motion				
		day	ET / hr:mn / PT	
☿	℞	5	**8:06 am**	5:06 am
♃	℞	7	**11:40 pm**	8:40 pm
☿	D	25	**4:50 pm**	1:50 pm

1 FRIDAY
☽△☿ **12:33 am**
☽⚹♀ **7:05 am** 4:05 am
☽⚻♆ **5:03 pm** 2:03 pm
☽□☉ 9:30 pm
☽⚹♄ 9:35 pm
☉⚺♄ 10:35 pm

2 SATURDAY
☽□☉ **12:30 am**
☽⚹♄ **12:35 am**
☉⚺♄ **1:35 am**
☽□♇ **8:23 am** 5:23 am
☽☍♅ **11:23 am** 8:23 am
☽⚺♃ 9:50 pm

3 SUNDAY
☽⚺♃ **12:50 am**
☽☌♂ **2:51 pm** 11:51 am
☽□☿ **4:12 pm** 1:12 pm
☽⚺♀ 11:53 pm

4 MONDAY
☽⚺♀ **2:53 am**
☽△♆ **5:56 am** 2:56 am
☽⚺♄ **1:46 pm** 10:46 am
☽⚹☉ **6:43 pm** 3:43 pm
☽⚹♇ **8:59 pm** 5:59 pm
☽⚻♅ **11:47 pm** 8:47 pm

5 TUESDAY
☿□♂ **7:00 am** 4:00 am

♀□♆ **9:33 am** 6:33 am
☽⚹♃ **12:47 pm** 9:47 am
☉☌♇ **10:28 pm** 7:28 pm

6 WEDNESDAY
☽⚹☿ **3:49 am** 12:49 am
☽⚺♂ **4:54 am** 1:54 am
☽□♆ **4:39 pm** 1:39 pm
☽☌♀ **7:54 pm** 4:54 pm
☽☌♄ 9:27 pm

7 THURSDAY
☽☌♄ **12:27 am**
☽⚺♇ **6:57 am** 3:57 am
☉□♅ **7:22 am** 4:22 am
☽△♅ **9:29 am** 6:29 am
☽⚺☉ **9:39 am** 6:39 am
☽□♃ **9:44 pm** 6:44 pm

8 FRIDAY
☽⚺☿ **10:19 am** 7:19 am
☽⚹♂ **3:20 pm** 12:20 pm
♀☌♄ **11:11 pm** 8:11 pm
☽⚹♆ 9:07 pm

9 SATURDAY
☽⚹♆ **12:07 am**
☽⚺♄ **7:48 am** 4:48 am
☽⚺♀ **8:35 am** 5:35 am
☽☌♇ **1:40 pm** 10:40 am
☽□♅ **3:58 pm** 12:58 pm
☽☌☉ **8:31 pm** 5:31 pm

10 SUNDAY
☽△♃ **3:33 am** 12:33 am
☽☌☿ **12:39 pm** 9:39 am
☽□♂ **10:31 pm** 7:31 pm

11 MONDAY
☽⚺♆ **4:55 am** 1:55 am
☽⚹♄ **12:35 pm** 9:35 am
☽⚹♀ **5:59 pm** 2:59 pm
☽⚺♇ **6:00 pm** 3:00 pm
♀⚺♇ **6:18 pm** 3:18 pm
☽⚹♅ **8:09 pm** 5:09 pm

12 TUESDAY
☽⚺☉ **4:34 am** 1:34 am
☽⚻♃ **7:19 am** 4:19 am
☽⚺☿ **12:27 pm** 9:27 am
♀△♅ **7:11 pm** 4:11 pm

13 WEDNESDAY
☽△♂ **3:56 am** 12:56 am
☽☌♆ **8:17 am** 5:17 am
☽□♄ **4:06 pm** 1:06 pm
☉△♃ **5:49 pm** 2:49 pm
☽⚹♇ **9:13 pm** 6:13 pm
☽⚺♅ **11:17 pm** 8:17 pm
☽□♀ 10:54 pm

14 THURSDAY
☽□♀ **1:54 am**
☉☌☿ **9:05 am** 6:05 am
☽☍♃ **10:13 am** 7:13 am
☽⚹☿ **11:09 am** 8:09 am

☽⚹☉ **11:31 am** 8:31 am
☿△♃ **9:15 pm** 6:15 pm

15 FRIDAY
☽⚻♂ **8:50 am** 5:50 am
☽⚺♆ **11:16 am** 8:16 am
☽△♄ **7:21 pm** 4:21 pm
☽□♇ 9:15 pm
☽☌♅ 11:15 pm

16 SATURDAY
☽□♇ **12:15 am**
☽☌♅ **2:15 am**
☽△♀ **9:39 am** 6:39 am
☽□☿ **9:47 am** 6:47 am
☿⚺♀ **10:25 am** 7:25 am
☽⚻♃ **1:05 pm** 10:05 am
☽□☉ **6:26 pm** 3:26 pm

17 SUNDAY
☽☍♂ **1:53 pm** 10:53 am
☽⚹♆ **2:28 pm** 11:28 am
☽⚻♄ **10:51 pm** 7:51 pm
♀□♃ 9:10 pm

18 MONDAY
♀□♃ **12:10 am**
☽△♇ **3:33 am** 12:33 am
☽⚺♅ **5:30 am** 2:30 am
♂△♆ **6:01 am** 3:01 am
☽△☿ **9:03 am** 6:03 am
☽△♃ **4:15 pm** 1:15 pm
☽⚻♀ **5:51 pm** 2:51 pm
☽△☉ 10:50 pm

19 TUESDAY
☽△☉ **1:50 am**
☽□♆ **6:09 pm** 3:09 pm
☽⚻♂ **7:30 pm** 4:30 pm
☽☍♄ 11:54 pm

20 WEDNESDAY
☽☍♄ **2:54 am**
☽⚻♇ **7:27 am** 4:27 am
☽⚹♅ **9:24 am** 6:24 am
☽⚻☿ **9:37 am** 6:37 am
☿□♅ **1:26 pm** 10:26 am
☽□♃ **8:07 pm** 5:07 pm

21 THURSDAY
☽☍♀ **3:01 am** 12:01 am
☽⚻☉ **10:15 am** 7:15 am
☽△♆ **10:53 am** 7:53 pm
☽△♂ 11:15 pm

22 FRIDAY
☽△♂ **2:15 am**
☿☌♇ **4:59 am** 1:59 am
☽⚻♄ **8:07 am** 5:07 am
☽☍☿ **12:17 pm** 9:17 am
☽☍♇ **12:34 pm** 9:34 am
☽□♅ **2:32 pm** 11:32 am
☽⚹♃ 10:21 pm

23 SATURDAY
☽⚹♃ **1:21 am**
☽⚻♀ **2:14 pm** 11:14 am
☽☍☉ **8:46 pm** 5:46 pm

24 SUNDAY
☽⚻♆ **5:30 am** 2:30 am
☽□♂ **11:11 am** 8:11 am
☽△♄ **3:25 pm** 12:25 pm
☽⚻☿ **6:09 pm** 3:09 pm
☽⚻♇ **7:50 pm** 4:50 pm
☽△♅ **9:51 pm** 6:51 pm

25 MONDAY
☽⚺♃ **8:52 am** 5:52 am

26 TUESDAY
☽△♀ **4:50 am** 1:50 am
☽⚻☉ **10:36 am** 7:36 am
☽☍♆ **2:52 pm** 11:52 am
☽⚹♂ **11:12 pm** 8:12 pm
☽□♄ 10:33 pm

27 WEDNESDAY
☽□♄ **1:33 am**
☽△☿ **4:10 am** 1:10 am
☽△♇ **5:56 am** 2:56 am
☽⚻♅ **8:02 am** 5:02 am
☽☌♃ **7:11 pm** 4:11 pm

28 THURSDAY
☉⚺♆ **3:45 pm** 12:45 pm
☽□♀ **11:12 pm** 8:12 pm
☽⚻♆ 11:54 pm

29 FRIDAY
☽⚻♆ **2:54 am**
☽△☉ **3:55 am** 12:55 am
☽⚺♂ **2:02 pm** 11:02 am
☽⚹♄ **2:12 pm** 11:12 am

☽□☿ **6:11 pm** 3:11 pm
☽□♇ **6:27 pm** 3:27 pm
♂⚺♄ **6:56 pm** 3:56 pm
☽☍♅ **8:34 pm** 5:34 pm
☿☌♇ 9:58 pm

30 SATURDAY
☿☌♇ **12:58 am**
☽⚺♃ **7:29 am** 4:29 am
♀⚹♆ **11:44 am** 8:44 am

31 SUNDAY
☽△♆ **3:58 pm** 12:58 pm
☽⚹♀ **7:08 pm** 4:08 pm
☽□☉ **10:28 pm** 7:28 pm
☿□♅ **10:41 pm** 7:41 pm

Eastern time in bold type
Pacific time in medium type

JANUARY 2016

DATE	SID.TIME	SUN	MOON	NODE	MERCURY	VENUS	MARS	JUPITER	SATURN	URANUS	NEPTUNE	PLUTO	CERES	PALLAS	JUNO	VESTA	CHIRON
1 F	6 40 22	9 ♑ 58 56	26 ♍ 42	24 ♍ 53	0 ≈ 28	2 ♐ 02	28 ♎ 33	23 ♍ 12	11 ♐ 09	16 ♈ 34	7 ♓ 33	15 ♑ 05	19 ≈ 36	21 ♒ 58	6 ♏ 11	5 ♈ 58	17 ♓ 28
2 Sa	6 44 18	11 00 05	8 ♎ 56	24 53 ℞	0 49	3 16	29 07	23 13	11 15	16 35	7 34	15 05	19 58	22 20	6 27	6 14	17 30
3 Su	6 48 15	12 01 15	20 20	24 51	1 01	4 29	29 40	23 13	11 22	16 35	7 36	15 07	20 20	22 43	6 42	6 31	17 32
4 M	6 52 11	13 02 24	2 ♏ 11	24 47	1 07	5 42	0 ♏ 13	23 14	11 28	16 36	7 37	15 09	20 41	23 05	6 57	6 48	17 34
5 T	6 56 8	14 03 34	14 11	24 40	1 05 ℞	6 55	0 46	23 14	11 34	16 36	7 39	15 11	21 03	23 27	7 12	7 05	17 36
6 W	7 0 4	15 04 45	26 25	24 31	0 54	8 08	1 19	23 14	11 41	16 37	7 40	15 13	21 25	23 50	7 27	7 23	17 38
7 Th	7 4 1	16 05 55	8 ♐ 56	24 24	0 31	9 21	1 52	23 14	11 47	16 38	7 42	15 15	21 47	24 11	7 42	7 40	17 40
8 F	7 7 58	17 07 05	21 45	24 20	29 ♑ 57	10 35	2 25	23 14 ℞	11 53	16 39	7 43	15 17	22 09	24 34	7 56	7 58	17 42
9 Sa	7 11 54	18 08 16	4 ♑ 54	24 14	29 07	11 48	2 57	23 13	12 00	16 40	7 45	15 20	22 32	24 56	8 11	8 16	17 44
10 Su	7 15 51	19 09 26	18 22	24 07	28 10	13 01	3 30	23 12	12 06	16 40	7 47	15 22	22 54	25 18	8 25	8 34	17 47
11 M	7 19 47	20 10 36	2 ≈ 39	23 56	27 05	14 14	4 02	23 11	12 12	16 41	7 48	15 24	23 16	25 40	8 39	8 53	17 49
12 T	7 23 44	21 11 46	16 01	23 45	25 53	15 28	4 35	23 10	12 18	16 42	7 50	15 26	23 38	26 02	8 52	9 11	17 51
13 W	7 27 40	22 12 55	0 ♓ 04	23 37	24 36	16 41	5 07	23 08	12 24	16 43	7 52	15 28	24 01	26 24	9 06	9 30	17 54
14 Th	7 31 37	23 14 04	14 12	23 32	23 17	17 55	5 39	23 07	12 30	16 44	7 53	15 30	24 23	26 46	9 19	9 49	17 56
15 F	7 35 33	24 15 12	28 21	23 30 D	21 58	19 08	6 11	23 05	12 36	16 45	7 55	15 32	24 46	27 08	9 32	10 08	17 58
16 Sa	7 39 30	25 16 20	12 ♈ 29	23 30	20 42	20 22	6 43	23 03	12 42	16 46	7 57	15 34	25 08	27 31	9 45	10 27	18 01
17 Su	7 43 27	26 17 26	26 36	23 31 ℞	19 26	21 35	7 15	23 01	12 48	16 46	7 59	15 36	25 31	27 53	9 58	10 47	18 03
18 M	7 47 23	27 18 32	10 ♉ 39	23 31	18 26	22 49	7 47	22 58	12 53	16 47	8 00	15 38	25 53	28 15	10 11	11 06	18 06
19 T	7 51 20	28 19 37	24 39	23 30	17 28	24 02	8 18	22 56	12 59	16 48	8 02	15 40	26 16	28 37	10 23	11 26	18 08
20 W	7 55 16	29 20 41	8 Ⅱ 57	23 27	16 48	25 16	8 50	22 53	13 05	16 50	8 04	15 42	26 39	28 59	10 35	11 46	18 11
21 Th	7 59 13	0 ≈ 21 45	22 57	23 22	16 28	26 30	9 21	22 50	13 10	16 51	8 06	15 44	27 02	29 21	10 47	12 06	18 14
22 F	8 3 9	1 22 47	5 ♋ 57	23 14	16 01	27 43	9 52	22 47	13 16	16 52	8 08	15 46	27 24	29 43	10 59	12 27	18 16
23 Sa	8 7 6	2 23 49	19 22	23 05	15 42	28 57	10 24	22 44	13 21	16 54	8 10	15 48	27 47	0 ♓ 05	11 10	12 47	18 17
24 Su	8 11 3	3 24 50	2 ♌ 32	22 56	15 10	0 ♑ 11	10 55	22 41	13 27	16 55	8 12	15 50	28 10	0 26	11 22	13 07	18 19
25 M	8 14 59	4 25 51	15 26	22 47	14 58 D	1 24	11 25	22 38	13 32	16 56	8 14	15 52	28 33	0 48	11 33	13 28	18 22
26 T	8 18 56	5 26 50	28 03	22 40	14 55	2 38	11 56	22 35	13 37	16 58	8 16	15 54	28 56	1 10	11 43	13 49	18 25
27 W	8 22 52	6 27 49	10 ♍ 24	22 35	14 59	3 52	12 27	22 32	13 43	16 59	8 18	15 56	29 19	1 32	11 54	14 10	18 28
28 Th	8 26 49	7 28 47	22 31	22 32	15 11	5 06	12 57	22 30	13 48	17 01	8 20	15 58	29 42	1 54	12 04	14 31	18 31
29 F	8 30 45	8 29 44	4 ♎ 28	22 31 D	15 30	6 20	13 28	22 28	13 53	17 03	8 22	16 00	0 ♓ 05	2 16	12 14	14 52	18 34
30 Sa	8 34 42	9 30 41	16 18	22 33	15 55	7 34	13 58	22 26	13 58	17 04	8 24	16 02	0 28	2 37	12 24	15 14	18 40
31 Su	8 38 38	10 31 37	28 07	22 35	16 26	8 48	14 28	22 25	14 03	17 06	8 26	16 04	0 51	2 59	12 34	15 35	18 43

EPHEMERIS CALCULATED FOR 12 MIDNIGHT GREENWICH MEAN TIME. ALL OTHER DATA AND FACING ASPECTARIAN PAGE IN **EASTERN TIME (BOLD)** AND PACIFIC TIME (REGULAR).

FEBRUARY 2016

☽ Last Aspect / ☽ Ingress

day	ET / hr:mn / PT		asp	sign	day	ET / hr:mn / PT	
1	**7:35 pm**	4:35 pm	⚹ ♃	♐	2	**10:50 am**	7:50 am
4	**5:04 am**	2:04 am	□ ♃	♑	4	**7:44 pm**	4:44 pm
6	**10:54 am**	7:54 am	△ ♃	♒	6		9:59 pm
6	**10:54 am**	7:54 am	△ ♃	♒	7	**12:59 am**	
8	**9:39 am**	6:39 am	☌ ☉	♓	9	**3:31 am**	12:31 am
10	**11:25 pm**	8:25 pm	⚹ ☿	♈	11	**4:55 am**	1:55 am
13	**5:32 am**	2:32 am	□ ☿	♉	13	**6:36 am**	3:36 am
15	**5:54 am**	2:54 am	△ ♀	♊	15	**9:35 am**	6:35 am
17	**11:37 am**	8:37 am	△ ☉	♋	17	**2:24 pm**	11:24 am
19	**9:36 am**	6:36 am	△ ♂	♌	19	**9:17 pm**	6:17 pm
21	**8:17 pm**	5:17 pm	□ ♂	♍	22	**6:24 am**	3:24 am
24	**9:22 am**	6:22 am	⚹ ♂	♎	24	**5:41 pm**	2:41 pm
26	**6:18 am**	3:18 am	☍ ♅	♏	27	**6:26 am**	3:26 am
29	**2:55 pm**	11:55 am	☌ ♂	♐	29	**6:56 pm**	3:56 pm

☽ Phases & Eclipses

phase	day	ET / hr:mn / PT	
New Moon	8	**9:39 am**	6:39 am
2nd Quarter	14		11:46 pm
2nd Quarter	15	**2:46 am**	
Full Moon	22	**1:20 pm**	10:20 am

Planet Ingress

	day	ET / hr:mn / PT	
☿ ♒	13	**5:43 pm**	2:43 pm
♀ ♒	16	**11:17 pm**	8:17 pm
☉ ♓	18		9:34 pm
☉ ♓	19	**12:34 am**	

Planetary Motion

day	ET / hr:mn / PT

1 MONDAY
☽ ⚺ ♄ **3:25 am** 12:25 am
☽ ☌ ♂ **5:28 am** 2:28 am
☽ ⚹ ♇ **7:20 am** 4:20 am
☽ ⚻ ♅ **9:25 am** 6:25 am
☽ ⚹ ☿ **10:01 am** 7:01 am
☽ ⚹ ♃ **7:35 pm** 4:35 pm

2 TUESDAY
No Aspects.

3 WEDNESDAY
☽ □ ♆ **3:25 am** 12:25 am
♂ ⚹ ♇ **5:53 am** 2:53 am
☽ ⚺ ♀ **12:42 pm** 9:42 am
☉ ⚹ ♄ **1:17 pm** 10:17 am
☽ ☌ ♄ **2:31 pm** 11:31 am
☽ ⚹ ☉ **2:37 pm** 11:37 am
☽ ⚺ ♇ **6:00 pm** 3:00 pm
☽ ⚺ ♂ **6:28 pm** 3:28 pm
☽ △ ♅ **7:58 pm** 4:58 pm
☽ ⚺ ☿ 9:12 pm

4 THURSDAY
☽ ⚺ ☿ **12:12 am**
☽ □ ♃ **5:04 am** 2:04 am
♀ ⚺ ♄ **8:15 am** 5:15 am

5 FRIDAY
☉ ⚺ ♇ **10:12 am** 7:12 am
☽ ⚹ ♆ **11:24 am** 8:24 am
♂ ⚻ ♅ **12:31 pm** 9:31 am
♀ ☌ ♇ **8:15 pm** 5:15 pm
☽ ⚺ ♄ **9:56 pm** 6:56 pm
☽ ☌ ♇ 10:01 pm
☽ ☌ ♀ 10:29 pm
☽ ⚺ ☉ 11:10 pm
☽ □ ♅ 11:52 pm

6 SATURDAY
☽ ☌ ♇ **1:01 am**
☽ ☌ ♀ **1:29 am**
☽ ⚺ ☉ **2:10 am**
☽ □ ♅ **2:52 am**
☽ ⚹ ♂ **3:21 am** 12:21 am
☽ ☌ ☿ **10:39 am** 7:39 am
☽ △ ♃ **10:54 am** 7:54 am
☉ ⚹ ♅ **11:39 am** 8:39 am
☿ △ ♃ **1:45 pm** 10:45 am
♀ □ ♅ **5:03 pm** 2:03 pm

7 SUNDAY
☉ □ ♂ **7:08 am** 4:08 am
♀ ⚹ ♂ **10:01 am** 7:01 am
☽ ⚺ ♆ **3:52 pm** 12:52 pm
☉ ⚺ ♀ **4:59 pm** 1:59 pm
☽ ⚹ ♄ 10:58 pm

8 MONDAY
☽ ⚹ ♄ **1:58 am**
☽ ⚺ ♇ **4:44 am** 1:44 am
☽ ⚹ ♅ **6:30 am** 3:30 am
☽ □ ♂ **8:37 am** 5:37 am
☽ ☌ ☉ **9:39 am** 6:39 am
☽ ⚺ ♀ **9:56 am** 6:56 am
☽ ⚻ ♃ **1:42 pm** 10:42 am
☽ ⚺ ☿ **5:47 pm** 2:47 pm

9 TUESDAY
☽ ☌ ♆ **6:02 pm** 3:02 pm
♀ △ ♃ 11:54 pm

10 WEDNESDAY
♀ △ ♃ **2:54 am**
☽ □ ♄ **3:59 am** 12:59 am
☽ ⚹ ♇ **6:33 am** 3:33 am
☽ ⚺ ♅ **8:18 am** 5:18 am
☽ △ ♂ **11:55 am** 8:55 am
☉ ⚻ ♃ **2:28 pm** 11:28 am
☽ ☍ ♃ **2:56 pm** 11:56 am
☽ ⚺ ☉ **2:58 pm** 11:58 am
☽ ⚹ ♀ **4:07 pm** 1:07 pm
☽ ⚹ ☿ **11:25 pm** 8:25 pm

11 THURSDAY
☽ ⚺ ♆ **7:30 pm** 4:30 pm

12 FRIDAY
☽ △ ♄ **5:35 am** 2:35 am
☽ □ ♇ **8:03 am** 5:03 am
☽ ☌ ♅ **9:50 am** 6:50 am
☽ ⚻ ♂ **3:00 pm** 12:00 pm
☽ ⚻ ♃ **4:03 pm** 1:03 pm
☽ ⚹ ☉ **8:10 pm** 5:10 pm
☽ □ ♀ **10:15 pm** 7:15 pm

13 SATURDAY
☽ □ ☿ **5:32 am** 2:32 am
♂ ⚹ ♃ **5:59 pm** 2:59 pm
☽ ⚹ ♆ **9:37 pm** 6:37 pm

14 SUNDAY
☽ ⚻ ♄ **8:03 am** 5:03 am
☽ △ ♇ **10:27 am** 7:27 am
☽ ⚺ ♅ **12:20 pm** 9:20 am
☽ △ ♃ **6:13 pm** 3:13 pm
☽ ☍ ♂ **7:13 pm** 4:13 pm
☽ □ ☉ 11:46 pm

15 MONDAY
☽ □ ☉ **2:46 am**
☽ △ ♀ **5:54 am** 2:54 am
☽ △ ☿ **1:36 pm** 10:36 am
☽ □ ♆ 10:15 pm

16 TUESDAY
☽ □ ♆ **1:15 am**
☽ ☍ ♄ **12:10 pm** 9:10 am
☽ ⚻ ♇ **2:30 pm** 11:30 am
☽ ⚹ ♅ **4:31 pm** 1:31 pm
☽ □ ♃ **10:02 pm** 7:02 pm
☽ ⚻ ♂ 10:18 pm

17 WEDNESDAY
☽ ⚻ ♂ **1:18 am**
☽ △ ☉ **11:37 am** 8:37 am
☽ ⚻ ♀ **3:56 pm** 12:56 pm
☽ ⚻ ☿ 9:26 pm

18 THURSDAY
☽ ⚻ ☿ **12:26 am**
☽ △ ♆ **6:49 am** 3:49 am
☽ ⚻ ♄ **6:15 pm** 3:15 pm
☽ ☍ ♇ **8:34 pm** 5:34 pm
☽ □ ♅ **10:42 pm** 7:42 pm

19 FRIDAY
☽ ⚹ ♃ **3:48 am** 12:48 am
☽ △ ♂ **9:36 am** 6:36 am
☽ ⚻ ☉ **11:03 pm** 8:03 pm

20 SATURDAY
☽ ☍ ♀ **4:45 am** 1:45 am
☽ ☍ ☿ **2:28 pm** 11:28 am
☽ ⚻ ♆ **2:33 pm** 11:33 am
☿ ⚺ ♆ **3:13 pm** 12:13 pm
☽ △ ♄ 11:31 pm

21 SUNDAY
☽ △ ♄ **2:31 am**
☽ ⚻ ♇ **4:48 am** 1:48 am
☽ △ ♅ **7:06 am** 4:06 am
☽ ⚺ ♃ **11:41 am** 8:41 am
☽ □ ♂ **8:17 pm** 5:17 pm

22 MONDAY
☽ ☍ ☉ **1:20 pm** 10:20 am
☽ ⚻ ♀ **8:36 pm** 5:36 pm
☽ ☍ ♆ 9:32 pm

23 TUESDAY
☽ ☍ ♆ **12:32 am**
☽ ⚻ ☿ **7:57 am** 4:57 am
☽ □ ♄ **1:02 pm** 10:02 am
☽ △ ♇ **3:17 pm** 12:17 pm
☽ ⚻ ♅ **5:46 pm** 2:46 pm
☽ ☌ ♃ **9:44 pm** 6:44 pm

24 WEDNESDAY
☽ ⚹ ♂ **9:22 am** 6:22 am
♀ ⚺ ♆ **12:32 pm** 9:32 am

25 THURSDAY
☿ ⚹ ♄ **3:05 am** 12:05 am
☽ ⚻ ☉ **6:20 am** 3:20 am
☽ ⚻ ♆ **12:35 pm** 9:35 am
☽ △ ♀ **3:17 pm** 12:17 pm
☿ ⚺ ♇ **8:53 pm** 5:53 pm
☽ ⚹ ♄ 10:29 pm

26 FRIDAY
☽ ⚹ ♄ **1:29 am**
☽ □ ♇ **3:40 am** 12:40 am
☽ △ ☿ **4:38 am** 1:38 am
☽ ☍ ♅ **6:18 am** 3:18 am
☽ ⚺ ♃ **9:30 am** 6:30 am
☿ ⚹ ♅ **6:02 pm** 3:02 pm
☽ ⚺ ♂ 9:12 pm

27 SATURDAY
☽ ⚺ ♂ **12:12 am**
☿ ⚻ ♃ **3:56 pm** 12:56 pm
☽ △ ☉ 9:51 pm
☽ △ ♆ 10:40 pm

28 SUNDAY
☽ △ ☉ **12:51 am**
☽ △ ♆ **1:40 am**
☉ ☌ ♆ **10:47 am** 7:47 am
☽ □ ♀ **11:16 am** 8:16 am
☽ ⚺ ♄ **2:35 pm** 11:35 am
☽ ⚹ ♇ **4:39 pm** 1:39 pm
☽ ⚻ ♅ **7:24 pm** 4:24 pm
☽ ⚹ ♃ **9:42 pm** 6:42 pm
☽ □ ☿ 11:30 pm

29 MONDAY
☽ □ ☿ **2:30 am**
☽ ☌ ♂ **2:55 pm** 11:55 am
♀ ⚹ ♄ **8:07 pm** 5:07 pm

Eastern time in bold type
Pacific time in medium type

FEBRUARY 2016

DATE	SID.TIME	SUN	MOON	NODE	MERCURY	VENUS	MARS	JUPITER	SATURN	URANUS	NEPTUNE	PLUTO	CERES	PALLAS	JUNO	VESTA	CHIRON
1 M	8 42 35	11 ≈32 32	9 ♍ 58	22 ♏ 55 R	17 ♑ 02	10 ♑ 02	14 ♍ 58	22 ♍ 20	14 ♐ 08	17 ♈ 08	8 ♓ 28	16 ♑ 06	1 ♓ 15	3 ≈ 21	12 ♏ 43	15 ♈ 57	18 ♓ 46
2 T	8 46 31	12 33 27	21 58	22 35	17 43	11 16	15 28	22 16 R	14 12	17 10	8 30	16 08	1 38	3 42	12 52	16 18	18 49
3 W	8 50 28	13 34 21	4 ♐ 12	22 33	18 28	12 30	15 57	22 11	14 17	17 12	8 32	16 10	2 01	4 04	13 01	16 40	18 52
4 Th	8 54 25	14 35 14	16 43	22 29	19 18	13 44	16 27	22 06	14 22	17 14	8 34	16 12	2 24	4 26	13 10	17 02	18 55
5 F	8 58 21	15 36 06	29 36	22 23	20 10	14 58	16 56	22 01	14 26	17 16	8 36	16 13	2 48	4 47	13 18	17 24	18 58
6 Sa	9 2 18	16 36 57	12 ♑ 52	22 17	21 06	16 12	17 25	21 56	14 31	17 18	8 38	16 15	3 11	5 09	13 26	17 46	19 02
7 Su	9 6 14	17 37 47	26 32	22 11	22 05	17 26	17 54	21 51	14 35	17 20	8 41	16 17	3 34	5 30	13 34	18 09	19 05
8 M	9 10 11	18 38 36	10 ≈ 33	22 06	23 07	18 40	18 23	21 46	14 40	17 22	8 43	16 19	3 58	5 52	13 41	18 31	19 08
9 T	9 14 7	19 39 24	24 52	22 00	24 11	19 54	18 51	21 40	14 44	17 24	8 45	16 21	4 21	6 13	13 49	18 54	19 11
10 W	9 18 4	20 40 11	9 ♓ 22	22 00 D	25 18	21 08	19 20	21 34	14 48	17 26	8 47	16 23	4 44	6 34	13 55	19 16	19 15
11 Th	9 22 0	21 40 56	23 58	21 59	26 27	22 22	19 48	21 28	14 52	17 28	8 49	16 24	5 08	6 56	14 02	19 39	19 18
12 F	9 25 57	22 41 40	8 ♈ 34	22 00	27 37	23 36	20 16	21 22	14 56	17 31	8 52	16 26	5 31	7 17	14 08	20 02	19 21
13 Sa	9 29 54	23 42 22	23 03	22 02	28 50	24 50	20 44	21 16	15 00	17 33	8 54	16 28	5 55	7 38	14 15	20 25	19 25
14 Su	9 33 50	24 43 02	7 ♉ 23	22 03	0 ≈ 04	26 04	21 11	21 10	15 04	17 35	8 56	16 30	6 18	7 59	14 20	20 48	19 28
15 M	9 37 47	25 43 41	21 31	22 04 R	1 20	27 18	21 39	21 04	15 08	17 38	8 58	16 32	6 42	8 20	14 26	21 11	19 32
16 T	9 41 43	26 44 18	5 ♊ 26	22 04	2 37	28 33	22 06	20 57	15 12	17 40	9 00	16 33	7 05	8 41	14 31	21 34	19 35
17 W	9 45 40	27 44 53	19 07	22 02	3 56	29 47	22 33	20 50	15 15	17 43	9 03	16 35	7 29	9 03	14 36	21 57	19 39
18 Th	9 49 36	28 45 27	2 ♋ 34	22 00	5 16	1 ≈ 01	23 00	20 44	15 19	17 45	9 05	16 36	7 52	9 23	14 40	22 21	19 42
19 F	9 53 33	29 45 59	15 47	21 57	6 38	2 15	23 26	20 37	15 22	17 48	9 07	16 38	8 16	9 44	14 45	22 44	19 45
20 Sa	9 57 29	0 ♓46 29	28 46	21 53	8 01	3 29	23 53	20 30	15 26	17 50	9 09	16 40	8 40	10 05	14 49	23 08	19 49
21 Su	10 1 26	1 46 57	11 ♌ 29	21 50	9 25	4 43	24 19	20 23	15 29	17 53	9 12	16 41	9 03	10 26	14 52	23 31	19 53
22 M	10 5 23	2 47 23	24 06	21 47	10 50	5 58	24 45	20 16	15 32	17 55	9 14	16 43	9 27	10 47	14 55	23 55	19 56
23 T	10 9 19	3 47 48	6 ♍ 28	21 46	12 16	7 12	25 10	20 09	15 35	17 58	9 16	16 44	9 50	11 07	14 58	24 19	20 00
24 W	10 13 16	4 48 12	18 38	21 45 D	13 44	8 26	25 36	20 01	15 38	18 01	9 19	16 46	10 14	11 28	15 01	24 43	20 03
25 Th	10 17 12	5 48 33	0 ♎ 39	21 45	15 12	9 40	26 01	19 54	15 41	18 03	9 21	16 47	10 38	11 49	15 03	25 07	20 07
26 F	10 21 9	6 48 53	12 33	21 46	16 42	10 54	26 26	19 47	15 44	18 06	9 23	16 49	11 01	12 09	15 05	25 31	20 10
27 Sa	10 25 5	7 49 12	24 22	21 47	18 13	12 09	26 51	19 39	15 47	18 09	9 25	16 50	11 25	12 30	15 07	25 55	20 14
28 Su	10 29 2	8 49 29	6 ♏ 11	21 49	19 44	13 23	27 15	19 32	15 50	18 12	9 28	16 52	11 49	12 50	15 08	26 19	20 18
29 M	10 32 58	9 49 45	18 03	21 50	21 17	14 37	27 39	19 24	15 52	18 15	9 30	16 53	12 12	13 10	15 09	26 43	20 21

EPHEMERIS CALCULATED FOR 12 MIDNIGHT GREENWICH MEAN TIME. ALL OTHER DATA AND FACING ASPECTARIAN PAGE IN EASTERN TIME (BOLD) AND PACIFIC TIME (REGULAR).

MARCH 2016

☽ Last Aspect day	ET / hr:mn / PT	asp	☽ Ingress sign	day	ET / hr:mn / PT
2	**9:55 pm** 6:55 pm	⚹ ☿	♑	3	**5:01 am** 2:01 am
5	**11:05 am** 8:05 am	⚹ ♂	♒	5	**11:22 am** 8:22 am
7	**3:46 am** 12:46 am	☌ ♀	♓	7	**2:08 pm** 11:08 am
8	**8:54 pm** 5:54 pm	☌ ☉	♈	9	**2:40 pm** 11:40 am
11	**1:24 pm** 10:24 am	⚹ ♀	♉	11	**2:44 pm** 11:44 am
13	**5:46 am** 2:46 am	⚹ ☉	♊	13	**5:03 pm** 2:03 pm
15	**1:03 pm** 10:03 am	□ ☉	♋	15	**8:57 pm** 5:57 pm
17	9:09 pm	△ ☉	♌	18	12:54 am
18	**12:09 am**	△ ☉	♌	18	**3:54 am**
19	**4:43 pm** 1:43 pm	△ ♅	♍	20	**1:39 pm** 10:39 am
21	**11:55 pm** 8:55 pm	△ ♇	♎	22	10:23 pm
21	**11:55 pm** 8:55 pm	△ ♇	♎	23	**1:23 am**
24	**4:55 pm** 1:55 pm	☍ ♅	♏	25	**2:09 pm** 11:09 am
27	**3:25 am** 12:25 am	△ ♀	♐	27	11:46 pm
27	**3:25 am** 12:25 am	△ ♀	♐	28	**2:46 am**
29	**9:55 pm** 6:55 pm	□ ♀	♑	30	**1:45 pm** 10:45 am

☽ Phases & Eclipses phase	day	ET / hr:mn / PT
4th Quarter	1	**6:11 pm** 3:11 pm
New Moon	8	**8:54 pm** 5:54 pm
● (eclipse)	8	18° ♓ 55'
2nd Quarter	15	**1:03 pm** 10:03 am
Full Moon	23	**8:01 am** 5:01 am
● (eclipse)	23	3° ♎ 10'
4th Quarter	31	**11:17 am** 8:17 am

Planet Ingress		day	ET / hr:mn / PT
☿	♓	5	**5:23 am** 2:23 am
♂	♐	5	**9:29 pm** 6:29 pm
⚵	♉	7	**7:53 pm** 4:53 pm
♀	♓	12	**5:24 am** 2:24 am
☉	♈	19	9:30 pm
☉	♈	20	**12:30 am**
☿	♈	21	**8:19 pm** 5:19 pm

Planetary Motion		day	ET / hr:mn / PT
⚵	R	2	**5:40 am** 2:40 am
♄	R	25	**6:01 am** 3:01 am

1 TUESDAY
- ☽ □ ♆ **1:49 pm** 10:49 am
- ♀ ⚺ ♇ **3:50 pm** 12:50 pm
- ☽ □ ☉ **6:11 pm** 3:11 pm
- ☽ ☌ ♄ 11:15 pm

2 WEDNESDAY
- ☽ ☌ ♄ **2:15 am**
- ☽ ⚺ ♇ **4:09 am** 1:09 am
- ☽ ⚹ ♀ **5:29 am** 2:29 am
- ☽ △ ♅ **6:54 am** 3:54 am
- ☽ □ ♃ **8:15 am** 5:15 am
- ♀ ⚹ ♅ **8:13 pm** 5:13 pm
- ☽ ⚹ ☿ **9:55 pm** 6:55 pm

3 THURSDAY
- ☽ ⚺ ♂ **3:04 am** 12:04 am
- ♀ ⚻ ♃ **7:04 am** 4:04 am
- ☽ ⚹ ♆ **10:57 pm** 7:57 pm

4 FRIDAY
- ☽ ⚹ ☉ **7:32 am** 4:32 am
- ☽ ⚺ ♄ **10:35 am** 7:35 am
- ☽ ☌ ♇ **12:17 pm** 9:17 am
- ☽ □ ♅ **2:58 pm** 11:58 am
- ☽ △ ♃ **3:30 pm** 12:30 pm
- ☽ ⚺ ♀ **7:08 pm** 4:08 pm
- ☿ □ ♂ 9:43 pm

5 SATURDAY
- ☿ □ ♂ **12:43 am**
- ☽ ⚹ ♂ **11:05 am** 8:05 am
- ☽ ⚺ ☿ **12:11 pm** 9:11 am
- ☉ □ ♄ 10:04 pm

6 SUNDAY
- ☉ □ ♄ **1:04 am**
- ☽ ⚺ ♆ **4:12 am** 1:12 am
- ♃ ⚻ ♅ **6:45 am** 3:45 am
- ☽ ⚹ ♄ **3:01 pm** 12:01 pm
- ☽ ⚺ ☉ **4:03 pm** 1:03 pm
- ☽ ⚺ ♇ **4:34 pm** 1:34 pm
- ☽ ⚻ ♃ **7:01 pm** 4:01 pm
- ☽ ⚹ ♅ **7:11 pm** 4:11 pm
- ☉ ⚹ ♇ **11:41 pm** 8:41 pm

7 MONDAY
- ☽ ☌ ♀ **3:46 am** 12:46 am
- ☽ □ ♂ **3:11 pm** 12:11 pm
- ☽ ☌ ☿ **9:29 pm** 6:29 pm

8 TUESDAY
- ☉ ☍ ♃ **5:57 am** 2:57 am
- ☽ ☌ ♆ **6:11 am** 3:11 am
- ☉ ⚺ ♅ **2:58 pm** 11:58 am
- ☽ □ ♄ **4:29 pm** 1:29 pm
- ☽ ⚹ ♇ **5:56 pm** 2:56 pm
- ☽ ☍ ♃ **7:47 pm** 4:47 pm
- ☽ ⚺ ♅ **8:32 pm** 5:32 pm
- ☽ ☌ ☉ **8:54 pm** 5:54 pm

9 WEDNESDAY
- ☽ ⚺ ♀ **9:01 am** 6:01 am
- ☽ △ ♂ **4:51 pm** 1:51 pm

10 THURSDAY
- ☽ ⚺ ☿ **4:05 am** 1:05 am
- ☽ ⚺ ♆ **6:29 am** 3:29 am
- ☽ △ ♄ **4:36 pm** 1:36 pm
- ☽ □ ♇ **6:02 pm** 3:02 pm
- ☽ ⚻ ♃ **7:24 pm** 4:24 pm
- ☽ ☌ ♅ **8:43 pm** 5:43 pm
- ☽ ⚺ ☉ 9:22 pm
- ☿ ☌ ♆ 10:01 pm

11 FRIDAY
- ☽ ⚺ ☉ **12:22 am**
- ☿ ☌ ♆ **1:01 am**
- ☽ ⚹ ♀ **1:24 pm** 10:24 am
- ☽ ⚻ ♂ **6:04 pm** 3:04 pm

12 SATURDAY
- ☽ ⚹ ♆ **6:54 am** 3:54 am
- ☽ ⚹ ☿ **10:56 am** 7:56 am
- ☽ ⚻ ♄ **5:14 pm** 2:14 pm
- ☽ △ ♇ **6:41 pm** 3:41 pm
- ☽ △ ♃ **7:36 pm** 4:36 pm
- ☽ ⚺ ♅ **9:34 pm** 6:34 pm

13 SUNDAY
- ☽ ⚹ ☉ **5:46 am** 2:46 am
- ☽ □ ♀ **8:21 pm** 5:21 pm
- ☽ ☍ ♂ **9:42 pm** 6:42 pm

14 MONDAY
- ☽ □ ♆ **10:06 am** 7:06 am
- ☿ □ ♄ **3:26 pm** 12:26 pm
- ♀ □ ♂ **4:48 pm** 1:48 pm
- ☽ ☍ ♄ **8:54 pm** 5:54 pm
- ☽ □ ☿ **9:44 pm** 6:44 pm
- ☽ ⚻ ♇ **10:25 pm** 7:25 pm
- ☽ □ ♃ **10:51 pm** 7:51 pm
- ☽ ⚹ ♅ 10:36 pm
- ☿ ⚹ ♇ 11:58 pm

15 TUESDAY
- ☽ ⚹ ♅ **1:36 am**
- ☿ ⚹ ♇ **2:58 am**
- ☿ ☍ ♃ **5:42 am** 2:42 am
- ☽ □ ☉ **1:03 pm** 10:03 am

16 WEDNESDAY
- ☽ ⚻ ♂ **3:07 am** 12:07 am
- ☿ ⚺ ♅ **3:22 am** 12:22 am
- ☽ △ ♀ **5:44 am** 2:44 am
- ☽ △ ♆ **3:09 pm** 12:09 pm
- ♃ △ ♇ **4:06 pm** 1:06 pm
- ☽ ⚻ ♄ 11:31 pm

17 THURSDAY
- ☽ ⚻ ♄ **2:31 am**
- ☽ ⚹ ♃ **4:00 am** 1:00 am
- ☽ ☍ ♇ **4:08 am** 1:08 am
- ☽ □ ♅ **7:39 am** 4:39 am
- ☽ △ ☿ **12:17 pm** 9:17 am
- ☽ △ ☉ 9:09 pm

18 FRIDAY
- ☽ △ ☉ **12:09 am**
- ☽ △ ♂ **11:46 am** 8:46 am
- ☽ ⚻ ♀ **7:13 pm** 4:13 pm
- ☽ ⚻ ♆ **11:17 pm** 8:17 pm

19 SATURDAY
- ☽ △ ♄ **11:08 am** 8:08 am
- ☽ ⚺ ♃ **12:04 pm** 9:04 am
- ☽ ⚻ ♇ **12:51 pm** 9:51 am
- ☽ △ ♅ **4:43 pm** 1:43 pm

20 SUNDAY
- ☽ ⚻ ☿ **7:50 am** 4:50 am
- ♀ ☌ ♆ **1:45 pm** 10:45 am
- ☽ ⚻ ☉ **2:49 pm** 11:49 am
- ☽ □ ♂ **11:13 pm** 8:13 pm

21 MONDAY
- ☽ ☍ ♆ **9:59 am** 6:59 am
- ☽ ☍ ♀ **12:14 pm** 9:14 am
- ☽ □ ♄ **10:07 pm** 7:07 pm
- ☽ ☌ ♃ **10:27 pm** 7:27 pm
- ☽ △ ♇ **11:55 pm** 8:55 pm

22 TUESDAY
- ☽ ⚻ ♅ **4:07 am** 1:07 am

23 WEDNESDAY
- ♃ □ ♄ **6:15 am** 3:15 am
- ☽ ☍ ☿ **7:11 am** 4:11 am
- ☽ ☍ ☉ **8:01 am** 5:01 am
- ☽ ⚹ ♂ **12:33 pm** 9:33 am
- ☉ ☌ ☿ **4:11 pm** 1:11 pm
- ☽ ⚻ ♆ **10:22 pm** 7:22 pm

24 THURSDAY
- ☽ ⚻ ♀ **7:30 am** 4:30 am
- ☽ ⚺ ♃ **10:16 am** 7:16 am
- ☽ ⚹ ♄ **10:33 am** 7:33 am
- ☽ □ ♇ **12:26 pm** 9:26 am
- ☽ ☍ ♅ **4:55 pm** 1:55 pm
- ☿ △ ♂ **6:45 pm** 3:45 pm

25 FRIDAY
- ♀ ☍ ♃ **7:58 am** 4:58 am
- ♀ □ ♄ **12:48 pm** 9:48 am
- ☽ ⚻ ☉ 11:23 pm
- ☽ ⚺ ♂ 11:39 pm

26 SATURDAY
- ☽ ⚻ ☉ **2:23 am**
- ☽ ⚺ ♂ **2:39 am**
- ☉ △ ♂ **6:33 am** 3:33 am
- ♀ ⚹ ♇ **7:12 am** 4:12 am
- ☽ ⚻ ☿ **8:28 am** 5:28 am
- ☽ △ ♆ **11:25 am** 8:25 am
- ☽ ⚹ ♃ **10:31 pm** 7:31 pm
- ☽ ⚺ ♄ **11:24 pm** 8:24 pm
- ☽ ⚹ ♇ 10:20 pm
- ☿ ⚺ ♆ 10:55 pm

27 SUNDAY
- ☽ ⚹ ♇ **1:20 am**
- ☿ ⚺ ♆ **1:55 am**
- ☽ △ ♀ **3:25 am** 12:25 am
- ☽ ⚻ ♅ **6:02 am** 3:02 am

28 MONDAY
- ♀ ⚺ ♅ **5:34 am** 2:34 am
- ☽ ☌ ♂ **4:12 pm** 1:12 pm
- ☽ △ ☉ **8:11 pm** 5:11 pm
- ☽ □ ♆ **11:49 pm** 8:49 pm

29 TUESDAY
- ☽ △ ☿ **8:56 am** 5:56 am
- ☽ □ ♃ **9:55 am** 6:55 am
- ☽ ☌ ♄ **11:18 am** 8:18 am
- ☽ ⚺ ♇ **1:15 pm** 10:15 am
- ☿ ⚻ ♃ **2:36 pm** 11:36 am
- ☽ △ ♅ **6:02 pm** 3:02 pm
- ☽ □ ♀ **9:55 pm** 6:55 pm
- ☿ △ ♄ **11:02 pm** 8:02 pm

30 WEDNESDAY
- ☿ □ ♇ **10:53 am** 7:53 am
- ☉ ⚺ ♆ **6:08 pm** 3:08 pm

31 THURSDAY
- ☽ ⚺ ♂ **3:31 am** 12:31 am
- ☽ ⚹ ♆ **10:00 am** 7:00 am
- ☽ □ ☉ **11:17 am** 8:17 am
- ☿ ☌ ♅ **4:49 pm** 1:49 pm
- ☽ △ ♃ **6:57 pm** 3:57 pm
- ☽ ⚺ ♄ **8:41 pm** 5:41 pm
- ☽ ☌ ♇ **10:37 pm** 7:37 pm

Eastern time in bold type
Pacific time in medium type

MARCH 2016

DATE	SID.TIME	SUN	MOON	NODE	MERCURY	VENUS	MARS	JUPITER	SATURN	URANUS	NEPTUNE	PLUTO	CERES	PALLAS	JUNO	VESTA	CHIRON
1 T	10 36 55	10 ♓ 49 59	0 ♈ 02	21 ♏ 50	22 ≈ 51	15 ≈ 51	28 ♏ 03	19 ♍ 16 R	15 ♐ 55	18 ♈ 17	9 ♓ 32	16 ♑ 54	12 ♓ 36	13 ≈ 31	15 ♏ 10 R	27 ♈ 07	20 ♓ 25
2 W	10 40 52	11 50 11	12 13	21 51 R	24 26	17 05	28 26	19 09	15 57	18 20	9 34	16 56	13 00	13 51	15 10	27 32	20 28
3 Th	10 44 48	12 50 22	24 42	21 50	26 02	18 20	28 50	19 01	15 59	18 23	9 37	16 57	13 23	14 11	15 10	27 56	20 32
4 F	10 48 45	13 50 32	7 ♉ 31	21 50	27 39	19 34	29 13	18 53	16 01	18 26	9 39	16 59	13 47	14 31	15 10	28 21	20 36
5 Sa	10 52 41	14 50 40	20 44	21 49	29 17	20 48	29 35	18 45	16 03	18 29	9 41	17 00	14 11	14 51	15 09	28 45	20 39
6 Su	10 56 38	15 50 47	4 ♊ 23	21 48	0 ♓ 56	22 02	29 58	18 38	16 05	18 32	9 44	17 01	14 34	15 11	15 08	29 10	20 43
7 M	11 0 34	16 50 51	18 29	21 48	2 37	23 17	0 ♐ 20	18 30	16 07	18 35	9 46	17 02	14 58	15 31	15 07	29 34	20 47
8 T	11 4 31	17 50 54	2 ♋ 58	21 47	4 18	24 31	0 41	18 22	16 09	18 38	9 48	17 04	15 21	15 51	15 05	29 59	20 50
9 W	11 8 27	18 50 55	17 45	21 47 D	6 01	25 45	1 03	18 14	16 11	18 41	9 50	17 05	15 45	16 10	15 03	0 ♉ 24	20 54
10 Th	11 12 24	19 50 55	2 ♌ 43	21 47	7 44	26 59	1 24	18 06	16 12	18 44	9 53	17 05	16 09	16 30	15 01	0 49	20 58
11 F	11 16 21	20 50 52	17 43	21 47 R	9 29	28 14	1 44	17 58	16 14	18 48	9 55	17 07	16 32	16 49	14 58	1 14	21 01
12 Sa	11 20 17	21 50 47	2 ♍ 39	21 47	11 15	29 28	2 05	17 51	16 15	18 51	9 57	17 08	16 56	17 09	14 55	1 38	21 05
13 Su	11 24 14	22 50 40	17 21	21 47	13 02	0 ♓ 42	2 25	17 43	16 17	18 54	9 59	17 09	17 20	17 28	14 51	2 03	21 09
14 M	11 28 10	23 50 31	1 ♎ 45	21 47	14 50	1 56	2 44	17 35	16 18	18 57	10 02	17 10	17 43	17 48	14 47	2 28	21 12
15 T	11 32 7	24 50 20	15 48	21 47 D	16 40	3 11	3 03	17 27	16 19	19 00	10 04	17 11	18 07	18 07	14 43	2 54	21 16
16 W	11 36 3	25 50 06	29 28	21 47	18 30	4 25	3 22	17 20	16 20	19 03	10 06	17 12	18 30	18 26	14 38	3 19	21 20
17 Th	11 40 0	26 49 50	12 ♏ 47	21 47	20 22	5 39	3 40	17 12	16 21	19 06	10 08	17 13	18 54	18 45	14 33	3 44	21 23
18 F	11 43 56	27 49 32	25 47	21 48	22 15	6 53	3 58	17 04	16 21	19 10	10 10	17 14	19 18	19 04	14 28	4 09	21 27
19 Sa	11 47 53	28 49 12	8 ♐ 30	21 48	24 09	8 07	4 16	16 57	16 22	19 13	10 13	17 15	19 41	19 23	14 23	4 34	21 31
20 Su	11 51 49	29 48 49	20 58	21 49	26 04	9 22	4 33	16 49	16 23	19 16	10 15	17 16	20 05	19 41	14 17	5 00	21 34
21 M	11 55 46	0 ♈ 48 24	3 ♑ 14	21 50	28 01	10 36	4 49	16 42	16 23	19 20	10 17	17 17	20 28	20 00	14 10	5 25	21 38
22 T	11 59 43	1 47 57	15 20	21 50 R	29 58	11 50	5 06	16 34	16 24	19 23	10 19	17 18	20 52	20 19	14 04	5 50	21 41
23 W	12 3 39	2 47 28	27 19	21 50	1 ♈ 57	13 04	5 21	16 27	16 24	19 26	10 21	17 19	21 15	20 37	13 57	6 16	21 45
24 Th	12 7 36	3 46 57	9 ♒ 13	21 50	3 57	14 18	5 37	16 20	16 24	19 30	10 23	17 19	21 39	20 55	13 50	6 41	21 49
25 F	12 11 32	4 46 23	21 04	21 48	5 57	15 32	5 51	16 13	16 24 R	19 33	10 26	17 20	22 02	21 14	13 42	7 07	21 52
26 Sa	12 15 29	5 45 48	2 ♓ 53	21 47	7 58	16 47	6 06	16 06	16 24	19 36	10 28	17 21	22 25	21 32	13 34	7 32	21 56
27 Su	12 19 25	6 45 11	14 43	21 44	10 00	18 01	6 20	15 59	16 24	19 40	10 30	17 22	22 49	21 50	13 26	7 58	21 59
28 M	12 23 22	7 44 32	26 37	21 42	12 02	19 15	6 33	15 52	16 24	19 43	10 32	17 22	23 12	22 08	13 18	8 23	22 03
29 T	12 27 18	8 43 52	8 ♈ 37	21 40	14 05	20 29	6 46	15 45	16 24	19 46	10 34	17 23	23 36	22 26	13 09	8 49	22 07
30 W	12 31 15	9 43 09	20 50	21 38	16 08	21 43	6 58	15 39	16 23	19 50	10 36	17 23	23 59	22 44	13 00	9 14	22 10
31 Th	12 35 12	10 42 25	3 ♉ 16	21 37 D	18 10	22 57	7 10	15 32	16 23	19 53	10 38	17 24	24 22	23 01	12 50	9 40	22 14

EPHEMERIS CALCULATED FOR 12 MIDNIGHT GREENWICH MEAN TIME. ALL OTHER DATA AND FACING ASPECTARIAN PAGE IN **EASTERN TIME (BOLD)** AND PACIFIC TIME (REGULAR).

APRIL 2016

☽ Last Aspect day	ET / hr:mn / PT	asp	☽ Ingress sign	day	ET / hr:mn / PT
1	**12:39 pm** 9:39 am	⚹ ♀	♒	1	**9:37 pm** 6:37 pm
3	**7:16 pm** 4:16 pm	⚹ ☿	♓	3	10:45 pm
3	**7:16 pm** 4:16 pm	⚹ ☿	♓	4	**1:45 am**
5	**6:33 am** 3:33 am	⚹ ♇	♈	5	11:46 pm
5	**6:33 am** 3:33 am	⚹ ♇	♈	6	**2:46 am**
7	**10:56 am** 7:56 am	☌ ♅	♉	7	11:10 pm
7	**10:56 am** 7:56 am	☌ ♅	♉	8	**2:10 am**
9	**5:49 am** 2:49 am	△ ♇	♊	9	10:59 pm
9	**5:49 am** 2:49 am	△ ♇	♊	10	**1:59 am**
11	**2:57 pm** 11:57 am	⚹ ☉	♋	12	**4:07 am** 1:07 am
13	**11:59 pm** 8:59 pm	□ ☉	♌	14	**9:53 am** 6:53 am
16	**1:48 pm** 10:48 am	△ ☉	♍	16	**7:23 pm** 4:23 pm
18	**8:29 am** 5:29 am	△ ☿	♎	19	**7:24 am** 4:24 am
20	11:13 am	☍ ♅	♏	21	**8:17 pm** 5:17 pm
21	**2:13 am**	☍ ♅	♏	21	**8:17 pm** 5:17 pm
23	**5:46 pm** 2:46 pm	☍ ☿	♐	24	**8:46 am** 5:46 am
26	**11:51 am** 8:51 am	△ ♀	♑	26	**7:54 pm** 4:54 pm
29	**3:07 am** 12:07 am	□ ♀	♒	29	**4:47 am** 1:47 am
30	**10:56 pm** 7:56 pm	□ ☿	♓	5/1	**10:33 am** 7:33 am

☽ Phases & Eclipses phase	day	ET / hr:mn / PT
New Moon	7	**7:24 am** 4:24 am
2nd Quarter	13	**11:59 pm** 8:59 pm
Full Moon	21	10:24 pm
Full Moon	22	**1:24 am**
4th Quarter	29	**11:29 pm** 8:29 pm

Planet Ingress		day	ET / hr:mn / PT
♀	♈	5	**12:50 pm** 9:50 am
☿	♉	5	**7:09 pm** 4:09 pm
⚳	♈	14	**10:52 am** 7:52 am
☉	♉	19	**11:29 am** 8:29 am
♀	♓	26	**3:54 am** 12:54 am
♀	♉	29	**8:36 pm** 5:36 pm

Planetary Motion	day	ET / hr:mn / PT
♂ ℞	17	**8:14 am** 5:14 am
♇ ℞	18	**3:26 am** 12:26 am
☿ ℞	28	**1:20 pm** 10:20 am

1 FRIDAY
☽ □ ♅ **3:20 am** 12:20 am
☽ □ ☿ **5:13 am** 2:13 am
☽ ⚹ ♀ **12:39 pm** 9:39 am

2 SATURDAY
☽ ⚹ ♂ **11:14 am** 8:14 am
☽ ⚺ ♆ **4:41 pm** 1:41 pm
☽ ⚹ ☉ **9:58 pm** 6:58 pm
☽ ⚻ ♃ 9:30 pm
☽ ⚹ ♄ 11:28 pm

3 SUNDAY
☽ ⚻ ♃ **12:30 am**
☽ ⚹ ♄ **2:28 am**
☽ ⚺ ♇ **4:21 am** 1:21 am
☽ ⚹ ♅ **8:56 am** 5:56 am
☽ ⚹ ☿ **7:16 pm** 4:16 pm
☽ ⚺ ♀ **10:26 pm** 7:26 pm

4 MONDAY
☉ ⚻ ♃ **6:19 am** 3:19 am
☽ □ ♂ **3:01 pm** 12:01 pm
☽ ☌ ♆ **7:42 pm** 4:42 pm
☽ ☍ ♃ 11:34 pm

5 TUESDAY
☽ ☍ ♃ **2:34 am**
☽ ⚺ ☉ **4:09 am** 1:09 am
☽ □ ♄ **4:42 am** 1:42 am
☽ ⚹ ♇ **6:33 am** 3:33 am

☽ ⚺ ♅ **11:02 am** 8:02 am
☉ △ ♄ **12:09 pm** 9:09 am

6 WEDNESDAY
☽ ⚺ ☿ **3:51 am** 12:51 am
☽ ☌ ♀ **4:00 am** 1:00 am
☿ ⚺ ♀ **7:14 am** 4:14 am
☽ △ ♂ **3:51 pm** 12:51 pm
☉ □ ♇ **4:13 pm** 1:13 pm
☽ ⚺ ♆ **8:01 pm** 5:01 pm
☽ ⚻ ♃ 11:14 pm

7 THURSDAY
☽ ⚻ ♃ **2:14 am**
☽ △ ♄ **4:33 am** 1:33 am
☽ □ ♇ **6:25 am** 3:25 am
☽ ☌ ☉ **7:24 am** 4:24 am
☽ ☌ ♅ **10:56 am** 7:56 am

8 FRIDAY
☽ ⚺ ♀ **7:35 am** 4:35 am
☽ ☌ ☿ **9:41 am** 6:41 am
☽ ⚻ ♂ **3:31 pm** 12:31 pm
☽ ⚹ ♆ **7:26 pm** 4:26 pm
☽ △ ♃ 10:18 pm

9 SATURDAY
☽ △ ♃ **1:18 am**
☽ ⚻ ♄ **3:51 am** 12:51 am
☽ △ ♇ **5:49 am** 2:49 am
☽ ⚺ ☉ **10:07 am** 7:07 am
☽ ⚺ ♅ **10:34 am** 7:34 am
☉ ☌ ♅ **5:27 pm** 2:27 pm

10 SUNDAY
☽ ⚹ ♀ **11:59 am** 8:59 am
☽ ⚺ ☿ **4:01 pm** 1:01 pm
☽ ☍ ♂ **4:06 pm** 1:06 pm
☿ ⚻ ♂ **4:46 pm** 1:46 pm
☽ □ ♆ **7:59 pm** 4:59 pm
☽ □ ♃ 10:44 pm

11 MONDAY
☽ □ ♃ **1:44 am**
☽ ☍ ♄ **4:36 am** 1:36 am
☽ ⚻ ♇ **6:47 am** 3:47 am
☽ ⚹ ♅ **11:58 am** 8:58 am
☽ ⚹ ☉ **2:57 pm** 11:57 am

12 TUESDAY
☿ ⚹ ♆ **5:40 am** 2:40 am
♀ △ ♂ **3:16 pm** 12:16 pm
☽ ⚻ ♂ **7:26 pm** 4:26 pm
☽ □ ♀ **7:50 pm** 4:50 pm
☽ △ ♆ **11:28 pm** 8:28 pm
☽ ⚹ ☿ 10:35 pm

13 WEDNESDAY
☽ ⚹ ☿ **1:35 am**
☽ ⚹ ♃ **5:13 am** 2:13 am
☽ ⚻ ♄ **8:29 am** 5:29 am
☽ ☍ ♇ **10:58 am** 7:58 am
☽ □ ♅ **4:45 pm** 1:45 pm
☽ □ ☉ **11:59 pm** 8:59 pm

14 THURSDAY
☿ △ ♃ **11:27 am** 8:27 am

♀ ⚺ ♆ **12:36 pm** 9:36 am
☽ △ ♂ 11:32 pm

15 FRIDAY
☽ △ ♂ **2:32 am**
☽ ⚻ ♆ **6:48 am** 3:48 am
☽ △ ♀ **8:44 am** 5:44 am
☽ ⚺ ♃ **12:31 pm** 9:31 am
☽ □ ☿ **3:30 pm** 12:30 pm
☽ △ ♄ **4:12 pm** 1:12 pm
☽ ⚻ ♇ **6:59 pm** 3:59 pm
☿ ⚻ ♄ **10:28 pm** 7:28 pm
☽ △ ♅ 10:26 pm

16 SATURDAY
☽ △ ♅ **1:26 am**
☽ △ ☉ **1:48 pm** 10:48 am
♀ ⚻ ♃ **9:26 pm** 6:26 pm

17 SUNDAY
☿ △ ♇ **5:23 am** 2:23 am
☽ □ ♂ **1:00 pm** 10:00 am
☽ ☍ ♆ **5:34 pm** 2:34 pm
☽ ☌ ♃ **11:04 pm** 8:04 pm
☽ ⚻ ♀ 11:10 pm

18 MONDAY
☽ ⚻ ♀ **2:10 am**
☽ □ ♄ **3:04 am** 12:04 am
☽ △ ♇ **6:10 am** 3:10 am
☽ △ ☿ **8:29 am** 5:29 am
♀ △ ♄ **10:37 am** 7:37 am
☽ ⚻ ♅ **1:08 pm** 10:08 am

19 TUESDAY
☽ ⚻ ☉ **7:02 am** 4:02 am
♀ □ ♇ **4:51 pm** 1:51 pm
☽ ⚹ ♂ 10:21 pm

20 WEDNESDAY
☽ ⚹ ♂ **1:21 am**
☽ ⚻ ♆ **6:14 am** 3:14 am
☽ ⚺ ♃ **11:23 am** 8:23 am
☽ ⚹ ♄ **3:32 pm** 12:32 pm
☽ □ ♇ **6:52 pm** 3:52 pm
☽ ☍ ♀ **9:54 pm** 6:54 pm
☽ ⚻ ☿ 10:55 pm
☽ ☍ ♅ 11:13 pm

21 THURSDAY
☽ ⚻ ☿ **1:55 am**
☽ ☍ ♅ **2:13 am**
☿ ⚺ ♅ **7:27 am** 4:27 am
☽ ☍ ☉ 10:24 pm

22 FRIDAY
☽ ☍ ☉ **1:24 am**
☽ ⚺ ♂ **1:59 pm** 10:59 am
♀ ☌ ♅ **5:00 pm** 2:00 pm
☽ △ ♆ **7:14 pm** 4:14 pm
☽ ⚹ ♃ **11:57 pm** 8:57 pm

23 SATURDAY
☽ ⚺ ♄ **4:08 am** 1:08 am
☽ ⚹ ♇ **7:38 am** 4:38 am
☽ ⚻ ♅ **3:13 pm** 12:13 pm
☽ ⚻ ♀ **5:39 pm** 2:39 pm

☽ ☍ ☿ **5:46 pm** 2:46 pm
☿ ⚺ ♀ **7:18 pm** 4:18 pm

24 SUNDAY
☽ ⚻ ☉ **7:06 pm** 4:06 pm
☽ ☌ ♂ 10:46 pm

25 MONDAY
☽ ☌ ♂ **1:46 am**
☽ □ ♆ **7:26 am** 4:26 am
☽ □ ♃ **11:42 am** 8:42 am
☽ ☌ ♄ **3:47 pm** 12:47 pm
☽ ⚺ ♇ **7:26 pm** 4:26 pm

26 TUESDAY
☽ △ ♅ **3:06 am** 12:06 am
☽ ⚻ ☿ **6:59 am** 3:59 am
☽ △ ♀ **11:51 am** 8:51 am

27 WEDNESDAY
☽ △ ☉ **10:53 am** 7:53 am
☽ ⚺ ♂ **11:50 am** 8:50 am
☽ ⚹ ♆ **5:56 pm** 2:56 pm
☉ ⚻ ♂ **9:42 pm** 6:42 pm
☽ △ ♃ **9:45 pm** 6:45 pm
☽ ⚺ ♄ 10:38 pm

28 THURSDAY
☽ ⚺ ♄ **1:38 am**
☽ ☌ ♇ **5:21 am** 2:21 am
☽ □ ♅ **12:59 pm** 9:59 am
☽ △ ☿ **4:53 pm** 1:53 pm

29 FRIDAY
☽ □ ♀ **3:07 am** 12:07 am
☽ ⚹ ♂ **7:19 pm** 4:19 pm
☽ □ ☉ **11:29 pm** 8:29 pm
☽ ⚺ ♆ 10:48 pm

30 SATURDAY
☽ ⚺ ♆ **1:48 am**
☽ ⚻ ♃ **5:11 am** 2:11 am
☽ ⚹ ♄ **8:46 am** 5:46 am
☽ ⚺ ♇ **12:28 pm** 9:28 am
☽ ⚹ ♅ **7:55 pm** 4:55 pm
☽ □ ☿ **10:56 pm** 7:56 pm

Eastern time in bold type
Pacific time in medium type

APRIL 2016

DATE	SID.TIME	SUN	MOON	NODE	MERCURY	VENUS	MARS	JUPITER	SATURN	URANUS	NEPTUNE	PLUTO	CERES	PALLAS	JUNO	VESTA	CHIRON
1 F	12 39 8	11 ♈ 41 39	16 ♑ 00	21 ♍ 37	20 ♈ 12	26 ♓ 40	7 ♐ 21	15 ♍ 26	16 ♐ 22	19 ♈ 57	10 ♓ 40	17 ♑ 25	24 ♓ 46	23 ≈ 19	12 ♏ 41	10 ♉ 06	22 ♓ 17
2 Sa	12 43 5	12 40 51	29 06	21 37	22 14	27 54	7 31	15 19 R	16 21 R	20 00	10 42	17 25	25 09	23 36	12 31 R	10 31	22 21
3 Su	12 47 1	13 40 01	12 ≈ 37	21 39	24 14	29 08	7 41	15 13	16 21	20 03	10 44	17 26	25 32	23 53	12 20	10 57	22 24
4 M	12 50 58	14 39 10	26 35	21 40	26 12	0 ♈ 22	7 51	15 07	16 19	20 07	10 46	17 26	25 55	24 11	12 10	11 23	22 27
5 T	12 54 54	15 38 16	10 ♓ 59	21 41 R	28 09	1 36	8 00	15 01	16 18	20 10	10 48	17 26	26 19	24 28	11 59	11 49	22 31
6 W	12 58 51	16 37 21	25 48	21 40	0 ♉ 04	2 50	8 08	14 55	16 18	20 14	10 50	17 27	26 42	24 45	11 48	12 15	22 34
7 Th	13 2 47	17 36 24	10 ♈ 51	21 40	1 56	4 04	8 15	14 50	16 16	20 17	10 52	17 27	27 05	25 02	11 37	12 40	22 38
8 F	13 6 44	18 35 25	26 05	21 38	3 45	5 18	8 22	14 44	16 15	20 21	10 54	17 27	27 28	25 18	11 25	13 06	22 41
9 Sa	13 10 40	19 34 24	11 ♉ 17	21 35	5 31	6 33	8 28	14 39	16 14	20 24	10 56	17 28	27 51	25 35	11 14	13 32	22 44
10 Su	13 14 37	20 33 21	26 18	21 31	7 13	7 47	8 34	14 34	16 12	20 27	10 57	17 28	28 14	25 51	11 02	13 58	22 48
11 M	13 18 34	21 32 16	11 ♊ 00	21 27	8 51	9 01	8 39	14 29	16 11	20 31	10 59	17 28	28 37	26 08	10 50	14 24	22 51
12 T	13 22 30	22 31 08	25 17	21 23	10 25	10 15	8 43	14 24	16 09	20 34	11 01	17 29	29 00	26 24	10 37	14 50	22 54
13 W	13 26 27	23 29 58	9 ♋ 06	21 21	11 55	11 29	8 47	14 19	16 07	20 38	11 03	17 29	29 23	26 40	10 25	15 16	22 58
14 Th	13 30 23	24 28 46	22 28	21 D 20	13 19	12 43	8 50	14 14	16 06	20 41	11 05	17 29	29 46	26 56	10 12	15 42	23 01
15 F	13 34 20	25 27 32	5 ♌ 25	21 20	14 39	13 57	8 52	14 10	16 04	20 44	11 06	17 29	0 ♈ 09	27 12	9 59	16 08	23 04
16 Sa	13 38 16	26 26 15	18 00	21 22	15 54	15 11	8 53	14 06	16 02	20 48	11 08	17 29	0 32	27 27	9 47	16 34	23 07
17 Su	13 42 13	27 24 56	0 ♍ 19	21 23	17 03	16 25	8 54 R	14 01	15 59	20 51	11 10	17 29	0 54	27 43	9 33	17 00	23 11
18 M	13 46 9	28 23 35	12 25	21 25 R	18 07	17 39	8 54	13 58	15 57	20 55	11 12	17 29 R	1 17	27 58	9 20	17 26	23 14
19 T	13 50 6	29 22 11	24 22	21 24	19 06	18 53	8 53	13 55	15 55	20 58	11 13	17 29	1 40	28 13	9 07	17 52	23 17
20 W	13 54 3	0 ♉ 20 46	6 ♎ 13	21 24	19 59	20 07	8 52	13 50	15 53	21 02	11 15	17 29	2 02	28 28	8 54	18 19	23 20
21 Th	13 57 59	1 19 18	18 02	21 21	20 46	21 21	8 50	13 47	15 50	21 05	11 17	17 29	2 25	28 43	8 40	18 45	23 23
22 F	14 1 56	2 17 49	29 51	21 16	21 27	22 35	8 47	13 43	15 48	21 08	11 18	17 29	2 47	28 58	8 27	19 11	23 26
23 Sa	14 5 52	3 16 18	11 ♏ 43	21 09	22 03	23 49	8 43	13 40	15 45	21 12	11 20	17 29	3 10	29 13	8 13	19 37	23 29
24 Su	14 9 49	4 14 45	23 37	21 01	22 33	25 02	8 38	13 37	15 42	21 15	11 21	17 29	3 32	29 27	7 59	20 03	23 32
25 M	14 13 45	5 13 10	5 ♐ 41	20 53	22 57	26 16	8 33	13 35	15 40	21 19	11 23	17 28	3 55	29 41	7 46	20 29	23 35
26 T	14 17 42	6 11 33	17 46	20 45	23 15	27 30	8 27	13 32	15 37	21 22	11 24	17 28	4 17	29 55	7 32	20 55	23 38
27 W	14 21 38	7 09 55	0 ♑ 03	20 38	23 28	28 44	8 20	13 30	15 34	21 25	11 26	17 28	4 40	0 ♓ 09	7 18	21 21	23 41
28 Th	14 25 35	8 08 15	12 32	20 33	23 35 R	29 58	8 13	13 28	15 31	21 29	11 27	17 28	5 02	0 23	7 04	21 48	23 43
29 F	14 29 32	9 06 34	25 16	20 30	23 36	1 ♉ 12	8 05	13 26	15 28	21 32	11 29	17 27	5 24	0 37	6 51	22 14	23 46
30 Sa	14 33 28	10 04 51	8 ≈ 18	20 29 D	23 32	2 26	7 56	13 24	15 25	21 35	11 30	17 27	5 46	0 50	6 37	22 40	23 49

EPHEMERIS CALCULATED FOR 12 MIDNIGHT GREENWICH MEAN TIME. ALL OTHER DATA AND FACING ASPECTARIAN PAGE IN **EASTERN TIME (BOLD)** AND PACIFIC TIME (REGULAR).

MAY 2016

☽ Last Aspect day	ET / hr:mn / PT		asp	☽ Ingress sign	day	ET / hr:mn / PT	
4/30	**10:56 pm**	7:56 pm	□ ☿	♓	1	**10:33 am**	7:33 am
2		10:08 pm	✶ ☿	♈	3	**1:04 pm**	10:04 am
3	**1:08 am**		✶ ☿	♈	3	**1:04 pm**	10:04 am
4		9:17 pm	☌ ♅	♉	5	**1:10 pm**	10:10 am
5	**12:17 am**		☌ ♅	♉	5	**1:10 pm**	10:10 am
6	**10:10 pm**	7:10 am	☌ ☿	♊	7	**12:35 pm**	9:35 am
8		9:15 pm	✶ ♅	♋	9	**1:24 pm**	10:24 am
9	**12:15 am**		✶ ♅	♋	9	**1:24 pm**	10:24 am
11	**3:34 am**	12:34 am	□ ♅	♌	11	**5:32 pm**	2:32 pm
13	**1:02 pm**	10:02 am	□ ☉	♍	13		10:52 pm

☽ Last Aspect day	ET / hr:mn / PT		asp	☽ Ingress sign	day	ET / hr:mn / PT	
13	**1:02 pm**	10:02 am	□ ☉	♍	14	**1:52 am**	
16	**5:20 am**	2:20 am	△ ☉	♎	16	**1:33 pm**	10:33 am
18	**11:23 am**	8:23 am	☍ ♅	♏	18		11:29 pm
18	**11:23 am**	8:23 am	☍ ♅	♏	19	**2:29 am**	
21	**7:40 am**	4:40 am	☍ ♀	♐	21	**2:48 pm**	11:48 am
23	**11:37 am**	8:37 am	△ ♅	♑	23		10:34 pm
23	**11:37 am**	8:37 am	△ ♅	♑	24	**1:34 am**	
25	**9:11 pm**	6:11 pm	□ ♅	♒	26	**10:27 am**	7:27 am
28	**4:19 pm**	1:19 pm	□ ♂	♓	28	**5:06 pm**	2:06 pm
30	**7:10 pm**	4:10 pm	△ ♂	♈	30	**9:09 pm**	6:09 pm

☽ Phases & Eclipses

phase	day	ET / hr:mn / PT	
New Moon	6	**3:30 pm**	12:30 pm
2nd Quarter	13	**1:02 pm**	10:02 am
Full Moon	21	**5:14 pm**	2:14 pm
4th Quarter	29	**8:12 am**	5:12 am

Planet Ingress

	day	ET / hr:mn / PT	
⚵ ♊	16	**2:29 pm**	11:29 am
☉ ♊	20	**10:36 am**	7:36 am
♀ ♊	24	**5:45 am**	2:45 am
♂ ♏	27	**9:51 am**	6:51 am

Planetary Motion

	day	ET / hr:mn / PT	
♃ D	9	**8:14 am**	5:14 am
☿ D	22	**9:20 am**	6:20 am

1 SUNDAY
☉ ✶ ♆ **8:00 am** 5:00 am
☽ ✶ ♀ **2:16 pm** 11:16 am
☽ □ ♂ **11:35 pm** 8:35 pm

2 MONDAY
☽ ☌ ♆ **6:23 am** 3:23 am
☽ ✶ ☉ **7:59 am** 4:59 am
☽ ☍ ♃ **9:23 am** 6:23 am
☽ □ ♄ **12:38 pm** 9:38 am
☽ ✶ ♇ **4:17 pm** 1:17 pm
☽ ⚺ ♅ **11:29 pm** 8:29 pm
☽ ✶ ☿ 10:08 pm

3 TUESDAY
☽ ✶ ☿ **1:08 am**
☉ △ ♃ **3:58 am** 12:58 am
☽ ⚺ ♀ **9:09 pm** 6:09 pm
☽ △ ♂ 9:43 pm

4 WEDNESDAY
☽ △ ♂ **12:43 am**
☽ ⚺ ♆ **7:53 am** 4:53 am
☽ ⚻ ♃ **10:35 am** 7:35 am
☽ ⚺ ☉ **12:45 pm** 9:45 am
☽ △ ♄ **1:34 pm** 10:34 am
☽ □ ♇ **5:12 pm** 2:12 pm
☽ ☌ ♅ 9:17 pm
☽ ⚺ ☿ 9:22 pm
☉ ⚻ ♄ 9:39 pm
☿ ⚺ ♅ 11:31 pm

5 THURSDAY
☽ ☌ ♅ **12:17 am**
☽ ⚺ ☿ **12:22 am**
☉ ⚻ ♄ **12:39 am**
☿ ⚺ ♅ **2:31 am**
♀ ⚻ ♂ **10:11 am** 7:11 am
☽ ⚻ ♂ **11:47 pm** 8:47 pm
☽ ☌ ♀ 10:12 pm

6 FRIDAY
☽ ☌ ♀ **1:12 am**
☽ ✶ ♆ **7:32 am** 4:32 am
☽ △ ♃ **10:06 am** 7:06 am
☽ ⚻ ♄ **12:53 pm** 9:53 am
☽ ☌ ☉ **3:30 pm** 12:30 pm
☽ △ ♇ **4:37 pm** 1:37 pm
☽ ☌ ☿ **10:10 pm** 7:10 pm
☽ ⚺ ♅ **11:51 pm** 8:51 pm

7 SATURDAY
☉ △ ♇ **9:03 am** 6:03 am
☽ ☍ ♂ **10:34 pm** 7:34 pm

8 SUNDAY
☽ ⚺ ♀ **5:03 am** 2:03 am
☽ □ ♆ **7:18 am** 4:18 am
☽ □ ♃ **9:51 am** 6:51 am
☽ ☍ ♄ **12:32 pm** 9:32 am
☽ ⚻ ♇ **4:33 pm** 1:33 pm
☽ ⚺ ☉ **6:48 pm** 3:48 pm
☽ ⚺ ☿ **8:29 pm** 5:29 pm
☽ ✶ ♅ 9:15 pm

9 MONDAY
☽ ✶ ♅ **12:15 am**
♀ ✶ ♆ **8:41 am** 5:41 am
☉ ☌ ☿ **11:12 am** 8:12 am
☽ ⚻ ♂ **11:02 pm** 8:02 pm

10 TUESDAY
☽ △ ♆ **9:18 am** 6:18 am
☽ ✶ ♀ **11:39 am** 8:39 am
☽ ✶ ♃ **11:56 am** 8:56 am
☽ ⚻ ♄ **2:34 pm** 11:34 am
♀ △ ♃ **3:00 pm** 12:00 pm
☽ ☍ ♇ **7:04 pm** 4:04 pm
☽ ✶ ☿ **9:10 pm** 6:10 pm
☽ ✶ ☉ 10:23 pm

11 WEDNESDAY
☽ ✶ ☉ **1:23 am**
☽ □ ♅ **3:34 am** 12:34 am
♀ ⚻ ♄ **7:08 pm** 4:08 pm
☽ △ ♂ 11:50 pm

12 THURSDAY
☽ △ ♂ **2:50 am**
☉ ⚺ ♅ **9:44 am** 6:44 am
☽ ⚻ ♆ **3:07 pm** 12:07 pm
☽ ⚺ ♃ **5:57 pm** 2:57 pm
☽ △ ♄ **8:29 pm** 5:29 pm
☿ △ ♇ **10:45 pm** 7:45 pm
☽ □ ♀ **11:20 pm** 8:20 pm
☽ □ ☿ 10:28 pm
☽ ⚻ ♇ 10:35 pm

13 FRIDAY
☽ □ ☿ **1:28 am**
☽ ⚻ ♇ **1:35 am**
☽ △ ♅ **11:02 am** 8:02 am
☽ □ ☉ **1:02 pm** 10:02 am
☿ ☌ ♀ **3:10 pm** 12:10 pm
♀ △ ♇ **10:20 pm** 7:20 pm

14 SATURDAY
☽ □ ♂ **10:28 am** 7:28 am
☽ ☍ ♆ 10:02 pm

15 SUNDAY
☽ ☍ ♆ **1:02 am**
☽ ☌ ♃ **4:02 am** 1:02 am
☽ □ ♄ **6:21 am** 3:21 am
☽ △ ☿ **9:31 am** 6:31 am
☽ △ ♇ **12:00 pm** 9:00 am
☽ △ ♀ **4:21 pm** 1:21 pm
☽ ⚻ ♅ **10:17 pm** 7:17 pm

16 MONDAY
☽ △ ☉ **5:20 am** 2:20 am
☽ ✶ ♂ **8:54 pm** 5:54 pm

17 TUESDAY
☽ ⚻ ♆ **1:34 pm** 10:34 am
☽ ⚺ ♃ **4:40 pm** 1:40 pm
☽ ✶ ♄ **6:34 pm** 3:34 pm
☽ ⚻ ☿ **8:11 pm** 5:11 pm
☽ □ ♇ 9:37 pm

18 WEDNESDAY
☽ □ ♇ **12:37 am**
♀ ⚺ ♅ **4:14 am** 1:14 am
☽ ☍ ♅ **11:23 am** 8:23 am
☽ ⚻ ♀ **12:11 pm** 9:11 am
☽ ⚻ ☉ **11:39 pm** 8:39 pm

19 THURSDAY
☽ ⚺ ♂ **8:11 am** 5:11 am
☽ △ ♆ 11:31 pm

20 FRIDAY
☽ △ ♆ **2:31 am**
☽ ✶ ♃ **5:39 am** 2:39 am
☽ ⚺ ♄ **7:03 am** 4:03 am
☽ ☍ ☿ **7:48 am** 4:48 am
☽ ✶ ♇ **1:18 pm** 10:18 am
☽ ⚻ ♅ 9:13 pm

21 SATURDAY
☽ ⚻ ♅ **12:13 am**
☽ ☍ ♀ **7:40 am** 4:40 am
☽ ☍ ☉ **5:14 pm** 2:14 pm
☽ ☌ ♂ **6:43 pm** 3:43 pm

22 SUNDAY
☉ ☍ ♂ **7:17 am** 4:17 am
☽ □ ♆ **2:20 pm** 11:20 am
☽ □ ♃ **5:31 pm** 2:31 pm
☽ ☌ ♄ **6:20 pm** 3:20 pm
☽ ⚻ ☿ **7:07 pm** 4:07 pm
☽ ⚺ ♇ 9:42 pm

23 MONDAY
☽ ⚺ ♇ **12:42 am**
☽ △ ♅ **11:37 am** 8:37 am
☽ ⚻ ♀ 10:06 pm

24 TUESDAY
☽ ⚻ ♀ **1:06 am**
☽ ⚺ ♂ **3:46 am** 12:46 am
☽ ⚻ ☉ **8:50 am** 5:50 am
♀ ☍ ♂ **10:38 pm** 7:38 pm
☽ ✶ ♆ 9:26 pm

25 WEDNESDAY
☽ ✶ ♆ **12:26 am**
☽ △ ♃ **3:39 am** 12:39 am
☽ ⚺ ♄ **3:56 am** 12:56 am
☽ △ ☿ **5:35 am** 2:35 am
☽ ☌ ♇ **10:21 am** 7:21 am
☽ □ ♅ **9:11 pm** 6:11 pm

26 THURSDAY
♃ □ ♄ **8:28 am** 5:28 am
☽ ✶ ♂ **11:04 am** 8:04 am
☽ △ ♀ **3:59 pm** 12:59 pm
☽ △ ☉ **9:58 pm** 6:58 pm

27 FRIDAY
☽ ⚺ ♆ **8:31 am** 5:31 am
☽ ✶ ♄ **11:32 am** 8:32 am
☽ ⚻ ♃ **11:48 am** 8:48 am
☽ □ ☿ **2:44 pm** 11:44 am
☽ ⚺ ♇ **5:56 pm** 2:56 pm

28 SATURDAY
☽ ✶ ♅ **4:36 am** 1:36 am
☽ □ ♂ **4:19 pm** 1:19 pm

29 SUNDAY
☽ □ ♀ **3:48 am** 12:48 am
☽ □ ☉ **8:12 am** 5:12 am
☽ ☌ ♆ **2:12 pm** 11:12 am
☽ □ ♄ **4:45 pm** 1:45 pm
☽ ☍ ♃ **5:30 pm** 2:30 pm
☽ ✶ ☿ **9:58 pm** 6:58 pm
☽ ✶ ♇ **11:04 pm** 8:04 pm

30 MONDAY
☽ ⚺ ♅ **9:26 am** 6:26 am
☽ △ ♂ **7:10 pm** 4:10 pm
☿ △ ♇ **11:09 pm** 8:09 pm

31 TUESDAY
☽ ✶ ♀ **12:09 pm** 9:09 am
☽ ✶ ☉ **3:10 pm** 12:10 pm
☽ ⚺ ♆ **5:15 pm** 2:15 pm
☽ △ ♄ **7:23 pm** 4:23 pm
☽ ⚻ ♃ **8:35 pm** 5:35 pm
☽ □ ♇ 10:35 pm
☽ ⚺ ☿ 11:53 pm

Eastern time in bold type
Pacific time in medium type

MAY 2016

DATE	SID.TIME	SUN	MOON	NODE	MERCURY	VENUS	MARS	JUPITER	SATURN	URANUS	NEPTUNE	PLUTO	CERES	PALLAS	JUNO	VESTA	CHIRON
1 Su	14 37 25	11 ♉ 03 06	21 ≈ 41	20 ♍ 30	23 ♉ 08 ℞	1 ♉ 02	7 ♐ 46 ℞	13 ♍ 22	15 ♐ 21 ℞	21 ♈ 38	11 ♓ 32	17 ♑ 27 ℞	6 ♉ 08	1 ♈ 03	6 ♏ 23	23 ♉ 06	23 ♓ 52
2 M	14 41 21	12 01 20	5 ♓ 33	20 31	22 50	2 26	7 35	13 21 ℞	15 18	21 42	11 33	17 26	6 30	1 17	6 10 ℞	23 32	23 54
3 T	14 45 18	12 59 33	19 40	20 31 ℞	22 27	3 40	7 24	13 19	15 15	21 45	11 34	17 26	6 52	1 30	5 56	23 59	23 57
4 W	14 49 14	13 57 44	4 ♈ 15	20 30	22 00	4 54	7 12	13 17	15 11	21 48	11 36	17 25	7 14	1 42	5 43	24 25	24 00
5 Th	14 53 11	14 55 53	19 11	20 28	21 30	6 08	6 59	13 16	15 08	21 52	11 37	17 25	7 36	1 55	5 29	24 51	24 02
6 F	14 57 7	15 54 01	4 ♉ 20	20 22	20 58	7 22	6 46	13 16	15 04	21 55	11 38	17 25	7 58	2 07	5 16	25 17	24 05
7 Sa	15 1 4	16 52 08	19 33	20 15	20 24	8 35	6 32	13 16	15 01	21 58	11 39	17 24	8 20	2 19	5 03	25 44	24 07
8 Su	15 5 1	17 50 13	4 ♊ 39	20 07	20 04	9 49	6 17	13 16	14 57	22 01	11 40	17 23	8 42	2 31	4 50	26 10	24 10
9 M	15 8 57	18 48 16	19 29	19 58	19 48	11 03	6 01	13 15 D	14 53	22 04	11 42	17 23	9 03	2 43	4 37	26 36	24 12
10 T	15 12 54	19 46 17	3 ♋ 56	19 50	19 12	12 17	5 45	13 15	14 50	22 07	11 43	17 22	9 25	2 55	4 25	27 02	24 15
11 W	15 16 50	20 44 17	17 ♋ 41	19 44	18 35	13 31	5 29	13 16	14 46	22 11	11 44	17 22	9 46	3 06	4 12	27 29	24 17
12 Th	15 20 47	21 42 14	1 ♌ 22	19 40	17 59	14 45	5 12	13 16	14 42	22 14	11 45	17 21	10 08	3 17	4 00	27 55	24 19
13 F	15 24 43	22 40 10	14 22	19 38 D	17 24	15 59	4 54	13 16	14 38	22 17	11 46	17 21	10 29	3 28	3 47	28 21	24 22
14 Sa	15 28 40	23 38 04	26 59	19 37	16 51	17 12	4 36	13 17	14 34	22 20	11 47	17 20	10 51	3 39	3 35	28 47	24 24
15 Su	15 32 36	24 35 57	9 ♍ 15	19 38 ℞	16 20	18 26	4 17	13 18	14 30	22 23	11 48	17 19	11 12	3 49	3 24	29 14	24 26
16 M	15 36 33	25 33 47	21 18	19 37	15 52	19 40	3 58	13 19	14 26	22 26	11 49	17 18	11 33	4 00	3 12	29 40	24 28
17 T	15 40 30	26 31 36	3 ♎ 11	19 34	15 27	20 54	3 39	13 20	14 22	22 29	11 50	17 17	11 54	4 10	3 01	0 ♊ 06	24 30
18 W	15 44 26	27 29 23	15 00	19 29	15 06	22 07	3 19	13 22	14 18	22 32	11 51	17 16	12 15	4 20	2 50	0 32	24 32
19 Th	15 48 23	28 27 08	26 48	19 21	14 48	23 21	2 59	13 24	14 14	22 35	11 51	17 16	12 36	4 29	2 39	0 58	24 34
20 F	15 52 19	29 24 52	8 ♏ 39	19 11	14 35	24 35	2 39	13 25	14 09	22 38	11 52	17 15	12 57	4 39	2 28	1 25	24 36
21 Sa	15 56 16	0 ♊ 22 35	20 35	19 10	14 26	25 49	2 18	13 27	14 05	22 41	11 53	17 14	13 18	4 48	2 18	1 51	24 38
22 Su	16 0 12	1 20 16	2 ♐ 37	18 58	14 21 D	27 03	1 57	13 29	14 01	22 43	11 54	17 13	13 38	4 57	2 08	2 17	24 40
23 M	16 4 9	2 17 56	14 48	18 45	14 21	28 16	1 36	13 32	13 57	22 46	11 55	17 12	13 59	5 06	1 58	2 43	24 42
24 T	16 8 5	3 15 35	27 07	18 33	14 24	29 30	1 15	13 34	13 52	22 49	11 55	17 11	14 19	5 14	1 48	3 09	24 44
25 W	16 12 2	4 13 12	9 ♑ 37	18 22	14 34	0 ♊ 44	0 54	13 37	13 48	22 52	11 56	17 10	14 40	5 22	1 39	3 36	24 46
26 Th	16 15 59	5 10 49	22 17	18 13	14 47	1 58	0 33	13 40	13 44	22 55	11 57	17 09	15 00	5 30	1 30	4 02	24 47
27 F	16 19 55	6 08 24	5 ≈ 09	18 08	15 05	3 11	0 12	13 43	13 39	22 57	11 57	17 08	15 21	5 38	1 21	4 28	24 49
28 Sa	16 23 52	7 05 59	18 15	18 04	15 27	4 25	29 ♏ 51	13 46	13 35	23 00	11 58	17 07	15 41	5 45	1 12	4 54	24 51
29 Su	16 27 48	8 03 33	1 ♓ 36	18 03 D	15 53	5 39	29 30	13 49	13 30	23 03	11 58	17 06	16 01	5 53	1 04	5 20	24 52
30 M	16 31 45	9 01 05	15 19	18 03 ℞	16 24	6 53	29 09	13 53	13 26	23 05	11 59	17 05	16 21	6 00	0 56	5 46	24 54
31 T	16 35 41	9 58 37	29 14	18 03	16 59	8 06	28 49	13 56	13 22	23 08	11 59	17 04	16 41	6 06	0 49	6 13	24 55

EPHEMERIS CALCULATED FOR 12 MIDNIGHT GREENWICH MEAN TIME. ALL OTHER DATA AND FACING ASPECTARIAN PAGE IN **EASTERN TIME (BOLD)** AND PACIFIC TIME (REGULAR).

JUNE 2016

☽ Last Aspect day	ET / hr:mn / PT		asp	☽ Ingress sign	day	ET / hr:mn / PT	
1	**11:42 am**	8:42 am	☌ ♅	♉	1	**10:46 pm**	7:46 pm
3	**7:02 pm**	4:02 pm	☍ ♂	♊	3	**11:01 pm**	8:01 pm
5	**12:47 pm**	9:47 am	⚹ ♅	♋	5	**11:41 pm**	8:41 pm
7	**8:18 pm**	5:18 pm	△ ♂	♌	7		11:47 pm
7	**8:18 pm**	5:18 pm	△ ♂	♌	8	**2:47 am**	
10	**3:14 am**	12:14 am	□ ☿	♍	10	**9:46 am**	6:46 am
12	**10:47 am**	7:47 am	⚹ ♂	♎	12	**8:33 pm**	5:33 pm
15	**3:00 am**	12:00 am	△ ♀	♏	15	**9:18 am**	6:18 am
17	**9:52 am**	6:52 am	☌ ♂	♐	17	**9:34 pm**	6:34 pm
20	**7:02 am**	4:02 am	☍ ☉	♑	20	**7:55 am**	4:55 am
22	**4:57 am**	1:57 am	□ ♅	♒	22	**4:08 pm**	1:08 pm
24	**11:48 am**	8:48 am	⚹ ♅	♓	24	**10:30 pm**	7:30 pm
26	**3:55 pm**	12:55 pm	□ ☿	♈	27	**3:08 am**	12:08 am
29	**3:46 am**	12:46 am	⚹ ☿	♉	29	**6:03 am**	3:03 am
30	**8:19 pm**	5:19 pm	☍ ♂	♊	7/1	**7:44 am**	4:44 am

☽ Phases & Eclipses phase	day	ET / hr:mn / PT	
New Moon	4	**11:00 pm**	8:00 pm
2nd Quarter	12	**4:10 am**	1:10 am
Full Moon	20	**7:02 am**	4:02 am
4th Quarter	27	**2:19 pm**	11:19 am

Planet Ingress	day	ET / hr:mn / PT	
⚳ ♎	7	**7:03 pm**	4:03 pm
☿ ♊	12	**7:22 pm**	4:22 pm
♀ ♋	17	**3:39 pm**	12:39 pm
☉ ♋	20	**6:34 pm**	3:34 pm
☿ ♋	29	**7:24 pm**	4:24 pm

Planetary Motion	day	ET / hr:mn / PT	
♆ ℞	13	**4:43 pm**	1:43 pm
♀ ℞	21	**9:21 am**	6:21 am
⚳ D	22	**4:01 pm**	1:01 pm
⚷ ℞	27	**7:10 am**	4:10 am
♂ D	29	**7:38 pm**	4:38 pm

1 WEDNESDAY
- ☽ □ ♇ **1:35 am**
- ☽ ⚺ ☿ **2:53 am**
- ☽ ☌ ♅ **11:42 am** 8:42 am
- ☽ ⚻ ♂ **7:46 pm** 4:46 pm
- ☉ □ ♆ **10:42 pm** 7:42 pm

2 THURSDAY
- ☽ ⚺ ♀ **5:37 pm** 2:37 pm
- ☽ ⚹ ♆ **6:10 pm** 3:10 pm
- ☽ ⚺ ☉ **7:29 pm** 4:29 pm
- ☽ ⚻ ♄ **7:59 pm** 4:59 pm
- ☽ △ ♃ **9:36 pm** 6:36 pm
- ♀ □ ♆ 9:14 pm
- ☽ △ ♇ 11:11 pm
- ☉ ☍ ♄ 11:37 pm

3 FRIDAY
- ♀ □ ♆ **12:14 am**
- ☽ △ ♇ **2:11 am**
- ☉ ☍ ♄ **2:37 am**
- ☽ ☌ ☿ **6:07 am** 3:07 am
- ☽ ⚺ ♅ **12:16 pm** 9:16 am
- ☽ ☍ ♂ **7:02 pm** 4:02 pm
- ♀ ☍ ♄ **8:47 pm** 5:47 pm

4 SATURDAY
- ☉ □ ♃ **6:57 am** 3:57 am
- ☽ □ ♆ **6:21 pm** 3:21 pm
- ☽ ☍ ♄ **7:55 pm** 4:55 pm
- ♀ □ ♃ **8:49 pm** 5:49 pm
- ☽ □ ♃ **10:02 pm** 7:02 pm
- ☽ ☌ ♀ **10:08 pm** 7:08 pm
- ☽ ☌ ☉ **11:00 pm** 8:00 pm
- ☽ ⚻ ♇ 11:22 pm

5 SUNDAY
- ☽ ⚻ ♇ **2:22 am**
- ☽ ⚺ ☿ **9:33 am** 6:33 am
- ☽ ⚹ ♅ **12:47 pm** 9:47 am
- ☽ ⚻ ♂ **6:35 pm** 3:35 pm

6 MONDAY
- ☉ ☌ ♀ **5:39 pm** 2:39 pm
- ☽ △ ♆ **7:47 pm** 4:47 pm
- ☽ ⚻ ♄ **9:09 pm** 6:09 pm
- ☽ ⚹ ♃ **11:54 pm** 8:54 pm
- ♀ ⚻ ♇ 9:13 pm
- ☉ ⚻ ♇ 11:02 pm

7 TUESDAY
- ♀ ⚻ ♇ **12:13 am**
- ☉ ⚻ ♇ **2:02 am**
- ☽ ☍ ♇ **4:06 am** 1:06 am
- ☽ ⚺ ☉ **4:15 am** 1:15 am
- ☽ ⚺ ♀ **4:28 am** 1:28 am
- ☿ ⚺ ♅ **10:14 am** 7:14 am
- ☽ □ ♅ **3:20 pm** 12:20 pm
- ☽ ⚹ ☿ **3:45 pm** 12:45 pm
- ☽ △ ♂ **8:18 pm** 5:18 pm

8 WEDNESDAY
- ☽ ⚻ ♆ 9:20 pm
- ☽ △ ♄ 10:30 pm

9 THURSDAY
- ☽ ⚻ ♆ **12:20 am**
- ☽ △ ♄ **1:30 am**
- ☽ ⚺ ♃ **5:06 am** 2:06 am
- ☽ ⚻ ♇ **9:12 am** 6:12 am
- ☿ ☍ ♂ **1:01 pm** 10:01 am
- ☽ ⚹ ☉ **1:40 pm** 10:40 am
- ☽ ⚹ ♀ **3:15 pm** 12:15 pm
- ☽ △ ♅ **9:34 pm** 6:34 pm
- ☽ □ ♂ 10:37 pm

10 FRIDAY
- ☽ □ ♂ **1:37 am**
- ☽ □ ☿ **3:14 am** 12:14 am

11 SATURDAY
- ☽ ☍ ♆ **8:58 am** 5:58 am
- ☽ □ ♄ **9:52 am** 6:52 am
- ☽ ☌ ♃ **2:29 pm** 11:29 am
- ☽ △ ♇ **6:21 pm** 3:21 pm

12 SUNDAY
- ☽ □ ☉ **4:10 am** 1:10 am
- ☽ □ ♀ **7:26 am** 4:26 am
- ☽ ⚻ ♅ **7:49 am** 4:49 am
- ☽ ⚹ ♂ **10:47 am** 7:47 am
- ♀ ⚹ ♅ **11:13 am** 8:13 am
- ☽ △ ☿ **8:42 pm** 5:42 pm

13 MONDAY
- ♀ ⚻ ♂ **11:39 am** 8:39 am
- ☽ ⚻ ♆ **8:51 pm** 5:51 pm
- ☽ ⚹ ♄ **9:25 pm** 6:25 pm

14 TUESDAY
- ☽ ⚺ ♃ **3:03 am** 12:03 am
- ☉ ⚹ ♅ **3:53 am** 12:53 am
- ☽ □ ♇ **6:26 am** 3:26 am
- ☽ ☍ ♅ **8:32 pm** 5:32 pm
- ☽ △ ☉ **9:57 pm** 6:57 pm
- ☽ ⚺ ♂ **10:18 pm** 7:18 pm
- ☉ ⚻ ♂ 10:31 pm

15 WEDNESDAY
- ☉ ⚻ ♂ **1:31 am**
- ☽ △ ♀ **3:00 am** 12:00 am
- ☽ ⚻ ☿ **5:50 pm** 2:50 pm

16 THURSDAY
- ☽ △ ♆ **9:39 am** 6:39 am
- ☽ ⚺ ♄ **9:52 am** 6:52 am
- ☽ ⚹ ♃ **4:21 pm** 1:21 pm
- ☽ ⚹ ♇ **7:04 pm** 4:04 pm

17 FRIDAY
- ☽ ⚻ ♅ **9:14 am** 6:14 am
- ☽ ☌ ♂ **9:52 am** 6:52 am
- ☽ ⚻ ☉ **3:39 pm** 12:39 pm
- ☽ ⚻ ♀ **10:14 pm** 7:14 pm
- ♄ □ ♆ **11:29 pm** 8:29 pm

18 SATURDAY
- ☽ ☍ ☿ **2:48 pm** 11:48 am
- ☽ ☌ ♄ **9:07 pm** 6:07 pm
- ☽ □ ♆ **9:14 pm** 6:14 pm
- ♂ ⚻ ♅ 10:55 pm

19 SUNDAY
- ♂ ⚻ ♅ **1:55 am**
- ☽ □ ♃ **4:15 am** 1:15 am
- ☽ ⚺ ♇ **6:14 am** 3:14 am
- ☽ ⚺ ♂ **7:56 pm** 4:56 pm
- ☽ △ ♅ **8:11 pm** 5:11 pm

20 MONDAY
- ☽ ☍ ☉ **7:02 am** 4:02 am
- ☿ ☍ ♄ **10:55 am** 7:55 am
- ☿ □ ♆ **1:11 pm** 10:11 am
- ☽ ☍ ♀ **2:51 pm** 11:51 am

21 TUESDAY
- ☽ ⚺ ♄ **6:17 am** 3:17 am
- ☽ ⚹ ♆ **6:41 am** 3:41 am
- ☽ ⚻ ☿ **9:30 am** 6:30 am
- ☽ △ ♃ **1:59 pm** 10:59 am
- ☽ ☌ ♇ **3:16 pm** 12:16 pm

22 WEDNESDAY
- ☽ ⚹ ♂ **4:03 am** 1:03 am
- ☽ □ ♅ **4:57 am** 1:57 am
- ☿ □ ♃ **6:59 pm** 3:59 pm
- ☽ ⚻ ☉ **7:44 pm** 4:44 pm
- ☿ ⚻ ♇ 10:39 pm

23 THURSDAY
- ☿ ⚻ ♇ **1:39 am**
- ☽ ⚻ ♀ **4:38 am** 1:38 am
- ☽ ⚹ ♄ **1:28 pm** 10:28 am
- ☽ ⚺ ♆ **2:07 pm** 11:07 am
- ☽ ⚻ ♃ **9:41 pm** 6:41 pm
- ☽ ⚺ ♇ **10:21 pm** 7:21 pm
- ☽ △ ☿ 10:48 pm

24 FRIDAY
- ☽ △ ☿ **1:48 am**
- ☽ □ ♂ **10:26 am** 7:26 am
- ☽ ⚹ ♅ **11:48 am** 8:48 am

25 SATURDAY
- ☽ △ ☉ **6:07 am** 3:07 am
- ☽ △ ♀ **3:58 pm** 12:58 pm
- ☽ □ ♄ **6:54 pm** 3:54 pm
- ☽ ☌ ♆ **7:46 pm** 4:46 pm

26 SUNDAY
- ☽ ☍ ♃ **3:36 am** 12:36 am
- ☽ ⚹ ♇ **3:39 am** 12:39 am
- ♃ △ ♇ **8:30 am** 5:30 am
- ☿ ⚻ ♂ **11:16 am** 8:16 am
- ☽ △ ♂ **3:14 pm** 12:14 pm
- ☽ □ ☿ **3:55 pm** 12:55 pm
- ☽ ⚺ ♅ **4:52 pm** 1:52 pm
- ☿ ⚹ ♅ **10:31 pm** 7:31 pm
- ♀ ⚻ ♄ **11:00 pm** 8:00 pm

27 MONDAY
- ♀ △ ♆ **9:53 am** 6:53 am
- ☽ □ ☉ **2:19 pm** 11:19 am
- ☽ △ ♄ **10:37 pm** 7:37 pm
- ☽ ⚺ ♆ **11:40 pm** 8:40 pm
- ☽ □ ♀ 9:59 pm

28 TUESDAY
- ☽ □ ♀ **12:59 am**
- ☽ □ ♇ **7:14 am** 4:14 am
- ☽ ⚻ ♃ **7:44 am** 4:44 am
- ☽ ⚻ ♂ **6:25 pm** 3:25 pm
- ☽ ☌ ♅ **8:12 pm** 5:12 pm

29 WEDNESDAY
- ☽ ⚹ ☿ **3:46 am** 12:46 am
- ☽ ⚹ ☉ **8:29 pm** 5:29 pm
- ☽ ⚻ ♄ 9:46 pm
- ☽ ⚹ ♆ 10:59 pm

30 THURSDAY
- ☽ ⚻ ♄ **12:46 am**
- ☽ ⚹ ♆ **1:59 am**
- ☽ ⚹ ♀ **7:57 am** 4:57 am
- ☽ △ ♇ **9:18 am** 6:18 am
- ☽ △ ♃ **10:20 am** 7:20 am
- ☽ ☍ ♂ **8:19 pm** 5:19 pm
- ☽ ⚺ ♅ **10:09 pm** 7:09 pm
- ♀ ☍ ♇ **11:32 pm** 8:32 pm

Eastern time in bold type
Pacific time in medium type

JUNE 2016

DATE	SID.TIME	SUN	MOON	NODE	MERCURY	VENUS	MARS	JUPITER	SATURN	URANUS	NEPTUNE	PLUTO	CERES	PALLAS	JUNO	VESTA	CHIRON
1 W	16 39 38	10 Ⅱ 56 09	13 ♈ 39	18 ℧ 11 R	17 ♉ 38	9 Ⅱ 20	28 ♏ 29	14 ♍ 00	13 ♐ 17	23 ♈ 10	12 ♓ 00	17 ♑ 01	17 ♈ 01	6 ♓ 13	0 ♏ 42	6 Ⅱ 39	24 ♓ 56
2 Th	16 43 34	11 53 39	28 18	17 57 R	18 20	10 34	28 09 R	14 04	13 13 R	23 13	12 00	17 02 R	17 21	6 19	0 35 R	7 05	24 58
3 F	16 47 31	12 51 09	13 ♉ 09	17 51	19 07	11 47	27 49	14 08	13 08	23 15	12 00	17 01	17 40	6 25	0 28	7 31	24 59
4 Sa	16 51 28	13 48 38	28 07	17 42	19 57	13 01	27 30	14 13	13 04	23 18	12 01	16 59	18 00	6 30	0 22	7 57	25 00
5 Su	16 55 24	14 46 06	13 Ⅱ 02	17 31	20 51	14 15	27 12	14 17	12 59	23 20	12 01	16 59	18 19	6 36	0 16	8 23	25 02
6 M	16 59 21	15 43 33	27 46	17 19	21 48	15 29	26 53	14 22	12 55	23 23	12 01	16 57	18 39	6 41	0 10	8 49	25 03
7 T	17 3 17	16 40 59	12 ⊚ 10	17 09	22 49	16 43	26 35	14 27	12 50	23 25	12 02	16 56	18 58	6 45	0 05	9 15	25 04
8 W	17 7 14	17 38 24	26 08	17 00	23 53	17 56	26 18	14 32	12 46	23 27	12 02	16 54	19 17	6 50	0 00	9 41	25 05
9 Th	17 11 10	18 35 48	9 ♌ 39	16 54	25 00	19 10	26 02	14 37	12 42	23 30	12 02	16 53	19 36	6 54	29 ♍ 55	10 07	25 06
10 F	17 15 7	19 33 11	22 42	16 51	26 11	20 24	25 46	14 42	12 37	23 32	12 02	16 52	19 55	6 58	29 51	10 33	25 07
11 Sa	17 19 3	20 30 33	5 ♍ 21	16 49 D	27 25	21 37	25 30	14 47	12 33	23 34	12 02	16 51	20 14	7 01	29 47	10 59	25 08
12 Su	17 23 0	21 27 54	17 40	16 49 R	28 42	22 51	25 16	14 53	12 28	23 36	12 02	16 49	20 33	7 04	29 43	11 25	25 09
13 M	17 26 57	22 25 14	29 43	16 49	0 Ⅱ 02	24 05	25 02	14 59	12 24	23 39	12 02 R	16 48	20 51	7 07	29 40	11 51	25 09
14 T	17 30 53	23 22 33	11 ♎ 41	16 48	1 25	25 19	24 48	15 05	12 19	23 41	12 02	16 47	21 10	7 10	29 37	12 17	25 10
15 W	17 34 50	24 19 51	23 27	16 45	2 52	26 32	24 36	15 11	12 15	23 43	12 02	16 45	21 28	7 12	29 34	12 43	25 11
16 Th	17 38 46	25 17 09	5 ♏ 17	16 40	4 21	27 46	24 24	15 17	12 11	23 45	12 02	16 44	21 46	7 14	29 32	13 09	25 11
17 F	17 42 43	26 14 25	17 11	16 32	5 53	29 00	24 13	15 23	12 07	23 47	12 02	16 43	22 04	7 16	29 30	13 35	25 12
18 Sa	17 46 39	27 11 41	29 13	16 21	7 28	0 ⊚ 13	24 03	15 29	12 03	23 49	12 02	16 41	22 22	7 17	29 28	14 01	25 13
19 Su	17 50 36	28 08 56	11 ♐ 24	16 09	9 06	1 27	23 53	15 36	11 59	23 51	12 02	16 40	22 40	7 18	29 27	14 27	25 13
20 M	17 54 32	29 06 11	23 47	15 56	10 48	2 41	23 45	15 43	11 54	23 53	12 02	16 39	22 58	7 19	29 26	14 52	25 14
21 T	17 58 29	0 ⊚ 03 25	6 ♑ 22	15 44	12 31	3 54	23 37	15 49	11 50	23 54	12 01	16 37	23 15	7 19 R	29 25	15 18	25 14
22 W	18 2 26	1 00 38	19 08	15 33	14 18	5 08	23 30	15 56	11 46	23 56	12 01	16 36	23 33	7 19	29 24 D	15 44	25 14
23 Th	18 6 22	1 57 52	2 ≈ 16	15 25	16 08	6 22	23 24	16 03	11 42	23 58	12 00	16 34	23 50	7 18	29 24	16 10	25 14
24 F	18 10 19	2 55 05	15 15	15 19	18 00	7 36	23 18	16 11	11 38	24 00	12 00	16 33	24 07	7 18	29 24	16 35	25 15
25 Sa	18 14 15	3 52 18	28 36	15 16	19 55	8 49	23 14	16 18	11 34	24 01	12 00	16 31	24 24	7 17	29 25	17 01	25 15
26 Su	18 18 12	4 49 31	12 ♓ 08	15 15 D	21 52	10 03	23 10	16 25	11 30	24 03	12 00	16 30	24 41	7 16	29 26	17 27	25 15
27 M	18 22 8	5 46 43	25 53	15 15 R	23 52	11 17	23 07	16 33	11 26	24 04	11 59	16 29	24 58	7 14	29 27	17 53	25 15 R
28 T	18 26 5	6 43 56	9 ♈ 50	15 15	25 54	12 30	23 05 D	16 41	11 23	24 06	11 59	16 27	25 14	7 12	29 28	18 18	25 15
29 W	18 30 1	7 41 09	24 00	15 14	27 58	13 44	23 04 D	16 48	11 19	24 07	11 59	16 26	25 31	7 10	29 30	18 44	25 15
30 Th	18 33 58	8 38 22	8 ♉ 22	15 11	0 ⊚ 03	14 58	23 03	16 56	11 15	24 09	11 58	16 24	25 47	7 07	29 32	19 09	25 15

EPHEMERIS CALCULATED FOR 12 MIDNIGHT GREENWICH MEAN TIME. ALL OTHER DATA AND FACING ASPECTARIAN PAGE IN **EASTERN TIME (BOLD)** AND PACIFIC TIME (REGULAR).

JULY 2016

☽ Last Aspect day	ET / hr:mn / PT		asp	☽ Ingress sign	day	ET / hr:mn / PT	
6/30	8:19 pm	5:19 pm	☍♂	♊	1	7:44 am	4:44 am
2	11:43 pm	8:43 pm	✱♅	♋	3	9:20 am	6:20 am
4		11:29 pm	□♅	♌	5	12:28 pm	9:28 am
5	2:29 am		□♅	♌	5	12:28 pm	9:28 am
7	8:07 am	5:07 am	△♅	♍	7	6:41 pm	3:41 pm
9	11:28 pm	8:28 pm	✱♀	♎	10	4:32 am	1:32 am
12	11:01 am	8:01 am	□☿	♏	12	4:52 pm	1:52 pm
14	6:22 pm	3:22 pm	☌♂	♐	15	5:14 am	2:14 am
17	4:57 am	1:57 am	△♅	♑	17	3:33 pm	12:33 pm
19	6:57 pm	3:57 pm	☍☉	♒	19	11:10 pm	8:10 pm
21	9:56 pm	6:56 pm	□♂	♓	22	4:35 am	1:35 am
24	3:06 am	12:06 am	△♂	♈	24	8:33 am	5:33 am
25		11:19 pm	☌♅	♉	26	11:37 am	8:37 am
26	2:19 am		☌♅	♉	26	11:37 am	8:37 am
28	11:13 am	8:13 am	☍♂	♊	28	2:17 pm	11:17 am
30	7:46 am	4:46 am	✱♅	♋	30	5:09 pm	2:09 pm

☽ Phases & Eclipses phase	day	ET / hr:mn / PT	
New Moon	4	7:01 am	4:01 am
2nd Quarter	11	8:52 pm	5:52 pm
Full Moon	19	6:57 pm	3:57 pm
4th Quarter	26	7:00 pm	4:00 pm

Planet Ingress		day	ET / hr:mn / PT	
⚵	♏	7	11:45 pm	8:45 pm
♀	♌	11		10:34 pm
♀	♌	12	1:34 am	
☿	♌	13	8:47 pm	5:47 pm
⚷	♉	16		9:10 pm
⚷	♉	17	12:10 am	
☉	♌	22	5:30 am	2:30 am
⚳	♋	25	5:21 pm	2:21 pm
☿	♍	30	2:18 pm	11:18 am

Planetary Motion		day	ET / hr:mn / PT	
♅	℞	29	5:06 pm	2:06 pm

1 FRIDAY
☽⚺☿ **1:56 pm** 10:56 am
♀✱♃ **3:18 pm** 12:18 pm
☽⚺☉ 10:28 pm
☽☍♄ 11:03 pm

2 SATURDAY
☽⚺☉ **1:28 am**
☽☍♄ **2:03 am**
☽□♆ **3:25 am** 12:25 am
☉⚻♄ **9:52 am** 6:52 am
☽⚻♇ **10:40 am** 7:40 am
☽□♃ **12:15 pm** 9:15 am
☽⚺♀ **1:59 pm** 10:59 am
☽⚻♂ **9:53 pm** 6:53 pm
☽✱♅ **11:43 pm** 8:43 pm

3 SUNDAY
☉△♆ **7:01 am** 4:01 am
☽☌☿ 9:29 pm

4 MONDAY
☽☌☿ **12:29 am**
☽⚻♄ **3:48 am** 12:48 am
☽△♆ **5:23 am** 2:23 am
☽☌☉ **7:01 am** 4:01 am
☽☍♇ **12:48 pm** 9:48 am
☽✱♃ **3:02 pm** 12:02 pm
☽☌♀ **9:09 pm** 6:09 pm
☿⚻♄ **9:42 pm** 6:42 pm

☽△♂ 9:44 pm
☽□♅ 11:29 pm

5 TUESDAY
☽△♂ **12:44 am**
☽□♅ **2:29 am**
☿△♆ **8:19 am** 5:19 am

6 WEDNESDAY
☽△♄ **7:42 am** 4:42 am
☽⚻♆ **9:33 am** 6:33 am
☽⚺☿ **2:29 pm** 11:29 am
☽⚺☉ **3:21 pm** 12:21 pm
♀△♂ **4:17 pm** 1:17 pm
☽⚻♇ **5:21 pm** 2:21 pm
☽⚺♃ **8:25 pm** 5:25 pm
☉☌☿ **11:24 pm** 8:24 pm

7 THURSDAY
☽□♂ **6:30 am** 3:30 am
☽⚺♀ **7:52 am** 4:52 am
☿☍♇ **7:55 am** 4:55 am
☽△♅ **8:07 am** 5:07 am
♀□♅ **10:25 am** 7:25 am
☉☍♇ **6:27 pm** 3:27 pm

8 FRIDAY
☿✱♃ **5:05 am** 2:05 am
☽□♄ **3:01 pm** 12:01 pm
☽☍♆ **5:10 pm** 2:10 pm
☽△♇ 10:27 pm

9 SATURDAY
☽△♇ **1:27 am**
☽✱☉ **4:07 am** 1:07 am
☽☌♃ **5:32 am** 2:32 am
☽✱☿ **10:19 am** 7:19 am
☽✱♂ **4:09 pm** 1:09 pm
☽⚻♅ **5:23 pm** 2:23 pm
☽✱♀ **11:28 pm** 8:28 pm
☉✱♃ 10:41 pm

10 SUNDAY
☉✱♃ **1:41 am**
☿△♂ **10:00 pm** 7:00 pm
☽✱♄ 10:45 pm

11 MONDAY
☽✱♄ **1:45 am**
☿□♅ **3:29 am** 12:29 am
☽⚻♆ **4:11 am** 1:11 am
☽□♇ **12:47 pm** 9:47 am
☽⚺♃ **5:55 pm** 2:55 pm
☽□☉ **8:52 pm** 5:52 pm

12 TUESDAY
☽⚺♂ **4:54 am** 1:54 am
☽☍♅ **5:30 am** 2:30 am
☽□☿ **11:01 am** 8:01 am
☽□♀ **6:39 pm** 3:39 pm

13 WEDNESDAY
☽⚺♄ **2:09 pm** 11:09 am
☽△♆ **4:46 pm** 1:46 pm
♂⚻♅ 10:13 pm
☽✱♇ 10:20 pm

14 THURSDAY
♂⚻♅ **1:13 am**
☽✱♇ **1:20 am**
☽✱♃ **7:23 am** 4:23 am
☽△☉ **2:45 pm** 11:45 am
☽⚻♅ **6:07 pm** 3:07 pm
☽☌♂ **6:22 pm** 3:22 pm

15 FRIDAY
☽△☿ **11:42 am** 8:42 am
☽△♀ **1:46 pm** 10:46 am
☽☌♄ 10:45 pm

16 SATURDAY
☽☌♄ **1:45 am**
☽□♆ **4:25 am** 1:25 am
☉□♅ **9:32 am** 6:32 am
☽⚺♇ **12:39 pm** 9:39 am
☿☌♀ **5:59 pm** 2:59 pm
☽□♃ **7:22 pm** 4:22 pm
☉△♂ **11:45 pm** 8:45 pm

17 SUNDAY
☽△♅ **4:57 am** 1:57 am
☽⚺♂ **6:08 am** 3:08 am
☽⚻☉ **6:32 am** 3:32 am

18 MONDAY
☽⚻♀ **5:52 am** 2:52 am
☽⚻☿ **8:12 am** 5:12 am
☽⚺♄ **10:56 am** 7:56 am
☽✱♆ **1:36 pm** 10:36 am
☽☌♇ **9:25 pm** 6:25 pm
☿△♄ 11:28 pm

19 TUESDAY
☿△♄ **2:28 am**
☽△♃ **4:39 am** 1:39 am
☽□♅ **1:06 pm** 10:06 am
☽✱♂ **3:12 pm** 12:12 pm
☽☍☉ **6:57 pm** 3:57 pm
☿⚻♆ **8:44 pm** 5:44 pm

20 WEDNESDAY
♀△♄ **9:19 am** 6:19 am
☽✱♄ **5:34 pm** 2:34 pm
☽☍♀ **6:26 pm** 3:26 pm
☽⚺♆ **8:12 pm** 5:12 pm
☽☍☿ **11:58 pm** 8:58 pm

21 THURSDAY
☽⚺♇ **3:40 am** 12:40 am
☽⚻♃ **11:24 am** 8:24 am
♀⚻♆ **1:33 pm** 10:33 am
☽✱♅ **6:54 pm** 3:54 pm
☽□♂ **9:56 pm** 6:56 pm

22 FRIDAY
☿⚻♇ **3:11 am** 12:11 am
☽⚻☉ **4:31 am** 1:31 am
☽□♄ **10:17 pm** 7:17 pm
☽☌♆ 9:54 pm

23 SATURDAY
☽☌♆ **12:54 am**
☽⚻♀ **4:23 am** 1:23 am
☽✱♇ **8:08 am** 5:08 am
☽⚻☿ **12:27 pm** 9:27 am
☽☍♃ **4:25 pm** 1:25 pm

☽⚺♅ **11:05 pm** 8:05 pm

24 SUNDAY
☽△♂ **3:06 am** 12:06 am
☽△☉ **12:17 pm** 9:17 am
♀⚻♇ **9:57 pm** 6:57 pm
☿⚺♃ **11:26 pm** 8:26 pm
☽△♄ 10:46 pm

25 MONDAY
☽△♄ **1:46 am**
☽⚺♆ **4:23 am** 1:23 am
☽□♇ **11:29 am** 8:29 am
☽△♀ **12:48 pm** 9:48 am
☽⚻♃ **8:22 pm** 5:22 pm
☽△☿ **10:55 pm** 7:55 pm
☽☌♅ 11:19 pm

26 TUESDAY
☽☌♅ **2:19 am**
☽⚻♂ **7:22 am** 4:22 am
☽□☉ **7:00 pm** 4:00 pm

27 WEDNESDAY
☿△♅ **3:45 am** 12:45 am
☽⚻♄ **4:33 am** 1:33 am
☽✱♆ **7:10 am** 4:10 am
☽△♇ **2:12 pm** 11:12 am
☽□♀ **8:23 pm** 5:23 pm
☽△♃ **11:44 pm** 8:44 pm

28 THURSDAY
☽⚺♅ **5:01 am** 2:01 am
☽□☿ **8:17 am** 5:17 am
☽☍♂ **11:13 am** 8:13 am

☽✱☉ 10:17 pm

29 FRIDAY
☽✱☉ **1:17 am**
☽☍♄ **7:06 am** 4:06 am
☽□♆ **9:44 am** 6:44 am
☽⚻♇ **4:47 pm** 1:47 pm
☿□♂ **4:49 pm** 1:49 pm
♀⚺♃ **5:03 pm** 2:03 pm

30 SATURDAY
☽□♃ **3:06 am** 12:06 am
☽✱♀ **3:55 am** 12:55 am
☽✱♅ **7:46 am** 4:46 am
☽⚻♂ **3:19 pm** 12:19 pm
☽✱☿ **5:30 pm** 2:30 pm

31 SUNDAY
☽⚺☉ **8:04 am** 5:04 am
☽⚻♄ **10:09 am** 7:09 am
☽△♆ **12:51 pm** 9:51 am
☽☍♇ **8:03 pm** 5:03 pm
♀△♅ 9:09 pm

Eastern time in bold type
Pacific time in medium type

JULY 2016

DATE	SID. TIME	SUN	MOON	NODE	MERCURY	VENUS	MARS	JUPITER	SATURN	URANUS	NEPTUNE	PLUTO	CERES	PALLAS	JUNO	VESTA	CHIRON
1 F	18 37 55	9 ♋ 35 35	22 ♉ 52	15 ♍ 06	2 ♋ 10	16 ♋ 12	23 ♏ 04 R	17 ♍ 04	11 ♐ 12 R	24 ♈ 10	11 ♓ 58	16 ♑ 23 R	26 ♋ 03	7 ♋ 04 R	29 ♌ 35	19 ♊ 35	25 ♓ 15
2 Sa	18 41 51	10 32 49	7 ♊ 27	14 58 R	4 19	17 25	23 05	17 13	11 08	24 12	11 57 R	16 21 R	26 19	7 01 R	29 37	20 00	25 14 R
3 Su	18 45 48	11 30 02	21 59	14 49	6 28	18 39	23 07	17 21	11 04	24 13	11 57	16 20	26 35	6 57	29 40	20 26	25 14
4 M	18 49 44	12 27 16	6 ♋ 22	14 39	8 38	19 53	23 10	17 29	11 01	24 14	11 56	16 18	26 51	6 53	29 43	20 51	25 13
5 T	18 53 41	13 24 30	20 30	14 28	10 48	21 07	23 14	17 38	10 58	24 15	11 55	16 17	27 06	6 48	29 47	21 17	25 13
6 W	18 57 37	14 21 43	4 ♌ 17	14 23	12 58	22 20	23 18	17 46	10 54	24 17	11 55	16 15	27 22	6 43	29 51	21 42	25 13
7 Th	19 1 34	15 18 56	17 42	14 17	15 09	23 34	23 24	17 55	10 51	24 18	11 54	16 14	27 37	6 38	29 55	22 08	25 12
8 F	19 5 31	16 16 10	0 ♍ 42	14 14	17 18	24 48	23 30	18 04	10 48	24 19	11 54	16 13	27 52	6 33	29 59	22 33	25 12
9 Sa	19 9 27	17 13 23	13 21	14 13 D	19 27	26 02	23 37	18 13	10 45	24 20	11 53	16 11	28 06	6 27	0 ♍ 04	22 58	25 11
10 Su	19 13 24	18 10 36	25 41	14 14	21 36	27 15	23 44	18 22	10 41	24 21	11 52	16 09	28 21	6 20	0 09	23 24	25 11
11 M	19 17 20	19 07 49	7 ♎ 46	14 15	23 43	28 29	23 53	18 31	10 38	24 22	11 51	16 08	28 35	6 14	0 14	23 49	25 10
12 T	19 21 17	20 05 02	19 41	14 15 R	25 49	29 43	24 02	18 40	10 36	24 23	11 51	16 06	28 50	6 07	0 20	24 14	25 09
13 W	19 25 13	21 02 15	1 ♏ 33	14 15	27 53	0 ♌ 57	24 12	18 50	10 33	24 24	11 50	16 05	29 04	6 00	0 25	24 39	25 09
14 Th	19 29 10	21 59 28	13 25	14 12	29 56	2 10	24 22	18 59	10 30	24 24	11 49	16 03	29 17	5 52	0 31	25 04	25 08
15 F	19 33 6	22 56 41	25 22	14 08	1 ♌ 57	3 24	24 33	19 09	10 27	24 25	11 48	16 02	29 31	5 44	0 38	25 29	25 07
16 Sa	19 37 3	23 53 54	7 ♐ 28	14 01	3 57	4 38	24 45	19 18	10 25	24 26	11 47	16 01	29 44	5 36	0 44	25 54	25 06
17 Su	19 40 59	24 51 07	19 47	13 54	5 55	5 52	24 58	19 28	10 22	24 26	11 46	15 59	29 58	5 27	0 51	26 19	25 05
18 M	19 44 56	25 48 21	2 ♑ 21	13 45	7 52	7 05	25 11	19 38	10 20	24 27	11 45	15 58	0 ♌ 11	5 18	0 58	26 44	25 04
19 T	19 48 53	26 45 35	15 10	13 37	9 46	8 19	25 25	19 48	10 17	24 28	11 44	15 56	0 24	5 09	1 05	27 09	25 03
20 W	19 52 49	27 42 49	28 15	13 30	11 39	9 33	25 40	19 58	10 15	24 28	11 43	15 55	0 36	4 59	1 13	27 34	25 02
21 Th	19 56 46	28 40 04	11 ♒ 34	13 24	13 30	10 47	25 55	20 08	10 13	24 29	11 42	15 53	0 49	4 49	1 21	27 59	25 01
22 F	20 0 42	29 37 20	25 07	13 21	15 19	12 00	26 11	20 18	10 11	24 29	11 41	15 52	1 01	4 39	1 29	28 24	25 00
23 Sa	20 4 39	0 ♌ 34 36	8 ♓ 50	13 20 D	17 06	13 14	26 28	20 28	10 09	24 29	11 39	15 50	1 13	4 28	1 37	28 49	24 59
24 Su	20 8 35	1 31 52	22 42	13 20	18 52	14 28	26 45	20 39	10 07	24 30	11 38	15 49	1 24	4 17	1 45	29 13	24 57
25 M	20 12 32	2 29 10	6 ♈ 42	13 21	20 36	15 41	27 02	20 49	10 05	24 30	11 37	15 48	1 36	4 06	1 54	29 38	24 55
26 T	20 16 28	3 26 28	20 47	13 22 R	22 18	16 55	27 20	21 00	10 03	24 30	11 36	15 46	1 47	3 55	2 03	0 ♋ 03	24 54
27 W	20 20 25	4 23 48	4 ♉ 57	13 23	23 58	18 09	27 39	21 10	10 01	24 30	11 34	15 45	1 58	3 43	2 12	0 27	24 52
28 Th	20 24 22	5 21 08	19 10	13 22	25 37	19 23	27 59	21 21	10 00	24 30 R	11 33	15 43	2 09	3 31	2 21	0 52	24 51
29 F	20 28 18	6 18 30	3 ♊ 23	13 20	27 14	20 36	28 18	21 32	9 58	24 30	11 32	15 42	2 19	3 19	2 31	1 16	24 49
30 Sa	20 32 15	7 15 53	17 35	13 16	28 49	21 50	28 39	21 42	9 57	24 30	11 31	15 41	2 30	3 06	2 41	1 41	24 48
31 Su	20 36 11	8 13 17	1 ♋ 40	13 11	0 ♍ 22	23 04	29 00	21 53	9 55	24 30	11 29	15 39	2 40	2 54	2 51	2 05	24 46

EPHEMERIS CALCULATED FOR 12 MIDNIGHT GREENWICH MEAN TIME. ALL OTHER DATA AND FACING ASPECTARIAN PAGE IN **EASTERN TIME (BOLD)** AND PACIFIC TIME (REGULAR).

AUGUST 2016

☽ Last Aspect day	ET / hr:mn / PT		asp	☽ Ingress sign	day	ET / hr:mn / PT	
1	**8:44 pm**	5:44 pm	△♂	♌	1	**9:12 pm**	6:12 pm
3		9:13 pm	☌♀	♍	4	**3:34 am**	12:34 am
4	**12:13 am**		☌♀	♍	4	**3:34 am**	12:34 am
5	**11:20 pm**	8:20 pm	☌♃	♎	6	**12:57 pm**	9:57 am
8	**1:41 pm**	10:41 am	☍♅	♏	8		9:51 pm
8	**1:41 pm**	10:41 am	☍♅	♏	9	**12:51 am**	
10		10:22 pm	⚹♃	♐	11	**1:24 pm**	10:24 am
11	**1:22 am**		⚹♃	♐	11	**1:24 pm**	10:24 am
13	**1:37 pm**	10:37 am	□♃	♑	13		9:11 pm
13	**1:37 pm**	10:37 am	□♃	♑	14	**12:11 am**	

☽ Last Aspect day	ET / hr:mn / PT		asp	☽ Ingress sign	day	ET / hr:mn / PT	
15	**10:45 pm**	7:45 pm	△♃	♒	16	**7:52 am**	4:52 am
18	**5:27 am**	2:27 am	☍☉	♓	18	**12:34 pm**	9:34 am
20	**8:21 am**	5:21 am	☍♃	♈	20	**3:18 pm**	12:18 pm
22	**7:48 am**	4:48 am	☌♅	♉	22	**5:19 pm**	2:19 pm
24	**3:38 pm**	12:38 pm	△☿	♊	24	**7:40 pm**	4:40 pm
26	**8:30 pm**	5:30 pm	□☿	♋	26	**11:06 pm**	8:06 pm
28		11:23 pm	⚹☿	♌	29	**4:11 am**	1:11 am
29	**2:23 am**		⚹☿	♌	29	**4:11 am**	1:11 am
30		9:20 pm	△♅	♍	31	**11:22 am**	8:22 am
31	**12:20 am**		△♅	♍	31	**11:22 am**	8:22 am

☽ Phases & Eclipses phase	day	ET / hr:mn / PT	
New Moon	2	**4:45 pm**	1:45 pm
2nd Quarter	10	**2:21 pm**	11:21 am
Full Moon	18	**5:27 am**	2:27 am
4th Quarter	24	**11:41 pm**	8:41 pm

Planet Ingress		day	ET / hr:mn / PT	
♂	♐	2	**1:49 pm**	10:49 am
♀	♍	5	**11:27 am**	8:27 am
⚴	♒	12	**3:03 am**	12:03 am
☉	♍	22	**12:38 pm**	9:38 am
♀	♎	29	**10:07 pm**	7:07 pm

Planetary Motion		day	ET / hr:mn / PT	
♄	D	13	**5:50 am**	2:50 am
☿	℞	30	**9:04 am**	6:04 am
⚳	℞	31	**3:09 am**	12:09 am

1 MONDAY
♀ △ ♅ **12:09 am**
☽ ⚹ ♃ **7:25 am** 4:25 am
☽ □ ♅ **11:31 am** 8:31 am
☽ ⚺ ♀ **12:39 pm** 9:39 am
☉ △ ♄ **1:49 pm** 10:49 am
☽ △ ♂ **8:44 pm** 5:44 pm

2 TUESDAY
☽ ⚺ ☿ **4:05 am** 1:05 am
☽ △ ♄ **2:47 pm** 11:47 am
☽ ☌ ☉ **4:45 pm** 1:45 pm
☽ ⚻ ♆ **5:34 pm** 2:34 pm
☽ ⚻ ♇ 10:05 pm

3 WEDNESDAY
☽ ⚻ ♇ **1:05 am**
☉ ⚻ ♆ **4:02 am** 1:02 am
☽ ⚺ ♃ **1:51 pm** 10:51 am
☽ △ ♅ **5:23 pm** 2:23 pm
☽ ☌ ♀ 9:13 pm

4 THURSDAY
☽ ☌ ♀ **12:13 am**
☽ □ ♂ **4:43 am** 1:43 am
☽ ☌ ☿ **5:44 pm** 2:44 pm
☽ □ ♄ **10:02 pm** 7:02 pm
☽ ☍ ♆ 9:57 pm

5 FRIDAY
☽ ☍ ♆ **12:57 am**
☽ ⚺ ☉ **4:44 am** 1:44 am
☽ △ ♇ **8:54 am** 5:54 am
☽ ☌ ♃ **11:20 pm** 8:20 pm
☽ ⚻ ♅ 11:10 pm

6 SATURDAY
☽ ⚻ ♅ **2:10 am**
☿ □ ♄ **9:18 am** 6:18 am
☽ ⚺ ♀ **3:48 pm** 12:48 pm
☽ ⚹ ♂ **4:06 pm** 1:06 pm
♀ □ ♂ **8:20 pm** 5:20 pm

7 SUNDAY
☽ ⚹ ♄ **8:19 am** 5:19 am
☉ ⚻ ♇ **10:12 am** 7:12 am
☽ ⚺ ☿ **11:11 am** 8:11 am
☽ ⚻ ♆ **11:19 am** 8:19 am
☿ ☍ ♆ **12:24 pm** 9:24 am
☽ □ ♇ **7:38 pm** 4:38 pm
☽ ⚹ ☉ **8:29 pm** 5:29 pm

8 MONDAY
☽ ⚺ ♃ **11:45 am** 8:45 am
☽ ☍ ♅ **1:41 pm** 10:41 am

9 TUESDAY
☽ ⚺ ♂ **6:19 am** 3:19 am
☽ ⚹ ♀ **10:43 am** 7:43 am
☽ ⚺ ♄ **8:40 pm** 5:40 pm
☽ △ ♆ **11:37 pm** 8:37 pm

10 WEDNESDAY
☽ ⚹ ☿ **6:47 am** 3:47 am
☽ ⚹ ♇ **8:05 am** 5:05 am
☽ □ ☉ **2:21 pm** 11:21 am
☿ △ ♇ **7:25 pm** 4:25 pm
☽ ⚹ ♃ 10:22 pm
☽ ⚻ ♅ 11:15 pm

11 THURSDAY
☽ ⚹ ♃ **1:22 am**
☽ ⚻ ♅ **2:15 am**
☽ ☌ ♂ **9:04 pm** 6:04 pm

12 FRIDAY
☽ □ ♀ **5:58 am** 2:58 am
☽ ☌ ♄ **8:51 am** 5:51 am
☽ □ ♆ **11:38 am** 8:38 am
☽ ⚺ ♇ **7:53 pm** 4:53 pm
☽ □ ☿ 9:59 pm

13 SATURDAY
☽ □ ☿ **12:59 am**
♃ ⚻ ♅ **5:02 am** 2:02 am
☽ △ ☉ **7:05 am** 4:05 am
♀ □ ♄ **10:31 am** 7:31 am
☽ △ ♅ **1:28 pm** 10:28 am
☽ □ ♃ **1:37 pm** 10:37 am

14 SUNDAY
☽ ⚺ ♂ **9:41 am** 6:41 am
♀ ☍ ♆ **1:03 pm** 10:03 am
☽ ⚺ ♄ **6:42 pm** 3:42 pm
☽ ⚹ ♆ **9:14 pm** 6:14 pm
☽ △ ♀ **10:07 pm** 7:07 pm

15 MONDAY
☽ ☌ ♇ **5:04 am** 2:04 am
☽ △ ☿ **2:59 pm** 11:59 am
☽ ⚻ ☉ **8:13 pm** 5:13 pm
☽ □ ♅ **9:42 pm** 6:42 pm
☽ △ ♃ **10:45 pm** 7:45 pm

16 TUESDAY
☉ △ ♅ **4:23 pm** 1:23 pm
☽ ⚹ ♂ **6:50 pm** 3:50 pm
☽ ⚹ ♄ 10:21 pm

17 WEDNESDAY
☽ ⚹ ♄ **1:21 am**
☽ ⚺ ♆ **3:37 am** 12:37 am
☽ ⚻ ♀ **9:57 am** 6:57 am
☽ ⚺ ♇ **11:04 am** 8:04 am
☉ ⚺ ♃ **3:26 pm** 12:26 pm
♀ △ ♇ **10:17 pm** 7:17 pm
☽ ⚻ ☿ 9:27 pm
☽ ⚹ ♅ 11:50 pm

18 THURSDAY
☽ ⚻ ☿ **12:27 am**
☽ ⚹ ♅ **2:50 am**
☽ ⚻ ♃ **4:40 am** 1:40 am
☽ ☍ ☉ **5:27 am** 2:27 am
☽ □ ♂ 9:53 pm

19 FRIDAY
☽ □ ♂ **12:53 am**
☽ □ ♄ **5:19 am** 2:19 am
☽ ☌ ♆ **7:21 am** 4:21 am
☽ ⚹ ♇ **2:33 pm** 11:33 am
☿ ⚻ ♅ **2:55 pm** 11:55 am
☽ ☍ ♀ **6:24 pm** 3:24 pm

20 SATURDAY
☽ ⚺ ♅ **5:48 am** 2:48 am
☽ ☍ ☿ **6:41 am** 3:41 am
☽ ☍ ♃ **8:21 am** 5:21 am
☽ ⚻ ☉ **12:03 pm** 9:03 am

21 SUNDAY
☽ △ ♂ **5:09 am** 2:09 am
☽ △ ♄ **7:43 am** 4:43 am
☽ ⚺ ♆ **9:36 am** 6:36 am
☽ □ ♇ **4:43 pm** 1:43 pm
☽ ⚻ ♀ 10:15 pm

22 MONDAY
☽ ⚻ ♀ **1:15 am**
☿ ☌ ♃ **5:05 am** 2:05 am
☽ ☌ ♅ **7:48 am** 4:48 am
☽ ⚻ ♃ **11:06 am** 8:06 am
☽ ⚻ ☿ **11:18 am** 8:18 am
☽ △ ☉ **5:39 pm** 2:39 pm

23 TUESDAY
☽ ⚻ ♂ **9:00 am** 6:00 am
☽ ⚻ ♄ **9:47 am** 6:47 am
☽ ⚹ ♆ **11:32 am** 8:32 am
☽ △ ♇ **6:43 pm** 3:43 pm

24 WEDNESDAY
♂ ☌ ♄ **7:26 am** 4:26 am
☽ △ ♀ **8:06 am** 5:06 am
☽ ⚺ ♅ **9:56 am** 6:56 am
☽ △ ♃ **2:06 pm** 11:06 am
☽ △ ☿ **3:38 pm** 12:38 pm
☽ □ ☉ **11:41 pm** 8:41 pm

25 THURSDAY
♀ ⚻ ♅ **5:08 am** 2:08 am
☽ ☍ ♄ **12:29 pm** 9:29 am
☽ ☍ ♂ **1:34 pm** 10:34 am
☽ □ ♆ **2:06 pm** 11:06 am
☽ ⚻ ♇ **9:29 pm** 6:29 pm
♂ □ ♆ 11:56 pm

26 FRIDAY
♂ □ ♆ **2:56 am**
☽ ⚹ ♅ **1:03 pm** 10:03 am
☽ □ ♀ **4:12 pm** 1:12 pm
☽ □ ♃ **6:09 pm** 3:09 pm
☽ □ ☿ **8:30 pm** 5:30 pm

27 SATURDAY
☽ ⚹ ☉ **7:08 am** 4:08 am
☽ ⚻ ♄ **4:30 pm** 1:30 pm
☽ △ ♆ **5:58 pm** 2:58 pm
♀ ☌ ♃ **6:29 pm** 3:29 pm
☽ ⚻ ♂ **7:39 pm** 4:39 pm
☽ ☍ ♇ 10:39 pm

28 SUNDAY
☽ ☍ ♇ **1:39 am**
☽ □ ♅ **5:41 pm** 2:41 pm
☽ ⚹ ♃ **11:54 pm** 8:54 pm
☽ ⚹ ♀ 11:23 pm
☽ ⚹ ☿ 11:23 pm
☿ ☌ ♀ 11:32 pm

29 MONDAY
☽ ⚹ ♀ **2:23 am**
☽ ⚹ ☿ **2:23 am**
☿ ☌ ♀ **2:32 am**
☽ ⚺ ☉ **4:43 pm** 1:43 pm
☽ △ ♄ **10:20 pm** 7:20 pm
☽ ⚻ ♆ **11:39 pm** 8:39 pm

30 TUESDAY
☽ △ ♂ **3:51 am** 12:51 am
☽ ⚻ ♇ **7:41 am** 4:41 am
☽ △ ♅ 9:20 pm

31 WEDNESDAY
☽ △ ♅ **12:20 am**
☽ ⚺ ♃ **7:49 am** 4:49 am
☽ ⚺ ☿ **9:32 am** 6:32 am
☽ ⚺ ♀ **3:20 pm** 12:20 pm

Eastern time in bold type
Pacific time in medium type

AUGUST 2016

DATE	SID. TIME	SUN	MOON	NODE	MERCURY	VENUS	MARS	JUPITER	SATURN	URANUS	NEPTUNE	PLUTO	CERES	PALLAS	JUNO	VESTA	CHIRON
1 M	20 40 42	9♌10 42	15♋36	13♍06	1♍54	24♌18	29♏21	22♍04	9♐54 Rx	24♈30	11♓27 Rx	15♑38 Rx	2♊50	2♒41	3♏01	2♋30	24♓44 Rx
2 T	20 44 44	10 08 07	29 19	13 01 Rx	3 23	25 31	29 43	22 15	9 53 Rx	24 30 Rx	11 27 Rx	15 37 Rx	2 59	2 27 Rx	3 11	2 54	24 43 Rx
3 W	20 48 1	11 05 34	12♌46	12 57	4 51	26 45	0♐06	22 26	9 52	24 30	11 25	15 35	3 08	2 14	3 22	3 18	24 41
4 Th	20 51 58	12 03 02	25 55	12 54	6 17	27 59	0 29	22 38	9 51	24 30	11 24	15 34	3 17	2 00	3 33	3 42	24 39
5 F	20 55 54	13 00 30	8♍46	12 53 D	7 42	29 13	0 52	22 49	9 50	24 29	11 23	15 33	3 26	1 46	3 44	4 06	24 37
6 Sa	20 59 51	13 57 59	21 18	12 53	9 04	0♍26	1 16	23 00	9 49	24 29	11 21	15 31	3 34	1 32	3 55	4 31	24 35
7 Su	21 3 47	14 55 29	3♎35	12 54	10 25	1 40	1 41	23 11	9 49	24 29	11 20	15 30	3 42	1 18	4 06	4 55	24 33
8 M	21 7 44	15 53 00	15 40	12 56	11 43	2 54	2 06	23 23	9 48	24 28	11 18	15 29	3 50	1 04	4 18	5 18	24 31
9 T	21 11 40	16 50 32	27 36	12 58	13 00	4 07	2 31	23 34	9 48	24 28	11 17	15 28	3 58	0 49	4 29	5 42	24 29
10 W	21 15 37	17 48 04	9♏28	12 59 Rx	14 15	5 21	2 57	23 46	9 47	24 28	11 15	15 27	4 05	0 34	4 41	6 06	24 27
11 Th	21 19 33	18 45 38	21 20	12 59	15 28	6 35	3 23	23 58	9 47	24 27	11 14	15 25	4 12	0 19	4 53	6 30	24 25
12 F	21 23 30	19 43 12	3♐18	12 58	16 38	7 49	3 49	24 09	9 47	24 27	11 13	15 24	4 19	0 04	5 06	6 54	24 23
13 Sa	21 27 26	20 40 47	15 26	12 56	17 46	9 02	4 16	24 21	9 47 D	24 26	11 11	15 23	4 25	29♑49	5 18	7 17	24 21
14 Su	21 31 23	21 38 24	27 49	12 54	18 51	10 16	4 44	24 33	9 47	24 26	11 09	15 22	4 31	29 34	5 31	7 41	24 19
15 M	21 35 20	22 36 01	10♑27	12 51	19 55	11 30	5 12	24 45	9 47	24 25	11 08	15 21	4 37	29 19	5 43	8 04	24 17
16 T	21 39 16	23 33 39	23 27	12 48	20 55	12 43	5 40	24 56	9 47	24 24	11 06	15 20	4 42	29 04	5 56	8 28	24 14
17 W	21 43 13	24 31 19	6♒46	12 46	21 53	13 57	6 08	25 08	9 47	24 23	11 05	15 19	4 48	28 48	6 10	8 51	24 12
18 Th	21 47 9	25 28 59	20 25	12 44	22 49	15 10	6 37	25 20	9 48	24 23	11 03	15 18	4 52	28 33	6 23	9 14	24 10
19 F	21 51 6	26 26 41	4♓20	12 43 D	23 41	16 24	7 06	25 32	9 48	24 22	11 02	15 17	4 57	28 18	6 36	9 38	24 07
20 Sa	21 55 2	27 24 25	18 30	12 43	24 30	17 37	7 36	25 44	9 49	24 21	11 00	15 16	5 01	28 02	6 50	10 01	24 05
21 Su	21 58 59	28 22 09	2♈48	12 44	25 16	18 51	8 06	25 57	9 50	24 19	10 58	15 15	5 05	27 47	7 04	10 24	24 03
22 M	22 2 55	29 19 56	17 12	12 45	25 58	20 05	8 36	26 09	9 50	24 18	10 57	15 14	5 08	27 31	7 17	10 47	24 00
23 T	22 6 52	0♍17 44	1♉36	12 46	26 37	21 19	9 07	26 21	9 51	24 17	10 55	15 13	5 11	27 16	7 31	11 10	23 58
24 W	22 10 49	1 15 33	16♉02	12 46 Rx	27 12	22 32	9 38	26 33	9 52	24 15	10 54	15 12	5 14	27 01	7 46	11 33	23 55
25 Th	22 14 45	2 13 25	0♊12	12 46	27 42	23 46	10 09	26 45	9 53	24 14	10 52	15 11	5 17	26 45	8 00	11 56	23 53
26 F	22 18 42	3 11 18	14 18	12 46	28 08	24 59	10 41	26 58	9 54	24 13	10 50	15 10	5 19	26 30	8 14	12 18	23 50
27 Sa	22 22 38	4 09 14	28 13	12 45	28 30	26 13	11 12	27 10	9 56	24 12	10 49	15 09	5 20	26 15	8 29	12 41	23 48
28 Su	22 26 35	5 07 11	11♋56	12 45	28 46	27 26	11 45	27 23	9 57	24 10	10 47	15 08	5 22	26 00	8 44	13 03	23 45
29 M	22 30 31	6 05 09	25 27	12 44	28 58	28 40	12 17	27 35	9 58	24 09	10 45	15 07	5 23	25 45	8 59	13 26	23 42
30 T	22 34 28	7 03 10	8♌43	12 43	29 04 Rx	29 54	12 50	27 47	10 00	24 08	10 44	15 07	5 24	25 30	9 14	13 48	23 40
31 W	22 38 24	8 01 12	21 46	12 43	29 04	1♎07	13 23	28 00	10 02	24 06	10 42	15 06	5 24 Rx	25 15	9 29	14 10	23 37

EPHEMERIS CALCULATED FOR 12 MIDNIGHT GREENWICH MEAN TIME. ALL OTHER DATA AND FACING ASPECTARIAN PAGE IN EASTERN TIME (**BOLD**) AND PACIFIC TIME (REGULAR).

SEPTEMBER 2016

☽ Last Aspect day	ET / hr:mn / PT		asp	☽ Ingress sign	day	ET / hr:mn / PT	
2	**6:13 pm**	3:13 pm	☌ ♃	♎	2	**8:55 pm**	5:55 pm
4	**8:30 pm**	5:30 pm	☍ ♅	♏	5	**8:38 am**	5:38 am
7	**8:43 pm**	5:43 pm	⚹ ♃	♐	7	**9:20 pm**	6:20 pm
9	**8:51 pm**	5:51 pm	△ ♅	♑	10	**8:55 am**	5:55 am
12	**6:00 am**	3:00 am	□ ♅	♒	12	**5:28 pm**	2:28 pm
14	**11:31 am**	8:31 am	⚹ ♅	♓	14	**10:23 pm**	7:23 pm
16	**3:05 pm**	12:05 pm	☍ ☉	♈	16		9:22 pm
16	**3:05 pm**	12:05 pm	☍ ☉	♈	17	**12:22 am**	
18	**4:11 pm**	1:11 pm	△ ♂	♉	18		9:58 pm
18	**4:11 pm**	1:11 pm	△ ♂	♉	19	**12:58 am**	
20	**11:32 pm**	8:32 pm	△ ☉	♊	20		10:53 pm
20	**11:32 pm**	8:32 pm	△ ☉	♊	21	**1:53 am**	
23	**3:57 am**	12:57 am	△ ♀	♋	23	**4:33 am**	1:33 am
24	**9:42 pm**	6:42 pm	□ ♅	♌	25	**9:48 am**	6:48 am
27	**4:52 am**	1:52 am	△ ♅	♍	27	**5:43 pm**	2:43 pm
29	**6:05 am**	3:05 am	☌ ☿	♎	30	**3:52 am**	12:52 am

☽ Phases & Eclipses phase	day	ET / hr:mn / PT	
New Moon	1	**5:03 am**	2:03 am
●	1	9° ♍ 21'	
2nd Quarter	9	**7:49 am**	4:49 am
Full Moon	16	**3:05 pm**	12:05 pm
●	16	24° ♓ 20'	
4th Quarter	23	**5:56 am**	2:56 am
New Moon	30	**8:11 pm**	5:11 pm

Planet Ingress	day	ET / hr:mn / PT	
♃ ♎	9	**7:18 am**	4:18 am
☉ ♎	22	**10:21 am**	7:21 am
♀ ♏	23	**10:51 am**	7:51 am
♂ ♑	27	**4:07 am**	1:07 am

Planetary Motion	day	ET / hr:mn / PT	
☿ D	21		10:31 pm
☿ D	22	**1:31 am**	
♇ D	26	**11:01 am**	8:01 am

1 THURSDAY

☽ ☌ ☉	**5:03 am**	2:03 am
☽ □ ♄	**6:25 am**	3:25 am
☽ ☍ ♆	**7:33 am**	4:33 am
☽ □ ♂	**2:39 pm**	11:39 am
☽ △ ♇	**3:59 pm**	12:59 pm
☉ □ ♄	**11:22 pm**	8:22 pm

2 FRIDAY

☽ ⚻ ♅	**9:18 am**	6:18 am
☉ ☍ ♆	**12:38 pm**	9:38 am
☿ ☌ ♃	**1:18 pm**	10:18 am
☽ ☌ ☿	**6:00 pm**	3:00 pm
☽ ☌ ♃	**6:13 pm**	3:13 pm
♂ ⚺ ♇	**7:54 pm**	4:54 pm

3 SATURDAY

☽ ☌ ♀	**7:30 am**	4:30 am
☽ ⚹ ♄	**4:55 pm**	1:55 pm
☽ ⚻ ♆	**5:48 pm**	2:48 pm
☽ ⚺ ☉	**8:25 pm**	5:25 pm
☽ □ ♇		11:39 pm

4 SUNDAY

☽ □ ♇	**2:39 am**	
☽ ⚹ ♂	**4:13 am**	1:13 am
☽ ☍ ♅	**8:30 pm**	5:30 pm

5 MONDAY

☽ ⚺ ☿	**3:22 am**	12:22 am
☽ ⚺ ♃	**6:55 am**	3:55 am
☽ ⚺ ♀		11:25 pm

Eastern time in bold type
Pacific time in medium type

6 TUESDAY

☽ ⚺ ♀	**2:25 am**	
☽ ⚺ ♄	**5:20 am**	2:20 am
☽ △ ♆	**5:55 am**	2:55 am
☽ ⚹ ☉	**2:06 pm**	11:06 am
☽ ⚹ ♇	**3:02 pm**	12:02 pm
☽ ⚺ ♂	**7:46 pm**	4:46 pm
☉ △ ♇		10:19 pm

7 WEDNESDAY

☉ △ ♇	**1:19 am**	
♀ ⚹ ♄	**7:34 am**	4:34 am
☽ ⚻ ♅	**9:00 am**	6:00 am
♀ ⚻ ♆	**11:39 am**	8:39 am
☽ ⚹ ☿	**12:38 pm**	9:38 am
☽ ⚹ ♃	**8:43 pm**	5:43 pm

8 THURSDAY

☽ ☌ ♄	**6:06 pm**	3:06 pm
☽ □ ♆	**6:20 pm**	3:20 pm
☽ ⚹ ♀	**9:54 pm**	6:54 pm

9 FRIDAY

☽ ⚺ ♇	**3:24 am**	12:24 am
☽ □ ☉	**7:49 am**	4:49 am
☽ ☌ ♂	**11:11 am**	8:11 am
☿ ⚻ ♅	**2:58 pm**	11:58 am
☽ □ ☿	**8:26 pm**	5:26 pm
☽ △ ♅	**8:51 pm**	5:51 pm

10 SATURDAY

♄ □ ♆	**9:04 am**	6:04 am
☽ □ ♃	**9:22 am**	6:22 am

11 SUNDAY

♀ □ ♇	**3:47 am**	12:47 am
☽ ⚹ ♆	**4:54 am**	1:54 am
☽ ⚺ ♄	**5:01 am**	2:01 am
☽ ☌ ♇	**1:37 pm**	10:37 am
☽ □ ♀	**2:40 pm**	11:40 am
☽ △ ☉	**10:36 pm**	7:36 pm
☽ ⚺ ♂	**11:51 pm**	8:51 pm
☽ △ ☿		10:37 pm

12 MONDAY

☽ △ ☿	**1:37 am**	
☽ □ ♅	**6:00 am**	3:00 am
☿ □ ♂	**2:58 pm**	11:58 am
☽ △ ♃	**6:50 pm**	3:50 pm
☉ ☌ ☿	**7:40 pm**	4:40 pm

13 TUESDAY

☽ ⚺ ♆	**12:05 pm**	9:05 am
☽ ⚹ ♄	**12:30 pm**	9:30 am
☉ □ ♂	**4:39 pm**	1:39 pm
☽ ⚺ ♇	**8:18 pm**	5:18 pm
☽ △ ♀		11:41 pm

14 WEDNESDAY

☽ △ ♀	**2:41 am**	
☽ ⚻ ☿	**3:53 am**	12:53 am
☽ ⚹ ♂	**8:23 am**	5:23 am
☽ ⚻ ☉	**8:50 am**	5:50 am
☿ ⚺ ♀	**10:44 am**	7:44 am
☽ ⚹ ♅	**11:31 am**	8:31 am
☽ ⚻ ♃		9:28 pm

15 THURSDAY

☽ ⚻ ♃	**12:28 am**	
☽ ☌ ♆	**3:45 pm**	12:45 pm
☽ □ ♄	**4:25 pm**	1:25 pm
☉ ⚻ ♅	**9:51 pm**	6:51 pm
☽ ⚹ ♇	**11:35 pm**	8:35 pm

16 FRIDAY

☽ ☍ ☿	**3:46 am**	12:46 am
☽ ⚻ ♀	**10:18 am**	7:18 am
☽ □ ♂	**1:17 pm**	10:17 am
☽ ⚺ ♅	**1:54 pm**	10:54 am
☽ ☍ ☉	**3:05 pm**	12:05 pm

17 SATURDAY

♂ △ ♅	**3:04 am**	12:04 am
☽ ☍ ♃	**3:06 am**	12:06 am
☽ ⚺ ♆	**4:59 pm**	1:59 pm
☽ △ ♄	**5:54 pm**	2:54 pm
☽ □ ♇		9:39 pm
☽ ⚻ ☿		11:27 pm

18 SUNDAY

☽ □ ♇	**12:39 am**	
☽ ⚻ ☿	**2:27 am**	
♀ ☍ ♅	**4:06 am**	1:06 am
☽ ☌ ♅	**2:32 pm**	11:32 am
☽ ☍ ♀	**3:30 pm**	12:30 pm
☽ △ ♂	**4:11 pm**	1:11 pm
☽ ⚻ ☉	**7:14 pm**	4:14 pm

19 MONDAY

☽ ⚻ ♃	**4:24 am**	1:24 am
♀ ⚹ ♂	**7:53 am**	4:53 am
☽ ⚹ ♆	**5:25 pm**	2:25 pm
☽ ⚻ ♄	**6:36 pm**	3:36 pm
☽ △ ♇		10:11 pm
☽ △ ☿		10:32 pm

20 TUESDAY

☽ △ ♇	**1:11 am**	
☽ △ ☿	**1:32 am**	
☽ ⚺ ♅	**3:08 pm**	12:08 pm
☽ ⚻ ♂	**7:07 pm**	4:07 pm
☽ ⚻ ♀	**8:40 pm**	5:40 pm
☿ △ ♇	**9:26 pm**	6:26 pm
☽ △ ☉	**11:32 pm**	8:32 pm

21 WEDNESDAY

☽ △ ♃	**6:08 am**	3:08 am
☽ □ ♆	**6:42 pm**	3:42 pm
☽ ☍ ♄	**8:13 pm**	5:13 pm
☽ □ ☿		11:38 pm
☽ ⚻ ♇		11:49 pm

22 THURSDAY

☽ □ ☿	**2:38 am**	
☽ ⚻ ♇	**2:49 am**	
☽ ⚹ ♅	**5:11 pm**	2:11 pm
☽ ☍ ♂	**11:53 pm**	8:53 pm

23 FRIDAY

☽ △ ♀	**3:57 am**	12:57 am
☿ △ ♇	**4:51 am**	1:51 am
☽ □ ☉	**5:56 am**	2:56 am
☽ □ ♃	**9:49 am**	6:49 am
☽ △ ♆	**10:06 pm**	7:06 pm
☽ ⚻ ♄		9:01 pm

24 SATURDAY

☽ ⚻ ♄	**12:01 am**	
☽ ☍ ♇	**6:42 am**	3:42 am
☽ ⚹ ☿	**7:15 am**	4:15 am
☽ □ ♅	**9:42 pm**	6:42 pm

25 SUNDAY

☽ ⚻ ♂	**7:37 am**	4:37 am
☽ □ ♀	**2:36 pm**	11:36 am
☽ ⚹ ☉	**3:33 pm**	12:33 pm
☽ ⚹ ♃	**4:14 pm**	1:14 pm

26 MONDAY

☉ ☌ ♃	**3:00 am**	12:00 am
☽ ⚻ ♆	**4:09 am**	1:09 am
☽ △ ♄	**6:34 am**	3:34 am
♀ ⚺ ♃	**11:35 am**	8:35 am
☽ ⚻ ♇	**1:19 pm**	10:19 am
☽ ⚺ ☿	**4:20 pm**	1:20 pm

27 TUESDAY

☽ △ ♅	**4:52 am**	1:52 am
☉ ⚺ ♀	**3:14 pm**	12:14 pm
☽ △ ♂	**6:27 pm**	3:27 pm
☽ ⚺ ♃		10:25 pm

28 WEDNESDAY

☽ ⚺ ♃	**1:25 am**	
☽ ⚺ ☉	**4:30 am**	1:30 am
☽ ⚹ ♀	**4:46 am**	1:46 am
☽ ☍ ♆	**12:46 pm**	9:46 am
☽ □ ♄	**3:42 pm**	12:42 pm
☽ △ ♇	**10:24 pm**	7:24 pm

29 THURSDAY

☽ ☌ ☿	**6:05 am**	3:05 am
☽ ⚻ ♅	**2:24 pm**	11:24 am

30 FRIDAY

☽ □ ♂	**7:58 am**	4:58 am
☽ ☌ ♃	**12:54 pm**	9:54 am
☽ ☌ ☉	**8:11 pm**	5:11 pm
☽ ⚺ ♀	**9:51 pm**	6:51 pm
☽ ⚻ ♆	**11:26 pm**	8:26 pm
☽ ⚹ ♄		11:55 pm

SEPTEMBER 2016

DATE	SID.TIME	SUN	MOON	NODE	MERCURY	VENUS	MARS	JUPITER	SATURN	URANUS	NEPTUNE	PLUTO	CERES	PALLAS	JUNO	VESTA	CHIRON
1 Th	22 42 21	8 ♍ 59 16	4 ♈ 35	12 ♍ 43 D	28 ♍ 58	2 ♎ 21	13 ♐ 56	28 ♍ 13	10 ♐ 03	24 ♈ 05	10 ♓ 40	15 ♑ 05	5 ♉ 24	25 ≈ 01	9 ♍ 44	14 ♋ 33	23 ♓ 35 ℞
2 F	22 46 18	9 57 22	17 10	12 43	28 47 ℞	3 34	14 30	28 25	10 05	24 03 ℞	10 39 ℞	15 04 ℞	5 23 ℞	24 47 ℞	9 59	14 55	23 32 ℞
3 Sa	22 50 14	10 55 29	29 32	12 43	28 29	4 48	15 04	28 38	10 07	24 02	10 37	15 04	5 22	24 32	10 15	15 17	23 29
4 Su	22 54 11	11 53 38	11 ♉ 42	12 43 ℞	28 04	6 01	15 38	28 50	10 09	24 00	10 35	15 03	5 21	24 18	10 31	15 39	23 27
5 M	22 58 7	12 51 48	23 43	12 43	27 34	7 15	16 13	29 03	10 11	23 58	10 34	15 02	5 20	24 04	10 46	16 00	23 24
6 T	23 2 4	13 50 00	5 ♊ 38	12 43	26 57	8 28	16 47	29 16	10 14	23 57	10 32	15 02	5 18	23 51	11 02	16 22	23 21
7 W	23 6 0	14 48 14	17 29	12 42	26 15	9 42	17 22	29 28	10 16	23 55	10 31	15 01	5 15	23 37	11 18	16 44	23 18
8 Th	23 9 57	15 46 29	29 21	12 42	25 15	10 55	17 57	29 41	10 18	23 53	10 29	15 01	5 13	23 24	11 34	17 05	23 16
9 F	23 13 53	16 44 45	11 ♋ 17	12 42 D	24 34	12 08	18 33	29 54	10 21	23 51	10 27	15 00	5 10	23 11	11 51	17 26	23 13
10 Sa	23 17 50	17 43 03	23 24	12 42	23 38	13 22	19 08	0 ♎ 07	10 23	23 50	10 26	15 00	5 08	22 59	12 07	17 48	23 10
11 Su	23 21 47	18 41 23	5 ♌ 44	12 42	22 39	14 35	19 44	0 20	10 26	23 48	10 24	14 59	5 02	22 46	12 23	18 09	23 08
12 M	23 25 43	19 39 44	18 23	12 44	21 38	15 49	20 20	0 32	10 29	23 46	10 22	14 59	4 58	22 34	12 40	18 30	23 05
13 T	23 29 40	20 38 07	1 ♍ 23	12 44	20 36	17 02	20 57	0 45	10 32	23 44	10 21	14 58	4 54	22 22	12 57	18 51	23 02
14 W	23 33 36	21 36 32	14 48	12 44	19 36	18 15	21 33	0 58	10 34	23 42	10 19	14 58	4 49	22 10	13 13	19 11	22 59
15 Th	23 37 33	22 34 58	28 36	12 45 ℞	18 38	19 29	22 10	1 11	10 37	23 40	10 18	14 58	4 44	21 59	13 30	19 32	22 57
16 F	23 41 29	23 33 26	12 ♎ 48	12 45	17 45	20 42	22 47	1 24	10 41	23 38	10 16	14 57	4 38	21 48	13 47	19 53	22 54
17 Sa	23 45 26	24 31 55	27 20	12 44	16 56	21 55	23 24	1 37	10 44	23 36	10 14	14 57	4 32	21 37	14 04	20 13	22 51
18 Su	23 49 22	25 30 27	12 ♏ 04	12 44	16 14	23 09	24 02	1 50	10 47	23 34	10 13	14 57	4 26	21 27	14 21	20 33	22 48
19 M	23 53 19	26 29 00	26 56	12 41	15 40	24 22	24 39	2 03	10 50	23 32	10 11	14 56	4 19	21 17	14 39	20 54	22 45
20 T	23 57 15	27 27 36	11 ♐ 45	12 38	15 14	25 35	25 17	2 16	10 54	23 30	10 10	14 56	4 12	21 07	14 56	21 14	22 43
21 W	0 1 12	28 26 14	26 26	12 38	14 57	26 48	25 55	2 28	10 57	23 28	10 08	14 56	4 04	20 57	15 13	21 34	22 40
22 Th	0 5 9	29 24 54	10 ♑ 53	12 37 D	14 50 D	28 02	26 33	2 41	11 01	23 26	10 07	14 56	3 57	20 48	15 31	21 53	22 37
23 F	0 9 5	0 ♎ 23 36	25 02	12 37	14 52	29 15	27 12	2 54	11 05	23 23	10 05	14 56	3 48	20 39	15 49	22 13	22 35
24 Sa	0 13 2	1 22 21	8 ♒ 52	12 37	15 05	0 ♏ 28	27 50	3 07	11 08	23 21	10 03	14 56	3 40	20 31	16 06	22 32	22 32
25 Su	0 16 58	2 21 08	22 22	12 38	15 27	1 41	28 29	3 20	11 12	23 19	10 02	14 56 D	3 31	20 23	16 24	22 52	22 29
26 M	0 20 55	3 19 57	5 ♓ 35	12 39	15 59	2 54	29 08	3 33	11 16	23 17	10 00	14 56	3 22	20 15	16 42	23 11	22 26
27 T	0 24 51	4 18 49	18 30	12 41	16 40	4 07	29 47	3 46	11 20	23 14	9 59	14 56	3 13	20 07	17 00	23 30	22 24
28 W	0 28 48	5 17 42	1 ♈ 12	12 42 ℞	17 26	5 21	0 ♑ 26	3 59	11 24	23 12	9 58	14 56	3 03	20 00	17 18	23 49	22 21
29 Th	0 32 44	6 16 38	13 41	12 42	18 26	6 34	1 05	4 12	11 28	23 10	9 56	14 56	2 53	19 53	17 36	24 08	22 18
30 F	0 36 41	7 15 36	26 00	12 42	19 31	7 47	1 45	4 25	11 33	23 08	9 55	14 56	2 42	19 46	17 54	24 26	22 16

EPHEMERIS CALCULATED FOR 12 MIDNIGHT GREENWICH MEAN TIME. ALL OTHER DATA AND FACING ASPECTARIAN PAGE IN **EASTERN TIME (BOLD)** AND PACIFIC TIME (REGULAR).

OCTOBER 2016

☽ Last Aspect day	ET / hr:mn / PT	asp	☽ Ingress sign day	ET / hr:mn / PT
1	10:43 pm	☍ ♅	♏ 2	**3:43 pm** 12:43 pm
2	**1:43 am**	☍ ♅	♏ 2	**3:43 pm** 12:43 pm
4	**9:04 pm** 6:04 pm	⚹ ☿	♐ 5	**4:26 am** 1:26 am
6	11:26 pm	△ ♅	♑ 7	**4:40 pm** 1:40 pm
7	**2:26 am**	△ ♅	♑ 7	**4:40 pm** 1:40 pm
9	**12:51 pm** 9:51 am	□ ♅	♒ 9	11:33 pm
9	**12:51 pm** 9:51 am	□ ♅	♒ 10	**2:33 am**
11	**7:49 pm** 4:49 pm	⚹ ♅	♓ 12	**8:43 am** 5:43 am
14	**3:13 am** 12:13 am	△ ♀	♈ 14	**11:08 am** 8:08 am
15	9:23 pm	☍ ☉	♉ 16	**11:04 am** 8:04 am
16	**12:23 am**	☍ ☉	♉ 16	**11:04 am** 8:04 am
17	**10:47 am** 7:47 am	△ ♇	♊ 18	**10:30 am** 7:30 am
20	**7:17 am** 4:17 am	△ ☉	♋ 20	**11:28 am** 8:28 am
22	**3:14 pm** 12:14 pm	□ ☉	♌ 22	**3:34 pm** 12:34 pm
24	**8:21 am** 5:21 am	△ ♅	♍ 24	**11:16 pm** 8:16 pm
26	**2:33 pm** 11:33 am	△ ♂	♎ 27	**9:51 am** 6:51 am
29	**6:09 am** 3:09 am	□ ♂	♏ 29	**10:01 pm** 7:01 pm
31	**10:44 pm** 7:44 pm	⚹ ♂	♐ 11/1	**10:43 am** 7:43 am

☽ Phases & Eclipses phase	day	ET / hr:mn / PT
2nd Quarter	8	9:33 pm
2nd Quarter	9	**12:33 am**
Full Moon	15	9:23 pm
Full Moon	16	**12:23 am**
4th Quarter	22	**3:14 pm** 12:14 pm
New Moon	30	**1:38 pm** 10:38 am

Planet Ingress	day	ET / hr:mn / PT
☿ ♎	7	**3:56 am** 12:56 am
⚳ ♈	13	**6:41 am** 3:41 am
♀ ♐	18	**3:01 am** 12:01 am
⚵ ♌	19	**9:06 pm** 6:06 pm
☉ ♏	22	**7:46 pm** 4:46 pm
☿ ♏	24	**4:46 pm** 1:46 pm

Planetary Motion	day	ET / hr:mn / PT
♀ D	17	**3:31 pm** 12:31 pm

1 SATURDAY
☽ ⚹ ♄ **2:55 am**
☽ □ ♇ **9:29 am** 6:29 am
♀ △ ♆ **1:13 pm** 10:13 am
☽ ⚺ ☿ 9:02 pm
☽ ☍ ♅ 10:43 pm

2 SUNDAY
☽ ⚺ ☿ **12:02 am**
☽ ☍ ♅ **1:43 am**
☉ ⚻ ♆ **11:11 am** 8:11 am
☿ ⚻ ♅ **2:19 pm** 11:19 am
☽ ⚹ ♂ **11:27 pm** 8:27 pm
☽ ⚺ ♃ 11:03 pm
♀ ⚺ ♄ 11:59 pm

3 MONDAY
☽ ⚺ ♃ **2:03 am**
♀ ⚺ ♄ **2:59 am**
☽ △ ♆ **11:33 am** 8:33 am
☽ ⚺ ☉ **1:49 pm** 10:49 am
☽ ⚺ ♄ **3:36 pm** 12:36 pm
☽ ☌ ♀ **4:57 pm** 1:57 pm
☽ ⚹ ♇ **9:55 pm** 6:55 pm

4 TUESDAY
☉ ⚹ ♄ **12:59 pm** 9:59 am
☽ ⚻ ♅ **2:08 pm** 11:08 am
☽ ⚹ ☿ **9:04 pm** 6:04 pm

5 WEDNESDAY
☽ ⚺ ♂ **3:51 pm** 12:51 pm
☽ ⚹ ♃ **3:56 pm** 12:56 pm
♀ ⚹ ♇ **5:22 pm** 2:22 pm
♂ □ ♃ **5:45 pm** 2:45 pm
☽ □ ♆ 9:12 pm

6 THURSDAY
☽ □ ♆ **12:12 am**
☽ ☌ ♄ **4:44 am** 1:44 am
☽ ⚹ ☉ **8:02 am** 5:02 am
☽ ⚺ ♇ **10:38 am** 7:38 am
☽ ⚺ ♀ **12:35 pm** 9:35 am
☽ △ ♅ 11:26 pm

7 FRIDAY
☽ △ ♅ **2:26 am**
☉ □ ♇ **3:33 pm** 12:33 pm
☽ □ ☿ **6:40 pm** 3:40 pm

8 SATURDAY
☽ □ ♃ **4:56 am** 1:56 am
☽ ☌ ♂ **7:18 am** 4:18 am
☽ ⚹ ♆ **11:46 am** 8:46 am
☽ ⚺ ♄ **4:38 pm** 1:38 pm
☽ ☌ ♇ **9:57 pm** 6:57 pm
☽ □ ☉ 9:33 pm

9 SUNDAY
☽ □ ☉ **12:33 am**
☽ ⚹ ♀ **6:10 am** 3:10 am
☽ □ ♅ **12:51 pm** 9:51 am

10 MONDAY
☽ △ ☿ **1:07 pm** 10:07 am
☽ △ ♃ **3:05 pm** 12:05 pm
☽ ⚺ ♂ **7:30 pm** 4:30 pm
☽ ⚺ ♆ **8:27 pm** 5:27 pm
☽ ⚹ ♄ 10:28 pm

11 TUESDAY
☽ ⚹ ♄ **1:28 am**
☿ ☌ ♃ **5:45 am** 2:45 am
☽ ⚺ ♇ **6:06 am** 3:06 am
☽ △ ☉ **12:58 pm** 9:58 am
♂ ⚹ ♆ **1:03 pm** 10:03 am
☽ □ ♀ **7:15 pm** 4:15 pm
☽ ⚹ ♅ **7:49 pm** 4:49 pm
♀ ⚻ ♅ 10:16 pm

12 WEDNESDAY
♀ ⚻ ♅ **1:16 am**
☿ ⚻ ♆ **7:59 pm** 4:59 pm
☽ ⚻ ♃ **9:11 pm** 6:11 pm
☽ ☌ ♆ 10:16 pm
☽ ⚻ ☿ 11:01 pm

13 THURSDAY
☽ ☌ ♆ **1:16 am**
☽ ⚻ ☿ **2:01 am**
☽ ⚹ ♂ **3:10 am** 12:10 am
☽ □ ♄ **6:19 am** 3:19 am
☽ ⚹ ♇ **10:20 am** 7:20 am
☿ □ ♂ **5:00 pm** 2:00 pm
☽ ⚻ ☉ **8:30 pm** 5:30 pm
☽ ⚺ ♅ **10:56 pm** 7:56 pm

14 FRIDAY
☽ △ ♀ **3:13 am** 12:13 am
☿ ⚹ ♄ **2:47 pm** 11:47 am
☽ ☍ ♃ **11:34 pm** 8:34 pm
☽ ⚺ ♆ 11:38 pm

15 SATURDAY
☽ ⚺ ♆ **2:38 am**
☉ ☍ ♅ **6:43 am** 3:43 am
☽ □ ♂ **6:54 am** 3:54 am
☽ △ ♄ **7:46 am** 4:46 am
☽ ☍ ☿ **9:53 am** 6:53 am
☽ □ ♇ **11:20 am** 8:20 am
☿ □ ♇ **10:29 pm** 7:29 pm
☽ ☌ ♅ **11:11 pm** 8:11 pm
☽ ☍ ☉ 9:23 pm

16 SUNDAY
☽ ☍ ☉ **12:23 am**
♂ ⚺ ♄ **4:14 am** 1:14 am
☽ ⚻ ♀ **7:37 am** 4:37 am
☽ ⚻ ♃ **11:51 pm** 8:51 pm
☽ ⚹ ♆ 11:08 pm

17 MONDAY
☽ ⚹ ♆ **2:08 am**
☽ ⚻ ♄ **7:31 am** 4:31 am
☽ △ ♂ **8:39 am** 5:39 am
☽ △ ♇ **10:47 am** 7:47 am
☽ ⚻ ☿ **3:25 pm** 12:25 pm
☽ ⚺ ♅ **10:25 pm** 7:25 pm

18 TUESDAY
☽ ⚻ ☉ **3:04 am** 12:04 am

☽ ☍ ♀ **11:09 am** 8:09 am
☽ △ ♃ 9:11 pm
☽ □ ♆ 10:47 pm

19 WEDNESDAY
☽ △ ♃ **12:11 am**
☽ □ ♆ **1:47 am**
♂ ☌ ♇ **7:22 am** 4:22 am
☽ ☍ ♄ **7:40 am** 4:40 am
☽ ⚻ ♇ **10:46 am** 7:46 am
☽ ⚻ ♂ **10:56 am** 7:56 am
☽ △ ☿ **9:59 pm** 6:59 pm
☽ ⚹ ♅ **10:41 pm** 7:41 pm

20 THURSDAY
☿ ☍ ♅ **3:48 am** 12:48 am
☽ △ ☉ **7:17 am** 4:17 am
☽ ⚻ ♀ **4:43 pm** 1:43 pm
☽ □ ♃ 11:41 pm

21 FRIDAY
☽ □ ♃ **2:41 am**
☽ △ ♆ **3:33 am** 12:33 am
☽ ⚻ ♄ **10:13 am** 7:13 am
☽ ☍ ♇ **1:13 pm** 10:13 am
☽ ☍ ♂ **4:04 pm** 1:04 pm
☽ □ ♅ 10:44 pm

22 SATURDAY
☽ □ ♅ **1:44 am**
☽ □ ☿ **8:30 am** 5:30 am
☽ □ ☉ **3:14 pm** 12:14 pm
☽ △ ♀ 11:28 pm

23 SUNDAY
☽ △ ♀ **2:28 am**
☽ ⚹ ♃ **8:44 am** 5:44 am
☽ ⚻ ♆ **8:44 am** 5:44 am
♃ ⚻ ♆ **9:33 am** 6:33 am
☽ △ ♄ **4:20 pm** 1:20 pm
☽ ⚻ ♇ **7:12 pm** 4:12 pm
☽ ⚻ ♂ 10:22 pm

24 MONDAY
☽ ⚻ ♂ **1:22 am**
☽ △ ♅ **8:21 am** 5:21 am
☽ ⚹ ☿ 9:16 pm

25 TUESDAY
☽ ⚹ ☿ **12:16 am**
☽ ⚹ ☉ **3:43 am** 12:43 am
☽ □ ♀ **4:55 pm** 1:55 pm
☽ ☍ ♆ **5:24 pm** 2:24 pm
☽ ⚺ ♃ **6:26 pm** 3:26 pm
♀ □ ♆ **9:54 pm** 6:54 pm
☽ □ ♄ 10:56 pm

26 WEDNESDAY
☽ □ ♄ **1:56 am**
☽ △ ♇ **4:34 am** 1:34 am
♀ ⚹ ♃ **11:19 am** 8:19 am
☽ △ ♂ **2:33 pm** 11:33 am
☽ ⚻ ♅ **6:06 pm** 3:06 pm

27 THURSDAY
☉ ☌ ☿ **12:16 pm** 9:16 am
☽ ⚺ ☉ **7:46 pm** 4:46 pm
☽ ⚺ ☿ **8:14 pm** 5:14 pm

28 FRIDAY
☽ ⚻ ♆ **4:33 am** 1:33 am
☽ ☌ ♃ **6:43 am** 3:43 am
☽ ⚹ ♀ **10:44 am** 7:44 am
☽ ⚹ ♄ **1:54 pm** 10:54 am
☽ □ ♇ **4:11 pm** 1:11 pm
♂ □ ♅ 9:06 pm

29 SATURDAY
♂ □ ♅ **12:06 am**
☽ ☍ ♅ **5:46 am** 2:46 am
☽ □ ♂ **6:09 am** 3:09 am
♀ ☌ ♄ **8:45 pm** 5:45 pm

30 SUNDAY
☿ △ ♆ **8:57 am** 5:57 am
☽ ☌ ☉ **1:38 pm** 10:38 am
☽ △ ♆ **4:56 pm** 1:56 pm
♀ ⚺ ♇ **5:27 pm** 2:27 pm
☽ ☌ ☿ **6:12 pm** 3:12 pm
☽ ⚺ ♃ **8:14 pm** 5:14 pm
☽ ⚺ ♄ 11:57 pm

31 MONDAY
☽ ⚺ ♄ **2:57 am**
☽ ⚹ ♇ **4:49 am** 1:49 am
☽ ⚺ ♀ **6:05 am** 3:05 am
☿ ⚺ ♃ **10:54 am** 7:54 am
☽ ⚻ ♅ **6:13 pm** 3:13 pm
☽ ⚹ ♂ **10:44 pm** 7:44 pm

Eastern time in bold type
Pacific time in medium type

OCTOBER 2016

DATE	SID. TIME	SUN	MOON	NODE	MERCURY	VENUS	MARS	JUPITER	SATURN	URANUS	NEPTUNE	PLUTO	CERES	PALLAS	JUNO	VESTA	CHIRON
1 Sa	0 40 38	8 ♎ 14 36	8 ♎ 09	12 ♍ 40	20 ♍ 42	9 ♏ 00	2 ♐ 25	4 ♎ 38	11 ♐ 37	23 ♈ 05	9 ♓ 53	14 ♑ 56	2 ♉ 32	19 ♈ 41	18 ♍ 13	24 ♋ 45	22 ♓ 13
2 Su	0 44 34	9 13 38	20 11	12 36 Rx	21 59	10 13	3 05	4 51	11 41	23 03 Rx	9 52 Rx	14 56	2 21 Rx	19 35 Rx	18 31	25 03	22 10 Rx
3 M	0 48 31	10 12 42	2 ♏ 00	12 32	23 21	11 26	3 45	5 04	11 46	23 01	9 50	14 56	2 10	19 30	18 49	25 21	22 08
4 T	0 52 27	11 11 48	14 00	12 27	24 47	12 39	4 25	5 17	11 50	22 58	9 49	14 57	1 58	19 25	19 06	25 39	22 05
5 W	0 56 24	12 10 55	25 50	12 22	26 18	13 52	5 05	5 30	11 55	22 56	9 48	14 57	1 47	19 20	19 26	25 57	22 03
6 Th	1 0 20	13 10 05	7 ♐ 42	12 17	27 51	15 05	5 46	5 43	12 00	22 53	9 46	14 57	1 35	19 16	19 45	26 14	22 00
7 F	1 4 17	14 09 17	19 37	12 13	29 28	16 18	6 26	5 56	12 04	22 51	9 45	14 57	1 23	19 12	20 04	26 32	21 58
8 Sa	1 8 13	15 08 30	1 ♑ 41	12 10	1 ♎ 06	17 31	7 07	6 09	12 09	22 49	9 44	14 58	1 10	19 08	20 23	26 49	21 55
9 Su	1 12 10	16 07 45	13 58	12 10 D	2 46	18 44	7 48	6 22	12 14	22 46	9 43	14 58	0 58	19 05	20 42	27 06	21 53
10 M	1 16 7	17 07 02	26 31	12 10	4 28	19 57	8 29	6 35	12 19	22 44	9 41	14 58	0 45	19 02	21 00	27 23	21 50
11 T	1 20 3	18 06 21	9 ♒ 26	12 11	6 11	21 10	9 10	6 47	12 24	22 41	9 40	14 59	0 32	18 59	21 19	27 39	21 48
12 W	1 24 0	19 05 41	22 45	12 13	7 54	22 22	9 51	7 00	12 29	22 39	9 39	14 59	0 19	18 57	21 39	27 56	21 46
13 Th	1 27 56	20 05 03	6 ♓ 32	12 14 Rx	9 38	23 35	10 33	7 13	12 34	22 36	9 38	15 00	0 06	18 55	21 58	28 12	21 43
14 F	1 31 53	21 04 27	20 47	12 14	11 22	24 48	11 14	7 26	12 40	22 34	9 37	15 00	29 ♈ 53	18 54	22 17	28 28	21 41
15 Sa	1 35 49	22 03 53	5 ♈ 28	12 12	13 06	26 01	11 56	7 39	12 45	22 32	9 36	15 01	29 39	18 53	22 36	28 44	21 39
16 Su	1 39 46	23 03 21	20 28	12 08	14 51	27 13	12 38	7 51	12 50	22 29	9 34	15 01	29 26	18 52	22 55	28 59	21 36
17 M	1 43 42	24 02 51	5 ♉ 40	12 02	16 35	28 26	13 20	8 04	12 56	22 27	9 33	15 02	29 12	18 52 D	23 15	29 15	21 34
18 T	1 47 39	25 02 23	20 53	11 55	18 19	29 39	14 01	8 17	13 01	22 24	9 32	15 02	28 58	18 52	23 34	29 30	21 32
19 W	1 51 35	26 01 57	5 ♊ 56	11 49	20 02	0 ♐ 51	14 44	8 30	13 07	22 19	9 31	15 03	28 45	18 52	23 54	29 45	21 30
20 Th	1 55 32	27 01 33	20 42	11 44	21 44	2 04	15 26	8 42	13 12	22 17	9 30	15 03	28 31	18 53	24 13	29 59	21 28
21 F	1 59 29	28 01 12	5 ♋ 03	11 40	23 28	3 17	16 08	8 55	13 18	22 14	9 29	15 04	28 17	18 54	24 33	0 ♌ 14	21 26
22 Sa	2 3 25	29 00 53	18 58	11 37 D	25 11	4 29	16 50	9 07	13 23	22 12	9 29	15 05	28 03	18 54	24 52	0 28	21 24
23 Su	2 7 22	0 ♏ 00 36	2 ♌ 28	11 37	26 52	5 42	17 33	9 20	13 29	22 10	9 28	15 06	27 50	18 56	25 12	0 42	21 22
24 M	2 11 18	1 00 21	15 33	11 38	28 33	6 54	18 16	9 32	13 35	22 07	9 27	15 07	27 36	18 58	25 32	0 56	21 20
25 T	2 15 15	2 00 09	28 17	11 39	0 ♏ 14	8 07	18 58	9 45	13 41	22 05	9 26	15 08	27 22	19 00	25 51	1 09	21 18
26 W	2 19 11	2 59 59	10 ♍ 45	11 39 Rx	1 54	9 19	19 41	9 57	13 47	22 02	9 25	15 09	27 09	19 03	26 11	1 22	21 16
27 Th	2 23 8	3 59 51	23 00	11 39	3 33	10 32	20 24	10 10	13 53	22 00	9 24	15 10	26 55	19 05	26 31	1 35	21 14
28 F	2 27 4	4 59 45	5 ♎ 06	11 38	5 12	11 44	21 07	10 22	13 59	21 58	9 23	15 10	26 41	19 09	26 51	1 48	21 12
29 Sa	2 31 1	5 59 41	17 05	11 36	6 51	12 56	21 50	10 35	14 05	21 55	9 23	15 11	26 28	19 12	27 11	2 00	21 10
30 Su	2 34 58	6 59 40	29 00	11 22	8 29	14 09	22 33	10 47	14 11	21 55	9 22	15 12	26 15	19 16	27 31	2 12	21 09
31 M	2 38 54	7 59 40	10 ♏ 55	11 12	10 06	15 21	23 16	10 59	14 17	21 53	9 21	15 13	26 02	19 20	27 51	2 24	21 07

EPHEMERIS CALCULATED FOR 12 MIDNIGHT GREENWICH MEAN TIME. ALL OTHER DATA AND FACING ASPECTARIAN PAGE IN EASTERN TIME (**BOLD**) AND PACIFIC TIME (REGULAR).

NOVEMBER 2016

☽ Last Aspect day	ET / hr:mn / PT		asp	☽ Ingress sign	day	ET / hr:mn / PT	
31	**10:44 pm**	7:44 pm	⚹♂	♐	1	**10:43 am**	7:43 am
3	**6:35 am**	3:35 am	△♅	♑	3	**11:05 pm**	8:05 pm
6	**4:56 am**	1:56 am	☌♂	♒	6	**8:55 am**	5:55 am
8	**8:54 am**	5:54 am	⚹♀	♓	8	**4:45 pm**	1:45 pm
10	**6:16 pm**	3:16 pm	□♀	♈	10	**8:45 pm**	5:45 pm
12	**7:45 am**	4:45 am	☌♅	♉	12	**9:24 pm**	6:24 pm
14	**8:52 am**	5:52 am	☍☉	♊	14	**8:23 pm**	5:23 pm
16	**5:58 am**	2:58 am	⚹♅	♋	16	**7:57 pm**	4:57 pm
18	**5:02 pm**	2:02 pm	△☉	♌	18	**10:14 pm**	7:14 pm
21	**3:33 am**	12:33 am	□☉	♍	21	**4:34 am**	1:34 am
22	**12:41 pm**	9:41 am	□♄	♎	23	**2:42 pm**	11:42 am
25	**8:52 am**	5:52 am	☍♅	♏	26	**3:01 am**	12:01 am
27	**4:48 pm**	1:48 pm	⚹♀	♐	28	**3:46 pm**	12:46 pm
30	**11:08 pm**	8:08 pm	☌☿	♑	12/1	**3:52 am**	12:52 am

☽ Phases & Eclipses phase	day	ET / hr:mn / PT	
2nd Quarter	7	**2:51 pm**	11:51 am
Full Moon	14	**8:52 am**	5:52 am
4th Quarter	21	**3:33 am**	12:33 am
New Moon	29	**7:18 am**	4:18 am

Planet Ingress		day	ET / hr:mn / PT	
⚳	♐	6	**4:40 am**	1:40 am
♂	♒	8		9:51 pm
♂	♒	9	**12:51 am**	
♀	♑	11	**11:54 pm**	8:54 pm
☿	♐	12	**9:40 am**	6:40 am
☉	♐	21	**4:22 pm**	1:22 pm

Planetary Motion		day	ET / hr:mn / PT	
♆	D	19	**11:38 pm**	8:38 pm

1 TUESDAY
☉△♆ **4:17 am** 1:17 am

2 WEDNESDAY
☽□♆ **5:34 am** 2:34 am
☽⊻☉ **7:55 am** 4:55 am
☽⚹♃ **9:58 am** 6:58 am
☿⊻♄ **2:29 pm** 11:29 am
☽☌♄ **4:09 pm** 1:09 pm
☽⊻☿ **4:24 pm** 1:24 pm
☽⊻♇ **5:34 pm** 2:34 pm
☿⚹♇ 10:10 pm
☽☌♀ 10:32 pm

3 THURSDAY
☿⚹♇ **1:10 am**
☽☌♀ **1:32 am**
☽△♅ **6:35 am** 3:35 am
☉⊻♃ **1:54 pm** 10:54 am
☽⊻♂ **3:09 pm** 12:09 pm

4 FRIDAY
☽⚹♆ **5:34 pm** 2:34 pm
☽□♃ **10:56 pm** 7:56 pm
☽⚹☉ 10:18 pm
♀△♅ 11:23 pm

5 SATURDAY
☽⚹☉ **1:18 am**
♀△♅ **2:23 am**
☽⊻♄ **4:29 am** 1:29 am
☽☌♇ **5:25 am** 2:25 am

☽⚹☿ **1:06 pm** 10:06 am
☽□♅ **5:48 pm** 2:48 pm
☽⊻♀ **7:31 pm** 4:31 pm

6 SUNDAY
☽☌♂ **4:56 am** 1:56 am
☉⊻♄ **7:15 pm** 4:15 pm
☿⊼♅ 9:11 pm
☽⊻♆ 11:35 pm

7 MONDAY
☿⊼♅ **12:11 am**
☽⊻♆ **2:35 am**
☉⚹♇ **3:25 am** 12:25 am
☽△♃ **8:38 am** 5:38 am
☽⚹♄ **1:29 pm** 10:29 am
☽⊻♇ **1:59 pm** 10:59 am
☽□☉ **2:51 pm** 11:51 am
☽⚹♅ 10:27 pm

8 TUESDAY
☽⚹♅ **1:27 am**
☽□☿ **4:57 am** 1:57 am
☽⚹♀ **8:54 am** 5:54 am
☽⊻♂ **4:17 pm** 1:17 pm

9 WEDNESDAY
☽☌♆ **9:14 am** 6:14 am
☽⊼♃ **3:41 pm** 12:41 pm
☽□♄ **7:50 pm** 4:50 pm
☽⚹♇ **7:57 pm** 4:57 pm
☽△☉ 9:52 pm

10 THURSDAY
☽△☉ **12:52 am**
☽⊻♅ **6:24 am** 3:24 am
♄⊻♇ **2:39 pm** 11:39 am
☽△☿ **4:17 pm** 1:17 pm
☽□♀ **6:16 pm** 3:16 pm
☽⚹♂ **11:06 pm** 8:06 pm

11 FRIDAY
☽⊻♆ **12:03 pm** 9:03 am
☽☍♃ **6:46 pm** 3:46 pm
☽□♇ **10:09 pm** 7:09 pm
☽△♄ **10:20 pm** 7:20 pm

12 SATURDAY
☽⊼☉ **6:16 am** 3:16 am
☽☌♅ **7:45 am** 4:45 am
☽⊼☿ **10:43 pm** 7:43 pm
☽△♀ **11:14 pm** 8:14 pm
☽□♂ 11:06 pm

13 SUNDAY
☽□♂ **2:06 am**
☉⊼♅ **3:38 am** 12:38 am
☽⚹♆ **11:58 am** 8:58 am
☽⊼♃ **7:01 pm** 4:01 pm
☿⊻♀ **7:43 pm** 4:43 pm
☽△♇ **9:45 pm** 6:45 pm
☽⊼♄ **10:13 pm** 7:13 pm

14 MONDAY
☽⊻♅ **6:54 am** 3:54 am
☽☍☉ **8:52 am** 5:52 am

☽⊼♀ 11:10 pm
☽☍☿ 11:54 pm

15 TUESDAY
☽⊼♀ **2:10 am**
☽☍☿ **2:54 am**
☽△♂ **3:25 am** 12:25 am
☽□♆ **10:53 am** 7:53 am
☿⚹♂ **12:22 pm** 9:22 am
☽△♃ **6:35 pm** 3:35 pm
☽⊼♇ **8:49 pm** 5:49 pm
☽☍♄ **9:34 pm** 6:34 pm

16 WEDNESDAY
☽⚹♅ **5:58 am** 2:58 am
☽⊼☉ **11:29 am** 8:29 am
♀⊻♂ **6:38 pm** 3:38 pm

17 THURSDAY
☽⊼♂ **5:49 am** 2:49 am
☽☍♀ **6:11 am** 3:11 am
☽⊼☿ **8:17 am** 5:17 am
☽△♆ **11:04 am** 8:04 am
☽□♃ **7:50 pm** 4:50 pm
☽☍♇ **9:39 pm** 6:39 pm
☽⊼♄ **10:45 pm** 7:45 pm

18 FRIDAY
☽□♅ **7:10 am** 4:10 am
☿□♆ **11:04 am** 8:04 am
☽△☉ **5:02 pm** 2:02 pm

19 SATURDAY
☽☍♂ **11:48 am** 8:48 am
☽⊼♀ **2:11 pm** 11:11 am

☽⊼♆ **2:31 pm** 11:31 am
☽△☿ **6:00 pm** 3:00 pm
♀⚹♆ **6:03 pm** 3:03 pm
☽⚹♃ 9:44 pm
☽⊼♇ 11:04 pm

20 SUNDAY
☽⚹♃ **12:44 am**
☽⊼♇ **2:04 am**
☽△♄ **3:36 am** 12:36 am
☽△♅ **12:08 pm** 9:08 am

21 MONDAY
☽□☉ **3:33 am** 12:33 am
♂⊻♆ **1:06 pm** 10:06 am
☽☍♆ **10:08 pm** 7:08 pm
☽⊼♂ **10:42 pm** 7:42 pm

22 TUESDAY
☽△♀ **3:36 am** 12:36 am
☽□☿ **9:32 am** 6:32 am
☽⊻♃ **9:56 am** 6:56 am
☽△♇ **10:38 am** 7:38 am
☽□♄ **12:41 pm** 9:41 am
☿⚹♃ **1:19 pm** 10:19 am
☿⊻♇ **6:48 pm** 3:48 pm
☽⊼♅ **9:08 pm** 6:08 pm

23 WEDNESDAY
☿☌♄ **1:44 pm** 10:44 am
☽⚹☉ **6:56 pm** 3:56 pm

24 THURSDAY
☽⊼♆ **9:09 am** 6:09 am
☽△♂ **1:40 pm** 10:40 am

♃□♇ **6:00 pm** 3:00 pm
☽□♀ **9:22 pm** 6:22 pm
☽□♇ **10:17 pm** 7:17 pm
☽☌♃ **10:21 pm** 7:21 pm
☽⚹♄ 9:52 pm

25 FRIDAY
☽⚹♄ **12:52 am**
☽⚹☿ **5:28 am** 2:28 am
♀☌♇ **6:50 am** 3:50 am
♀□♃ **8:45 am** 5:45 am
☽☍♅ **8:52 am** 5:52 am

26 SATURDAY
☿△♅ **8:38 am** 5:38 am
♀⊻♄ **12:13 pm** 9:13 am
☽⊻☉ **12:59 pm** 9:59 am
☽△♆ **9:47 pm** 6:47 pm

27 SUNDAY
☽□♂ **6:24 am** 3:24 am
☽⚹♇ **11:09 am** 8:09 am
☽⊻♃ **11:59 am** 8:59 am
☽⊻♄ **2:13 pm** 11:13 am
☽⚹♀ **4:48 pm** 1:48 pm
☽⊼♅ **9:30 pm** 6:30 pm
☽⊻☿ 11:44 pm

28 MONDAY
☽⊻☿ **2:44 am**

29 TUESDAY
☽☌☉ **7:18 am** 4:18 am
☽□♆ **10:26 am** 7:26 am
♀□♅ **3:20 pm** 12:20 pm

☽⚹♂ **10:59 pm** 7:59 pm
☽⊻♇ **11:47 pm** 8:47 pm
☽⚹♃ 10:20 pm

30 WEDNESDAY
☽⚹♃ **1:20 am**
☽☌♄ **3:16 am** 12:16 am
☽△♅ **9:45 am** 6:45 am
☽⊻♀ **11:47 am** 8:47 am
♂⊻♇ **12:15 pm** 9:15 am
☉□♆ **8:17 pm** 5:17 pm
☽☌☿ **11:08 pm** 8:08 pm

Eastern time in bold type
Pacific time in medium type

NOVEMBER 2016

DATE	SID.TIME	SUN	MOON	NODE	MERCURY	VENUS	MARS	JUPITER	SATURN	URANUS	NEPTUNE	PLUTO	CERES	PALLAS	JUNO	VESTA	CHIRON
1 T	2 42 51	8 ♏ 59 42	22 ♏ 44	11 ♏ 01	11 ♏ 43	16 ✗ 33	24 ♑ 00	11 ♎ 11	14 ✗ 23	21 ♈ 51 ℞	9 ✗ 21	15 ♑ 14	25 ♈ 49	19 ♒ 24	28 ♏ 11	2 ♌ 36	21 ✗ 05
2 W	2 46 47	9 59 46	4 ✗ 35	10 49 ℞	13 20	17 45	24 43	11 24	14 36	21 48 ℞	9 20 ℞	15 16	25 36 ℞	19 29	28 31	2 47	21 04 ℞
3 Th	2 50 44	10 59 52	16 29	10 38	14 56	18 58	25 27	11 36	14 48	21 46	9 19	15 17	25 23	19 34	28 51	2 58	21 02
4 F	2 54 40	11 59 59	28 27	10 30	16 32	20 10	26 10	11 48	14 42	21 44	9 19	15 18	25 11	19 39	29 11	3 09	21 01
5 Sa	2 58 37	13 00 08	10 ♑ 32	10 21	18 07	21 22	26 54	12 00	14 48	21 42	9 18	15 19	24 58	19 45	29 32	3 19	20 59
6 Su	3 2 33	14 00 19	22 47	10 16	19 42	22 34	27 38	12 12	14 55	21 39	9 18	15 20	24 46	19 51	29 52	3 29	20 58
7 M	3 6 30	15 00 31	5 ♒ 17	10 14 D	21 16	23 46	28 21	12 24	15 01	21 37	9 17	15 21	24 35	19 57	0 ✗ 12	3 39	20 57
8 T	3 10 27	16 00 45	18 05	10 13	22 51	24 58	29 05	12 36	15 08	21 35	9 17	15 22	24 23	20 03	0 33	3 48	20 55
9 W	3 14 23	17 01 00	1 ✗ 15	10 14 ℞	24 24	26 10	29 49	12 47	15 14	21 33	9 17	15 24	24 12	20 10	0 53	3 57	20 54
10 Th	3 18 20	18 01 16	14 52	10 14	25 58	27 22	0 ♒ 33	12 59	15 21	21 31	9 16	15 25	24 01	20 17	1 13	4 06	20 53
11 F	3 22 16	19 01 34	28 57	10 12	27 31	28 34	1 17	13 11	15 27	21 29	9 16	15 26	23 50	20 24	1 34	4 14	20 52
12 Sa	3 26 13	20 01 53	13 ♑ 31	10 09	29 04	29 45	2 01	13 22	15 34	21 27	9 16	15 28	23 39	20 31	1 54	4 22	20 51
13 Su	3 30 9	21 02 14	28 29	10 02	0 ✗ 36	0 ♑ 57	2 46	13 34	15 40	21 25	9 15	15 29	23 29	20 39	2 14	4 30	20 50
14 M	3 34 6	22 02 37	13 ♉ 45	9 53	2 08	2 09	3 30	13 45	15 47	21 23	9 15	15 30	23 19	20 47	2 35	4 37	20 49
15 T	3 38 2	23 03 01	29 07	9 43	3 40	3 20	4 14	13 57	15 54	21 21	9 15	15 32	23 10	20 55	2 55	4 44	20 48
16 W	3 41 59	24 03 27	14 ♊ 24	9 32	5 11	4 32	4 58	14 08	16 01	21 19	9 15	15 33	23 00	21 04	3 16	4 51	20 47
17 Th	3 45 56	25 03 54	29 25	9 23	6 43	5 43	5 43	14 19	16 07	21 17	9 15	15 34	22 51	21 12	3 36	4 57	20 46
18 F	3 49 52	26 04 23	14 ♋ 01	9 14	8 14	6 55	6 27	14 31	16 14	21 15	9 15	15 36	22 43	21 21	3 57	5 03	20 45
19 Sa	3 53 49	27 04 55	28 08	9 09	9 44	8 06	7 12	14 42	16 21	21 13	9 14	15 37	22 35	21 30	4 18	5 08	20 45
20 Su	3 57 45	28 05 27	11 ♌ 45	9 06	11 15	9 17	7 56	14 53	16 28	21 11	9 14 D	15 39	22 27	21 40	4 38	5 13	20 44
21 M	4 1 42	29 06 02	24 53	9 05 D	12 45	10 28	8 41	15 04	16 35	21 09	9 14	15 40	22 19	21 49	4 59	5 18	20 43
22 T	4 5 38	0 ✗ 06 38	7 ♍ 37	9 05 ℞	14 15	11 40	9 25	15 15	16 42	21 08	9 15	15 42	22 12	21 59	5 19	5 22	20 43
23 W	4 9 35	1 07 16	20 01	9 04	15 44	12 51	10 10	15 26	16 48	21 06	9 15	15 44	22 05	22 09	5 40	5 26	20 42
24 Th	4 13 31	2 07 56	2 ♎ 11	9 03	17 13	14 02	10 55	15 36	16 55	21 04	9 15	15 45	21 59	22 20	6 01	5 30	20 42
25 F	4 17 28	3 08 37	14 09	8 58	18 42	15 13	11 40	15 47	17 02	21 03	9 15	15 47	21 52	22 30	6 21	5 33	20 41
26 Sa	4 21 25	4 09 20	26 02	8 51	20 10	16 23	12 24	15 58	17 09	21 01	9 15	15 48	21 47	22 41	6 42	5 36	20 41
27 Su	4 25 21	5 10 04	7 ♏ 53	8 41	21 38	17 34	13 09	16 08	17 16	21 00	9 15	15 50	21 41	22 52	7 03	5 38	20 41
28 M	4 29 18	6 10 50	19 44	8 28	23 05	18 45	13 54	16 19	17 23	20 58	9 16	15 52	21 36	23 03	7 23	5 40	20 41
29 T	4 33 14	7 11 37	1 ✗ 36	8 13	24 32	19 56	14 39	16 29	17 30	20 57	9 16	15 53	21 32	23 14	7 44	5 41	20 40
30 W	4 37 11	8 12 26	13 32	7 58	25 58	21 06	15 24	16 39	17 37	20 55	9 16	15 55	21 28	23 26	8 05	5 42	20 40

EPHEMERIS CALCULATED FOR 12 MIDNIGHT GREENWICH MEAN TIME. ALL OTHER DATA AND FACING ASPECTARIAN PAGE IN EASTERN TIME (**BOLD**) AND PACIFIC TIME (REGULAR).

DECEMBER 2016

☽ Last Aspect day	ET / hr:mn / PT		asp	☽ Ingress sign	day	ET / hr:mn / PT	
11/30	**11:08 pm**	8:08 pm	☌ ☿	♑	1	**3:52 am**	12:52 am
3	**5:16 pm**	2:16 pm	☌ ♀	♒	3	**2:44 pm**	11:44 am
5	**6:23 am**	3:23 am	✶ ♅	♓	5	**11:31 pm**	8:31 pm
7	**9:05 am**	6:05 am	□ ♄	♈	8	**5:15 am**	2:15 am
9	**8:06 pm**	5:06 pm	✶ ♂	♉	10	**7:41 am**	4:41 am
11	**11:04 pm**	8:04 pm	□ ♂	♊	12	**7:41 am**	4:41 am
13		9:58 pm	△ ♂	♋	14	**7:09 am**	4:09 am
14	**12:58 am**		△ ♂	♋	14	**7:09 am**	4:09 am
15	**4:37 pm**	1:37 pm	□ ♅	♌	16	**8:15 am**	5:15 am
18	**11:55 am**	8:55 am	☍ ♂	♍	18	**12:52 pm**	9:52 am

☽ Last Aspect day	ET / hr:mn / PT		asp	☽ Ingress sign	day	ET / hr:mn / PT	
20	**8:56 pm**	5:56 pm	□ ☉	♎	20	**9:40 pm**	6:40 pm
22	**2:31 pm**	11:31 am	☍ ♅	♏	23	**9:32 am**	6:32 am
24		11:22 pm	□ ♀	♐	25	**10:19 pm**	7:19 pm
25	**2:22 am**		□ ♀	♐	25	**10:19 pm**	7:19 pm
27	**8:45 pm**	5:45 pm	✶ ♀	♑	28	**10:12 am**	7:12 am
30	**3:07 am**	12:07 am	□ ♃	♒	30	**8:29 pm**	5:29 pm

☽ Phases & Eclipses phase	day	ET / hr:mn / PT	
2nd Quarter	7	**4:03 am**	1:03 am
Full Moon	13	**7:06 pm**	4:06 pm
4th Quarter	20	**8:56 pm**	5:56 pm
New Moon	28		10:53 pm
New Moon	29	**1:53 am**	

Planet Ingress		day	ET / hr:mn / PT	
☿	♑	2	**4:18 pm**	1:18 pm
♀	♒	7	**9:51 am**	6:51 am
♂	♓	19	**4:23 am**	1:23 am
☉	♑	21	**5:44 am**	2:44 am
♀	♓	27	**7:23 pm**	4:23 pm

Planetary Motion		day	ET / hr:mn / PT	
⚷	D	1	**4:53 am**	1:53 am
⚵	R	1	**10:38 am**	7:38 am
⚳	D	9	**7:26 pm**	4:26 pm
☿	R	19	**5:55 am**	2:55 am
♅	D	29	**4:29 am**	1:29 am

1 THURSDAY
- ☽ ✶ ♆ **10:15 pm** 7:15 pm
- ♂ △ ♃ **10:46 pm** 7:46 pm
- ☽ ⊻ ☉ 9:36 pm

2 FRIDAY
- ☽ ⊻ ☉ **12:36 am**
- ☽ ☌ ♇ **11:27 am** 8:27 am
- ☽ □ ♃ **1:40 pm** 10:40 am
- ☽ ⊻ ♂ **2:25 pm** 11:25 am
- ☽ ⊻ ♄ **3:18 pm** 12:18 pm
- ☽ □ ♅ **8:57 pm** 5:57 pm

3 SATURDAY
- ☽ ☌ ♀ **5:16 am** 2:16 am
- ♂ ✶ ♄ **7:15 am** 4:15 am
- ☽ ⊻ ☿ **5:30 pm** 2:30 pm

4 SUNDAY
- ☽ ⊻ ♆ **8:36 am** 5:36 am
- ☽ ✶ ☉ **3:56 pm** 12:56 pm
- ☽ ⊻ ♇ **9:28 pm** 6:28 pm
- ☽ △ ♃ 9:13 pm
- ☽ ✶ ♄ 10:34 pm

5 MONDAY
- ☽ △ ♃ **12:13 am**
- ☽ ✶ ♄ **1:34 am**
- ☽ ☌ ♂ **3:49 am** 12:49 am
- ☽ ✶ ♅ **6:23 am** 3:23 am
- ☽ ⊻ ♀ **8:08 pm** 5:08 pm

6 TUESDAY
- ☽ ✶ ☿ **8:28 am** 5:28 am
- ☽ ☌ ♆ **4:34 pm** 1:34 pm
- ♂ ✶ ♅ **10:30 pm** 7:30 pm

7 WEDNESDAY
- ☽ □ ☉ **4:03 am** 1:03 am
- ☽ ✶ ♇ **4:51 am** 1:51 am
- ☽ ⚻ ♃ **7:58 am** 4:58 am
- ☽ □ ♄ **9:05 am** 6:05 am
- ☽ ⊻ ♅ **1:04 pm** 10:04 am
- ☽ ⊻ ♂ **1:56 pm** 10:56 am
- ☉ ⊻ ♇ **2:51 pm** 11:51 am

8 THURSDAY
- ☽ ✶ ♀ **7:02 am** 4:02 am
- ☽ □ ☿ **6:43 pm** 3:43 pm
- ☽ ⊻ ♆ **9:18 pm** 6:18 pm

9 FRIDAY
- ☽ □ ♇ **8:52 am** 5:52 am
- ☽ △ ☉ **11:59 am** 8:59 am
- ☽ ☍ ♃ **12:16 pm** 9:16 am
- ☽ △ ♄ **1:10 pm** 10:10 am
- ☽ ☌ ♅ **4:24 pm** 1:24 pm
- ☉ ✶ ♃ **4:39 pm** 1:39 pm
- ☽ ✶ ♂ **8:06 pm** 5:06 pm

10 SATURDAY
- ☿ ✶ ♆ **3:25 am** 12:25 am
- ☉ ☌ ♄ **6:51 am** 3:51 am
- ☽ □ ♀ **1:38 pm** 10:38 am

- ☽ ✶ ♆ **10:51 pm** 7:51 pm
- ☽ △ ☿ 9:19 pm

11 SUNDAY
- ☽ △ ☿ **12:19 am**
- ☽ △ ♇ **9:54 am** 6:54 am
- ☽ ⚻ ♃ **1:32 pm** 10:32 am
- ☽ ⚻ ♄ **2:17 pm** 11:17 am
- ☽ ⚻ ☉ **4:17 pm** 1:17 pm
- ☽ ⊻ ♅ **4:57 pm** 1:57 pm
- ☽ □ ♂ **11:04 pm** 8:04 pm
- ☉ △ ♅ 10:56 pm

12 MONDAY
- ☉ △ ♅ **1:56 am**
- ☽ △ ♀ **5:22 pm** 2:22 pm
- ☽ □ ♆ **10:30 pm** 7:30 pm

13 TUESDAY
- ☽ ⚻ ☿ **3:02 am** 12:02 am
- ☽ ⚻ ♇ **9:27 am** 6:27 am
- ☽ △ ♃ **1:24 pm** 10:24 am
- ☽ ☍ ♄ **2:04 pm** 11:04 am
- ☽ ✶ ♅ **4:18 pm** 1:18 pm
- ☽ ☍ ☉ **7:06 pm** 4:06 pm
- ☽ △ ♂ 9:58 pm

14 WEDNESDAY
- ☽ △ ♂ **12:58 am**
- ☽ ⚻ ♀ **8:57 pm** 5:57 pm
- ☽ △ ♆ **10:17 pm** 7:17 pm

15 THURSDAY
- ☽ ☍ ☿ **5:25 am** 2:25 am
- ☽ ☍ ♇ **9:38 am** 6:38 am

- ☽ □ ♃ **2:08 pm** 11:08 am
- ♀ ⊻ ♆ **2:24 pm** 11:24 am
- ☽ ⚻ ♄ **2:43 pm** 11:43 am
- ☽ □ ♅ **4:37 pm** 1:37 pm
- ☽ ⚻ ☉ **11:15 pm** 8:15 pm

16 FRIDAY
- ☽ ⚻ ♂ **4:26 am** 1:26 am
- ☽ ⚻ ♆ 9:23 pm

17 SATURDAY
- ☽ ⚻ ♆ **12:23 am**
- ☽ ☍ ♀ **3:23 am** 12:23 am
- ☽ ⚻ ☿ **9:45 am** 6:45 am
- ☽ ⚻ ♇ **12:36 pm** 9:36 am
- ☽ ✶ ♃ **5:51 pm** 2:51 pm
- ☽ △ ♄ **6:24 pm** 3:24 pm
- ☽ △ ♅ **7:57 pm** 4:57 pm

18 SUNDAY
- ☽ △ ☉ **7:27 am** 4:27 am
- ☽ ☍ ♂ **11:55 am** 8:55 am

19 MONDAY
- ☽ ☍ ♆ **6:23 am** 3:23 am
- ☽ ⚻ ♀ **2:52 pm** 11:52 am
- ☽ △ ☿ **4:59 pm** 1:59 pm
- ☽ △ ♇ **7:41 pm** 4:41 pm
- ☽ ⊻ ♃ 10:48 pm
- ☽ □ ♄ 11:19 pm

20 TUESDAY
- ☽ ⊻ ♃ **1:48 am**
- ☽ □ ♄ **2:19 am**
- ☽ ⚻ ♅ **3:26 am** 12:26 am

- ☿ ⊻ ♀ **11:58 am** 8:58 am
- ☽ □ ☉ **8:56 pm** 5:56 pm
- ☽ ⚻ ♂ 9:22 pm

21 WEDNESDAY
- ☽ ⚻ ♂ **12:22 am**
- ☽ ⚻ ♆ **4:26 pm** 1:26 pm
- ♀ ⊻ ♇ **10:36 pm** 7:36 pm
- ☽ □ ☿ 11:05 pm

22 THURSDAY
- ☽ □ ☿ **2:05 am**
- ☽ □ ♇ **6:35 am** 3:35 am
- ☽ △ ♀ **7:23 am** 4:23 am
- ☽ ☌ ♃ **1:30 pm** 10:30 am
- ☽ ✶ ♄ **1:59 pm** 10:59 am
- ☽ ☍ ♅ **2:31 pm** 11:31 am

23 FRIDAY
- ☽ ✶ ☉ **2:25 pm** 11:25 am
- ☽ △ ♂ **4:25 pm** 1:25 pm

24 SATURDAY
- ☽ △ ♆ **4:57 am** 1:57 am
- ☽ ✶ ☿ **10:58 am** 7:58 am
- ♄ △ ♅ **7:21 pm** 4:21 pm
- ☽ ✶ ♇ **7:25 pm** 4:25 pm
- ☽ □ ♀ 11:22 pm
- ☽ ⊻ ♃ 11:52 pm

25 SUNDAY
- ☽ □ ♀ **2:22 am**
- ☽ ⊻ ♃ **2:52 am**
- ☽ ⚻ ♅ **3:14 am** 12:14 am
- ☽ ⊻ ♄ **3:19 am** 12:19 am

- ♀ △ ♃ **8:23 am** 5:23 am
- ♀ ✶ ♅ **11:35 am** 8:35 am
- ♀ ✶ ♄ **1:33 pm** 10:33 am

26 MONDAY
- ☽ ⊻ ☉ **8:50 am** 5:50 am
- ☽ □ ♂ **9:16 am** 6:16 am
- ♃ ☍ ♅ **1:35 pm** 10:35 am
- ☽ □ ♆ **5:41 pm** 2:41 pm
- ☽ ⊻ ☿ **6:14 pm** 3:14 pm
- ☿ ✶ ♆ **11:19 pm** 8:19 pm

27 TUESDAY
- ☉ ✶ ♂ **3:07 am** 12:07 am
- ☽ ⊻ ♇ **8:00 am** 5:00 am
- ☽ △ ♅ **3:30 pm** 12:30 pm
- ☽ ✶ ♃ **3:46 pm** 12:46 pm
- ☽ ☌ ♄ **4:11 pm** 1:11 pm
- ☽ ✶ ♀ **8:45 pm** 5:45 pm

28 WEDNESDAY
- ☉ ☌ ☿ **1:47 pm** 10:47 am
- ☿ ✶ ♂ **6:06 pm** 3:06 pm
- ☽ ☌ ☿ **11:46 pm** 8:46 pm
- ☽ ✶ ♂ 9:49 pm
- ☽ ☌ ☉ 10:53 pm

29 THURSDAY
- ☽ ✶ ♂ **12:49 am**
- ☽ ☌ ☉ **1:53 am**
- ☽ ✶ ♆ **5:11 am** 2:11 am
- ☽ ☌ ♇ **7:12 pm** 4:12 pm
- ☽ □ ♅ 11:19 pm

30 FRIDAY
- ☽ □ ♅ **2:19 am**
- ☽ □ ♃ **3:07 am** 12:07 am
- ☽ ⊻ ♄ **3:32 am** 12:32 am
- ☽ ⊻ ♀ **1:04 pm** 10:04 am
- ☉ ✶ ♆ **6:25 pm** 3:25 pm

31 SATURDAY
- ☽ ⊻ ☿ **4:10 am** 1:10 am
- ☽ ⊻ ♂ **2:20 pm** 11:20 am
- ☽ ⊻ ♆ **3:00 pm** 12:00 pm
- ☽ ⊻ ☉ **4:46 pm** 1:46 pm
- ♂ ☌ ♆ 10:53 pm

Eastern time in bold type
Pacific time in medium type

DECEMBER 2016

DATE	SID.TIME	SUN	MOON	NODE	MERCURY	VENUS	MARS	JUPITER	SATURN	URANUS	NEPTUNE	PLUTO	CERES	PALLAS	JUNO	VESTA	CHIRON
1 Th	4 41 7	9 ✗ 13 15	25 ♒ 32	7 ♍ 43	27 ✗ 22	22 ♑ 16	16 ♒ 00	16 ♎ 54	17 ✗ 44	20 ♈ 54	9 ♓ 16	15 ♑ 57	21 ♈ 24	23 ♒ 38	8 ♓ 26	5 ♌ 42 ℞	20 ♓ 40 D
2 F	4 45 4	10 14 06	7 ♓ 38	7 30 ℞	28 46	23 27	16 54	16 59	17 51	20 52 ℞	9 17	15 59	21 21 ℞	23 50	8 46	5 43	20 40
3 Sa	4 49 0	11 14 58	19 51	7 20	0 ♑ 09	24 37	17 39	17 09	17 58	20 51	9 17	16 00	21 18	24 02	9 07	5 42	20 40
4 Su	4 52 57	12 15 51	2 ♈ 13	7 13	1 31	25 47	18 24	17 19	18 05	20 50	9 18	16 02	21 15	24 14	9 28	5 41	20 40
5 M	4 56 54	13 16 45	14 46	7 09	2 51	26 57	19 09	17 29	18 13	20 49	9 18	16 04	21 13	24 27	9 49	5 40	20 41
6 T	5 0 50	14 17 39	27 34	7 08 D	4 09	28 07	19 54	17 39	18 20	20 47	9 19	16 06	21 11	24 39	10 09	5 38	20 41
7 W	5 4 47	15 18 34	10 ♉ 40	7 07	5 25	29 17	20 39	17 48	18 27	20 46	9 19	16 07	21 10	24 52	10 30	5 36	20 41
8 Th	5 8 43	16 19 30	24 07	7 07	6 39	0 ♒ 27	21 25	17 58	18 34	20 45	9 20	16 09	21 09	25 05	10 51	5 34	20 41
9 F	5 12 40	17 20 26	8 ♊ 00	7 06	7 50	1 36	22 10	18 07	18 41	20 44	9 21	16 11	21 08	25 19	11 12	5 30	20 42
10 Sa	5 16 36	18 21 23	22 17	7 02	8 58	2 45	22 55	18 16	18 48	20 43	9 21	16 13	21 08 D	25 32	11 32	5 27	20 42
11 Su	5 20 33	19 22 21	6 ♋ 58	6 56	10 03	3 55	23 40	18 25	18 55	20 42	9 22	16 15	21 08	25 46	11 53	5 23	20 43
12 M	5 24 29	20 23 20	21 59	6 47	11 03	5 04	24 25	18 34	19 02	20 41	9 23	16 17	21 09	25 59	12 14	5 18	20 43
13 T	5 28 26	21 24 19	7 ♌ 10	6 37	11 58	6 13	25 11	18 43	19 09	20 40	9 24	16 19	21 10	26 13	12 35	5 14	20 44
14 W	5 32 23	22 25 19	22 22	6 25	12 48	7 22	25 56	18 52	19 16	20 40	9 24	16 21	21 11	26 27	12 55	5 08	20 45
15 Th	5 36 19	23 26 19	7 ♍ 29	6 15	13 32	8 30	26 41	19 01	19 23	20 39	9 25	16 23	21 13	26 42	13 16	5 02	20 45
16 F	5 40 16	24 27 21	22 05	6 06	14 09	9 39	27 26	19 09	19 31	20 38	9 26	16 24	21 15	26 56	13 37	4 56	20 46
17 Sa	5 44 12	25 28 23	6 ♎ 19	6 00	14 37	10 47	28 12	19 18	19 38	20 37	9 27	16 26	21 17	27 11	13 58	4 50	20 47
18 Su	5 48 9	26 29 26	20 05	5 57	14 57	11 55	28 57	19 26	19 45	20 37	9 28	16 28	21 20	27 25	14 18	4 42	20 48
19 M	5 52 5	27 30 30	3 ♏ 21	5 56 D	15 07 ℞	13 03	29 42	19 34	19 52	20 36	9 29	16 30	21 23	27 40	14 39	4 35	20 49
20 T	5 56 2	28 31 35	16 11	5 56	15 06	14 11	0 ♓ 28	19 42	19 59	20 36	9 30	16 32	21 27	27 55	15 00	4 27	20 50
21 W	5 59 58	29 32 40	28 38	5 56 ℞	14 55	15 19	1 13	19 50	20 06	20 35	9 31	16 34	21 31	28 10	15 20	4 18	20 51
22 Th	6 3 55	0 ♑ 33 46	10 ✗ 49	5 56	14 31	16 26	1 58	19 58	20 13	20 35	9 32	16 36	21 35	28 25	15 41	4 09	20 52
23 F	6 7 52	1 34 53	22 48	5 53	13 56	17 34	2 44	20 06	20 20	20 34	9 33	16 38	21 40	28 41	16 01	4 00	20 53
24 Sa	6 11 48	2 36 01	4 ♑ 40	5 48	13 10	18 41	3 29	20 13	20 27	20 34	9 34	16 40	21 45	28 56	16 22	3 50	20 54
25 Su	6 15 45	3 37 09	16 30	5 41	12 12	19 48	4 14	20 21	20 34	20 34	9 35	16 42	21 50	29 12	16 43	3 40	20 56
26 M	6 19 41	4 38 18	28 22	5 31	11 06	20 54	4 59	20 28	20 41	20 34	9 36	16 44	21 56	29 28	17 03	3 30	20 57
27 T	6 23 38	5 39 28	10 ♒ 17	5 19	9 52	22 01	5 45	20 35	20 48	20 33 D	9 38	16 46	22 02	29 44	17 24	3 19	20 58
28 W	6 27 34	6 40 38	22 19	5 07	8 32	23 07	6 30	20 42	20 55	20 33	9 39	16 48	22 08	0 ♓ 00	17 44	3 08	21 00
29 Th	6 31 31	7 41 48	4 ♓ 28	4 56	7 11	24 13	7 15	20 49	21 02	20 33	9 40	16 50	22 15	0 16	18 05	2 56	21 01
30 F	6 35 28	8 42 58	16 47	4 46	5 49	25 19	8 01	20 56	21 08	20 33	9 41	16 52	22 22	0 32	18 25	2 44	21 03
31 Sa	6 39 24	9 44 09	29 14	4 38	4 30	26 24	8 46	21 02	21 15	20 34	9 43	16 54	22 30	0 49	18 46	2 31	21 05

JANUARY 2017

☽ Last Aspect day	ET / hr:mn / PT	asp	☽ Ingress sign day	ET / hr:mn / PT
1	11:59 pm	☌ ♀	♓ 2	**4:57 am** 1:57 am
2	**2:59 am**	☌ ♀	♓ 2	**4:57 am** 1:57 am
4	**11:14 am** 8:14 am	□ ☿	♈ 4	**11:20 am** 8:20 am
6	**1:41 pm** 10:41 am	△ ☿	♉ 6	**3:18 pm** 12:18 pm
7	**9:23 pm** 6:23 pm	△ ☉	♊ 8	**5:06 pm** 2:06 pm
10	**4:38 pm** 1:38 pm	☍ ☿	♋ 10	**5:49 pm** 2:49 pm
12	**6:34 am** 3:34 am	☍ ☉	♌ 12	**7:08 pm** 4:08 pm
14	**10:17 am** 7:17 am	△ ♄	♍ 14	**10:52 pm** 7:52 pm
16	10:09 pm	△ ☉	♎ 17	**6:16 am** 3:16 am
17	**1:09 am**	△ ☉	♎ 17	**6:16 am** 3:16 am
19	**3:55 am** 12:55 am	⚹ ♄	♏ 19	**5:09 pm** 2:09 pm
21	**8:24 pm** 5:24 pm	△ ♂	♐ 22	**5:45 am** 2:45 am
24	**12:33 pm** 9:33 am	□ ♂	♑ 24	**5:43 pm** 2:43 pm
26	11:18 pm	⚹ ♂	♒ 27	**3:37 am** 12:37 am
27	**2:18 am**	⚹ ♂	♒ 27	**3:37 am** 12:37 am
28	9:52 pm	⚹ ♄	♓ 29	**11:10 am** 8:10 am
29	**12:52 am**	⚹ ♄	♓ 29	**11:10 am** 8:10 am
31	**12:36 pm** 9:36 am	☌ ♂	♈ 31	**4:46 pm** 1:46 pm

☽ Phases & Eclipses phase	day	ET / hr:mn / PT
2nd Quarter	5	**2:47 pm** 11:47 am
Full Moon	12	**6:34 am** 3:34 am
4th Quarter	19	**5:13 pm** 2:13 pm
New Moon	27	**7:07 pm** 4:07 pm

Planet Ingress	day	ET / hr:mn / PT
♀ ♓	2	11:47 pm
♀ ♓	3	**2:47 am**
☿ ♐	4	**9:17 am** 6:17 am
⚳ ♋	10	**1:11 pm** 10:11 am
☿ ♑	12	**9:03 am** 6:03 am
☉ ♒	19	**4:24 pm** 1:24 pm
♂ ♈	27	9:39 pm
♂ ♈	28	**12:39 am**

Planetary Motion	day	ET / hr:mn / PT
☿ D	8	**4:43 am** 1:43 am

1 SUNDAY
♂ ☌ ♆ **1:53 am**
☽ ⚺ ♇ **4:38 am** 1:38 am
☽ ⚹ ♅ **11:24 am** 8:24 am
☽ △ ♃ **12:38 pm** 9:38 am
☽ ⚹ ♄ **1:04 pm** 10:04 am
☽ ☌ ♀ 11:59 pm ☽

2 MONDAY
☽ ☌ ♀ **2:59 am** ☽
☽ ⚹ ☿ **7:58 am** 4:58 am
☽ ☌ ♆ **10:56 pm** 7:56 pm
☽ ☌ ♂ 10:36 pm

3 TUESDAY
☽ ☌ ♂ **1:36 am**
☽ ⚹ ☉ **5:13 am** 2:13 am
☽ ⚹ ♇ **12:07 pm** 9:07 am
☿ ⚹ ♀ **2:41 pm** 11:41 am
☽ ⚺ ♅ **6:29 pm** 3:29 pm
☽ ⚻ ♃ **8:05 pm** 5:05 pm
☽ □ ♄ **8:33 pm** 5:33 pm

4 WEDNESDAY
☽ □ ☿ **11:14 am** 8:14 am ☽
☽ ⚺ ♀ **2:07 pm** 11:07 am

5 THURSDAY
☽ ⚺ ♆ **4:38 am** 1:38 am
☽ ⚺ ♂ **10:11 am** 7:11 am
☽ □ ☉ **2:47 pm** 11:47 am
☽ □ ♇ **5:16 pm** 2:16 pm
☽ ☌ ♅ **11:15 pm** 8:15 pm
☽ ☍ ♃ 10:06 pm
☽ △ ♄ 10:37 pm

6 FRIDAY
☽ ☍ ♃ **1:06 am**
☽ △ ♄ **1:37 am**
☽ △ ☿ **1:41 pm** 10:41 am ☽
☽ ⚹ ♀ **10:08 pm** 7:08 pm
☉ ☌ ♇ 10:45 pm

7 SATURDAY
☉ ☌ ♇ **1:45 am**
☽ ⚹ ♆ **7:56 am** 4:56 am
☽ ⚹ ♂ **3:57 pm** 12:57 pm
☽ △ ♇ **8:03 pm** 5:03 pm
☽ △ ☉ **9:23 pm** 6:23 pm ☽
☽ ⚺ ♅ 10:41 pm

8 SUNDAY
☽ ⚺ ♅ **1:41 am**
☽ ⚻ ♃ **3:45 am** 12:45 am
☽ ⚻ ♄ **4:19 am** 1:19 am
☽ ⚻ ☿ **3:15 pm** 12:15 pm

9 MONDAY
☽ □ ♀ **3:30 am** 12:30 am
☽ □ ♆ **9:18 am** 6:18 am
☽ □ ♂ **7:40 pm** 4:40 pm
☽ ⚻ ♇ **9:09 pm** 6:09 pm
☽ ⚻ ☉ 10:58 pm
☽ ⚹ ♅ 11:36 pm

10 TUESDAY
☽ ⚻ ☉ **1:58 am**
☽ ⚹ ♅ **2:36 am**
☽ △ ♃ **4:53 am** 1:53 am
☽ ☍ ♄ **5:32 am** 2:32 am
☉ □ ♅ **11:22 am** 8:22 am
☽ ☍ ☿ **4:38 pm** 1:38 pm ☽
♂ ⚹ ♇ 11:15 pm

11 WEDNESDAY
♂ ⚹ ♇ **2:15 am**
☽ △ ♀ **7:51 am** 4:51 am
☽ △ ♆ **10:06 am** 7:06 am
☽ ☍ ♇ **10:06 pm** 7:06 pm
☽ △ ♂ **11:08 pm** 8:08 pm
☉ □ ♃ **11:43 pm** 8:43 pm

12 THURSDAY
☽ □ ♅ **3:34 am** 12:34 am
☽ □ ♃ **6:07 am** 3:07 am
☽ ☍ ☉ **6:34 am** 3:34 am ☽
☽ ⚻ ♄ **6:53 am** 3:53 am
☉ ⚺ ♄ **11:32 am** 8:32 am
♀ ☌ ♆ **4:54 pm** 1:54 pm
☽ ⚻ ☿ **7:31 pm** 4:31 pm

13 FRIDAY
☽ ⚻ ♆ **12:08 pm** 9:08 am
☽ ⚻ ♀ **1:35 pm** 10:35 am
☽ ⚻ ♇ 9:44 pm

14 SATURDAY
☽ ⚻ ♇ **12:44 am**
☽ ⚻ ♂ **4:37 am** 1:37 am
☽ △ ♅ **6:26 am** 3:26 am
☽ ⚹ ♃ **9:21 am** 6:21 am
☽ △ ♄ **10:17 am** 7:17 am ☽
☽ ⚻ ☉ **1:39 pm** 10:39 am
☽ △ ☿ 10:59 pm

15 SUNDAY
☽ △ ☿ **1:59 am**
♂ ⚺ ♅ **2:29 pm** 11:29 am
☽ ☍ ♆ **5:08 pm** 2:08 pm
☽ ☍ ♀ **10:58 pm** 7:58 pm

16 MONDAY
☽ △ ♇ **6:40 am** 3:40 am
☽ ⚻ ♅ **12:41 pm** 9:41 am
☽ ☍ ♂ **2:02 pm** 11:02 am
☽ ⚺ ♃ **4:02 pm** 1:02 pm
☽ □ ♄ **5:13 pm** 2:13 pm
☽ △ ☉ 10:09 pm ☽

17 TUESDAY
☽ △ ☉ **1:09 am** ☽
☽ □ ☿ **1:37 pm** 10:37 am
☽ ⚻ ♆ 10:57 pm
♂ ⚻ ♃ 11:51 pm

18 WEDNESDAY
☽ ⚻ ♆ **1:57 am**
♂ ⚻ ♃ **2:51 am**
☽ ⚻ ♀ **1:01 pm** 10:01 am
☽ □ ♇ **4:23 pm** 1:23 pm
☽ ☍ ♅ **10:42 pm** 7:42 pm
☽ ☌ ♃ 11:27 pm

19 THURSDAY
☽ ☌ ♃ **2:27 am**
☽ ⚻ ♂ **3:54 am** 12:54 am
☽ ⚹ ♄ **3:55 am** 12:55 am ☽
♂ □ ♄ **4:16 am** 1:16 am
☽ □ ☉ **5:13 pm** 2:13 pm

20 FRIDAY
☽ ⚹ ☿ **6:14 am** 3:14 am
♀ ⚹ ♇ **8:57 am** 5:57 am
☽ △ ♆ **1:50 pm** 10:50 am

21 SATURDAY
☽ ⚹ ♇ **4:44 am** 1:44 am
☽ △ ♀ **6:24 am** 3:24 am
☽ ⚻ ♅ **11:07 am** 8:07 am
☽ ⚺ ♃ **3:07 pm** 12:07 pm
☽ ⚺ ♄ **4:52 pm** 1:52 pm
☽ △ ♂ **8:24 pm** 5:24 pm ☽

22 SUNDAY
☽ ⚹ ☉ **11:30 am** 8:30 am
☽ ⚺ ☿ 10:08 pm
☽ □ ♆ 11:37 pm

23 MONDAY
☽ ⚺ ☿ **1:08 am**
☽ □ ♆ **2:37 am**
☿ ⚹ ♆ **4:29 pm** 1:29 pm
☽ ⚺ ♇ **5:23 pm** 2:23 pm
♀ ⚺ ♅ **7:24 pm** 4:24 pm
☽ △ ♅ **11:36 pm** 8:36 pm
☽ □ ♀ **11:56 pm** 8:56 pm

24 TUESDAY
☽ ⚹ ♃ **3:38 am** 12:38 am
☽ ☌ ♄ **5:38 am** 2:38 am
☽ □ ♂ **12:33 pm** 9:33 am ☽

25 WEDNESDAY
☽ ⚺ ☉ **4:44 am** 1:44 am
☽ ⚹ ♆ **2:07 pm** 11:07 am
☽ ☌ ☿ **6:58 pm** 3:58 pm

26 THURSDAY
♀ ⚻ ♃ **3:02 am** 12:02 am
☽ ☌ ♇ **4:22 am** 1:22 am
☽ □ ♅ **10:18 am** 7:18 am
☽ □ ♃ **2:15 pm** 11:15 am
☽ ⚹ ♀ **3:05 pm** 12:05 pm
☽ ⚺ ♄ **4:28 pm** 1:28 pm
☽ ⚹ ♂ 11:18 pm ☽

27 FRIDAY
☽ ⚹ ♂ **2:18 am** ☽
♀ □ ♄ **12:50 pm** 9:50 am
☽ ☌ ☉ **7:07 pm** 4:07 pm
☽ ⚺ ♆ **11:19 pm** 8:19 pm

28 SATURDAY
☽ ⚺ ☿ **10:04 am** 7:04 am
☽ ⚺ ♇ **12:59 pm** 9:59 am
☽ ⚹ ♅ **6:39 pm** 3:39 pm
☽ △ ♃ **10:28 pm** 7:28 pm
☽ ⚹ ♄ 9:52 pm ☽

29 SUNDAY
☽ ⚹ ♄ **12:52 am** ☽
☽ ⚺ ♀ **3:09 am** 12:09 am
☽ ⚺ ♂ **1:14 pm** 10:14 am
☿ ☌ ♇ **3:21 pm** 12:21 pm
☉ ⚺ ♆ 11:03 pm

30 MONDAY
☉ ⚺ ♆ **2:03 am**
☽ ☌ ♆ **6:17 am** 3:17 am
☽ ⚺ ☉ **6:37 am** 3:37 am
☽ ⚹ ♇ **7:28 pm** 4:28 pm
☽ ⚹ ☿ **10:31 pm** 7:31 pm
☽ ⚺ ♅ 9:54 pm

31 TUESDAY
☽ ⚺ ♅ **12:54 am**
☽ ⚻ ♃ **4:34 am** 1:34 am
☽ □ ♄ **7:11 am** 4:11 am
☽ ☌ ♀ **12:36 pm** 9:36 am ☽
☽ ☌ ♂ **9:52 pm** 6:52 pm
☿ □ ♅ **10:32 pm** 7:32 pm

Eastern time in bold type
Pacific time in medium type

JANUARY 2017

DATE	SID. TIME	SUN	MOON	NODE	MERCURY	VENUS	MARS	JUPITER	SATURN	URANUS	NEPTUNE	PLUTO	CERES	PALLAS	JUNO	VESTA	CHIRON
1 Su	6 43 21	10 ♑ 45 19	11 ≈ 51	4 ♍ 32℞	3 ♑ 17	27 ≈ 22	9 ♓ 31	21 ♎ 29	21 ♐ 22	20 ♈ 34	9 ♓ 44	16 ♑ 57	22 ♈ 37	1 ♓ 05	19 ♐ 06	2 ♌ 19	21 ♓ 06
2 M	6 47 17	11 46 29	24 38	4 30 D	2 10℞	28 34	10 17	21 15	21 29	20 34	9 45	16 59	22 46	1 22	19 26	2 06℞	21 08
3 T	6 51 14	12 47 40	7 ♈ 38	4 29	1 12	29 39	11 02	21 21	21 36	20 34	9 47	17 01	22 54	1 39	19 47	1 52	21 10
4 W	6 55 10	13 48 50	20 51	4 30	0 24	0 ♓ 43	11 48	21 27	21 43	20 34	9 48	17 03	23 03	1 56	20 07	1 39	21 11
5 Th	6 59 7	14 49 59	4 ♉ 20	4 31℞	29 ♐ 46	1 48	12 33	21 33	21 49	20 35	9 50	17 05	23 12	2 13	20 27	1 25	21 13
6 F	7 3 3	15 51 09	18 07	4 32	29 18	2 51	13 18	21 39	21 56	20 35	9 51	17 07	23 21	2 30	20 48	1 11	21 15
7 Sa	7 7 0	16 52 17	2 ♊ 11	4 31	29 00	3 55	14 03	21 44	22 03	20 35	9 53	17 09	23 30	2 47	21 08	0 56	21 17
8 Su	7 10 56	17 53 26	16 33	4 27	28 52 D	4 58	14 48	21 49	22 09	20 36	9 54	17 11	23 40	3 04	21 28	0 41	21 19
9 M	7 14 53	18 54 34	1 ♋ 10	4 22	28 52	6 01	15 34	21 54	22 16	20 36	9 56	17 13	23 50	3 22	21 48	0 27	21 21
10 T	7 18 50	19 55 42	15 56	4 16	29 02	7 03	16 19	21 59	22 23	20 37	9 57	17 15	24 01	3 39	22 08	0 12	21 23
11 W	7 22 46	20 56 49	0 ♌ 44	4 09	29 19	8 05	17 04	22 04	22 29	20 38	9 59	17 17	24 12	3 57	22 28	29 ♋ 56	21 25
12 Th	7 26 43	21 57 56	15 26	4 02	29 43	9 06	17 49	22 09	22 36	20 38	10 01	17 19	24 23	4 14	22 48	29 41	21 27
13 F	7 30 39	22 59 02	29 55	3 56	0 ♑ 13	10 08	18 34	22 14	22 42	20 39	10 02	17 21	24 34	4 32	23 08	29 25	21 30
14 Sa	7 34 36	24 00 08	14 ♍ 04	3 53	0 50	11 08	19 20	22 18	22 48	20 40	10 04	17 23	24 46	4 50	23 28	29 10	21 32
15 Su	7 38 32	25 01 14	27 49	3 51 D	1 31	12 09	20 05	22 22	22 55	20 41	10 06	17 25	24 57	5 08	23 48	28 54	21 34
16 M	7 42 29	26 02 19	11 ♎ 09	3 51	2 18	13 09	20 50	22 26	23 01	20 42	10 08	17 27	25 09	5 26	24 08	28 38	21 37
17 T	7 46 26	27 03 24	24 04	3 52	3 08	14 08	21 35	22 30	23 08	20 42	10 09	17 29	25 22	5 44	24 28	28 22	21 39
18 W	7 50 22	28 04 29	6 ♏ 37	3 54	4 02	15 07	22 20	22 34	23 14	20 43	10 11	17 31	25 34	6 03	24 47	28 06	21 41
19 Th	7 54 19	29 05 34	18 53	3 56℞	5 00	16 05	23 05	22 37	23 20	20 44	10 13	17 34	25 47	6 21	25 07	27 50	21 44
20 F	7 58 15	0 ≈ 06 38	0 ♐ 55	3 56	6 00	17 03	23 50	22 40	23 26	20 46	10 15	17 36	26 00	6 39	25 27	27 33	21 46
21 Sa	8 2 12	1 07 42	12 50	3 55	7 05	18 01	24 35	22 43	23 32	20 47	10 17	17 38	26 14	6 58	25 46	27 19	21 49
22 Su	8 6 8	2 08 45	24 41	3 53	8 11	18 58	25 20	22 46	23 38	20 48	10 19	17 40	26 27	7 16	26 06	27 03	21 51
23 M	8 10 5	3 09 48	6 ♑ 34	3 49	9 19	19 54	26 05	22 49	23 44	20 50	10 20	17 42	26 41	7 35	26 25	26 47	21 54
24 T	8 14 1	4 10 51	18 32	3 44	10 30	20 50	26 50	22 52	23 50	20 52	10 22	17 44	26 55	7 54	26 44	26 31	21 57
25 W	8 17 58	5 11 53	0 ≈ 39	3 39	11 42	21 45	27 35	22 54	23 56	20 53	10 24	17 46	27 09	8 13	27 04	26 16	21 59
26 Th	8 21 55	6 12 55	12 57	3 34	12 56	22 39	28 20	22 56	24 02	20 55	10 26	17 48	27 24	8 32	27 23	26 00	22 02
27 F	8 25 51	7 13 55	25 28	3 30	14 12	23 33	29 05	22 58	24 08	20 56	10 28	17 50	27 38	8 50	27 42	25 45	22 05
28 Sa	8 29 48	8 14 55	8 ♓ 11	3 28	15 29	24 26	29 49	23 00	24 14	20 58	10 30	17 51	27 53	9 10	28 01	25 30	22 08
29 Su	8 33 44	9 15 54	21 09	3 25 D	16 47	25 18	0 ♈ 34	23 02	24 20	20 59	10 32	17 53	28 08	9 29	28 20	25 15	22 10
30 M	8 37 41	10 16 52	4 ♈ 19	3 24	18 07	26 10	1 19	23 03	24 25	21 01	10 34	17 55	28 24	9 48	28 39	25 00	22 13
31 T	8 41 37	11 17 49	17 42	3 25	19 28	27 01	2 04	23 05	24 31	21 01	10 36	17 57	28 39	10 07	28 58	24 45	22 16

EPHEMERIS CALCULATED FOR 12 MIDNIGHT GREENWICH MEAN TIME. ALL OTHER DATA AND FACING ASPECTARIAN PAGE IN **EASTERN TIME (BOLD)** AND PACIFIC TIME (REGULAR).

FEBRUARY 2017

☽ Last Aspect day	ET / hr:mn / PT		asp	☽ Ingress sign	day	ET / hr:mn / PT	
2	**11:50 am**	8:50 am	△ ♄	♉	2	**8:50 pm**	5:50 pm
4	**5:42 pm**	2:42 pm	△ ☿	♊	4	**11:44 pm**	8:44 pm
6	**5:53 pm**	2:53 pm	☍ ♄	♋	6		11:03 pm
6	**5:53 pm**	2:53 pm	☍ ♄	♋	7	**2:03 am**	
8	**5:00 pm**	2:00 pm	□ ♃	♌	9	**4:41 am**	1:41 am
10		9:52 pm	△ ♄	♍	11	**8:52 am**	5:52 am
11	**12:52 am**		△ ♄	♍	11	**8:52 am**	5:52 am
13	**7:36 am**	4:36 am	□ ♄	♎	13	**3:43 pm**	12:43 pm
15	**8:54 pm**	5:54 pm	△ ☉	♏	15		10:41 pm
15	**8:54 pm**	5:54 pm	△ ☉	♏	16	**1:41 am**	
17	**2:38 pm**	11:38 am	✶ ♇	♐	18	**1:52 pm**	10:52 am
20	**6:37 pm**	3:37 pm	☌ ♄	♑	20		11:08 pm
20	**6:37 pm**	3:37 pm	☌ ♄	♑	21	**2:08 am**	
22	**10:24 pm**	7:24 pm	□ ♃	♒	23	**12:17 pm**	9:17 am
25	**1:11 pm**	10:11 am	✶ ♄	♓	25	**7:24 pm**	4:24 pm
27	**6:08 pm**	3:08 pm	□ ♄	♈	27	**11:52 pm**	8:52 pm

☽ Phases & Eclipses phase	day	ET / hr:mn / PT	
2nd Quarter	3	**11:19 pm**	8:19 pm
Full Moon	10	**7:33 pm**	4:43 pm
●	10	22° ♌ 28'	
4th Quarter	18	**2:33 pm**	11:33 am
New Moon	25	**9:58 am**	6:58 am
●		8° ♓ 12'	

Planet Ingress	day	ET / hr:mn / PT	
⚵ ♑	2		10:47 pm
⚵ ♑	3	**1:47 am**	
♀ ♈	3	**10:51 am**	7:51 am
⚳ ♉	4	**7:17 pm**	4:17 pm
☿ ♒	7	**4:35 am**	1:35 am
☉ ♓	18	**6:31 am**	3:31 am
☿ ♓	26	**6:07 pm**	3:07 pm

Planetary Motion	day	ET / hr:mn / PT	
♃ ℞	5		10:52 pm
♃ ℞	6	**1:52 am**	

1 WEDNESDAY
☽ ⚺ ♆ **11:26 am** 8:26 am
☽ ✶ ☉ **3:50 pm** 12:50 pm
☽ □ ♇ 9:13 pm

2 THURSDAY
☽ □ ♇ **12:13 am**
☽ ☌ ♅ **5:30 am** 2:30 am
☽ □ ☿ **8:52 am** 5:52 am
☽ ☍ ♃ **9:01 am** 6:01 am
☿ □ ♃ **10:15 am** 7:15 am
☽ △ ♄ **11:50 am** 8:50 am ☽
☽ ⚺ ♀ **8:00 pm** 5:00 pm

3 FRIDAY
☽ ⚺ ♂ **4:42 am** 1:42 am
☽ ✶ ♆ **3:10 pm** 12:10 pm
☿ ⚺ ♄ **3:50 pm** 12:50 pm
☽ □ ☉ **11:19 pm** 8:19 pm

4 SATURDAY
☽ △ ♇ **3:38 am** 12:38 am
☽ ⚺ ♅ **8:48 am** 5:48 am
☽ ⚻ ♃ **12:10 pm** 9:10 am
☽ ⚻ ♄ **3:14 pm** 12:14 pm
☽ △ ☿ **5:42 pm** 2:42 pm ☽
☽ ✶ ♀ 10:51 pm

5 SUNDAY
☽ ✶ ♀ **1:51 am**
☽ ✶ ♂ **10:15 am** 7:15 am
☽ □ ♆ **5:53 pm** 2:53 pm

6 MONDAY
☽ △ ☉ **5:40 am** 2:40 am
☽ ⚻ ♇ **6:12 am** 3:12 am
☽ ✶ ♅ **11:19 am** 8:19 am
☉ ⚺ ♇ **1:34 pm** 10:34 am
☽ △ ♃ **2:33 pm** 11:33 am
☽ ☍ ♄ **5:53 pm** 2:53 pm ☽
☽ ⚻ ☿ 10:45 pm

7 TUESDAY
☽ ⚻ ☿ **1:45 am**
☽ □ ♀ **6:55 am** 3:55 am
☽ □ ♂ **3:18 pm** 12:18 pm
☽ △ ♆ **8:19 pm** 5:19 pm

8 WEDNESDAY
☽ ☍ ♇ **8:41 am** 5:41 am
☽ ⚻ ☉ **11:54 am** 8:54 am
☽ □ ♅ **1:52 pm** 10:52 am
☽ □ ♃ **5:00 pm** 2:00 pm ☽
☽ ⚻ ♄ **8:42 pm** 5:42 pm

9 THURSDAY
☽ ☍ ☿ **10:25 am** 7:25 am
☽ △ ♀ **12:20 pm** 9:20 am
☉ ✶ ♅ **4:16 pm** 1:16 pm
☽ △ ♂ **9:05 pm** 6:05 pm
☽ ⚻ ♆ **11:30 pm** 8:30 pm

10 FRIDAY
☽ ⚻ ♇ **12:14 pm** 9:14 am
☿ ✶ ♀ **4:19 pm** 1:19 pm
☽ △ ♅ **5:36 pm** 2:36 pm
☽ ☍ ☉ **7:33 pm** 4:33 pm
☽ ✶ ♃ **8:40 pm** 5:40 pm
☽ △ ♄ 9:52 pm ☽

11 SATURDAY
☽ △ ♄ **12:52 am** ☽
☉ △ ♃ **10:25 am** 7:25 am
☽ ⚻ ♀ **7:34 pm** 4:34 pm
♂ ⚺ ♆ **8:49 pm** 5:49 pm
☽ ⚻ ☿ **9:38 pm** 6:38 pm

12 SUNDAY
☽ ☍ ♆ **4:42 am** 1:42 am
☽ ⚻ ♂ **5:08 am** 2:08 am
☽ △ ♇ **6:03 pm** 3:03 pm
☽ ⚻ ♅ **11:44 pm** 8:44 pm
☽ ⚺ ♃ 11:45 pm

13 MONDAY
☽ ⚺ ♃ **2:45 am**
☽ ⚻ ☉ **6:15 am** 3:15 am
☽ □ ♄ **7:36 am** 4:36 am ☽
☉ ✶ ♄ 9:58 pm

14 TUESDAY
☉ ✶ ♄ **12:58 am**
☽ ☍ ♀ **5:51 am** 2:51 am
☿ ⚺ ♆ **10:50 am** 7:50 am
☽ ⚻ ♆ **12:52 pm** 9:52 am
☽ △ ☿ **1:09 pm** 10:09 am
☽ ☍ ♂ **4:42 pm** 1:42 pm
☽ □ ♇ 11:58 pm

15 WEDNESDAY
☽ □ ♇ **2:58 am**
☽ ☍ ♅ **9:01 am** 6:01 am
☽ ☌ ♃ **11:54 am** 8:54 am
☽ ✶ ♄ **5:30 pm** 2:30 pm
☽ △ ☉ **8:54 pm** 5:54 pm ☽

16 THURSDAY
☿ ✶ ♂ **1:15 pm** 10:15 am
☽ ⚻ ♀ **7:19 pm** 4:19 pm
☽ △ ♆ 9:02 pm

17 FRIDAY
☽ △ ♆ **12:02 am**
☽ ⚻ ♂ **7:43 am** 4:43 am
☽ □ ☿ **9:18 am** 6:18 am
☽ ✶ ♇ **2:38 pm** 11:38 am ☽
☽ ⚻ ♅ **8:57 pm** 5:57 pm
☽ ⚺ ♃ **11:34 pm** 8:34 pm

18 SATURDAY
☽ ⚺ ♄ **5:52 am** 2:52 am
☽ □ ☉ **2:33 pm** 11:33 am
☿ ⚺ ♇ 9:38 pm

19 SUNDAY
☿ ⚺ ♇ **12:38 am**
☽ △ ♀ **10:20 am** 7:20 am
☽ □ ♆ **12:43 pm** 9:43 am
☽ △ ♂ 9:13 pm

20 MONDAY
☽ △ ♂ **12:13 am**
☽ ⚺ ♇ **3:18 am** 12:18 am
☽ ✶ ☿ **7:31 am** 4:31 am
☽ △ ♅ **9:39 am** 6:39 am
☽ ✶ ♃ **11:49 am** 8:49 am
☽ ☌ ♄ **6:37 pm** 3:37 pm ☽
☿ ✶ ♅ **11:01 pm** 8:01 pm

21 TUESDAY
☽ ✶ ☉ **8:16 am** 5:16 am
☿ △ ♃ **1:27 pm** 10:27 am
☽ □ ♀ 9:08 pm
☽ ✶ ♆ 9:35 pm

22 WEDNESDAY
☽ □ ♀ **12:08 am**
☽ ✶ ♆ **12:35 am**
♂ □ ♇ **4:03 am** 1:03 am
☽ ☌ ♇ **2:34 pm** 11:34 am
☽ □ ♂ **3:13 pm** 12:13 pm
♀ ⚺ ♆ **4:58 pm** 1:58 pm
☽ □ ♅ **8:44 pm** 5:44 pm
☽ □ ♃ **10:24 pm** 7:24 pm ☽

23 THURSDAY
☽ ⚺ ☿ **3:43 am** 12:43 am
☽ ⚺ ♄ **5:26 am** 2:26 am
☿ ✶ ♄ **4:45 pm** 1:45 pm
☽ ⚺ ☉ **11:04 pm** 8:04 pm

24 FRIDAY
☽ ⚺ ♆ **9:47 am** 6:47 am
☽ ✶ ♀ **10:41 am** 7:41 am
☽ ⚺ ♇ **10:58 pm** 7:58 pm
☽ ✶ ♂ 11:46 pm

25 SATURDAY
☽ ✶ ♂ **2:46 am**
☽ ✶ ♅ **4:53 am** 1:53 am
☽ △ ♃ **6:02 am** 3:02 am
☽ ✶ ♄ **1:11 pm** 10:11 am ☽
☽ ☌ ☿ **7:36 pm** 4:36 pm

26 SUNDAY
☽ ☌ ☉ **9:58 am** 6:58 am
☽ ☌ ♆ **3:56 pm** 12:56 pm
☽ ⚺ ♀ **5:39 pm** 2:39 pm
♂ ☌ ♅ **7:19 pm** 4:19 pm

27 MONDAY
☽ ✶ ♇ **4:25 am** 1:25 am
♂ ☍ ♃ **9:24 am** 6:24 am
☽ ⚺ ♅ **10:08 am** 7:08 am
☽ ⚻ ♃ **10:49 am** 7:49 am
☽ ⚺ ♂ **10:54 am** 7:54 am
☽ □ ♄ **6:08 pm** 3:08 pm ☽

28 TUESDAY
☽ ⚺ ☿ **7:41 am** 4:41 am
☽ ⚺ ☉ **5:51 pm** 2:51 pm
☽ ⚺ ♆ **7:46 pm** 4:46 pm
☽ ☌ ♀ **9:55 pm** 6:55 pm

Eastern time in bold type
Pacific time in medium type

FEBRUARY 2017

DATE	SID. TIME	SUN	MOON	NODE	MERCURY	VENUS	MARS	JUPITER	SATURN	URANUS	NEPTUNE	PLUTO	CERES	PALLAS	JUNO	VESTA	CHIRON
1 W	8 45 34	12 ≈ 18 44	1 ♈ 16	3 ♍ 26	20 ♑ 50	27 ♈ 51	2 ♈ 49	23 ♎ 05	24 ♐ 36	21 ♈ 02	10 ♓ 38	17 ♑ 59	28 ♋ 55	10 ♏ 26	29 ♐ 17	24 ♋ 31	22 ♓ 19
2 Th	8 49 30	13 19 38	15 01	3 27	22 14	28 40	3 33	23 07	24 42	21 04	10 40	18 01	29 11	10 46	29 36	24 17 ℞	22 22
3 F	8 53 27	14 20 31	28 56	3 29	23 38	29 29	4 18	23 07	24 47	21 06	10 42	18 03	29 27	11 05	29 55	24 03	22 25
4 Sa	8 57 24	15 21 23	13 ♉ 00	3 29 ℞	25 03	0 ♉ 16	5 03	23 08	24 53	21 08	10 44	18 05	29 43	11 25	0 ♑ 13	23 49	22 28
5 Su	9 1 20	16 22 13	27 11	3 29	26 29	1 03	5 47	23 08	24 58	21 09	10 47	18 07	0 ♌ 00	11 44	0 32	23 36	22 31
6 M	9 5 17	17 23 02	11 ♊ 28	3 28	27 57	1 48	6 32	23 08 ℞	25 03	21 11	10 49	18 09	0 16	12 04	0 50	23 23	22 34
7 T	9 9 13	18 23 49	25 48	3 26	29 25	2 33	7 16	23 08	25 08	21 13	10 51	18 10	0 33	12 23	1 09	23 11	22 37
8 W	9 13 10	19 24 35	10 ♋ 06	3 24	0 ≈ 54	3 16	8 01	23 08	25 13	21 15	10 53	18 12	0 50	12 43	1 27	22 58	22 41
9 Th	9 17 6	20 25 19	24 19	3 22	2 23	3 58	8 45	23 08	25 18	21 17	10 55	18 14	1 08	13 03	1 45	22 47	22 44
10 F	9 21 3	21 26 02	8 ♌ 21	3 21	3 54	4 40	9 30	23 07	25 23	21 19	10 57	18 16	1 25	13 23	2 03	22 35	22 47
11 Sa	9 24 59	22 26 43	22 09	3 20 D	5 25	5 20	10 14	23 06	25 28	21 21	11 00	18 18	1 43	13 43	2 21	22 24	22 50
12 Su	9 28 56	23 27 23	5 ♍ 40	3 20	6 58	5 58	10 58	23 05	25 33	21 24	11 02	18 19	2 00	14 03	2 39	22 13	22 53
13 M	9 32 53	24 28 02	18 52	3 20	8 31	6 36	11 43	23 04	25 38	21 26	11 04	18 21	2 18	14 23	2 57	22 03	22 57
14 T	9 36 49	25 28 39	1 ♎ 45	3 21	10 05	7 12	12 27	23 03	25 43	21 28	11 06	18 23	2 36	14 43	3 15	21 53	23 00
15 W	9 40 46	26 29 16	14 19	3 22	11 40	7 47	13 11	23 01	25 47	21 30	11 08	18 25	2 54	15 03	3 33	21 43	23 03
16 Th	9 44 42	27 29 50	26 37	3 23	13 16	8 20	13 56	22 59	25 52	21 33	11 11	18 26	3 13	15 23	3 50	21 34	23 07
17 F	9 48 39	28 30 24	8 ♏ 42	3 23 ℞	14 52	8 53	14 40	22 58	25 56	21 35	11 13	18 28	3 31	15 43	4 08	21 26	23 10
18 Sa	9 52 35	29 30 57	20 39	3 23	16 30	9 22	15 24	22 55	26 01	21 37	11 15	18 30	3 50	16 03	4 25	21 17	23 13
19 Su	9 56 32	0 ♓ 31 28	2 ♐ 32	3 23	18 08	9 51	16 08	22 53	26 05	21 40	11 17	18 31	4 09	16 23	4 42	21 10	23 17
20 M	10 0 28	1 31 58	14 26	3 23	19 48	10 18	16 52	22 51	26 09	21 42	11 19	18 33	4 28	16 44	5 00	21 02	23 20
21 T	10 4 25	2 32 26	26 25	3 23 D	21 28	10 43	17 36	22 48	26 13	21 45	11 22	18 35	4 47	17 04	5 17	20 55	23 23
22 W	10 8 21	3 32 54	8 ♑ 33	3 23	23 09	11 06	18 20	22 45	26 17	21 47	11 24	18 36	5 06	17 24	5 34	20 49	23 27
23 Th	10 12 18	4 33 20	20 55	3 23	24 51	11 28	19 04	22 42	26 21	21 50	11 26	18 38	5 25	17 45	5 50	20 43	23 30
24 F	10 16 15	5 33 44	3 ≈ 34	3 24	26 35	11 48	19 48	22 39	26 25	21 52	11 29	18 39	5 45	18 05	6 07	20 37	23 34
25 Sa	10 20 11	6 34 07	16 31	3 24	28 19	12 05	20 32	22 36	26 29	21 55	11 31	18 41	6 05	18 26	6 24	20 32	23 37
26 Su	10 24 8	7 34 28	29 46	3 24 ℞	0 ♓ 04	12 21	21 16	22 32	26 33	21 58	11 33	18 42	6 24	18 46	6 40	20 28	23 41
27 M	10 28 4	8 34 48	13 ♓ 20	3 24	1 50	12 34	22 00	22 28	26 37	22 00	11 35	18 44	6 44	19 07	6 57	20 23	23 44
28 T	10 32 1	9 35 06	27 10	3 23	3 37	12 46	22 43	22 24	26 40	22 03	11 38	18 45	7 04	19 27	7 13	20 20	23 48

EPHEMERIS CALCULATED FOR 12 MIDNIGHT GREENWICH MEAN TIME. ALL OTHER DATA AND FACING ASPECTARIAN PAGE IN **EASTERN TIME (BOLD)** AND PACIFIC TIME (REGULAR).

MARCH 2017

☽ Last Aspect day	ET / hr:mn	PT	asp	☽ Ingress sign	day	ET / hr:mn	PT
1	**9:18 pm**	6:18 pm	△♄	♉	1		11:43 pm
1	**9:18 pm**	6:18 pm	△♄	♉	2	**2:43 am**	
3	**10:20 am**	7:20 am	△♇	♊	4	**5:05 am**	2:05 am
6	**3:22 am**	12:22 am	✶♂	♋	6	**7:54 am**	4:54 am
8	**9:59 am**	6:59 am	□♂	♌	8	**11:45 am**	8:45 am
10	**12:06 pm**	9:06 am	△♄	♍	10	**5:07 pm**	2:07 pm
12	**10:36 pm**	7:36 pm	☍☿	♎	12		10:28 pm
12	**10:36 pm**	7:36 pm	☍☿	♎	13	**1:28 am**	
15	**6:05 am**	3:05 am	✶♄	♏	15	**11:11 am**	8:11 am
17	**5:56 pm**	2:56 pm	△☉	♐	17	**11:00 pm**	8:00 pm

☽ Last Aspect day	ET / hr:mn	PT	asp	☽ Ingress sign	day	ET / hr:mn	PT
20	**6:37 am**	3:37 am	☌♄	♑	20	**11:31 am**	8:31 am
22	**9:20 am**	6:20 am	□♅	♒	22	**10:28 pm**	7:28 pm
24		10:56 pm	✶♄	♓	25	**6:06 am**	3:06 am
25	**1:56 am**		✶♄	♓	25	**6:06 am**	3:06 am
27	**6:19 am**	3:19 am	□♄	♈	27	**10:11 am**	7:11 am
29	**8:07 am**	5:07 am	△♄	♉	29	**11:48 am**	8:48 am
30	**7:12 pm**	4:12 pm	△♇	♊	31	**12:40 pm**	9:40 am

☽ Phases & Eclipses phase	day	ET / hr:mn	PT
2nd Quarter	5	**6:32 am**	3:32 am
Full Moon	12	**10:54 am**	7:54 am
4th Quarter	20	**11:58 am**	8:58 am
New Moon	27	**10:57 pm**	7:57 pm

Planet Ingress		day	ET / hr:mn	PT
♂	♉	9	**7:34 pm**	4:34 pm
☿	♈	13	**5:07 pm**	2:07 pm
☉	♈	20	**6:29 am**	3:29 am
♀	♈	29		9:47 pm
♀	♈	30	**12:47 am**	
☿	♉	31	**1:31 pm**	10:31 am

Planetary Motion		day	ET / hr:mn	PT
♀	℞	4	**4:09 am**	1:09 am
⚵	D	7	**4:32 am**	1:32 am

1 WEDNESDAY
☽ □ ♇ **7:49 am** 4:49 am
☽ ☌ ♅ **1:27 pm** 10:27 am
☽ ☍ ♃ **1:43 pm** 10:43 am
☽ ☌ ♂ **4:48 pm** 1:48 pm
☽ △ ♄ **9:18 pm** 6:18 pm ☽
☉ ☌ ♆ **9:44 pm** 6:44 pm

2 THURSDAY
☽ ✶ ☿ **5:48 pm** 2:48 pm
♃ ☍ ♅ **8:15 pm** 5:15 pm
☽ ✶ ♆ **10:26 pm** 7:26 pm
☽ ✶ ☉ 9:14 pm
☽ ⚺ ♀ 9:44 pm

3 FRIDAY
☽ ✶ ☉ **12:14 am**
☽ ⚺ ♀ **12:44 am**
☉ ⚺ ♀ **7:49 am** 4:49 am
☽ △ ♇ **10:20 am** 7:20 am ☽
☽ ⚻ ♃ **3:52 pm** 12:52 pm
☽ ⚺ ♅ **4:02 pm** 1:02 pm
☽ ⚺ ♂ **9:54 pm** 6:54 pm
☽ ⚻ ♄ **11:53 pm** 8:53 pm

4 SATURDAY
☿ ☌ ♆ **6:10 am** 3:10 am
☿ ⚺ ♀ **11:17 pm** 8:17 pm
☽ □ ♆ 10:02 pm

5 SUNDAY
☽ □ ♆ **1:02 am**
☽ ✶ ♀ **3:14 am** 12:14 am
☽ □ ☿ **3:51 am** 12:51 am
☽ □ ☉ **6:32 am** 3:32 am
☽ ⚻ ♇ **12:59 pm** 9:59 am
♂ △ ♄ **3:46 pm** 12:46 pm
☽ △ ♃ **6:12 pm** 3:12 pm
☽ ✶ ♅ **6:50 pm** 3:50 pm
☽ ☍ ♄ 11:48 pm

6 MONDAY
☽ ☍ ♄ **2:48 am**
☽ ✶ ♂ **3:22 am** 12:22 am ☽
☉ ☌ ☿ **7:29 pm** 4:29 pm

7 TUESDAY
☽ △ ♆ **4:20 am** 1:20 am
☽ □ ♀ **6:08 am** 3:08 am
☽ △ ☉ **1:48 pm** 10:48 am
☽ △ ☿ **3:12 pm** 12:12 pm
☽ ☍ ♇ **4:28 pm** 1:28 pm
☽ □ ♃ **9:25 pm** 6:25 pm
☽ □ ♅ **10:33 pm** 7:33 pm
☿ ✶ ♇ 9:25 pm

8 WEDNESDAY
☿ ✶ ♇ **12:25 am**
☽ ⚻ ♄ **6:43 am** 3:43 am
☽ □ ♂ **9:59 am** 6:59 am ☽

9 THURSDAY
☉ ✶ ♇ **3:33 am** 12:33 am
☽ ⚻ ♆ **8:53 am** 5:53 am
☽ △ ♀ **9:55 am** 6:55 am
☿ ⚻ ♃ **9:57 am** 6:57 am
☿ ⚺ ♅ **8:55 pm** 5:55 pm
☽ ⚻ ♇ **9:18 pm** 6:18 pm
☽ ⚻ ☉ **10:42 pm** 7:42 pm
☽ ✶ ♃ 10:58 pm

10 FRIDAY
☽ ✶ ♃ **1:58 am**
☽ △ ♅ **3:42 am** 12:42 am
☽ ⚻ ☿ **4:49 am** 1:49 am
☽ △ ♄ **12:06 pm** 9:06 am ☽
☽ △ ♂ **6:22 pm** 3:22 pm

11 SATURDAY
♀ ⚺ ♆ **8:53 am** 5:53 am
☽ ⚻ ♀ **2:58 pm** 11:58 am
☉ ⚻ ♃ **3:00 pm** 12:00 pm
☽ ☍ ♆ **3:08 pm** 12:08 pm

12 SUNDAY
☽ △ ♇ **4:57 am** 12:57 am
☿ □ ♄ **8:10 am** 5:10 am
☽ ⚺ ♃ **9:18 am** 6:18 am
☽ ☍ ☉ **10:54 am** 7:54 am
☽ ⚻ ♅ **11:43 am** 8:43 am
☽ □ ♄ **8:25 pm** 5:25 pm
☉ ⚺ ♅ **10:04 pm** 7:04 pm
☽ ☍ ☿ **10:36 pm** 7:36 pm ☽

13 MONDAY
☽ ⚻ ♂ **6:05 am** 3:05 am
☽ ☍ ♀ **10:41 pm** 7:41 pm
☽ ⚻ ♆ 9:35 pm

14 TUESDAY
☽ ⚻ ♆ **12:35 am**
☽ □ ♇ **1:52 pm** 10:52 am
☽ ☌ ♃ **5:52 pm** 2:52 pm
☽ ☍ ♅ **9:05 pm** 6:05 pm
☽ ⚻ ☉ 10:00 pm

15 WEDNESDAY
☽ ⚻ ☉ **1:00 am**
☽ ✶ ♄ **6:05 am** 3:05 am ☽
☽ ⚻ ☿ **7:18 pm** 4:18 pm
☽ ☍ ♂ **7:38 pm** 4:38 pm
☿ ⚺ ♂ **10:21 pm** 7:21 pm

16 THURSDAY
☽ ⚻ ♀ **7:13 am** 4:13 am
☽ △ ♆ **11:25 am** 8:25 am
☽ ✶ ♇ 10:05 pm

17 FRIDAY
☽ ✶ ♇ **1:05 am**
☽ ⚺ ♃ **4:38 am** 1:38 am
☽ ⚻ ♅ **8:44 am** 5:44 am
☉ □ ♄ **5:48 pm** 2:48 pm
☽ ⚺ ♄ **5:56 pm** 2:56 pm
☽ △ ☉ **5:56 pm** 2:56 pm ☽

18 SATURDAY
☿ ☌ ♀ **8:27 am** 5:27 am
☽ ⚻ ♂ **11:31 am** 8:31 am
☽ △ ♀ **4:59 pm** 1:59 pm
☽ △ ☿ **7:06 pm** 4:06 pm
☽ □ ♆ **11:57 pm** 8:57 pm

19 SUNDAY
☽ ⚺ ♇ **1:41 pm** 10:41 am
☽ ✶ ♃ **4:36 pm** 1:36 pm
☽ △ ♅ **9:33 pm** 6:33 pm
☿ ⚺ ♆ 10:51 pm

20 MONDAY
☿ ⚺ ♆ **1:51 am**
☽ ☌ ♄ **6:37 am** 3:37 am ☽
☽ □ ☉ **11:58 am** 8:58 am
♀ ⚺ ♂ **4:22 pm** 1:22 pm
☽ □ ♀ 11:32 pm

21 TUESDAY
☽ □ ♀ **2:32 am**
☽ △ ♂ **3:43 am** 12:43 am
☽ ✶ ♆ **12:17 pm** 9:17 am
☽ □ ☿ **6:20 pm** 3:20 pm
☽ ☌ ♇ 10:32 pm

22 WEDNESDAY
☽ ☌ ♇ **1:32 am**
☽ □ ♃ **3:44 am** 12:44 am
☽ □ ♅ **9:20 am** 6:20 am ☽
☽ ⚺ ♄ **5:55 pm** 2:55 pm

23 THURSDAY
☽ ✶ ☉ **3:58 am** 12:58 am
☽ ✶ ♀ **10:06 am** 7:06 am
☽ □ ♂ **5:20 pm** 2:20 pm
☿ □ ♇ **8:45 pm** 5:45 pm
☽ ⚺ ♆ **10:10 pm** 7:10 pm

24 FRIDAY
☿ ☍ ♃ **8:45 am** 5:45 am
☽ ⚺ ♇ **10:33 am** 7:33 am
☽ △ ♃ **12:03 pm** 9:03 am
☽ ✶ ☿ **12:34 pm** 9:34 am
☽ ✶ ♅ **6:02 pm** 3:02 pm
☽ ✶ ♄ 10:56 pm ☽

25 SATURDAY
☽ ✶ ♄ **1:56 am** ☽
☉ ☌ ♀ **6:17 am** 3:17 am
☽ ⚺ ♀ **2:33 pm** 11:33 am
☽ ⚺ ☉ **3:37 pm** 12:37 pm
☽ ✶ ♂ 11:42 pm

26 SUNDAY
☽ ✶ ♂ **2:42 am**
☽ ☌ ♆ **4:23 am** 1:23 am
☿ ☌ ♅ **11:06 am** 8:06 am
☽ ✶ ♇ **3:52 pm** 12:52 pm
☽ ⚻ ♃ **4:47 pm** 1:47 pm
☽ ⚺ ♅ **11:03 pm** 8:03 pm
☽ ⚺ ☿ 9:25 pm

27 MONDAY
☽ ⚺ ☿ **12:25 am**
☽ □ ♄ **6:19 am** 3:19 am ☽
♂ ✶ ♆ **12:44 pm** 9:44 am
☽ ☌ ♀ **3:59 pm** 12:59 pm
☽ ☌ ☉ **10:57 pm** 7:57 pm

28 TUESDAY
☽ ⚺ ♆ **7:22 am** 4:22 am
☽ ⚺ ♂ **8:16 am** 5:16 am
☽ □ ♇ **6:14 pm** 3:14 pm
☽ ☍ ♃ **6:38 pm** 3:38 pm
☽ ☌ ♅ 10:15 pm

29 WEDNESDAY
☽ ☌ ♅ **1:15 am**
☽ ☌ ☿ **7:33 am** 4:33 am
☽ △ ♄ **8:07 am** 5:07 am ☽
☿ △ ♄ **2:16 pm** 11:16 am
☽ ⚺ ♀ **3:29 pm** 12:29 pm

30 THURSDAY
☽ ⚺ ☉ **3:45 am** 12:45 am
☽ ✶ ♆ **8:34 am** 5:34 am
☽ ☌ ♂ **11:49 am** 8:49 am
♃ □ ♇ **2:19 pm** 11:19 am
☽ ⚻ ♃ **7:09 pm** 4:09 pm
☽ △ ♇ **7:12 pm** 4:12 pm ☽
☽ ⚺ ♅ 11:20 pm

31 FRIDAY
☽ ⚺ ♅ **2:20 am**
☽ ⚻ ♄ **9:01 am** 6:01 am
☽ ⚺ ☿ **12:36 pm** 9:36 am
☽ ✶ ♀ **2:33 pm** 11:33 am

Eastern time in bold type
Pacific time in medium type

MARCH 2017

DATE	SID.TIME	SUN	MOON	NODE	MERCURY	VENUS	MARS	JUPITER	SATURN	URANUS	NEPTUNE	PLUTO	CERES	PALLAS	JUNO	VESTA	CHIRON
1 W	10 35 57	10 ♓ 36 06	11 ♈ 13	3 ♍ 23	5 ♓ 25	12 ♈ 55	23 ♈ 27	22 ♎ 16 ℞	26 ♐ 44	22 ♈ 06	11 ♓ 40	18 ♑ 47	7 ♑ 24	19 ♓ 48	7 ♈ 29	20 ♋ 14 ℞	23 ♓ 51
2 Th	10 39 54	11 36 11	25 25	3 22 ℞	7 14	13 02	24 11	22 12	26 47	22 08	11 42	18 48	7 45	20 19	7 45	20 12	23 55
3 F	10 43 50	12 36 15	9 ♉ 42	3 21	9 05	13 07	24 55	22 07	26 50	22 11	11 44	18 49	8 05	20 50	8 01	20 10	23 59
4 Sa	10 47 47	13 36 17	24 00	3 20	10 56	13 09 ℞	25 38	22 02	26 54	22 14	11 47	18 51	8 25	21 11	8 17	20 08	24 02
5 Su	10 51 44	14 36 16	8 ♊ 15	3 19 D	12 48	13 08	26 22	21 57	26 57	22 17	11 49	18 52	8 46	21 32	8 32	20 08	24 06
6 M	10 55 40	15 36 13	22 29	3 20	14 41	13 06	27 05	21 52	27 00	22 20	11 51	18 53	9 07	21 52	8 48	20 07 D	24 09
7 T	10 59 37	16 36 08	6 ♋ 29	3 21	16 35	13 00	27 49	21 47	27 03	22 23	11 54	18 55	9 28	22 13	9 03	20 07	24 13
8 W	11 3 33	17 36 01	20 23	3 22	18 30	12 53	28 32	21 42	27 06	22 26	11 56	18 56	9 49	22 34	9 18	20 08	24 16
9 Th	11 7 30	18 35 52	4 ♌ 08	3 23	20 26	12 42	29 16	21 36	27 08	22 29	11 58	18 57	10 10	22 55	9 33	20 09	24 20
10 F	11 11 26	19 35 42	17 41	3 24 ℞	22 23	12 29	29 59	21 31	27 11	22 32	12 00	18 58	10 31	23 16	9 48	20 10	24 24
11 Sa	11 15 23	20 35 29	1 ♍ 02	3 23	24 20	12 14	0 ♉ 42	21 25	27 14	22 35	12 03	19 00	10 52	23 37	10 03	20 12	24 27
12 Su	11 19 19	21 35 14	14 11	3 23	26 18	11 56	1 26	21 19	27 16	22 38	12 05	19 01	11 13	23 58	10 17	20 14	24 31
13 M	11 23 16	22 34 58	27 05	3 22	28 16	11 36	2 09	21 13	27 19	22 41	12 07	19 02	11 35	24 19	10 32	20 17	24 35
14 T	11 27 13	23 34 40	9 ♎ 46	3 20	0 ♈ 14	11 13	2 52	21 07	27 21	22 44	12 09	19 03	11 56	24 40	10 46	20 20	24 38
15 W	11 31 9	24 34 20	22 14	3 17	2 13	10 49	3 35	21 01	27 23	22 47	12 12	19 04	12 18	25 00	11 00	20 24	24 42
16 Th	11 35 6	25 33 58	4 ♏ 29	3 13	4 11	10 22	4 18	20 54	27 25	22 50	12 14	19 05	12 40	25 21	11 14	20 28	24 45
17 F	11 39 2	26 33 35	16 34	3 09	6 09	9 53	5 01	20 48	27 27	22 53	12 16	19 06	13 01	25 42	11 28	20 32	24 49
18 Sa	11 42 59	27 33 10	28 31	3 06	8 06	9 22	5 44	20 41	27 29	22 56	12 18	19 07	13 23	26 04	11 41	20 37	24 53
19 Su	11 46 55	28 32 43	10 ♐ 24	3 03	10 01	8 50	6 27	20 35	27 31	23 00	12 21	19 08	13 45	26 25	11 55	20 42	24 56
20 M	11 50 52	29 32 15	22 17	3 02 D	11 56	8 16	7 10	20 28	27 33	23 03	12 23	19 09	14 07	26 46	12 08	20 48	25 00
21 T	11 54 48	0 ♈ 31 44	4 ♑ 15	3 02	13 48	7 41	7 53	20 21	27 35	23 06	12 25	19 10	14 29	27 07	12 21	20 54	25 03
22 W	11 58 45	1 31 12	16 22	3 03	15 38	7 05	8 36	20 14	27 36	23 09	12 27	19 11	14 52	27 28	12 34	21 00	25 07
23 Th	12 2 42	2 30 38	28 43	3 04	17 25	6 28	9 19	20 07	27 38	23 13	12 29	19 12	15 14	27 49	12 47	21 07	25 11
24 F	12 6 38	3 30 02	11 ♒ 22	3 06	19 09	5 51	10 02	20 00	27 39	23 16	12 31	19 13	15 36	28 10	13 00	21 14	25 14
25 Sa	12 10 35	4 29 23	24 24	3 07 ℞	20 50	5 13	10 44	19 53	27 40	23 19	12 34	19 13	15 59	28 31	13 12	21 21	25 18
26 Su	12 14 31	5 28 43	7 ♓ 49	3 07	22 26	4 36	11 27	19 45	27 41	23 22	12 36	19 14	16 21	28 52	13 24	21 29	25 21
27 M	12 18 28	6 28 01	21 39	3 06	23 58	3 58	12 10	19 38	27 43	23 26	12 38	19 15	16 44	29 13	13 36	21 38	25 25
28 T	12 22 24	7 27 17	5 ♈ 51	3 03	25 25	3 21	12 52	19 31	27 43	23 29	12 40	19 16	17 07	29 35	13 48	21 46	25 28
29 W	12 26 21	8 26 31	20 21	2 59	26 47	2 45	13 35	19 23	27 44	23 32	12 42	19 16	17 30	29 56	13 59	21 55	25 32
30 Th	12 30 17	9 25 43	5 ♉ 02	2 53	28 03	2 09	14 17	19 16	27 45	23 36	12 44	19 17	17 52	0 ♈ 17	14 11	22 05	25 36
31 F	12 34 14	10 24 53	19 48	2 48	29 13	1 35	15 00	19 08	27 46	23 39	12 46	19 18	18 15	0 38	14 22	22 16	25 39

EPHEMERIS CALCULATED FOR 12 MIDNIGHT GREENWICH MEAN TIME. ALL OTHER DATA AND FACING ASPECTARIAN PAGE IN **EASTERN TIME (BOLD)** AND PACIFIC TIME (REGULAR).

APRIL 2017

☽ Last Aspect day	ET / hr:mn / PT		asp	☽ Ingress sign	day	ET / hr:mn / PT	
2	**10:43 am**	7:43 am	☍ ♄	♋	2	**2:27 pm**	11:27 am
4	**4:45 pm**	1:45 pm	△ ♀	♌	4	**6:13 pm**	3:13 pm
6	**8:16 pm**	5:16 pm	△ ♄	♍	6		9:20 pm
6	**8:16 pm**	5:16 pm	△ ♄	♍	7	**12:20 am**	
9	**4:21 am**	1:21 am	□ ♄	♎	9	**8:34 am**	5:34 am
11	**2:19 pm**	11:19 am	⚹ ♄	♏	11	**6:42 pm**	3:42 pm
13		9:18 pm	△ ♀	♐	14	**6:27 am**	3:27 am
14	**12:18 am**		△ ♀	♐	14	**6:27 am**	3:27 am
16	**2:26 pm**	11:26 am	☌ ♄	♑	16	**7:05 pm**	4:05 pm
19	**5:57 am**	2:57 am	□ ☉	♒	19	**6:52 am**	3:52 am

☽ Last Aspect day	ET / hr:mn / PT		asp	☽ Ingress sign	day	ET / hr:mn / PT	
21	**2:23 pm**	11:23 am	⚹ ☿	♓	21	**3:43 pm**	12:43 pm
23	**5:34 pm**	2:34 pm	☌ ♀	♈	23	**8:32 pm**	5:32 pm
25	**5:53 pm**	2:53 pm	△ ♄	♉	25	**9:56 pm**	6:56 pm
27	**9:18 pm**	6:18 pm	⚹ ♀	♊	27	**9:39 pm**	6:39 pm
29	**5:28 pm**	2:28 pm	☍ ♄	♋	29	**9:48 pm**	6:48 pm

☽ Phases & Eclipses phase	day	ET / hr:mn / PT	
2nd Quarter	3	**2:39 pm**	11:39 am
Full Moon	10		11:08 pm
Full Moon	11	**2:08 am**	
4th Quarter	19	**5:57 am**	2:57 am
New Moon	26	**8:16 am**	5:16 am

Planet Ingress		day	ET / hr:mn / PT	
♀	♓	2	**8:25 pm**	5:25 pm
☉	♉	19	**5:27 pm**	2:27 pm
☿	♈	20	**1:37 pm**	10:37 am
♂	♊	21	**6:32 am**	3:32 am
♀	♈	28	**9:13 am**	6:13 am
⚳	♊	29	**11:42 am**	8:42 am

Planetary Motion		day	ET / hr:mn / PT	
♄	℞	5		10:06 pm
♄	℞	6	**1:06 am**	
☿	℞	9	**7:14 pm**	4:14 pm
♀	D	15	**6:18 am**	3:18 am
♇	℞	20	**8:49 am**	5:49 am

1 SATURDAY
☿ ⚺ ♀ **7:53 am** 4:53 am
☽ ⚹ ☉ **8:20 am** 5:20 am
☽ □ ♆ **9:46 am** 6:46 am
☽ ⚺ ♂ **3:29 pm** 12:29 pm
☽ △ ♃ **8:01 pm** 5:01 pm
☽ ⚻ ♇ **8:32 pm** 5:32 pm

2 SUNDAY
☽ ⚹ ♅ **4:00 am** 1:00 am
☉ ⚺ ♆ **6:02 am** 3:02 am
☽ ☍ ♄ **10:43 am** 7:43 am ☽
☽ □ ♀ **2:39 pm** 11:39 am
☽ ⚹ ☿ **5:52 pm** 2:52 pm

3 MONDAY
☽ △ ♆ **12:25 pm** 9:25 am
☽ □ ☉ **2:39 pm** 11:39 am
☽ ⚹ ♂ **8:59 pm** 5:59 pm
☽ □ ♃ **10:31 pm** 7:31 pm
☽ ☍ ♇ **11:33 pm** 8:33 pm

4 TUESDAY
☽ □ ♅ **7:31 am** 4:31 am
☽ ⚻ ♄ **2:20 pm** 11:20 am
☽ △ ♀ **4:45 pm** 1:45 pm ☽
♂ ⚻ ♃ **10:53 pm** 7:53 pm
☽ □ ☿ 9:31 pm

5 WEDNESDAY
☽ □ ☿ **12:31 am**
☽ ⚻ ♆ **5:20 pm** 2:20 pm

☽ △ ☉ **11:46 pm** 8:46 pm
♂ △ ♇ 9:01 pm

6 THURSDAY
♂ △ ♇ **12:01 am**
☽ ⚹ ♃ **3:15 am** 12:15 am
☽ ⚻ ♇ **4:51 am** 1:51 am
☽ □ ♂ **5:08 am** 2:08 am
☽ △ ♅ **1:23 pm** 10:23 am
☽ △ ♄ **8:16 pm** 5:16 pm ☽
☽ ⚻ ♀ **9:16 pm** 6:16 pm

7 FRIDAY
☽ △ ☿ **8:40 am** 5:40 am
☉ ☍ ♃ **5:39 pm** 2:39 pm
☽ ☍ ♆ 9:32 pm

8 SATURDAY
☽ ☍ ♆ **12:32 am**
☽ ⚺ ♃ **10:09 am** 7:09 am
☽ ⚻ ☉ **11:42 am** 8:42 am
☽ △ ♇ **12:24 pm** 9:24 am
☽ △ ♂ **3:54 pm** 12:54 pm
♀ □ ♄ **4:28 pm** 1:28 pm
☉ □ ♇ **8:49 pm** 5:49 pm
☽ ⚻ ♅ **9:29 pm** 6:29 pm

9 SUNDAY
☽ ☍ ♀ **4:07 am** 1:07 am
☽ □ ♄ **4:21 am** 1:21 am ☽
☽ ⚻ ☿ **5:50 pm** 2:50 pm

10 MONDAY
☽ ⚻ ♆ **9:46 am** 6:46 am
☽ ☌ ♃ **6:58 pm** 3:58 pm
☽ □ ♇ **9:54 pm** 6:54 pm
☽ ☍ ☉ 11:08 pm

11 TUESDAY
☽ ☍ ☉ **2:08 am**
☽ ⚻ ♂ **4:58 am** 1:58 am
☽ ☍ ♅ **7:31 am** 4:31 am
☽ ⚻ ♀ **1:10 pm** 10:10 am
☽ ⚹ ♄ **2:19 pm** 11:19 am ☽

12 WEDNESDAY
☽ ☍ ☿ **3:40 am** 12:40 am
☽ △ ♆ **8:48 pm** 5:48 pm

13 THURSDAY
☽ ⚺ ♃ **5:29 am** 2:29 am
♂ ⚺ ♅ **5:37 am** 2:37 am
☽ ⚹ ♇ **9:09 am** 6:09 am
☽ ⚻ ☉ **6:46 pm** 3:46 pm
☽ ⚻ ♅ **7:17 pm** 4:17 pm
☽ ☍ ♂ **8:04 pm** 5:04 pm
☽ △ ♀ 9:18 pm ☽
☉ ☌ ♅ 10:30 pm
☽ ⚺ ♄ 10:54 pm

14 FRIDAY
☽ △ ♀ **12:18 am** ☽
☉ ☌ ♅ **1:30 am**
☽ ⚺ ♄ **1:54 am**
☽ ⚻ ☿ **1:54 pm** 10:54 am

15 SATURDAY
☽ □ ♆ **9:15 am** 6:15 am
☽ ⚹ ♃ **5:16 pm** 2:16 pm
☽ ⚺ ♇ **9:38 pm** 6:38 pm
☉ ⚺ ♂ **10:38 pm** 7:38 pm

16 SUNDAY
☽ △ ♅ **8:09 am** 5:09 am
☽ ⚻ ♂ **12:25 pm** 9:25 am
☽ △ ☉ **12:46 pm** 9:46 am
☽ □ ♀ **12:54 pm** 9:54 am
☉ ⚺ ♀ **2:26 pm** 11:26 am
☽ ☌ ♄ **2:26 pm** 11:26 am ☽
♀ ⚹ ♂ **9:26 pm** 6:26 pm
☽ △ ☿ **11:55 pm** 8:55 pm

17 MONDAY
☉ △ ♄ **8:43 am** 5:43 am
☽ ⚹ ♆ **9:55 pm** 6:55 pm
♂ ⚻ ♄ **10:14 pm** 7:14 pm

18 TUESDAY
☽ □ ♃ **5:03 am** 2:03 am
☽ ☌ ♇ **9:58 am** 6:58 am
☽ □ ♅ **8:32 pm** 5:32 pm
☽ ⚹ ♀ 10:21 pm
☽ ⚺ ♄ 11:16 pm

19 WEDNESDAY
☽ ⚹ ♀ **1:21 am**
☽ ⚺ ♄ **2:16 am**
☽ △ ♂ **4:00 am** 1:00 am
☽ □ ☉ **5:57 am** 2:57 am ☽
☽ □ ☿ **8:31 am** 5:31 am
☉ ☌ ☿ 10:54 pm

20 THURSDAY
☉ ☌ ☿ **1:54 am**
☽ ⚺ ♆ **8:45 am** 5:45 am
☽ △ ♃ **2:50 pm** 11:50 am
☽ ⚺ ♇ **8:04 pm** 5:04 pm
☿ ⚺ ♂ **10:00 pm** 7:00 pm

21 FRIDAY
☽ ⚹ ♅ **6:16 am** 3:16 am
♀ □ ♄ **7:09 am** 4:09 am
☽ ⚹ ♄ **11:19 am** 8:19 am
☽ ⚺ ♀ **11:23 am** 8:23 am
☽ ⚹ ☿ **2:23 pm** 11:23 am ☽
☽ □ ♂ **4:13 pm** 1:13 pm

22 SATURDAY
☽ ☌ ♆ **3:57 pm** 12:57 pm
☽ ⚻ ♃ **9:01 pm** 6:01 pm
☽ ⚹ ♇ 11:19 pm

23 SUNDAY
☽ ⚹ ♇ **2:19 am**
☿ ⚺ ♀ **6:39 am** 3:39 am
☽ ⚺ ♅ **12:00 pm** 9:00 am
☽ □ ♄ **4:22 pm** 1:22 pm
☽ ⚺ ☿ **4:52 pm** 1:52 pm
☽ ☌ ♀ **5:34 pm** 2:34 pm ☽
☽ ⚹ ♂ **11:43 pm** 8:43 pm

24 MONDAY
☽ ⚺ ☉ **3:50 am** 12:50 am
☿ △ ♄ **4:15 am** 1:15 am
☽ ⚺ ♆ **7:10 pm** 4:10 pm
☽ ☍ ♃ **11:24 pm** 8:24 pm

25 TUESDAY
☽ □ ♇ **4:46 am** 1:46 am
☽ ☌ ♅ **2:04 pm** 11:04 am
☽ ☌ ☿ **4:29 pm** 1:29 pm
☽ △ ♄ **5:53 pm** 2:53 pm ☽
☽ ⚺ ♀ **8:17 pm** 5:17 pm

26 WEDNESDAY
☽ ⚺ ♂ **3:20 am** 12:20 am
☽ ☌ ☉ **8:16 am** 5:16 am
☽ ⚹ ♆ **7:38 pm** 4:38 pm
☽ ⚻ ♃ **11:16 pm** 8:16 pm

27 THURSDAY
☽ △ ♇ **4:50 am** 1:50 am
☽ ⚺ ♅ **2:05 pm** 11:05 am
☽ ⚺ ☿ **2:44 pm** 11:44 am
☽ ⚻ ♄ **5:33 pm** 2:33 pm
☽ ⚹ ♀ **9:18 pm** 6:18 pm ☽

28 FRIDAY
☽ ☌ ♂ **5:16 am** 2:16 am
☿ ☌ ♅ **10:49 am** 7:49 am
☽ ⚺ ☉ **11:11 am** 8:11 am
☽ □ ♆ **7:22 pm** 4:22 pm
☽ △ ♃ **10:36 pm** 7:36 pm

29 SATURDAY
☽ ⚻ ♇ **4:35 am** 1:35 am
☽ ⚹ ☿ **1:29 pm** 10:29 am
☽ ⚹ ♅ **2:13 pm** 11:13 am
☽ ☍ ♄ **5:28 pm** 2:28 pm ☽
☽ □ ♀ **10:59 pm** 7:59 pm

30 SUNDAY
☽ ⚺ ♂ **8:04 am** 5:04 am
☽ ⚹ ☉ **3:20 pm** 12:20 pm
☽ △ ♆ **8:26 pm** 5:26 pm
☽ □ ♃ **11:23 pm** 8:23 pm

Eastern time in bold type
Pacific time in medium type

APRIL 2017

DATE	SID.TIME	SUN	MOON	NODE	MERCURY	VENUS	MARS	JUPITER	SATURN	URANUS	NEPTUNE	PLUTO	CERES	PALLAS	JUNO	VESTA	CHIRON
1 Sa	12 38 10	11 ♈ 27 16	4 ♊ 28	2 ♍ 42	0 ♉ 17	1 ♈ 02	15 ♉ 42	19 ♎ 02	27 ♐ 46	23 ♈ 42	12 ♓ 48	19 ♑ 18	18 ♌ 38	0 ♑ 38	14 ♑ 33	22 ♋ 15	25 ♓ 43
2 Su	12 42 7	12 26 29	19 00	2 39 ℞	1 14	0 30 ℞	16 25	19 01 ℞	27 47	23 46	12 50	19 19	19 01	0 59	14 44	22 25	25 46
3 M	12 46 4	13 25 40	3 ♋ 17	2 37	2 05	0 01	17 07	18 53	27 47	23 49	12 52	19 19	19 24	1 21	14 54	22 35	25 50
4 T	12 50 0	14 24 49	17 17	2 36	2 50	29 ♓ 33	17 49	18 45	27 47	23 53	12 54	19 20	19 48	1 42	15 04	22 46	25 53
5 W	12 53 57	15 23 55	1 ♌ 00	2 37	3 27	29 07	18 32	18 38	27 48	23 56	12 56	19 20	20 11	2 03	15 15	22 57	25 57
6 Th	12 57 53	16 22 58	14 27	2 38	3 58	28 43	19 14	18 30	27 48 ℞	23 59	12 58	19 21	20 34	2 24	15 24	23 08	26 00
7 F	13 1 50	17 22 00	27 39	2 39 ℞	4 21	28 21	19 56	18 22	27 48	24 03	13 00	19 21	20 58	2 45	15 34	23 20	26 03
8 Sa	13 5 46	18 20 59	10 ♍ 37	2 39	4 38	28 02	20 38	18 14	27 48	24 06	13 02	19 22	21 21	3 06	15 43	23 32	26 07
9 Su	13 9 43	19 19 56	23 23	2 37	4 48 ℞	27 45	21 20	18 07	27 47	24 10	13 04	19 22	21 44	3 27	15 53	23 44	26 10
10 M	13 13 39	20 18 50	5 ♎ 58	2 33	4 51	27 30	22 02	17 59	27 47	24 13	13 06	19 22	22 08	3 49	16 01	23 57	26 14
11 T	13 17 36	21 17 43	18 24	2 26	4 47	27 18	22 44	17 51	27 47	24 17	13 08	19 23	22 31	4 10	16 10	24 10	26 17
12 W	13 21 33	22 16 34	0 ♏ 40	2 18	4 38	27 09	23 26	17 44	27 46	24 20	13 10	19 23	22 55	4 31	16 19	24 23	26 20
13 Th	13 25 29	23 15 22	12 48	2 08	4 22	27 02	24 08	17 36	27 46	24 23	13 12	19 23	23 19	4 52	16 27	24 37	26 24
14 F	13 29 26	24 14 09	24 48	1 58	4 01	26 57	24 50	17 28	27 45	24 27	13 14	19 23	23 43	5 13	16 35	24 50	26 27
15 Sa	13 33 22	25 12 54	6 ♐ 43	1 49	3 35	26 55 D	25 32	17 21	27 44	24 30	13 15	19 23	24 06	5 34	16 42	25 04	26 30
16 Su	13 37 19	26 11 38	18 35	1 41	3 04	26 55	26 13	17 13	27 43	24 34	13 17	19 24	24 30	5 55	16 50	25 19	26 33
17 M	13 41 15	27 10 19	0 ♑ 27	1 35	2 30	26 57	26 55	17 06	27 42	24 37	13 19	19 24	24 54	6 17	16 57	25 33	26 37
18 T	13 45 12	28 08 59	12 24	1 32	1 52	27 02	27 37	16 58	27 41	24 41	13 21	19 24	25 18	6 38	17 03	25 48	26 40
19 W	13 49 8	29 07 37	24 28	1 30 D	1 12	27 09	28 19	16 51	27 40	24 44	13 23	19 24	25 42	6 59	17 10	26 03	26 43
20 Th	13 53 5	0 ♉ 06 14	6 ♒ 46	1 30	0 31	27 19	29 00	16 43	27 38	24 47	13 24	19 24 ℞	26 06	7 20	17 17	26 19	26 46
21 F	13 57 2	1 04 48	19 22	1 31 ℞	29 ♈ 49	27 30	29 42	16 36	27 37	24 51	13 26	19 24	26 30	7 41	17 23	26 34	26 49
22 Sa	14 0 58	2 03 21	2 ♓ 21	1 31	29 07	27 44	0 ♊ 23	16 29	27 36	24 54	13 28	19 24	26 54	8 02	17 29	26 50	26 52
23 Su	14 4 55	3 01 53	15 47	1 31	28 25	28 00	1 05	16 22	27 34	24 58	13 29	19 24	27 18	8 23	17 34	27 06	26 55
24 M	14 8 51	4 00 23	29 41	1 28	27 45	28 17	1 46	16 15	27 32	25 01	13 31	19 24	27 42	8 44	17 39	27 23	26 58
25 T	14 12 48	4 58 51	14 ♈ 03	1 22	27 07	28 37	2 28	16 08	27 31	25 05	13 32	19 23	28 07	9 05	17 44	27 39	27 01
26 W	14 16 44	5 57 17	28 48	1 14	26 32	28 58	3 09	16 01	27 29	25 08	13 34	19 23	28 31	9 26	17 49	27 56	27 04
27 Th	14 20 41	6 55 41	13 ♉ 49	1 05	26 00	29 21	3 50	15 54	27 27	25 11	13 36	19 23	28 55	9 47	17 53	28 13	27 07
28 F	14 24 37	7 54 04	28 58	0 55	25 32	29 46	4 32	15 47	27 25	25 15	13 37	19 23	29 20	10 08	17 57	28 30	27 10
29 Sa	14 28 34	8 52 25	14 ♊ 02	0 46	25 08	0 ♈ 12	5 13	15 41	27 23	25 18	13 39	19 23	29 44	10 29	18 01	28 48	27 13
30 Su	14 32 30	9 50 44	28 54	0 38	24 48	0 40	5 54	15 34	27 20	25 21	13 40	19 23	0 ♊ 08	10 50	18 04	29 06	27 16

EPHEMERIS CALCULATED FOR 12 MIDNIGHT GREENWICH MEAN TIME. ALL OTHER DATA AND FACING ASPECTARIAN PAGE IN EASTERN TIME (BOLD) AND PACIFIC TIME (REGULAR).

MAY 2017

☽ Last Aspect / ☽ Ingress

☽ Last Aspect			☽ Ingress		
day	ET / hr:mn / PT	asp	sign	day	ET / hr:mn / PT
1	4:23 am 1:23 am	□ ☿	♊	16	1:50 pm 10:50 am
1	4:23 am 1:23 am		♋	18	11:52 pm 8:52 pm
	9:35 am		♌	21	6:10 am 3:10 am
3		△ ♀	♍	23	8:33 am 5:33 am
4		△ ♀	♎	25	8:33 am 5:33 am
4	12:35 am		♏	25	8:33 am 5:33 am
6	8:42 am 5:42 am	⚹ ♂	♐	25	8:15 am 5:15 am
6	6:59 am 3:59 am	✶ ♂	♑	27	7:25 am 4:25 am
8	6:59 pm 3:59 pm	⚹ ♄	♒	27	7:25 am 4:25 am
10	5:42 pm 2:42 pm	♂ ♂	♓	29	8:12 pm 5:12 pm
13	10:14 am 7:14 am	□ ♀	♈	31	12:16 pm 9:16 am
13	10:14 am 7:14 am	△ ♀			

☽ Phases & Eclipses

phase	day	ET / hr:mn / PT
2nd Quarter	2	10:47 pm 7:47 pm
Full Moon	10	5:42 pm 2:42 pm
4th Quarter	18	8:33 pm 5:33 pm
New Moon	25	3:44 pm 12:44 pm

Planet Ingress

planet	sign	day	ET / hr:mn / PT
♀	♈	2	7:57 pm 4:57 pm
☿	♉	15	11:04 pm 9:07 pm
☉	♊	16	12:07 am
☉	♊	20	4:31 pm 1:31 pm

Planetary Motion

planet	day	ET / hr:mn / PT
☿ D	2	12:33 pm 9:33 am
♃ Rₓ	9	7:06 pm 4:06 pm

---

1 MONDAY

2 TUESDAY

3 WEDNESDAY

4 THURSDAY

5 FRIDAY

6 SATURDAY

7 SUNDAY

8 MONDAY

9 TUESDAY

10 WEDNESDAY

11 THURSDAY

12 FRIDAY

13 SATURDAY

14 SUNDAY

15 MONDAY

16 TUESDAY

17 WEDNESDAY

18 THURSDAY

19 FRIDAY

20 SATURDAY

21 SUNDAY

22 MONDAY

23 TUESDAY

24 WEDNESDAY

25 THURSDAY

26 FRIDAY

27 SATURDAY

28 SUNDAY

29 MONDAY

30 TUESDAY

31 WEDNESDAY

Eastern time in bold type
Pacific time in medium type

MAY 2017

DATE	SID.TIME	SUN	MOON	NODE	MERCURY	VENUS	MARS	JUPITER	SATURN	URANUS	NEPTUNE	PLUTO	CERES	PALLAS	JUNO	VESTA	CHIRON
1 M	14 36 27	10 ♉ 49 01	13 ♋ 26	0 ♍ 33 ℞	24 ♈ 17 ℞	1 ♈ 33	6 ♊ 35	15 ♎ 28 ℞	27 ♐ 18 ℞	25 ♈ 25	13 ♓ 41	19 ♑ 22	0 ♊ 33	11 ♈ 17	18 ♑ 07	29 ♋ 24	27 ♓ 19
2 T	14 40 24	11 47 16	27 34	0 31	24 17 D	1 40	7 17	15 21 ℞	27 16 ℞	25 28	13 43	19 22 ℞	0 57	11 32	18 10	29 42	27 22
3 W	14 44 20	12 45 28	11 ♌ 18	0 30 D	24 16	2 13	7 58	15 15	27 13	25 31	13 44	19 22	1 22	11 53	18 12	0 ♌ 00	27 25
4 Th	14 48 17	13 43 39	24 40	0 ♍ 30 ℞	24 16	2 46	8 39	15 09	27 11	25 35	13 46	19 21	1 46	12 14	18 15	0 19	27 27
5 F	14 52 13	14 41 48	7 ♍ 41	0 30	24 20	3 21	9 20	15 03	27 08	25 38	13 47	19 21	2 11	12 35	18 16	0 37	27 30
6 Sa	14 56 10	15 39 54	20 25	0 29	24 29	3 58	10 01	14 57	27 06	25 41	13 48	19 20	2 36	12 55	18 18	0 56	27 33
7 Su	15 0 6	16 37 59	2 ♎ 56	0 25	24 42	4 35	10 42	14 52	27 03	25 45	13 50	19 20	3 00	13 16	18 19	1 15	27 35
8 M	15 4 3	17 36 02	15 16	0 18	25 00	5 14	11 22	14 47	27 00	25 48	13 51	19 19	3 25	13 37	18 19	1 35	27 38
9 T	15 7 59	18 34 03	27 28	0 09	25 22	5 53	12 03	14 41	26 57	25 51	13 52	19 19	3 50	13 58	18 20 ℞	1 54	27 40
10 W	15 11 56	19 32 02	9 ♏ 33	29 ♌ 44	25 49	6 34	12 44	14 35	26 54	25 54	13 53	19 18	4 14	14 18	18 21	2 14	27 43
11 Th	15 15 52	20 30 00	21 33	29 44	26 19	7 16	13 25	14 30	26 51	25 57	13 54	19 18	4 39	14 39	18 20	2 34	27 45
12 F	15 19 49	21 27 56	3 ♐ 29	29 30	26 54	7 59	14 06	14 25	26 48	26 01	13 56	19 17	5 04	15 00	18 20	2 54	27 48
13 Sa	15 23 46	22 25 51	15 21	29 17	27 33	8 43	14 46	14 20	26 45	26 04	13 57	19 17	5 29	15 20	18 19	3 14	27 50
14 Su	15 27 42	23 23 45	27 13	29 05	28 15	9 27	15 27	14 16	26 41	26 07	13 58	19 16	5 54	15 41	18 18	3 34	27 53
15 M	15 31 39	24 21 37	9 ♑ 06	28 50	29 01	10 13	16 08	14 11	26 38	26 10	13 59	19 16	6 18	16 01	18 16	3 55	27 55
16 T	15 35 35	25 19 27	21 03	28 46	29 51	10 59	16 48	14 07	26 35	26 13	14 00	19 15	6 43	16 22	18 14	4 15	27 57
17 W	15 39 32	26 17 17	3 ≈ 07	28 46	0 ♉ 44	11 46	17 29	14 03	26 31	26 16	14 01	19 15	7 08	16 42	18 12	4 36	27 59
18 Th	15 43 28	27 15 05	15 24	28 45	1 40	12 34	18 09	13 59	26 28	26 19	14 02	19 14	7 33	17 03	18 09	4 57	28 02
19 F	15 47 25	28 12 52	27 57	28 45	2 40	13 23	18 50	13 55	26 24	26 22	14 03	19 13	7 58	17 23	18 07	5 18	28 04
20 Sa	15 51 22	29 10 38	10 ♓ 51	28 44	3 43	14 13	19 30	13 51	26 21	26 25	14 04	19 12	8 23	17 44	18 03	5 40	28 06
21 Su	15 55 18	0 ♊ 08 23	24 12	28 43	4 48	15 03	20 11	13 47	26 17	26 28	14 05	19 11	8 48	18 04	18 00	6 01	28 08
22 M	15 59 15	1 06 07	8 ♈ 06	28 40	5 56	15 54	20 51	13 44	26 13	26 31	14 06	19 11	9 13	18 24	17 56	6 23	28 10
23 T	16 3 11	2 03 49	22 20	28 34	7 08	16 45	21 31	13 41	26 09	26 34	14 07	19 10	9 38	18 45	17 51	6 45	28 12
24 W	16 7 8	3 01 31	7 ♉ 06	28 26	8 22	17 38	22 12	13 38	26 05	26 37	14 08	19 09	10 03	19 05	17 47	7 07	28 14
25 Th	16 11 4	3 59 12	22 12	28 15	9 39	18 30	22 52	13 35	26 02	26 40	14 08	19 08	10 28	19 25	17 42	7 29	28 16
26 F	16 15 1	4 56 51	7 ♊ 30	28 04	10 58	19 24	23 32	13 32	25 58	26 43	14 08	19 07	10 53	19 45	17 36	7 51	28 18
27 Sa	16 18 57	5 54 29	22 47	27 54	12 20	20 17	24 12	13 30	25 54	26 46	14 09	19 05	11 18	20 05	17 30	8 13	28 20
28 Su	16 22 54	6 52 06	7 ♋ 53	27 45	13 44	21 12	24 53	13 27	25 50	26 49	14 10	19 04	11 43	20 25	17 24	8 36	28 21
29 M	16 26 51	7 49 42	22 39	27 40	15 12	22 07	25 33	13 25	25 46	26 52	14 10	19 03	12 09	20 45	17 18	8 58	28 23
30 T	16 30 47	8 47 16	6 ♌ 59	27 38	16 41	23 02	26 13	13 23	25 41	26 54	14 11	19 02	12 34	21 05	17 11	9 21	28 25
31 W	16 34 44	9 44 49	21 ♌	27 35 D	18 13	23 58	26 53	13 21	25 37	26 57	14 11	19 01	12 59	21 25	17 04	9 44	28 26

EPHEMERIS CALCULATED FOR 12 MIDNIGHT GREENWICH MEAN TIME. ALL OTHER DATA AND FACING ASPECTARIAN PAGE IN **EASTERN TIME (BOLD)** AND PACIFIC TIME (REGULAR)

JUNE 2017

☽ Last Aspect day	ET / hr:mn / PT		asp	☽ Ingress sign	day	ET / hr:mn / PT	
2	**5:48 pm**	2:48 pm	☐♂	♎	2	**8:04 pm**	5:04 pm
5	**4:57 am**	1:57 am	☍♀	♏	5	**6:46 am**	3:46 am
6	**8:35 pm**	5:35 pm	✶♇	♐	7	**6:59 pm**	3:59 pm
9		11:20 pm	△♅	♑	10	**7:36 am**	4:36 am
10	**2:20 am**		△♅	♑	10	**7:36 am**	4:36 am
12	**2:45 pm**	11:45 am	☐♅	♒	12	**7:45 pm**	4:45 pm
14		10:40 pm	✶♅	♓	15	**6:17 am**	3:17 am
15	**1:40 am**		✶♅	♓	15	**6:17 am**	3:17 am
17	**7:33 am**	4:33 am	☐☉	♈	17	**1:55 pm**	10:55 am
19	**3:42 pm**	12:42 pm	✶☉	♉	19	**5:53 pm**	2:53 pm

☽ Last Aspect day	ET / hr:mn / PT		asp	☽ Ingress sign	day	ET / hr:mn / PT	
20		9:26 pm	△♇	♊	21	**6:44 pm**	3:44 pm
21	**12:26 am**		△♇	♊	21	**6:44 pm**	3:44 pm
23	**2:45 pm**	11:45 am	✶♅	♋	23	**6:07 pm**	3:07 pm
25	**2:44 pm**	11:44 am	☐♅	♌	25	**6:06 pm**	3:06 pm
27	**5:12 pm**	2:12 pm	△♅	♍	27	**8:41 pm**	5:41 pm
29	**4:35 pm**	1:35 pm	△♀	♎	30	**3:02 am**	12:02 am

☽ Phases & Eclipses phase	day	ET / hr:mn / PT	
2nd Quarter	1	**8:42 am**	5:42 am
Full Moon	9	**9:10 am**	6:10 am
4th Quarter	17	**7:33 am**	4:33 am
New Moon	23	**10:31 pm**	7:31 pm
2nd Quarter	30	**8:51 pm**	5:51 pm

Planet Ingress	day	ET / hr:mn / PT	
♂ ♋	4	**12:16 pm**	9:16 am
♀ ♉	6	**3:27 am**	12:27 am
☿ ♊	6	**6:15 pm**	3:15 pm
☉ ♋	20		9:24 pm
☉ ♋	21	**12:24 am**	
☿ ♋	21	**5:57 am**	2:57 am
♀ ♉	26	**10:34 pm**	7:34 pm

Planetary Motion	day	ET / hr:mn / PT	
♃ D	9	**10:03 am**	7:03 am
♆ ℞	16	**7:09 am**	4:09 am

1 THURSDAY
☽ ☐ ☉ **8:42 am** 5:42 am
♀ △ ♄ **11:23 am** 8:23 am
☽ ⚺ ♃ **12:35 pm** 9:35 am
☽ ☍ ♆ **2:15 pm** 11:15 am
☽ △ ♇ **11:10 pm** 8:10 pm

2 FRIDAY
☽ △ ☿ **4:54 am** 1:54 am
☽ ☐ ♄ **11:21 am** 8:21 am
☽ ⚻ ♀ **1:27 pm** 10:27 am
☽ ⚻ ♅ **2:28 pm** 11:28 am
☽ ☐ ♂ **5:48 pm** 2:48 pm☽

3 SATURDAY
♀ ☌ ♅ **3:32 am** 12:32 am
☉ △ ♃ **12:12 pm** 9:12 am
☽ ☌ ♃ **9:44 pm** 6:44 pm
☽ △ ☉ **10:33 pm** 7:33 pm
☽ ⚻ ♆ **11:37 pm** 8:37 pm

4 SUNDAY
☿ ⚻ ♄ **3:24 am** 12:24 am
☽ ☐ ♇ **8:52 am** 5:52 am
☉ ☐ ♆ **12:13 pm** 9:13 am
☽ ✶ ♄ **9:22 pm** 6:22 pm
☽ ⚻ ☿ 9:32 pm
☽ ☍ ♅ 10:10 pm

5 MONDAY
☽ ⚻ ☿ **12:32 am**
☽ ☍ ♅ **1:10 am**
☽ ☍ ♀ **4:57 am** 1:57 am☽
☿ ⚺ ♅ **4:58 am** 1:58 am
☽ △ ♂ **7:51 am** 4:51 am

6 TUESDAY
☽ ⚺ ♃ **9:13 am** 6:13 am
☽ △ ♆ **11:14 am** 8:14 am
☽ ⚻ ☉ **3:18 pm** 12:18 pm
☽ ✶ ♇ **8:35 pm** 5:35 pm☽

7 WEDNESDAY
☽ ⚺ ♄ **9:04 am** 6:04 am
☿ ⚺ ♀ **10:54 am** 7:54 am
☽ ⚻ ♅ **1:31 pm** 10:31 am
☽ ⚻ ♀ **10:33 pm** 7:33 pm
☽ ☍ ☿ **11:36 pm** 8:36 pm
☽ ⚻ ♂ **11:39 pm** 8:39 pm
☿ ⚺ ♂ 9:05 pm

8 THURSDAY
☿ ⚺ ♂ **12:05 am**
☽ ✶ ♃ **9:42 pm** 6:42 pm
☽ ☐ ♆ **11:47 pm** 8:47 pm

9 FRIDAY
☉ ⚻ ♇ **7:57 am** 4:57 am
☽ ⚺ ♇ **9:04 am** 6:04 am
☽ ☍ ☉ **9:10 am** 6:10 am
♀ ✶ ♂ **11:41 am** 8:41 am
☽ ☌ ♄ **9:19 pm** 6:19 pm
☽ △ ♅ 11:20 pm☽

10 SATURDAY
☽ △ ♅ **2:20 am** ☽
☽ ☍ ♂ **3:50 pm** 12:50 pm
☽ △ ♀ **4:42 pm** 1:42 pm
☽ ⚻ ☿ 9:03 pm

11 SUNDAY
☽ ⚻ ☿ **12:03 am**
☽ ☐ ♃ **10:14 am** 7:14 am
☽ ✶ ♆ **12:18 pm** 9:18 am
☽ ☌ ♇ **9:23 pm** 6:23 pm
☽ ⚻ ☉ 11:49 pm

12 MONDAY
☽ ⚻ ☉ **2:49 am**
☽ ⚺ ♄ **9:14 am** 6:14 am
☽ ☐ ♅ **2:45 pm** 11:45 am☽

13 TUESDAY
☽ ⚻ ♂ **7:17 am** 4:17 am
☽ ☐ ♀ **10:08 am** 7:08 am
☿ △ ♃ **11:45 am** 8:45 am
☽ △ ♃ **9:52 pm** 6:52 pm
☿ ☐ ♆ **11:29 pm** 8:29 pm
☽ ⚺ ♆ **11:52 pm** 8:52 pm
☽ △ ☿ **11:56 pm** 8:56 pm

14 WEDNESDAY
☽ ⚺ ♇ **8:35 am** 5:35 am
☽ △ ☉ **6:52 pm** 3:52 pm
☽ ✶ ♄ **7:49 pm** 4:49 pm
☽ ✶ ♅ 10:40 pm☽

15 THURSDAY
☽ ✶ ♅ **1:40 am** ☽
☉ ☍ ♄ **6:18 am** 3:18 am
☽ △ ♂ **8:32 pm** 5:32 pm
☽ ✶ ♀ 10:08 pm
☿ ⚻ ♇ 10:35 pm

16 FRIDAY
☽ ✶ ♀ **1:08 am**
☿ ⚻ ♇ **1:35 am**
☽ ⚻ ♃ **7:21 am** 4:21 am
☽ ☌ ♆ **9:10 am** 6:10 am
☽ ✶ ♇ **5:20 pm** 2:20 pm
☽ ☐ ☿ **8:29 pm** 5:29 pm

17 SATURDAY
☽ ☐ ♄ **3:44 am** 12:44 am
☽ ☐ ☉ **7:33 am** 4:33 am☽
☽ ⚺ ♅ **9:43 am** 6:43 am

18 SUNDAY
☽ ☐ ♂ **6:03 am** 3:03 am
☽ ⚺ ♀ **12:01 pm** 9:01 am
☽ ☍ ♃ **1:28 pm** 10:28 am
☉ ✶ ♅ **2:47 pm** 11:47 am
☽ ⚺ ♆ **3:04 pm** 12:04 pm
☿ ☍ ♄ **3:07 pm** 12:07 pm
☽ ☐ ♇ **10:37 pm** 7:37 pm

19 MONDAY
♀ ⚻ ♃ **7:49 am** 4:49 am
☽ △ ♄ **8:07 am** 5:07 am
☽ ✶ ☿ **11:20 am** 8:20 am
☽ ☌ ♅ **2:05 pm** 11:05 am
☽ ✶ ☉ **3:42 pm** 12:42 pm☽

20 TUESDAY
♀ ✶ ♆ **4:25 am** 1:25 am
☿ ✶ ♅ **5:30 am** 2:30 am
☽ ✶ ♂ **11:21 am** 8:21 am
☽ ⚻ ♃ **4:01 pm** 1:01 pm
☽ ✶ ♆ **5:25 pm** 2:25 pm
☽ ☌ ♀ **6:24 pm** 3:24 pm
☽ △ ♇ 9:26 pm☽

21 WEDNESDAY
☽ △ ♇ **12:26 am** ☽
☽ ⚻ ♄ **9:14 am** 6:14 am
☉ ☌ ☿ **10:14 am** 7:14 am
☽ ⚺ ♅ **3:15 pm** 12:15 pm
☽ ⚺ ☉ **7:59 pm** 4:59 pm
☽ ⚺ ☿ **8:55 pm** 5:55 pm

22 THURSDAY
☽ ⚺ ♂ **1:38 pm** 10:38 am
☽ △ ♃ **4:05 pm** 1:05 pm
☽ ☐ ♆ **5:18 pm** 2:18 pm
☽ ⚺ ♀ **9:51 pm** 6:51 pm
☽ ⚻ ♇ 9:03 pm

23 FRIDAY
☽ ⚻ ♇ **12:03 am**
☽ ☍ ♄ **8:31 am** 5:31 am
☽ ✶ ♅ **2:45 pm** 11:45 am☽
☽ ☌ ☉ **10:31 pm** 7:31 pm

24 SATURDAY
☽ ☌ ☿ **4:13 am** 1:13 am
♀ △ ♇ **4:59 am** 1:59 am
☽ ☌ ♂ **3:09 pm** 12:09 pm
☽ ☐ ♃ **3:36 pm** 12:36 pm
☽ △ ♆ **4:42 pm** 1:42 pm
☽ ☍ ♇ **11:29 pm** 8:29 pm
☽ ✶ ♀ 9:56 pm
♂ ☐ ♃ 11:07 pm

25 SUNDAY
☽ ✶ ♀ **12:56 am**
♂ ☐ ♃ **2:07 am**
☽ ⚻ ♄ **7:59 am** 4:59 am
☽ ☐ ♅ **2:44 pm** 11:44 am☽
☽ ⚺ ☉ 11:03 pm
♂ △ ♆ 11:18 pm

26 MONDAY
☽ ⚺ ☉ **2:03 am**
♂ △ ♆ **2:18 am**
☽ ⚺ ☿ **1:04 pm** 10:04 am
☽ ✶ ♃ **4:43 pm** 1:43 pm
☽ ⚻ ♆ **5:41 pm** 2:41 pm
☽ ⚺ ♂ **6:26 pm** 3:26 pm
☽ ⚻ ♇ 9:48 pm

27 TUESDAY
☽ ⚻ ♇ **12:48 am**
☽ ☐ ♀ **6:29 am** 3:29 am
☽ △ ♄ **9:38 am** 6:38 am
☿ ☐ ♃ **2:21 pm** 11:21 am
☽ △ ♅ **5:12 pm** 2:12 pm☽
☿ △ ♆ **8:22 pm** 5:22 pm

28 WEDNESDAY
☽ ✶ ☉ **9:03 am** 6:03 am
☿ ☌ ♂ **3:50 pm** 12:50 pm
♀ ⚻ ♄ **9:07 pm** 6:07 pm
☽ ⚺ ♃ **9:09 pm** 6:09 pm
☽ ☍ ♆ **9:57 pm** 6:57 pm
☽ ✶ ♂ 10:30 pm
☽ ✶ ☿ 11:44 pm

29 THURSDAY
☽ ✶ ♂ **1:30 am**
☽ ✶ ☿ **2:44 am**
☽ △ ♇ **5:32 am** 2:32 am
☽ ☐ ♄ **2:52 pm** 11:52 am
☽ △ ♀ **4:35 pm** 1:35 pm☽
☿ ☍ ♇ **8:36 pm** 5:36 pm
☽ ⚻ ♅ **11:24 pm** 8:24 pm

30 FRIDAY
☽ ☐ ☉ **8:51 pm** 5:51 pm

Eastern time in bold type
Pacific time in medium type

JUNE 2017

DATE	SID.TIME	SUN	MOON	NODE	MERCURY	VENUS	MARS	JUPITER	SATURN	URANUS	NEPTUNE	PLUTO	CERES	PALLAS	JUNO	VESTA	CHIRON
1 Th	16 38 40	10 Ⅱ 42 21	4 ♍ 17	27 ♌ 35	19 ♉ 48	24 ♈ 54	27 Ⅱ 33	13 ♎ 20	25 ♐ 33	27 ♈ 00	14 ♓ 12	19 ♑ 00	13 Ⅱ 24	21 ♈ 45	16 ♑ 57	10 ♌ 07	28 ♓ 28
2 F	16 42 37	11 39 51	17 18	27 35℞	21 25	25 51	28 13	13 18℞	25 29℞	27 03	14 12	18 59℞	13 49	22 05	16 49℞	10 30	28 29
3 Sa	16 46 33	12 37 20	29 58	27 34	23 05	26 48	28 54	13 17	25 25	27 05	14 13	18 58	14 14	22 24	16 41	10 53	28 31
4 Su	16 50 30	13 34 47	12 ♎ 22	27 31	24 47	27 46	29 33	13 16	25 20	27 08	14 13	18 57	14 40	22 44	16 33	11 17	28 32
5 M	16 54 26	14 32 13	24 35	27 25	26 32	28 43	0 ♋ 13	13 15	25 16	27 10	14 14	18 56	15 05	23 04	16 24	11 40	28 34
6 T	16 58 23	15 29 38	6 ♏ 38	27 17	28 19	29 42	0 53	13 14	25 12	27 13	14 14	18 55	15 30	23 23	16 15	12 04	28 35
7 W	17 2 20	16 27 03	18 36	27 06	0 Ⅱ 08	0 ♉ 41	1 33	13 14	25 07	27 15	14 14	18 53	15 55	23 43	16 06	12 27	28 36
8 Th	17 6 16	17 24 26	0 ♐ 30	26 54	2 00	1 40	2 12	13 13	25 03	27 18	14 15	18 52	16 20	24 02	15 56	12 51	28 38
9 F	17 10 13	18 21 48	12 23	26 41	3 54	2 39	2 52	13 13 D	24 59	27 20	14 15	18 51	16 46	24 22	15 46	13 15	28 39
10 Sa	17 14 9	19 19 09	24 15	26 29	5 51	3 39	3 32	13 13	24 54	27 23	14 15	18 50	17 11	24 41	15 36	13 39	28 40
11 Su	17 18 6	20 16 30	6 ♑ 09	26 19	7 49	4 39	4 12	13 13	24 50	27 25	14 15	18 48	17 36	25 00	15 25	14 03	28 41
12 M	17 22 2	21 13 50	18 06	26 11	9 50	5 39	4 51	13 14	24 46	27 28	14 16	18 47	18 01	25 19	15 15	14 28	28 42
13 T	17 25 59	22 11 09	0 ♒ 08	26 05	11 53	6 40	5 31	13 14	24 41	27 30	14 16	18 46	18 26	25 38	15 04	14 52	28 43
14 W	17 29 56	23 08 28	12 17	26 02	13 58	7 41	6 11	13 15	24 37	27 32	14 16	18 45	18 52	25 57	14 53	15 16	28 44
15 Th	17 33 52	24 05 47	24 38	26 01 D	16 04	8 43	6 50	13 16	24 32	27 34	14 16	18 43	19 17	26 16	14 41	15 41	28 45
16 F	17 37 49	25 03 05	7 ♓ 14	26 02℞	18 12	9 44	7 30	13 17	24 28	27 37	14 16℞	18 42	19 42	26 35	14 29	16 05	28 46
17 Sa	17 41 45	26 00 22	20 08	26 02℞	20 21	10 46	8 09	13 18	24 23	27 39	14 16	18 41	20 08	26 54	14 17	16 30	28 46
18 Su	17 45 42	26 57 39	3 ♈ 09	26 02	22 31	11 48	8 49	13 19	24 19	27 41	14 16	18 39	20 33	27 13	14 05	16 55	28 47
19 M	17 49 38	27 54 56	17 07	26 00	24 42	12 51	9 28	13 21	24 15	27 43	14 16	18 38	20 58	27 32	13 53	17 20	28 48
20 T	17 53 35	28 52 13	1 ♉ 16	25 57	26 54	13 54	10 08	13 23	24 10	27 45	14 15	18 37	21 23	27 50	13 40	17 45	28 49
21 W	17 57 31	29 49 30	15 51	25 51	29 05	14 57	10 47	13 25	24 06	27 47	14 15	18 35	21 49	28 09	13 28	18 10	28 49
22 Th	18 1 28	0 ♋ 46 46	0 Ⅱ 48	25 44	1 ♋ 17	16 00	11 27	13 27	24 01	27 49	14 15	18 34	22 14	28 27	13 15	18 36	28 50
23 F	18 5 25	1 44 02	15 58	25 38	3 28	17 03	12 06	13 29	23 57	27 51	14 15	18 33	22 39	28 46	13 01	19 01	28 50
24 Sa	18 9 21	2 41 18	1 ♋ 12	25 28	5 39	18 07	12 45	13 31	23 53	27 53	14 15	18 31	23 04	29 04	12 48	19 26	28 50
25 Su	18 13 18	3 38 34	16 19	25 22	7 49	19 11	13 25	13 34	23 48	27 55	14 15	18 30	23 30	29 22	12 35	19 52	28 51
26 M	18 17 14	4 35 49	1 ♌ 09	25 18	9 58	20 15	14 04	13 37	23 44	27 56	14 14	18 28	23 55	29 40	12 21	20 17	28 51
27 T	18 21 11	5 33 04	15 37	25 15 D	12 06	21 19	14 43	13 40	23 40	27 58	14 14	18 27	24 20	29 58	12 08	20 43	28 51
28 W	18 25 7	6 30 18	29 36	25 15	14 12	22 23	15 23	13 43	23 35	28 00	14 14	18 25	24 45	0 ♉ 16	11 54	21 09	28 52
29 Th	18 29 4	7 27 32	13 ♍ 08	25 16	16 16	23 28	16 02	13 46	23 31	28 02	14 13	18 24	25 11	0 34	11 40	21 35	28 52
30 F	18 33 0	8 24 45	26 14	25 17	18 20	24 33	16 41	13 50	23 27	28 03	14 13	18 23	25 36	0 51	11 26	22 01	28 52

EPHEMERIS CALCULATED FOR 12 MIDNIGHT GREENWICH MEAN TIME. ALL OTHER DATA AND FACING ASPECTARIAN PAGE IN **EASTERN TIME (BOLD)** AND PACIFIC TIME (REGULAR).

JULY 2017

☽ Last Aspect day	ET / hr:mn / PT	asp	☽ Ingress sign day	ET / hr:mn / PT
2	**9:16 am** 6:16 am	☍ ♅	♏ 2	**12:59 pm** 9:59 am
4	**9:34 pm** 6:34 pm	△ ☿	♐ 4	10:08 pm
4	**9:34 pm** 6:34 pm	△ ☿	♐ 5	**1:08 am**
7	**10:12 am** 7:12 am	△ ♅	♑ 7	**1:45 pm** 10:45 am
9	**10:12 pm** 7:12 pm	□ ♅	♒ 9	10:35 pm
9	**10:12 pm** 7:12 pm	□ ♅	♒ 10	**1:35 am**
12	**8:40 am** 5:40 am	✶ ♅	♓ 12	**11:51 am** 8:51 am
14	**1:00 pm** 10:00 am	△ ♂	♈ 14	**7:52 pm** 4:52 pm
16	**10:19 pm** 7:19 pm	☌ ♅	♉ 16	10:04 pm
16	**10:19 pm** 7:19 pm	☌ ♅	♉ 17	**1:04 am**

☽ Last Aspect day	ET / hr:mn / PT	asp	☽ Ingress sign day	ET / hr:mn / PT
18	11:11 pm	✶ ♂	♊ 19	**3:31 am** 12:31 am
19	**2:11 am**	✶ ♂	♊ 19	**3:31 am** 12:31 am
20	10:41 pm	✶ ♅	♋ 21	**4:09 am** 1:09 am
21	**1:41 am**	✶ ♅	♋ 21	**4:09 am** 1:09 am
22	11:05 pm	□ ♅	♌ 23	**4:34 am** 1:34 am
23	**2:05 am**	□ ♅	♌ 23	**4:34 am** 1:34 am
25	**5:22 am** 2:22 am	☌ ☿	♍ 25	**6:32 am** 3:32 am
27	**2:31 am**(11:31 pm)	□ ♀	♎ 27	**11:37 am** 8:37 am
29	**5:30 pm** 2:30 pm	☍ ♅	♏ 29	**8:23 pm** 5:23 pm
31	**7:10 am** 4:10 am	✶ ♇	♐ 8/1	**8:01 am** 5:01 am

☽ Phases & Eclipses phase	day	ET / hr:mn / PT
Full Moon	8	9:07 pm
Full Moon	9	**12:07 am**
4th Quarter	16	**3:26 pm** 12:26 pm
New Moon	23	**5:46 am** 2:46 am
2nd Quarter	30	**11:23 am** 8:23 am

Planet Ingress	day	ET / hr:mn / PT
♀ ♊	4	**8:11 pm** 5:11 pm
☿ ♌	5	**8:20 pm** 5:20 pm
⚳ ♋	10	**7:47 am** 4:47 am
⚶ ♍	17	**7:15 pm** 4:15 pm
♂ ♌	20	**8:19 am** 5:19 am
☉ ♌	22	**11:15 am** 8:15 am
☿ ♍	25	**7:41 pm** 4:41 pm
♀ ♋	31	**10:54 am** 7:54 am

Planetary Motion	day	ET / hr:mn / PT
⚷ ℞	1	**3:09 am** 12:09 am

1 SATURDAY
☽ ☌ ♃ **5:32 am** 2:32 am
☽ ⚻ ♆ **6:05 am** 3:05 am
☽ □ ♂ **1:03 pm** 10:03 am
☽ □ ♇ **2:06 pm** 11:06 am
☽ □ ☿ **10:16 pm** 7:16 pm
☽ ✶ ♄ **11:47 pm** 8:47 pm

2 SUNDAY
☿ ⚻ ♄ **7:29 am** 4:29 am
☽ ⚻ ♀ **7:32 am** 4:32 am
♂ ☍ ♇ **8:02 am** 5:02 am
☽ ☍ ♅ **9:16 am** 6:16 am ☽

3 MONDAY
♀ ⚺ ♅ **3:23 am** 12:23 am
☽ △ ☉ **12:46 pm** 9:46 am
☽ ⚺ ♃ **5:03 pm** 2:03 pm
☽ △ ♆ **5:16 pm** 2:16 pm
☽ ✶ ♇ 10:29 pm

4 TUESDAY
☽ ✶ ♇ **1:29 am**
☽ △ ♂ **3:58 am** 12:58 am
☽ ⚺ ♄ **11:16 am** 8:16 am
☿ □ ♅ **8:51 pm** 5:51 pm
☽ ⚻ ♅ **9:27 pm** 6:27 pm
☽ △ ☿ **9:34 pm** 6:34 pm ☽
♃ ⚻ ♆ 9:19 pm
☽ ☍ ♀ 10:38 pm

5 WEDNESDAY
♃ ⚻ ♆ **12:19 am**
☽ ☍ ♀ **1:38 am**
☉ △ ♆ **8:46 pm** 5:46 pm
☉ □ ♃ **10:44 pm** 7:44 pm

6 THURSDAY
☽ □ ♆ **5:46 am** 2:46 am
☽ ✶ ♃ **5:59 am** 2:59 am
☽ ⚻ ☉ **6:34 am** 3:34 am
☽ ⚺ ♇ **1:58 pm** 10:58 am
☽ ⚻ ♂ **8:06 pm** 5:06 pm
☽ ☌ ♄ **11:34 pm** 8:34 pm

7 FRIDAY
☿ ✶ ♀ **9:19 am** 6:19 am
☽ △ ♅ **10:12 am** 7:12 am ☽
☽ ⚻ ♀ **8:24 pm** 5:24 pm
☽ ⚻ ☿ **9:08 pm** 6:08 pm

8 SATURDAY
☽ ✶ ♆ **6:05 pm** 3:05 pm
☽ □ ♃ **6:45 pm** 3:45 pm
☽ ☍ ☉ 9:07 pm
☽ ☌ ♇ 11:06 pm

9 SUNDAY
☽ ☍ ☉ **12:07 am**
☽ ☌ ♇ **2:06 am**
♂ ⚻ ♄ **6:09 am** 3:09 am
☽ ⚺ ♄ **11:21 am** 8:21 am
☽ ☍ ♂ **11:40 am** 8:40 am

☽ □ ♅ **10:12 pm** 7:12 pm ☽
☉ ☍ ♇ 9:35 pm

10 MONDAY
☉ ☍ ♇ **12:35 am**
☽ △ ♀ **2:03 pm** 11:03 am
☽ ☍ ☿ **6:38 pm** 3:38 pm

11 TUESDAY
☽ ⚺ ♆ **5:13 am** 2:13 am
☽ △ ♃ **6:20 am** 3:20 am
☽ ⚺ ♇ **12:57 pm** 9:57 am
☽ ⚻ ☉ **4:03 pm** 1:03 pm
☽ ✶ ♄ **9:46 pm** 6:46 pm
☽ ⚻ ♂ 10:36 pm

12 WEDNESDAY
☽ ⚻ ♂ **1:36 am**
☽ ✶ ♅ **8:40 am** 5:40 am ☽

13 THURSDAY
☽ □ ♀ **5:28 am** 2:28 am
☽ ⚻ ☿ **12:46 pm** 9:46 am
☽ ☌ ♆ **2:27 pm** 11:27 am
☽ ⚻ ♃ **4:00 pm** 1:00 pm
☽ ✶ ♇ **9:50 pm** 6:50 pm
☿ ⚻ ♆ 11:19 pm

14 FRIDAY
☿ ⚻ ♆ **2:19 am**
☽ △ ☉ **5:26 am** 2:26 am
☽ □ ♄ **6:08 am** 3:08 am
☽ △ ♂ **1:00 pm** 10:00 am ☽
☉ ⚻ ♄ **2:29 pm** 11:29 am

☿ ✶ ♃ **4:46 pm** 1:46 pm
☽ ⚺ ♅ **4:54 pm** 1:54 pm

15 SATURDAY
☽ ✶ ♀ **5:40 pm** 2:40 pm
☽ ⚺ ♆ **9:08 pm** 6:08 pm
☽ ☍ ♃ **11:03 pm** 8:03 pm
☽ △ ☿ 11:38 pm

16 SUNDAY
☽ △ ☿ **2:38 am**
☽ □ ♇ **4:06 am** 1:06 am
☽ △ ♄ **11:50 am** 8:50 am
☽ □ ☉ **3:26 pm** 12:26 pm
☿ ⚻ ♇ **3:50 pm** 12:50 pm
☽ □ ♂ **9:12 pm** 6:12 pm
☽ ☌ ♅ **10:19 pm** 7:19 pm ☽

17 MONDAY
♀ □ ♆ **10:33 am** 7:33 am
♂ □ ♅ **9:37 pm** 6:37 pm
☽ ✶ ♆ 9:55 pm
☽ ⚺ ♀ 11:10 pm

18 TUESDAY
☽ ✶ ♆ **12:55 am**
☽ ⚺ ♀ **2:10 am**
☽ ⚻ ♃ **3:11 am** 12:11 am
☽ △ ♇ **7:30 am** 4:30 am
☽ □ ☿ **12:01 pm** 9:01 am
☽ ⚻ ♄ **2:44 pm** 11:44 am
♀ △ ♃ **4:09 pm** 1:09 pm
☽ ✶ ☉ **9:56 pm** 6:56 pm
☽ ⚺ ♅ 9:57 pm
☽ ✶ ♂ 11:11 pm ☽

19 WEDNESDAY
☽ ⚺ ♅ **12:57 am**
☽ ✶ ♂ **2:11 am** ☽
☿ △ ♄ **3:16 pm** 12:16 pm
☽ □ ♆ 11:19 pm

20 THURSDAY
☽ □ ♆ **2:19 am**
☽ △ ♃ **4:54 am** 1:54 am
☽ ☌ ♀ **7:39 am** 4:39 am
☽ ⚻ ♇ **8:38 am** 5:38 am
☽ ☍ ♄ **3:32 pm** 12:32 pm
☽ ✶ ☿ **6:04 pm** 3:04 pm
♀ ⚻ ♇ **8:17 pm** 5:17 pm
☉ □ ♅ **8:26 pm** 5:26 pm
☽ ✶ ♅ 10:41 pm ☽
☽ ⚺ ☉ 11:02 pm

21 FRIDAY
☽ ✶ ♅ **1:41 am** ☽
☽ ⚺ ☉ **2:02 am**
☽ ⚺ ♂ **5:03 am** 2:03 am
☽ △ ♆ 11:34 pm

22 SATURDAY
☽ △ ♆ **2:34 am**
☽ □ ♃ **5:34 am** 2:34 am
☽ ☍ ♇ **8:50 am** 5:50 am
☽ ⚺ ♀ **11:55 am** 8:55 am
☽ ⚻ ♄ **3:40 pm** 12:40 pm
☽ ⚺ ☿ **10:59 pm** 7:59 pm
☽ □ ♅ 11:05 pm ☽

23 SUNDAY
☽ □ ♅ **2:05 am** ☽ v/c
☽ ☌ ☉ **5:46 am** 2:46 am
☽ ☌ ♂ **7:41 am** 4:41 am

24 MONDAY
☽ ⚻ ♆ **3:25 am** 12:25 am
☽ ✶ ♃ **6:59 am** 3:59 am
☽ ⚻ ♇ **9:53 am** 6:53 am
♀ ☍ ♄ **10:54 am** 7:54 am
☿ △ ♅ **12:33 pm** 9:33 am
☽ △ ♄ **4:53 pm** 1:53 pm
☽ ✶ ♀ **5:26 pm** 2:26 pm

25 TUESDAY
☽ △ ♅ **3:58 am** 12:58 am
☽ ☌ ☿ **5:22 am** 2:22 am ☽
☽ ⚺ ☉ **11:28 am** 8:28 am
☽ ⚺ ♂ **12:16 pm** 9:16 am

26 WEDNESDAY
☽ ☍ ♆ **6:37 am** 3:37 am
☽ ⚺ ♃ **10:56 am** 7:56 am
☽ △ ♇ **1:28 pm** 10:28 am
☽ □ ♄ **8:51 pm** 5:51 pm
☉ ☌ ♂ **8:57 pm** 5:57 pm
☽ □ ♀ 11:31 pm ☽

27 THURSDAY
☽ □ ♀ **2:31 am** ☽
☽ ⚻ ♅ **8:53 am** 5:53 am
☽ ⚺ ☿ **3:17 pm** 12:17 pm
☽ ✶ ♂ **8:32 pm** 5:32 pm
☽ ✶ ☉ **9:09 pm** 6:09 pm

28 FRIDAY
☽ ⚻ ♆ **1:19 pm** 10:19 am
☽ ☌ ♃ **6:35 pm** 3:35 pm
☽ □ ♇ **8:38 pm** 5:38 pm

29 SATURDAY
☽ ✶ ♄ **4:27 am** 1:27 am
☽ △ ♀ **4:25 pm** 1:25 pm
☽ ☍ ♅ **5:30 pm** 2:30 pm ☽

30 SUNDAY
♀ ✶ ♅ **4:04 am** 1:04 am
☽ ✶ ☿ **5:21 am** 2:21 am
☽ □ ♂ **9:02 am** 6:02 am
☽ □ ☉ **11:23 am** 8:23 am
☽ △ ♆ **11:29 pm** 8:29 pm

31 MONDAY
☽ ⚺ ♃ **5:46 am** 2:46 am
☽ ✶ ♇ **7:10 am** 4:10 am ☽
☽ ⚺ ♄ **3:16 pm** 12:16 pm

Eastern time in bold type
Pacific time in medium type

JULY 2017

DATE	SID.TIME	SUN	MOON	NODE	MERCURY	VENUS	MARS	JUPITER	SATURN	URANUS	NEPTUNE	PLUTO	CERES	PALLAS	JUNO	VESTA	CHIRON
1 Sa	18 36 57	9 ♋ 21 58	8 ♎ 57	25 ♌ 21 R	20 ♋ 21	25 ♉ 38	17 ♋ 09	13 ♎ 53	23 ♐ 23	28 ♈ 05	14 ♓ 12	18 ♑ 21 R	26 ♊ 01	1 ♉ 09	11 ♑ 12	22 ♌ 27	28 ♓ 52 R
2 Su	18 40 54	10 19 10	21 22	25 17 R	22 20	26 43	17 59	13 57	23 19 R	28 06	14 12 R	18 20 R	26 26	1 27	10 58 R	22 53	28 52
3 M	18 44 50	11 16 22	3 ♏ 32	25 15	24 18	27 48	18 38	14 01	23 15	28 08	14 11	18 18	26 52	1 44	10 48	23 19	28 52
4 T	18 48 47	12 13 34	15 33	25 10	26 13	28 54	19 18	14 05	23 10	28 09	14 11	18 17	27 17	2 01	10 30	23 46	28 52
5 W	18 52 43	13 10 46	27 28	25 04	28 07	29 59	19 57	14 10	23 06	28 11	14 10	18 15	27 42	2 18	10 16	24 12	28 52
6 Th	18 56 40	14 07 57	9 ♐ 07	24 57	29 58	1 ♊ 05	20 36	14 14	23 02	28 12	14 10	18 14	28 07	2 35	10 02	24 38	28 51
7 F	19 0 36	15 05 08	21 12	24 50	1 ♌ 48	2 11	21 15	14 19	22 59	28 14	14 09	18 12	28 32	2 52	9 48	25 05	28 51
8 Sa	19 4 33	16 02 19	3 ♑ 07	24 43	3 36	3 18	21 54	14 23	22 55	28 15	14 09	18 11	28 57	3 09	9 34	25 31	28 51
9 Su	19 8 29	16 59 31	15 06	24 37	5 21	4 24	22 33	14 28	22 51	28 16	14 08	18 09	29 23	3 26	9 20	25 58	28 50
10 M	19 12 26	17 56 42	27 10	24 33	7 05	5 30	23 12	14 33	22 47	28 17	14 07	18 08	29 48	3 42	9 07	26 25	28 50
11 T	19 16 23	18 53 54	9 ♒ 23	24 30	8 46	6 37	23 51	14 38	22 43	28 18	14 06	18 06	0 ♋ 13	3 59	8 53	26 51	28 49
12 W	19 20 19	19 51 05	21 44	24 29 D	10 26	7 44	24 29	14 44	22 40	28 19	14 06	18 05	0 38	4 15	8 39	27 18	28 49
13 Th	19 24 16	20 48 18	4 ♓ 17	24 29	12 03	8 51	25 08	14 49	22 36	28 21	14 05	18 03	1 03	4 31	8 26	27 45	28 48
14 F	19 28 12	21 45 30	17 03	24 30	13 39	9 58	25 47	14 55	22 32	28 22	14 04	18 02	1 28	4 48	8 12	28 12	28 48
15 Sa	19 32 9	22 42 43	0 ♈ 04	24 32	15 12	11 05	26 26	15 01	22 29	28 23	14 03	18 01	1 53	5 03	7 59	28 39	28 47
16 Su	19 36 5	23 39 57	13 24	24 33 R	16 44	12 12	27 05	15 07	22 25	28 23	14 02	17 59	2 18	5 19	7 46	29 06	28 46
17 M	19 40 2	24 37 11	27 04	24 33	18 13	13 20	27 44	15 13	22 22	28 24	14 01	17 58	2 43	5 35	7 33	29 34	28 45
18 T	19 43 58	25 34 26	11 ♉ 05	24 33	19 41	14 27	28 23	15 19	22 19	28 25	14 00	17 56	3 08	5 50	7 20	0 ♍ 01	28 45
19 W	19 47 55	26 31 42	25 26	24 31	21 06	15 35	29 01	15 25	22 15	28 26	13 59	17 55	3 33	6 06	7 07	0 28	28 44
20 Th	19 51 52	27 28 59	10 ♊ 05	24 28	22 29	16 43	29 40	15 32	22 12	28 27	13 58	17 53	3 58	6 21	6 55	0 56	28 44
21 F	19 55 48	28 26 16	24 56	24 24	23 50	17 51	0 ♌ 19	15 38	22 09	28 27	13 57	17 52	4 23	6 36	6 43	1 23	28 42
22 Sa	19 59 45	29 23 34	9 ♋ 52	24 21	25 09	18 59	0 58	15 45	22 06	28 28	13 56	17 50	4 48	6 51	6 30	1 51	28 41
23 Su	20 3 41	0 ♌ 20 53	24 44	24 18	26 25	20 07	1 36	15 52	22 03	28 28	13 55	17 49	5 13	7 06	6 19	2 18	28 40
24 M	20 7 38	1 18 12	9 ♌ 25	24 16	27 40	21 16	2 15	15 59	22 00	28 29	13 54	17 47	5 38	7 20	6 07	2 46	28 39
25 T	20 11 34	2 15 32	23 48	24 16 D	28 51	22 24	2 54	16 06	21 57	28 29	13 53	17 46	6 03	7 35	5 56	3 13	28 37
26 W	20 15 31	3 12 52	7 ♍ 48	24 16	0 ♍ 01	23 33	3 32	16 14	21 54	28 30	13 52	17 45	6 28	7 49	5 45	3 41	28 36
27 Th	20 19 27	4 10 13	21 23	24 17	1 08	24 41	4 11	16 21	21 52	28 30	13 51	17 43	6 52	8 03	5 34	4 09	28 35
28 F	20 23 24	5 07 34	4 ♎ 33	24 19	2 12	25 50	4 50	16 29	21 49	28 31	13 50	17 42	7 17	8 17	5 23	4 37	28 34
29 Sa	20 27 21	6 04 56	17 21	24 20	3 14	26 59	5 28	16 36	21 46	28 31	13 48	17 40	7 42	8 30	5 13	5 05	28 32
30 Su	20 31 17	7 02 18	29 48	24 21 R	4 13	28 08	6 07	16 44	21 44	28 31	13 47	17 39	8 07	8 44	5 03	5 33	28 31
31 M	20 35 14	7 59 41	11 ♏ 21	24 21	5 09	29 17	6 45	16 52	21 42	28 31	13 46	17 38	8 31	8 57	4 53	6 01	28 29

EPHEMERIS CALCULATED FOR 12 MIDNIGHT GREENWICH MEAN TIME. ALL OTHER DATA AND FACING ASPECTARIAN PAGE IN **EASTERN TIME (BOLD)** AND PACIFIC TIME (REGULAR).

AUGUST 2017

☽ Last Aspect day	ET	PT	asp	☽ Ingress sign	day	ET	PT
7/31	**7:10 am**	4:10 am	⚹ ♇	♐	1	**8:01 am**	5:01 am
3	**5:38 pm**	2:38 pm	△ ♅	♑	3	**8:37 pm**	5:37 pm
6	**5:22 am**	2:22 am	□ ♅	♒	6	**8:15 am**	5:15 am
8	**3:07 pm**	12:07 pm	⚹ ♅	♓	8	**5:56 pm**	2:56 pm
10	**9:38 am**	6:38 am	□ ♄	♈	10		10:22 pm
10	**9:38 am**	6:38 am	□ ♄	♈	11	**1:22 am**	
13	**4:01 am**	1:01 am	☌ ♅	♉	13	**6:40 am**	3:40 am
14	**9:15 pm**	6:15 pm	□ ☉	♊	15	**10:06 am**	7:06 am
17	**9:38 am**	6:38 am	⚹ ♅	♋	17	**12:13 pm**	9:13 pm
19	**11:17 am**	8:17 am	□ ♅	♌	19	**1:55 pm**	10:55 am
21	**2:30 pm**	11:30 am	☌ ☉	♍	21	**4:25 pm**	1:25 pm
23	**4:02 pm**	1:02 pm	⚹ ♀	♎	23	**9:05 pm**	6:05 pm
25		10:39 pm	☍ ♅	♏	26	**4:53 am**	1:53 am
26	**1:39 am**		☍ ♅	♏	26	**4:53 am**	1:53 am
28	**5:38 am**	2:38 am	□ ♂	♐	28	**3:48 pm**	12:48 pm
30		9:42 pm	△ ♅	♑	31	**4:18 am**	1:18 am
31	**12:42 am**		△ ♅	♑	31	**4:18 am**	1:18 am

☽ Phases & Eclipses phase	day	ET	PT
Full Moon	7	**2:11 pm**	11:11 am
●●	7	15° ♒ 25'	
4th Quarter	14	**9:15 pm**	6:15 pm
New Moon	21	**2:30 pm**	11:30 am
●	21	8° ♓ 12'	
2nd Quarter	29	**4:13 am**	1:13 am

Planet Ingress	day	ET	PT
☉ ♍	22	**6:20 pm**	3:20 pm
♀ ♌	25		9:30 pm
♀ ♌	26	**12:30 am**	
☿ ♌	31	**11:28 am**	8:28 am

Planetary Motion	day	ET	PT
♅ ℞	2		10:31 pm
♅ ℞	3	**1:31 am**	
☿ ℞	12	**9:00 pm**	6:00 pm
♄ D	25	**8:08 am**	5:08 am
⚵ D	26	**1:14 pm**	10:14 am

1 TUESDAY
☽ ⚻ ♅ **5:03 am** 2:03 am
☽ ⚻ ♀ **10:17 am** 7:17 am
☽ □ ☿ **10:00 pm** 7:00 pm
☽ △ ♂ 9:30 pm

2 WEDNESDAY
☽ △ ♂ **12:30 am**
☽ △ ☉ **4:44 am** 1:44 am
☽ □ ♆ **11:43 am** 8:43 am
☽ ⚹ ♃ **6:55 pm** 3:55 pm
☽ ⚺ ♇ **7:31 pm** 4:31 pm

3 THURSDAY
☽ ☌ ♄ **3:37 am** 12:37 am
☽ △ ♅ **5:38 pm** 2:38 pm ☽

4 FRIDAY
☽ ☍ ♀ **5:22 am** 2:22 am
☽ △ ☿ **2:22 pm** 11:22 am
♃ □ ♇ **2:48 pm** 11:48 am
☽ ⚻ ♂ **4:24 pm** 1:24 pm
☽ ⚻ ☉ **10:24 pm** 7:24 pm
☽ ⚹ ♆ **11:58 pm** 8:58 pm

5 SATURDAY
☽ ☌ ♇ **7:37 am** 4:37 am
☽ □ ♃ **7:51 am** 4:51 am
☽ ⚺ ♄ **3:31 pm** 12:31 pm
☉ ⚻ ♆ **5:31 pm** 2:31 pm

6 SUNDAY
☽ □ ♅ **5:22 am** 2:22 am ☽
☽ ⚻ ♀ **10:57 pm** 7:57 pm

7 MONDAY
☽ ⚻ ☿ **4:15 am** 1:15 am
☽ ☍ ♂ **6:41 am** 3:41 am
☽ ⚺ ♆ **10:40 am** 7:40 am
☽ ☍ ☉ **2:11 pm** 11:11 am
☽ ⚺ ♇ **6:05 pm** 3:05 pm
☽ △ ♃ **7:06 pm** 4:06 pm
☽ ⚹ ♄ 10:40 pm

8 TUESDAY
☽ ⚹ ♄ **1:40 am**
☽ ⚹ ♅ **3:07 pm** 12:07 pm ☽

9 WEDNESDAY
☽ △ ♀ **1:45 pm** 10:45 am
☽ ☍ ☿ **2:51 pm** 11:51 am
☉ ⚻ ♇ **4:10 pm** 1:10 pm
☽ ⚻ ♂ **6:28 pm** 3:28 pm
☽ ☌ ♆ **7:14 pm** 4:14 pm
☽ ⚹ ♇ 11:22 pm

10 THURSDAY
☽ ⚹ ♇ **2:22 am**
☽ ⚻ ☉ **3:12 am** 12:12 am
☽ ⚻ ♃ **4:05 am** 1:05 am
☿ ⚹ ♀ **5:03 am** 2:03 am
♂ ⚻ ♆ **9:31 am** 6:31 am
☽ □ ♄ **9:38 am** 6:38 am ☽
☉ ⚹ ♃ **5:24 pm** 2:24 pm
☽ ⚺ ♅ **10:39 pm** 7:39 pm

11 FRIDAY
☽ ⚻ ☿ **10:13 pm** 7:13 pm
♀ △ ♆ 10:17 pm
☽ ⚺ ♆ 10:35 pm
☽ □ ♀ 10:36 pm

12 SATURDAY
♀ △ ♆ **1:17 am**
☽ ⚺ ♆ **1:35 am**
☽ □ ♀ **1:36 am**
☽ △ ♂ **3:39 am** 12:39 am
☽ □ ♇ **8:27 am** 5:27 am
☽ ☍ ♃ **10:48 am** 7:48 am
☽ △ ☉ **1:27 pm** 10:27 am
☽ △ ♄ **3:26 pm** 12:26 pm

13 SUNDAY
☽ ☌ ♅ **4:01 am** 1:01 am ☽
☉ △ ♄ **5:06 pm** 2:06 pm
☽ △ ☿ 11:42 pm
♀ ⚺ ♂ 11:43 pm

14 MONDAY
☽ △ ☿ **2:42 am**
♀ ⚺ ♂ **2:43 am**
☽ ⚹ ♆ **5:54 am** 2:54 am
☽ □ ♂ **10:30 am** 7:30 am
☽ ⚹ ♀ **10:49 am** 7:49 am
☽ △ ♇ **12:34 pm** 9:34 am
☽ ⚻ ♃ **3:29 pm** 12:29 pm
☽ ⚻ ♄ **7:18 pm** 4:18 pm
☽ □ ☉ **9:15 pm** 6:15 pm ☽

15 TUESDAY
♀ ☍ ♇ **7:17 am** 4:17 am
☽ ⚺ ♅ **7:30 am** 4:30 am

16 WEDNESDAY
☽ □ ☿ **4:49 am** 1:49 am
♂ ⚻ ♇ **6:37 am** 3:37 am
☽ □ ♆ **8:34 am** 5:34 am
☽ ⚻ ♇ **3:05 pm** 12:05 pm
☽ ⚹ ♂ **3:29 pm** 12:29 pm
☽ ⚺ ♀ **5:57 pm** 2:57 pm
☽ △ ♃ **6:35 pm** 3:35 pm
☽ ☍ ♄ **9:40 pm** 6:40 pm
♀ □ ♃ 11:40 pm

17 THURSDAY
♀ □ ♃ **2:40 am**
☽ ⚹ ☉ **3:13 am** 12:13 am
☽ ⚹ ♅ **9:38 am** 6:38 am ☽

18 FRIDAY
☽ ⚹ ☿ **5:19 am** 2:19 am
☽ △ ♆ **10:17 am** 7:17 am
♀ ⚻ ♄ **2:55 pm** 11:55 am
☽ ☍ ♇ **4:45 pm** 1:45 pm
☽ ⚺ ♂ **7:31 pm** 4:31 pm
☽ □ ♃ **8:52 pm** 5:52 pm
☽ ⚻ ♄ **11:20 pm** 8:20 pm
☽ ☌ ♀ 9:05 pm

19 SATURDAY
☽ ☌ ♀ **12:05 am**
☽ ⚺ ☉ **8:27 am** 5:27 am
☽ □ ♅ **11:17 am** 8:17 am ☽

20 SUNDAY
☽ ⚺ ☿ **5:12 am** 2:12 am
☽ ⚻ ♆ **12:04 pm** 9:04 am
♂ ⚹ ♃ **12:42 pm** 9:42 am
☽ ⚻ ♇ **6:41 pm** 3:41 pm
☽ ⚹ ♃ **11:32 pm** 8:32 pm
☽ ☌ ♂ **11:55 pm** 8:55 pm
☽ △ ♄ 10:26 pm
☉ △ ♅ 11:22 pm

21 MONDAY
☽ △ ♄ **1:26 am**
☉ △ ♅ **2:22 am**
☽ ⚺ ♀ **6:49 am** 3:49 am
☽ △ ♅ **1:40 pm** 10:40 am
☽ ☌ ☉ **2:30 pm** 11:30 am ☽

22 TUESDAY
☽ ☌ ☿ **5:41 am** 2:41 am
♂ △ ♄ **9:21 am** 6:21 am
☽ ☍ ♆ **3:17 pm** 12:17 pm
☽ △ ♇ **10:13 pm** 7:13 pm

23 WEDNESDAY
☽ ⚺ ♃ **4:01 am** 1:01 am
☽ □ ♄ **5:19 am** 2:19 am
☽ ⚺ ♂ **6:18 am** 3:18 am
☽ ⚹ ♀ **4:02 pm** 1:02 pm ☽
☽ ⚻ ♅ **6:07 pm** 3:07 pm
☽ ⚺ ☉ **11:10 pm** 8:10 pm

24 THURSDAY
☽ ⚺ ☿ **7:50 am** 4:50 am
♀ □ ♅ **3:01 pm** 12:01 pm
☽ ⚻ ♆ **9:08 pm** 6:08 pm

25 FRIDAY
☽ □ ♇ **4:32 am** 1:32 am
☽ ☌ ♃ **11:31 am** 8:31 am
☽ ⚹ ♄ **12:08 pm** 9:08 am
☽ ⚹ ♂ **4:05 pm** 1:05 pm
☽ ☍ ♅ 10:39 pm ☽

26 SATURDAY
☽ ☍ ♅ **1:39 am** ☽
☽ □ ♀ **5:21 am** 2:21 am
☽ ⚹ ☉ **11:48 am** 8:48 am
☽ ⚹ ☿ **12:29 pm** 9:29 am
☉ ☌ ☿ **4:42 pm** 1:42 pm

27 SUNDAY
☽ △ ♆ **6:16 am** 3:16 am
♃ ⚹ ♄ **8:15 am** 5:15 am
☽ ⚹ ♇ **2:08 pm** 11:08 am
☽ ⚺ ♄ **10:14 pm** 7:14 pm
☽ ⚺ ♃ **10:26 pm** 7:26 pm

28 MONDAY
☿ ⚺ ♀ **3:14 am** 12:14 am
☽ □ ♂ **5:38 am** 2:38 am ☽
☽ ⚻ ♅ **12:20 pm** 9:20 am
☽ □ ☿ **7:41 pm** 4:41 pm
☽ △ ♀ **10:48 pm** 7:48 pm

29 TUESDAY
☽ □ ☉ **4:13 am** 1:13 am
☽ □ ♆ **6:00 pm** 3:00 pm
☽ ⚺ ♇ 11:10 pm

30 WEDNESDAY
☽ ⚺ ♇ **2:10 am**
☽ ☌ ♄ **10:32 am** 7:32 am
☽ ⚹ ♃ **11:38 am** 8:38 am
☽ △ ♂ **9:27 pm** 6:27 pm
☽ △ ♅ 9:42 pm ☽

31 THURSDAY
☽ △ ♅ **12:42 am** ☽
☽ △ ☿ **4:40 am** 1:40 am
☽ ⚻ ♀ **6:07 pm** 3:07 pm
☽ △ ☉ **10:06 pm** 7:06 pm

Eastern time in bold type
Pacific time in medium type

AUGUST 2017

DATE	SID.TIME	SUN	MOON	NODE	MERCURY	VENUS	MARS	JUPITER	SATURN	URANUS	NEPTUNE	PLUTO	CERES	PALLAS	JUNO	VESTA	CHIRON
1 T	20 39 10	8 ♌ 57 04	24 ♏ 02	24 ♌ 20	6 ♍ 02	0 ♋ 26	7 ♌ 24	17 ♎ 00	21 ♐ 39	28 ♈ 31	13 ♓ 45	17 ♑ 36	8 ♋ 56	9 ♌ 10	4 ♐ 44	6 ♍ 29	28 ♓ 28
2 W	20 43 7	9 54 28	5 ♐ 56	24 19 R	6 51	1 36	8 01	17 08	21 37 R	28 32	13 43 R	17 35 R	9 21	9 23	4 35 R	6 57	28 26 R
3 Th	20 47 3	10 51 52	17 48	24 17	7 38	2 45	8 41	17 16	21 35	28 32 R	13 42	17 34	9 45	9 36	4 26	7 25	28 25
4 F	20 51 0	11 49 18	29 42	24 15	8 21	3 54	9 19	17 25	21 33	28 32	13 41	17 32	10 10	9 48	4 18	7 54	28 23
5 Sa	20 54 56	12 46 44	11 ♑ 40	24 14	9 00	5 04	9 58	17 33	21 31	28 31	13 39	17 31	10 34	10 01	4 10	8 22	28 21
6 Su	20 58 53	13 44 11	23 46	24 12	9 35	6 14	10 36	17 42	21 29	28 31	13 38	17 30	10 59	10 13	4 02	8 50	28 20
7 M	21 2 50	14 41 38	6 ♒ 01	24 11	10 07	7 23	11 15	17 51	21 27	28 31	13 37	17 29	11 23	10 24	3 55	9 19	28 18
8 T	21 6 46	15 39 07	18 27	24 11 D	10 34	8 33	11 53	17 59	21 26	28 31	13 35	17 27	11 48	10 36	3 48	9 47	28 16
9 W	21 10 43	16 36 37	1 ♓ 06	24 11	11 14	9 43	12 32	18 08	21 24	28 31	13 34	17 26	12 12	10 47	3 41	10 16	28 14
10 Th	21 14 39	17 34 08	13 58	24 11	11 27	10 53	13 10	18 17	21 22	28 30	13 32	17 25	12 37	10 59	3 35	10 44	28 12
11 F	21 18 36	18 31 40	27 03	24 12	11 36	12 04	13 48	18 26	21 21	28 30	13 31	17 24	13 01	11 09	3 29	11 13	28 10
12 Sa	21 22 32	19 29 13	10 ♈ 22	24 12	11 38 R	13 14	14 27	18 36	21 20	28 30	13 30	17 22	13 25	11 20	3 23	11 41	28 08
13 Su	21 26 29	20 26 48	23 54	24 13	11 36	14 24	15 05	18 45	21 18	28 29	13 28	17 21	13 49	11 31	3 18	12 10	28 06
14 M	21 30 25	21 24 24	7 ♉ 41	24 13 R	11 28	15 35	15 44	18 54	21 17	28 29	13 27	17 20	14 14	11 41	3 13	12 39	28 04
15 T	21 34 22	22 22 02	21 41	24 13 R	11 14	16 45	16 22	19 04	21 16	28 28	13 25	17 19	14 38	11 51	3 09	13 08	28 02
16 W	21 38 19	23 19 41	5 ♊ 53	24 13	10 55	17 56	17 00	19 14	21 15	28 28	13 24	17 18	15 02	12 00	3 04	13 36	28 00
17 Th	21 42 15	24 17 22	20 14	24 13	10 31	19 06	17 39	19 23	21 14	28 27	13 22	17 17	15 26	12 10	3 01	14 05	27 58
18 F	21 46 12	25 15 05	4 ♋ 42	24 12	10 01	20 17	18 17	19 33	21 14	28 26	13 21	17 15	15 50	12 19	2 57	14 34	27 56
19 Sa	21 50 8	26 12 49	19 12	24 11	9 25	21 28	18 55	19 43	21 13	28 26	13 19	17 14	16 14	12 27	2 54	15 03	27 54
20 Su	21 54 5	27 10 35	3 ♌ 40	24 13	8 45	22 39	19 34	19 53	21 12	28 25	13 17	17 13	16 38	12 36	2 51	15 32	27 51
21 M	21 58 1	28 08 22	17 59	24 13 R	8 01	23 50	20 12	20 03	21 12	28 24	13 16	17 12	17 02	12 44	2 49	16 01	27 49
22 T	22 1 58	29 06 11	2 ♍ 05	24 13	7 13	25 01	20 50	20 13	21 12	28 23	13 14	17 11	17 26	12 52	2 47	16 30	27 47
23 W	22 5 54	0 ♍ 04 01	15 55	24 13	6 22	26 13	21 28	20 24	21 11	28 22	13 13	17 10	17 50	12 59	2 46	17 00	27 45
24 Th	22 9 51	1 01 52	29 24	24 13	5 29	27 24	22 07	20 34	21 11	28 21	13 11	17 09	18 13	13 07	2 44	17 29	27 42
25 F	22 13 48	1 59 44	12 ♎ 33	24 12	4 34	28 35	22 45	20 45	21 11 D	28 20	13 09	17 08	18 37	13 14	2 44	17 58	27 40
26 Sa	22 17 44	2 57 38	25 21	24 11	3 40	29 47	23 23	20 55	21 11	28 19	13 08	17 07	19 01	13 20	2 43 D	18 27	27 37
27 Su	22 21 41	3 55 33	7 ♏ 50	24 10	2 47	0 ♌ 58	24 01	21 06	21 11	28 18	13 06	17 07	19 24	13 26	2 43	18 57	27 35
28 M	22 25 37	4 53 30	20 04	24 09	1 56	2 10	24 39	21 16	21 12	28 16	13 05	17 06	19 48	13 33	2 43	19 26	27 33
29 T	22 29 34	5 51 28	2 ♐ 06	24 08 D	1 08	3 21	25 18	21 27	21 12	28 15	13 03	17 05	20 11	13 38	2 44	19 55	27 30
30 W	22 33 30	6 49 27	14 01	24 08	0 25	4 33	25 56	21 38	21 12	28 14	13 01	17 04	20 34	13 43	2 45	20 25	27 28
31 Th	22 37 27	7 47 27	25 53	24 09	29 ♌ 48	5 45	26 34	21 49	21 12	28 13	13 00	17 03	20 58	13 48	2 46	20 54	27 25

EPHEMERIS CALCULATED FOR 12 MIDNIGHT GREENWICH MEAN TIME. ALL OTHER DATA AND FACING ASPECTARIAN PAGE IN **EASTERN TIME (BOLD)** AND PACIFIC TIME (REGULAR).

SEPTEMBER 2017

☽ Last Aspect day	ET / hr:mn / PT		asp	☽ Ingress sign	day	ET / hr:mn / PT	
2	**12:30 pm**	9:30 am	□ ♅	♒	2	**4:06 pm**	1:06 pm
4		10:15 pm	☍ ♂	♓	4		10:28 pm
5	**1:15 am**		☍ ♂	♓	5	**1:28 am**	
6	**4:29 pm**	1:29 pm	□ ♄	♈	7	**8:01 am**	5:01 am
9	**11:52 am**	8:52 am	△ ☿	♉	9	**12:23 pm**	9:23 am
10	**8:54 pm**	5:54 pm	□ ♀	♊	11	**3:29 pm**	12:29 pm
13	**2:35 pm**	11:35 am	✶ ♅	♋	13	**6:12 pm**	3:12 pm
15	**5:23 pm**	2:23 pm	□ ♅	♌	15	**9:09 pm**	6:09 pm
17	**8:55 pm**	5:55 pm	△ ♅	♍	17		9:52 pm
17	**8:55 pm**	5:55 pm	△ ♅	♍	18	**12:52 am**	
19		10:30 pm	☌ ☉	♎	20	**6:06 am**	3:06 am
20	**1:30 am**		☌ ☉	♎	20	**6:06 am**	3:06 am
22	**9:04 am**	6:04 am	☍ ♅	♏	22	**1:40 pm**	10:40 am
24	**3:33 am**	12:33 am	✶ ☿	♐	24		9:01 pm
24	**3:33 am**	12:33 am	✶ ☿	♐	25	**12:01 am**	
27	**7:08 am**	4:08 am	△ ♅	♑	27	**12:24 pm**	9:24 am
29	**8:14 pm**	5:14 pm	□ ♃	♒	29		9:40 pm
29	**8:14 pm**	5:14 pm	□ ♃	♒	30	**12:40 am**	

☽ Phases & Eclipses phase	day	ET / hr:mn / PT	
Full Moon	6	**3:03 am**	12:03 am
4th Quarter	12		11:25 pm
4th Quarter	13	**2:25 am**	
New Moon	19		10:30 pm
New Moon	20	**1:30 am**	
2nd Quarter	27	**10:54 pm**	7:54 pm

Planet Ingress		day	ET / hr:mn / PT	
♂	♍	5	**5:35 am**	2:35 am
☿	♍	9	**10:52 pm**	7:52 pm
⚵	♎	18	**3:50 am**	12:50 am
♀	♍	19	**9:15 pm**	6:15 pm
☉	♎	22	**4:02 pm**	1:02 pm
⚳	♌	23		10:45 pm
⚳	♌	24	**1:45 am**	
☿	♎	29	**8:42 pm**	5:42 pm

Planetary Motion		day	ET / hr:mn / PT	
☿	D	5	**7:29 am**	4:29 am
♀	R	11	**1:46 pm**	10:46 am
♇	D	28	**3:36 pm**	12:36 pm

1 FRIDAY
☽ ✶ ♆ **6:21 am** 3:21 am
☽ ☌ ♇ **2:29 pm** 11:29 am
☽ ⊻ ♄ **10:49 pm** 7:49 pm
☽ □ ♃ 9:47 pm

2 SATURDAY
☽ □ ♃ **12:47 am**
♂ △ ♅ **8:13 am** 5:13 am
☽ □ ♅ **12:30 pm** 9:30 am ☽
☽ ⊼ ♂ **12:44 pm** 9:44 am
☽ ⊼ ☿ **2:02 pm** 11:02 am

3 SUNDAY
☿ ☌ ♂ **5:38 am** 2:38 am
☽ ☍ ♀ **11:49 am** 8:49 am
☽ ⊼ ☉ **2:18 pm** 11:18 am
☽ ⊻ ♆ **5:06 pm** 2:06 pm
☽ ⊻ ♇ 9:58 pm

4 MONDAY
☽ ⊻ ♇ **12:58 am**
☽ ✶ ♄ **9:04 am** 6:04 am
☽ △ ♃ **11:44 am** 8:44 am
☽ ✶ ♅ **9:56 pm** 6:56 pm
☽ ☍ ☿ **10:33 pm** 7:33 pm
☽ ☍ ♂ 10:15 pm ☽
☉ ☍ ♆ 10:28 pm

5 TUESDAY
☽ ☍ ♂ **1:15 am** ☽
☉ ☍ ♆ **1:28 am**

♀ ⊼ ♆ **5:33 pm** 2:33 pm
☽ ☌ ♆ 10:07 pm
☽ ⊼ ♀ 10:54 pm

6 WEDNESDAY
☽ ☌ ♆ **1:07 am**
☽ ⊼ ♀ **1:54 am**
☽ ☍ ☉ **3:03 am** 12:03 am
☽ ✶ ♇ **8:40 am** 5:40 am
☽ □ ♄ **4:29 pm** 1:29 pm ☽
☽ ⊼ ♃ **7:44 pm** 4:44 pm

7 THURSDAY
☽ ⊻ ♅ **4:32 am** 1:32 am
☽ ⊼ ☿ **5:42 am** 2:42 am
☽ ⊼ ♂ **10:30 am** 7:30 am

8 FRIDAY
☽ ⊻ ♆ **6:31 am** 3:31 am
☽ △ ♀ **12:30 pm** 9:30 am
☽ ⊼ ☉ **12:31 pm** 9:31 am
☉ ⊻ ♀ **1:26 pm** 10:26 am
☽ □ ♇ **1:49 pm** 10:49 am
☽ △ ♄ **9:27 pm** 6:27 pm
☽ ☍ ♃ 10:15 pm

9 SATURDAY
☽ ☍ ♃ **1:15 am**
♀ ⊼ ♇ **3:23 am** 12:23 am
☉ △ ♇ **6:45 am** 3:45 am
☽ ☌ ♅ **8:54 am** 5:54 am
☽ △ ☿ **11:52 am** 8:52 am ☽
☽ △ ♂ **5:16 pm** 2:16 pm

10 SUNDAY
☽ ✶ ♆ **10:07 am** 7:07 am
☽ △ ♇ **5:19 pm** 2:19 pm
☽ △ ☉ **7:54 pm** 4:54 pm
☽ □ ♀ **8:54 pm** 5:54 pm ☽
☽ ⊼ ♄ 9:55 pm

11 MONDAY
☽ ⊼ ♄ **12:55 am**
☽ ⊼ ♃ **5:16 am** 2:16 am
☽ ⊻ ♅ **11:58 am** 8:58 am
☽ □ ☿ **5:54 pm** 2:54 pm
☽ □ ♂ **10:42 pm** 7:42 pm

12 TUESDAY
☽ □ ♆ **12:53 pm** 9:53 am
☽ ⊼ ♇ **8:05 pm** 5:05 pm
♀ △ ♄ **8:50 pm** 5:50 pm
☽ □ ☉ 11:25 pm

13 WEDNESDAY
☽ □ ☉ **2:25 am**
☽ ☍ ♄ **3:47 am** 12:47 am
☽ ✶ ♀ **4:25 am** 1:25 am
☽ △ ♃ **8:43 am** 5:43 am
☽ ✶ ♅ **2:35 pm** 11:35 am ☽
☉ □ ♄ **10:58 pm** 7:58 pm
☽ ✶ ☿ 9:41 pm

14 THURSDAY
☽ ✶ ☿ **12:41 am**
☽ ✶ ♂ **3:48 am** 12:48 am
☽ △ ♆ **3:31 pm** 12:31 pm
☽ ☍ ♇ **10:51 pm** 7:51 pm

15 FRIDAY
☽ ⊼ ♄ **6:43 am** 3:43 am
☽ ✶ ☉ **9:00 am** 6:00 am
☽ ⊻ ♀ **12:02 pm** 9:02 am
☽ □ ♃ **12:18 pm** 9:18 am
♀ ✶ ♃ **3:44 pm** 12:44 pm
☽ □ ♅ **5:23 pm** 2:23 pm ☽

16 SATURDAY
☽ ⊻ ☿ **8:54 am** 5:54 am
☽ ⊻ ♂ **9:16 am** 6:16 am
☿ ☌ ♂ **3:01 pm** 12:01 pm
☽ ⊼ ♆ **6:37 pm** 3:37 pm
☽ ⊼ ♇ 11:08 pm

17 SUNDAY
☽ ⊼ ♇ **2:08 am**
☽ △ ♄ **10:18 am** 7:18 am
☽ ⊻ ☉ **4:23 pm** 1:23 pm
☽ ✶ ♃ **4:37 pm** 1:37 pm
☉ ⊻ ♃ **8:17 pm** 5:17 pm
☽ ☌ ♀ **8:34 pm** 5:34 pm
☽ △ ♅ **8:55 pm** 5:55 pm ☽
♀ △ ♅ 9:27 pm

18 MONDAY
♀ △ ♅ **12:27 am**
☽ ☌ ♂ **3:48 pm** 12:48 pm
☽ ☌ ☿ **7:20 pm** 4:20 pm
☽ ☍ ♆ **10:46 pm** 7:46 pm

19 TUESDAY
☽ △ ♇ **6:35 am** 3:35 am
☽ □ ♄ **3:10 pm** 12:10 pm

☽ ⊻ ♃ **10:22 pm** 7:22 pm
☿ ☍ ♆ **11:50 pm** 8:50 pm
☽ ☌ ☉ 10:30 pm ☽
☽ ⊼ ♅ 10:52 pm

20 WEDNESDAY
☽ ☌ ☉ **1:30 am** ☽
☽ ⊼ ♅ **1:52 am**
☉ ⊼ ♅ **6:21 am** 3:21 am
☽ ⊻ ♀ **7:00 am** 4:00 am
☽ ⊻ ♂ 9:21 pm

21 THURSDAY
☽ ⊻ ♂ **12:21 am**
☽ ⊼ ♆ **4:46 am** 1:46 am
☽ ⊻ ☿ **9:08 am** 6:08 am
☽ □ ♇ **1:00 pm** 10:00 am
☽ ✶ ♄ **10:12 pm** 7:12 pm

22 FRIDAY
☽ ☌ ♃ **6:27 am** 3:27 am
☽ ☍ ♅ **9:04 am** 6:04 am ☽
☽ ⊻ ☉ **1:28 pm** 10:28 am
☿ △ ♇ **2:01 pm** 11:01 am
☽ ✶ ♀ **8:35 pm** 5:35 pm

23 SATURDAY
☽ ✶ ♂ **11:53 am** 8:53 am
☽ △ ♆ **1:22 pm** 10:22 am
☽ ✶ ♇ **10:08 pm** 7:08 pm

24 SUNDAY
☽ ✶ ☿ **3:33 am** 12:33 am ☽
☽ ⊻ ♄ **8:01 am** 5:01 am

♂ ☍ ♆ **3:49 pm** 12:49 pm
☽ ⊻ ♃ **5:27 pm** 2:27 pm
☽ ⊼ ♅ **7:02 pm** 4:02 pm

25 MONDAY
☽ ✶ ☉ **4:58 am** 1:58 am
☿ □ ♄ **10:36 am** 7:36 am
☽ □ ♀ **1:55 pm** 10:55 am
☽ □ ♆ 9:36 pm
☽ □ ♂ 11:31 pm

26 TUESDAY
☽ □ ♆ **12:36 am**
☽ □ ♂ **2:31 am**
☽ ⊻ ♇ **9:48 am** 6:48 am
☽ ☌ ♄ **8:15 pm** 5:15 pm
☽ □ ☿ 11:10 pm

27 WEDNESDAY
☽ □ ☿ **2:10 am**
☽ ✶ ♃ **6:46 am** 3:46 am
☽ △ ♅ **7:08 am** 4:08 am ☽
☽ □ ☉ **10:54 pm** 7:54 pm
♃ ☍ ♅ 9:25 pm

28 THURSDAY
♃ ☍ ♅ **12:25 am**
☽ △ ♀ **9:29 am** 6:29 am
☿ ⊼ ♅ **9:55 am** 6:55 am
☿ ⊻ ♃ **11:22 am** 8:22 am
☽ ✶ ♆ **1:08 pm** 10:08 am
☽ △ ♂ **6:35 pm** 3:35 pm
☽ ☌ ♇ **10:27 pm** 7:27 pm

29 FRIDAY
☽ ⊻ ♄ **9:05 am** 6:05 am
☽ □ ♅ **7:20 pm** 4:20 pm
♀ ☍ ♆ **8:12 pm** 5:12 pm
☽ □ ♃ **8:14 pm** 5:14 pm ☽
☽ △ ☿ 10:22 pm

30 SATURDAY
☽ △ ☿ **1:22 am**
☽ △ ☉ **4:06 pm** 1:06 pm
☽ ⊻ ♆ 9:30 pm

Eastern time in bold type
Pacific time in medium type

SEPTEMBER 2017

DATE	SID. TIME	SUN	MOON	NODE	MERCURY	VENUS	MARS	JUPITER	SATURN	URANUS	NEPTUNE	PLUTO	CERES	PALLAS	JUNO	VESTA	CHIRON
1 F	22 41 23	8 ♍ 45 29	7 ♑ 48	24 ♌ 10	29 ♌ 47	6 ♌ 57	27 ♌ 12	22 ♎ 12	21 ♐ 13	28 ♈ 12	12 ♓ 58	17 ♑ 02	21 ♋ 01	13 ♌ 53	2 ♑ 48	21 ♍ 24	27 ♓ 22
2 Sa	22 45 20	9 43 32	19 48	24 11	29 16 R	8 09	27 50	22 11	21 14	28 11 R	12 56 R	17 02 R	21 44	13 57	2 50	21 53	27 20 R
3 Su	22 49 16	10 41 37	1 ♒ 59	24 13	28 51	9 21	28 29	22 22	21 14	28 09	12 55	17 01	22 07	14 00	2 53	22 23	27 17
4 M	22 53 13	11 39 43	14 24	24 14 R	28 35	10 33	29 07	22 33	21 15	28 08	12 53	17 00	22 30	14 04	2 56	22 52	27 15
5 T	22 57 10	12 37 51	27 04	24 14	28 26 D	11 45	29 45	22 45	21 16	28 06	12 51	17 00	22 53	14 07	2 59	23 22	27 12
6 W	23 1 6	13 36 00	10 ♓ 02	24 13	28 27	12 57	0 ♍ 23	22 56	21 17	28 05	12 50	16 59	23 16	14 09	3 02	23 52	27 10
7 Th	23 5 3	14 34 11	23 16	24 12	28 36	14 10	1 01	23 07	21 19	28 03	12 48	16 58	23 39	14 12	3 06	24 21	27 07
8 F	23 8 59	15 32 24	6 ♈ 46	24 09	28 53	15 22	1 39	23 19	21 20	28 02	12 46	16 57	24 02	14 13	3 10	24 51	27 04
9 Sa	23 12 56	16 30 39	20 31	24 06	29 18	16 35	2 17	23 30	21 21	28 00	12 45	16 57	24 25	14 15	3 15	25 21	27 01
10 Su	23 16 52	17 28 55	4 ♉ 27	24 03	29 55	17 47	2 55	23 42	21 23	27 58	12 43	16 56	24 47	14 16	3 20	25 51	26 59
11 M	23 20 49	18 27 14	18 31	24 00	0 ♍ 39	19 00	3 33	23 54	21 24	27 57	12 42	16 56	25 10	14 16 R	3 25	26 20	26 56
12 T	23 24 45	19 25 35	2 ♊ 40	23 58	1 30	20 12	4 11	24 05	21 26	27 55	12 40	16 55	25 32	14 16	3 30	26 50	26 53
13 W	23 28 42	20 23 58	16 52	23 57 D	2 30	21 25	4 50	24 17	21 28	27 53	12 38	16 55	25 55	14 16	3 36	27 20	26 51
14 Th	23 32 39	21 22 23	1 ♋ 04	23 57	3 36	22 38	5 28	24 29	21 29	27 51	12 37	16 54	26 17	14 15	3 42	27 50	26 48
15 F	23 36 35	22 20 50	15 14	23 58	4 49	23 51	6 06	24 41	21 31	27 49	12 35	16 54	26 39	14 15	3 49	28 20	26 45
16 Sa	23 40 32	23 19 20	29 20	23 58	6 08	25 04	6 44	24 53	21 33	27 48	12 33	16 54	27 01	14 12	3 55	28 50	26 42
17 Su	23 44 28	24 17 52	13 ♌ 20	24 01 R	7 32	26 17	7 22	25 05	21 35	27 46	12 32	16 53	27 23	14 10	4 03	29 20	26 40
18 M	23 48 25	25 16 25	27 12	24 01	9 01	27 30	8 00	25 17	21 38	27 44	12 30	16 53	27 45	14 08	4 10	29 50	26 37
19 T	23 52 21	26 15 01	10 ♍ 54	24 00	10 34	28 43	8 38	25 29	21 40	27 42	12 29	16 53	28 07	14 06	4 18	0 ♎ 20	26 34
20 W	23 56 18	27 13 39	24 24	23 57	12 11	29 56	9 16	25 41	21 42	27 40	12 27	16 52	28 29	14 01	4 26	0 50	26 32
21 Th	0 0 14	28 12 18	7 ♎ 38	23 53 D	13 51	1 ♍ 09	9 54	25 53	21 45	27 38	12 25	16 52	28 51	13 57	4 34	1 21	26 29
22 F	0 4 11	29 11 00	20 37	23 47	15 31	2 23	10 32	26 06	21 47	27 36	12 24	16 52	29 12	13 52	4 43	1 51	26 26
23 Sa	0 8 8	0 ♎ 09 43	3 ♏ 20	23 41	17 18	3 36	11 10	26 18	21 50	27 34	12 22	16 51	29 34	13 47	4 52	2 21	26 23
24 Su	0 12 4	1 08 28	15 46	23 35	19 04	4 50	11 48	26 30	21 53	27 32	12 21	16 52	29 55	13 42	5 01	2 51	26 21
25 M	0 16 1	2 07 15	27 59	23 29	20 52	6 03	12 26	26 43	21 56	27 29	12 19	16 51	0 ♌ 16	13 36	5 10	3 22	26 18
26 T	0 19 57	3 06 04	10 ♐ 00	23 25	22 40	7 17	13 04	26 55	21 59	27 27	12 18	16 51	0 37	13 29	5 20	3 52	26 15
27 W	0 23 54	4 04 55	21 54	23 22	24 29	8 30	13 42	27 08	22 02	27 25	12 16	16 51	0 58	13 22	5 30	4 22	26 12
28 Th	0 27 50	5 03 47	3 ♑ 45	23 22	26 18	9 44	14 20	27 20	22 05	27 23	12 15	16 51 D	1 19	13 15	5 40	4 52	26 10
29 F	0 31 47	6 02 41	15 39	23 22 R	28 08	10 57	14 58	27 33	22 08	27 21	12 13	16 51	1 40	13 07	5 51	5 22	26 07
30 Sa	0 35 43	7 01 37	27 39	23 23	29 57	12 11	15 36	27 45	22 11	27 18	12 12	16 51	2 01	12 58	6 02	5 53	26 04

OCTOBER 2017

☽ Last Aspect day	ET / hr:mn / PT	asp	☽ Ingress sign	day	ET / hr:mn / PT
2	**7:13 am** 4:13 am	△ ♃	♓	2	**10:26 am** 7:26 am
4	**3:19 am** 12:19 am	□ ♄	♈	4	**4:40 pm** 1:40 pm
6	**6:38 pm** 3:38 pm	☍ ♃	♉	6	**7:56 pm** 4:56 pm
8	**9:45 am** 6:45 am	△ ♀	♊	8	**9:44 pm** 6:44 pm
10	**6:25 pm** 3:25 pm	⚹ ♅	♋	10	**11:38 pm** 8:38 pm
12	9:00 pm	⚹ ♀	♌	12	11:41 pm
13	**12:00 am**	⚹ ♀	♌	13	**2:41 am**
14	10:28 pm	△ ♅	♍	15	**7:19 am** 4:19 am
15	**1:28 am**	△ ♅	♍	15	**7:19 am** 4:19 am
17	**7:27 am** 4:27 am	☌ ♂	♎	17	**1:35 pm** 10:35 am
19	**3:12 pm** 12:12 pm	☌ ☉	♏	19	**9:41 pm** 6:41 pm
22	**7:35 am** 4:35 am	⚹ ♂	♐	22	**7:57 am** 4:57 am
24	**12:44 pm** 9:44 am	△ ♅	♑	24	**8:12 pm** 5:12 pm
26	10:22 pm	□ ♅	♒	27	**8:59 am** 5:59 am
27	**1:22 am**	□ ♅	♒	27	**8:59 am** 5:59 am
29	**12:22 pm** 9:22 am	⚹ ♅	♓	29	**7:46 pm** 4:46 pm
31	**5:08 pm** 2:08 pm	□ ♄	♈	31	11:43 pm
31	**5:08 pm** 2:08 pm	□ ♄	♈	11/1	**2:43 am**

☽ Phases & Eclipses phase	day	ET / hr:mn / PT
Full Moon	5	**2:40 pm** 11:40 am
4th Quarter	12	**8:25 am** 5:25 am
New Moon	19	**3:12 pm** 12:12 pm
2nd Quarter	27	**6:22 pm** 3:22 pm

Planet Ingress		day	ET / hr:mn / PT
♃	♏	10	**9:20 am** 6:20 am
♀	♎	14	**6:11 am** 3:11 am
☿	♏	17	**3:59 am** 12:59 am
♂	♎	22	**2:29 pm** 11:29 am
☉	♏	22	10:27 pm
☉	♏	23	**1:27 am**

Planetary Motion	day	ET / hr:mn / PT

1 SUNDAY
☽ ⚺ ♆ **12:30 am**
☽ ⚻ ♀ **3:40 am** 12:40 am
☽ ⚻ ♂ **9:00 am** 6:00 am
☽ ⚺ ♇ **9:33 am** 6:33 am
♂ △ ♇ **7:36 pm** 4:36 pm
☽ ⚹ ♄ **7:56 pm** 4:56 pm

2 MONDAY
☽ ⚹ ♅ **5:13 am** 2:13 am
☽ △ ♃ **7:13 am** 4:13 am ☽
☽ ⚻ ☿ **8:30 pm** 5:30 pm

3 TUESDAY
☽ ⚻ ☉ **5:35 am** 2:35 am
☽ ☌ ♆ **8:45 am** 5:45 am
♀ △ ♇ **3:09 pm** 12:09 pm
☽ ⚹ ♇ **5:20 pm** 2:20 pm
☽ ☍ ♀ **5:34 pm** 2:34 pm
☽ ☍ ♂ **7:36 pm** 4:36 pm

4 WEDNESDAY
☽ □ ♄ **3:19 am** 12:19 am ☽
☽ ⚺ ♅ **11:37 am** 8:37 am
☽ ⚻ ♃ **2:29 pm** 11:29 am
☉ ⚻ ♆ **11:09 pm** 8:09 pm

5 THURSDAY
☽ ☍ ☿ **10:00 am** 7:00 am
♀ ☌ ♂ **12:53 pm** 9:53 am
☽ ⚺ ♆ **1:33 pm** 10:33 am
☽ ☍ ☉ **2:40 pm** 11:40 am
☽ □ ♇ **9:46 pm** 6:46 pm

Eastern time in bold type
Pacific time in medium type

☽ ⚻ ♂ 11:21 pm
☽ ⚻ ♀ 11:58 pm

6 FRIDAY
☽ ⚻ ♂ **2:21 am**
☽ ⚻ ♀ **2:58 am**
☽ △ ♄ **7:26 am** 4:26 am
☿ ⚻ ♆ **1:44 pm** 10:44 am
☽ ☌ ♅ **2:58 pm** 11:58 am
☽ ☍ ♃ **6:38 pm** 3:38 pm ☽

7 SATURDAY
☽ ⚹ ♆ **3:58 pm** 12:58 pm
☽ ⚻ ☿ **7:37 pm** 4:37 pm
☽ ⚻ ☉ **8:49 pm** 5:49 pm
☽ △ ♇ 9:01 pm

8 SUNDAY
☽ △ ♇ **12:01 am**
☽ △ ♂ **6:46 am** 3:46 am
♀ □ ♄ **8:54 am** 5:54 am
☽ ⚻ ♄ **9:41 am** 6:41 am
☽ △ ♀ **9:45 am** 6:45 am ☽
☽ ⚺ ♅ **4:43 pm** 1:43 pm
☉ ☌ ☿ **4:54 pm** 1:54 pm
☽ ⚻ ♃ **9:12 pm** 6:12 pm

9 MONDAY
☿ □ ♇ **8:26 am** 5:26 am
☽ □ ♆ **5:34 pm** 2:34 pm
☉ □ ♇ **8:12 pm** 5:12 pm
☽ ⚻ ♇ 10:44 pm
☽ △ ☉ 11:08 pm

10 TUESDAY
☽ ⚻ ♇ **1:44 am**
☽ △ ☉ **2:08 am**
☽ △ ☿ **4:04 am** 1:04 am
☽ □ ♂ **10:47 am** 7:47 am
☽ ☍ ♄ **11:41 am** 8:41 am
☽ □ ♀ **4:12 pm** 1:12 pm
☽ ⚹ ♅ **6:25 pm** 3:25 pm ☽
☽ △ ♃ **11:51 pm** 8:51 pm

11 WEDNESDAY
♂ □ ♄ **9:37 am** 6:37 am
♀ ⚻ ♅ **5:04 pm** 2:04 pm
☽ △ ♆ **7:45 pm** 4:45 pm

12 THURSDAY
☽ ☍ ♇ **4:13 am** 1:13 am
☽ □ ☉ **8:25 am** 5:25 am
☽ □ ☿ **1:33 pm** 10:33 am
☽ ⚻ ♄ **2:39 pm** 11:39 am
☽ ⚹ ♂ **3:52 pm** 12:52 pm
☽ □ ♅ **9:10 pm** 6:10 pm
☿ ⚹ ♄ **11:02 pm** 8:02 pm
☽ ⚹ ♀ 9:00 pm ☽

13 FRIDAY
☽ ⚹ ♀ **12:00 am** ☽
☽ □ ♃ **3:43 am** 12:43 am
☿ ⚺ ♂ **7:07 pm** 4:07 pm
☽ ⚻ ♆ **11:20 pm** 8:20 pm

14 SATURDAY
☽ ⚻ ♇ **8:10 am** 5:10 am
☽ ⚹ ☉ **4:34 pm** 1:34 pm

☽ △ ♄ **7:11 pm** 4:11 pm
☽ ⚺ ♂ **10:43 pm** 7:43 pm
☽ ⚹ ☿ 10:07 pm
☽ △ ♅ 10:28 pm ☽
♀ ⚺ ♃ 10:45 pm

15 SUNDAY
☽ ⚹ ☿ **1:07 am**
☽ △ ♅ **1:28 am** ☽ v/c
♀ ⚺ ♃ **1:45 am**
☿ ☍ ♅ **3:52 am** 12:52 am
☽ ⚹ ♃ **9:14 am** 6:14 am
☽ ⚺ ♀ **9:52 am** 6:52 am

16 MONDAY
☽ ☍ ♆ **4:32 am** 1:32 am
☉ ⚹ ♄ **7:13 am** 4:13 am
☽ △ ♇ **1:44 pm** 10:44 am
☽ □ ♄ 10:23 pm
☽ ⚺ ☉ 11:45 pm

17 TUESDAY
☽ □ ♄ **1:23 am**
☽ ⚺ ☉ **2:45 am**
♂ ⚻ ♅ **6:03 am** 3:03 am
☽ ⚻ ♅ **7:22 am** 4:22 am
☽ ☌ ♂ **7:27 am** 4:27 am ☽
☽ ⚺ ☿ **2:57 pm** 11:57 am
☽ ⚺ ♃ **4:29 pm** 1:29 pm
☽ ☌ ♀ **9:57 pm** 6:57 pm

18 WEDNESDAY
☿ ☌ ♃ **4:54 am** 1:54 am
☽ ⚻ ♆ **11:24 am** 8:24 am
☽ □ ♇ **9:02 pm** 6:02 pm

19 THURSDAY
☽ ⚹ ♄ **9:24 am** 6:24 am
☉ ☍ ♅ **1:35 pm** 10:35 am
☽ ☍ ♅ **3:04 pm** 12:04 pm
☽ ☌ ☉ **3:12 pm** 12:12 pm ☽
☽ ⚺ ♂ **6:16 pm** 3:16 pm
☽ ☌ ♃ 10:41 pm

20 FRIDAY
☽ ☌ ♃ **1:41 am**
☽ ☌ ☿ **7:23 am** 4:23 am
☽ ⚺ ♀ **12:35 pm** 9:35 am
☽ △ ♆ **8:14 pm** 5:14 pm

21 SATURDAY
☽ ⚹ ♇ **6:23 am** 3:23 am
☽ ⚺ ♄ **7:34 pm** 4:34 pm
☽ ⚻ ♅ 9:53 pm

22 SUNDAY
☽ ⚻ ♅ **12:53 am**
☽ ⚺ ☉ **6:23 am** 3:23 am
☽ ⚹ ♂ **7:35 am** 4:35 am ☽
☽ ⚺ ♃ **1:10 pm** 10:10 am
☽ ⚺ ☿ 11:56 pm

23 MONDAY
☽ ⚺ ☿ **2:56 am**
☽ ⚹ ♀ **6:14 am** 3:14 am
☽ □ ♆ **7:17 am** 4:17 am
♀ ⚻ ♆ **4:11 pm** 1:11 pm
☽ ⚺ ♇ **5:56 pm** 2:56 pm
☉ ⚺ ♂ **8:27 pm** 5:27 pm

24 TUESDAY
☽ ☌ ♄ **7:55 am** 4:55 am
☿ △ ♆ **11:55 am** 8:55 am
☽ △ ♅ **12:44 pm** 9:44 am ☽
☽ □ ♂ **11:14 pm** 8:14 pm
☽ ⚹ ☉ 9:08 pm
☽ ⚹ ♃ 11:42 pm

25 WEDNESDAY
☽ ⚹ ☉ **12:08 am**
☽ ⚹ ♃ **2:42 am**
☽ ⚹ ♆ **7:55 am** 4:55 am
☽ ⚹ ☿ 9:49 pm
☽ □ ♀ 11:06 pm

26 THURSDAY
☽ ⚹ ☿ **12:49 am**
☽ □ ♀ **2:06 am**
☽ ☌ ♇ **6:49 am** 3:49 am
☉ ☌ ♃ **2:09 pm** 11:09 am
☽ ⚺ ♄ **9:13 pm** 6:13 pm
☽ □ ♅ 10:22 pm ☽

27 FRIDAY
☽ □ ♅ **1:22 am** ☽
☽ △ ♂ **3:21 pm** 12:21 pm
☽ □ ♃ **4:30 pm** 1:30 pm
☽ □ ☉ **6:22 pm** 3:22 pm
♀ □ ♇ **11:21 pm** 8:21 pm
☿ ⚹ ♇ **11:25 pm** 8:25 pm
☿ ⚺ ♀ **11:42 pm** 8:42 pm

28 SATURDAY
☽ ⚺ ♆ **8:10 am** 5:10 am
☽ ⚺ ♇ **6:51 pm** 3:51 pm
☽ △ ♀ **9:02 pm** 6:02 pm
☽ □ ☿ **9:35 pm** 6:35 pm
♂ ⚺ ♃ 9:16 pm

29 SUNDAY
♂ ⚺ ♃ **12:16 am**
☽ ⚹ ♄ **9:01 am** 6:01 am
☽ ⚹ ♅ **12:22 pm** 9:22 am ☽

30 MONDAY
☽ △ ♃ **3:54 am** 12:54 am
☽ ⚻ ♂ **4:50 am** 1:50 am
☽ △ ☉ **9:34 am** 6:34 am
☽ ☌ ♆ **5:32 pm** 2:32 pm

31 TUESDAY
☽ ⚹ ♇ **3:38 am** 12:38 am
☽ ⚻ ♀ **11:28 am** 8:28 am
☽ △ ☿ **1:21 pm** 10:21 am
☽ □ ♄ **5:08 pm** 2:08 pm ☽
☽ ⚺ ♅ **7:41 pm** 4:41 pm

OCTOBER 2017

DATE	SID.TIME	SUN	MOON	NODE	MERCURY	VENUS	MARS	JUPITER	SATURN	URANUS	NEPTUNE	PLUTO	CERES	PALLAS	JUNO	VESTA	CHIRON
1 Su	0 39 40	8 ≏00 34	9 ≈ 51	23 ♋ 25	1 ≏ 46	13 ♍ 25	16 ♍ 14	27 ≏ 58	22 ♐ 15	27 ♈ 16 R	12 ♓ 10	16 ♑ 51	2 ♌ 21	12 ♉ 49	6 ♍ 13	6 ≏ 23	26 ♓ 02
2 M	0 43 36	8 59 34	22 20	23 25 R	3 35	14 39	16 52	28 11	22 18	27 14 R	12 09	16 51	2 42	12 49 R	6 24	6 54	25 59 R
3 T	0 47 33	9 58 35	5 ♓ 09	23 25	5 23	15 53	17 30	28 23	22 22	27 12	12 07	16 52	3 02	12 30	6 36	7 24	25 56
4 W	0 51 30	10 57 38	18 20	23 22	7 11	17 07	18 08	28 36	22 25	27 09	12 06	16 52	3 22	12 19	6 48	7 54	25 54
5 Th	0 55 26	11 56 43	1 ♈ 55	23 17	8 58	18 21	18 46	28 49	22 29	27 07	12 05	16 52	3 42	12 09	7 00	8 25	25 51
6 F	0 59 23	12 55 49	15 50	23 10	10 44	19 35	19 24	29 01	22 33	27 05	12 03	16 52	4 02	11 57	7 12	8 55	25 49
7 Sa	1 3 19	13 54 58	0 ♉ 02	23 02	12 30	20 49	20 02	29 14	22 36	27 02	12 02	16 52	4 22	11 45	7 25	9 26	25 46
8 Su	1 7 16	14 54 09	14 27	22 54	14 15	22 03	20 40	29 27	22 40	27 00	12 01	16 52	4 42	11 33	7 38	9 56	25 43
9 M	1 11 12	15 53 23	28 57	22 46	15 59	23 17	21 18	29 40	22 44	26 55	11 59	16 53	5 01	11 20	7 51	10 27	25 41
10 T	1 15 9	16 52 38	13 ♊ 26	22 40	17 43	24 31	21 56	29 53	22 49	26 55	11 58	16 53	5 20	11 07	8 04	10 57	25 38
11 W	1 19 5	17 51 56	27 50	22 36	19 26	25 45	22 34	0 ♏ 06	22 53	26 53	11 57	16 53	5 40	10 53	8 18	11 28	25 36
12 Th	1 23 2	18 51 17	12 ♋ 04	22 35 D	21 08	27 00	23 12	0 19	22 57	26 50	11 55	16 54	5 59	10 39	8 32	11 59	25 33
13 F	1 26 59	19 50 39	26 07	22 35	22 49	28 14	23 49	0 32	23 01	26 48	11 54	16 54	6 18	10 24	8 46	12 29	25 31
14 Sa	1 30 55	20 50 04	9 ♌ 58	22 35 R	24 30	29 28	24 27	0 45	23 06	26 45	11 53	16 55	6 36	10 09	9 00	13 00	25 29
15 Su	1 34 52	21 49 31	23 38	22 36	26 10	0 ≏ 43	25 05	0 58	23 10	26 41	11 52	16 55	6 55	9 54	9 15	13 30	25 26
16 M	1 38 48	22 49 01	7 ♍ 06	22 35	27 49	1 57	25 43	1 11	23 15	26 41	11 51	16 56	7 13	9 38	9 29	14 01	25 24
17 T	1 42 45	23 48 33	20 23	22 32	29 27	3 12	26 21	1 24	23 19	26 38	11 50	16 56	7 32	9 22	9 44	14 32	25 22
18 W	1 46 41	24 48 07	3 ≏ 29	22 26	1 ♏ 05	4 26	26 59	1 37	23 24	26 36	11 48	16 57	7 50	9 05	9 59	15 02	25 19
19 Th	1 50 38	25 47 43	16 24	22 17	2 43	5 41	27 37	1 50	23 29	26 33	11 47	16 57	8 08	8 48	10 15	15 33	25 17
20 F	1 54 34	26 47 21	29 07	22 06	4 19	6 56	28 15	2 03	23 34	26 31	11 46	16 58	8 26	8 31	10 30	16 04	25 15
21 Sa	1 58 31	27 47 01	11 ♏ 38	21 54	5 55	8 10	28 53	2 16	23 38	26 28	11 45	16 59	8 43	8 13	10 46	16 34	25 13
22 Su	2 2 28	28 46 43	23 57	21 41	7 30	9 25	29 31	2 29	23 43	26 26	11 44	16 59	9 01	7 56	11 02	17 05	25 10
23 M	2 6 24	29 46 27	6 ♐ 04	21 30	9 05	10 40	0 ≏ 09	2 42	23 48	26 23	11 43	17 00	9 18	7 37	11 18	17 36	25 08
24 T	2 10 21	0 ♏46 13	18 02	21 20	10 40	11 54	0 47	2 55	23 54	26 19	11 41	17 01	9 35	7 19	11 35	18 07	25 06
25 W	2 14 17	1 46 00	29 54	21 13	12 13	13 09	1 25	3 08	23 59	26 19	11 41	17 02	9 52	7 00	11 51	18 37	25 04
26 Th	2 18 14	2 45 49	11 ♑ 43	21 08	13 46	14 24	2 02	3 21	24 04	26 16	11 41	17 02	10 08	6 42	12 08	19 08	25 02
27 F	2 22 10	3 45 41	23 33	21 06 D	15 19	15 39	2 40	3 34	24 09	26 14	11 40	17 03	10 25	6 23	12 25	19 38	25 00
28 Sa	2 26 7	4 45 33	5 ≈ 31	21 06	16 51	16 54	3 18	3 47	24 15	26 11	11 39	17 04	10 41	6 03	12 42	20 10	24 58
29 Su	2 30 3	5 45 28	17 40	21 06 R	18 23	18 09	3 56	4 00	24 20	26 09	11 38	17 05	10 57	5 44	12 59	20 40	24 56
30 M	2 34 0	6 45 24	0 ♓ 07	21 06	19 54	19 23	4 34	4 14	24 25	26 06	11 37	17 06	11 13	5 25	13 17	21 11	24 54
31 T	2 37 57	7 45 21	12 57	21 04	21 24	20 38	5 12	4 27	24 31	26 04	11 36	17 07	11 28	5 05	13 34	21 42	24 53

EPHEMERIS CALCULATED FOR 12 MIDNIGHT GREENWICH MEAN TIME. ALL OTHER DATA AND FACING ASPECTARIAN PAGE IN **EASTERN TIME (BOLD)** AND PACIFIC TIME (REGULAR).

NOVEMBER 2017

1 WEDNESDAY
11:07 am 8:07 am
1:42 am 10:42 am
7:40 am 4:40 pm
10:49 am 10:16 pm

2 THURSDAY
1:16 am
8:18 am 5:18 am
8:30 am 5:30 pm
9:02 am 6:02 pm
9:09 am 6:09 pm
11:03 am 8:03 pm
11:17 am 8:17 pm

3 FRIDAY
4:31 am 1:31 am
2:26 pm 11:26 am
3:23 pm 12:23 pm
6:22 pm 3:22 pm
9:42 pm
10:23 pm

4 SATURDAY
12:42 am
1:02 am
1:23 am
6:49 am
10:24 am 7:24 am

5 SUNDAY
1:56 am
4:29 am 1:29 am
2:36 am 11:36 am
7:53 pm
11:57 pm 8:57 pm

6 MONDAY
4:08 am 1:08 am
9:05 am 6:05 am
9:57 pm 6:57 pm
10:55 pm 7:55 pm

7 TUESDAY
5:40 am 2:40 pm
10:02 am 7:02 am
3:47 pm 12:47 pm
10:39 pm 7:39 pm
9:36 pm

8 WEDNESDAY
12:36 am
8:34 am 5:34 am
10:06 am 7:06 am
11:43 pm 8:43 pm
9:14 pm

9 THURSDAY
12:14 am
7:12 am 4:12 am

10 FRIDAY
12:15 pm 9:15 am
5:36 pm 2:36 pm
6:46 pm 3:46 pm
7:10 pm 4:10 pm

11 SATURDAY
3:12 am 12:12 am
3:35 am 12:35 am
7:07 am 4:07 am
1:17 pm 10:17 am
3:36 pm 12:36 pm

12 SUNDAY
3:55 am 12:55 am
3:55 am 12:55 am
4:45 am 1:45 am
10:07 pm 7:07 pm
9:26 pm

13 MONDAY
12:26 am
4:31 am 1:31 am
8:23 am 5:23 am
11:29 am 8:29 am
7:05 pm 4:05 pm
10:55 pm

14 TUESDAY
1:55 am
3:16 am 12:16 am
6:10 pm 3:10 pm
10:45 pm 7:45 pm
5:48 pm 2:48 pm

15 WEDNESDAY
8:40 am 5:40 am
11:20 am 8:20 am
12:59 pm 9:59 am
6:37 pm 3:37 pm
10:09 pm 7:09 pm

16 THURSDAY
3:12 am 12:12 am
3:07 pm 12:07 pm
6:36 pm 3:36 pm
7:50 pm 4:50 pm

17 FRIDAY
1:33 am
3:17 am 12:17 am
5:04 am 6:04 am
11:04 am 8:10 am
1:15 pm 10:15 am

18 SATURDAY
4:51 am 1:51 am
6:16 am 3:48 am
6:48 am 3:48 am
7:50 am 4:50 am
8:03 am 5:03 am

19 SUNDAY
7:14 am 4:14 am
7:15 am 4:15 am
12:51 pm 9:51 am
9:37 pm 6:37 pm
10:01 pm
10:58 pm

20 MONDAY
1:01 am
1:58 am
5:37 am 2:37 am
4:43 pm 1:43 pm
7:26 pm 4:26 pm
9:23 pm

21 TUESDAY
12:23 am
6:29 am 3:29 am
8:57 pm 5:57 pm
10:33 pm

22 WEDNESDAY
1:33 am
2:00 am 11:04 am
5:41 pm 2:41 pm
6:16 pm 3:16 pm
9:58 pm

23 THURSDAY
12:58 am
4:10 am 1:10 am
5:33 am 2:33 am

24 FRIDAY
10:56 am 7:56 am
2:23 pm 11:23 am
11:44 pm

25 SATURDAY
2:44 am
5:56 am 2:56 am
10:05 am 7:05 am
1:12 pm 10:12 am
5:35 pm 2:35 pm
6:32 pm 3:32 pm
9:37 pm 6:37 pm

26 SUNDAY
12:03 am 9:03 pm
10:52 pm 7:52 pm
10:08 pm

27 MONDAY
1:08 am
6:48 am 3:48 am
12:54 pm 9:54 am
10:37 pm 7:37 pm
10:58 pm
11:33 pm

28 TUESDAY
1:58 am
2:33 am
4:41 am 1:41 am
6:55 am 3:55 am

23 WEDNESDAY
12:22 am
6:11 am 3:11 am
6:41 am 3:41 am
7:57 am 4:57 am
6:53 pm 3:53 pm
10:00 pm

30 THURSDAY
1:00 am
6:13 am 3:13 am
7:16 am 4:16 am
11:50 am 8:50 am
1:37 pm 10:37 pm
2:25 pm 11:25 pm

9:01 am 6:01 am
7:05 pm 4:05 pm

7:09 am 4:09 am
9:22 am

Eastern time in **bold** type
Pacific time in medium type

NOVEMBER 2017

DATE	SID. TIME	SUN	MOON	NODE	MERCURY	VENUS	MARS	JUPITER	SATURN	URANUS	NEPTUNE	PLUTO	CERES	PALLAS	JUNO	VESTA	CHIRON
1 W	2 41 53	8 ♏ 45 20	26 ♓ 13	21 ♌ 00	22 ♏ 54	21 ♎ 53	5 ♎ 50	4 ♏ 40	24 ♐ 37	26 ♈ 02 ℞	11 ♓ 36 ℞	17 ♑ 08	11 ♌ 44	4 ♏ 46	13 ♑ 52	22 ♎ 13	24 ♓ 51 ℞
2 Th	2 45 50	9 45 21	9 ♈ 56	20 53 ℞	24 24	23 08	6 28	4 53	24 42	25 59 ℞	11 35 ℞	17 09	11 59	4 26 ℞	14 10	22 44	24 49 ℞
3 F	2 49 46	10 45 24	24 07	20 44	25 53	24 23	7 05	5 06	24 48	25 57	11 34	17 10	12 14	4 06	14 28	23 14	24 47
4 Sa	2 53 43	11 45 28	8 ♉ 41	20 32	27 22	25 38	7 43	5 19	24 54	25 55	11 34	17 11	12 28	3 47	14 47	23 45	24 46
5 Su	2 57 39	12 45 34	23 30	20 21	28 50	26 53	8 21	5 32	24 59	25 52	11 33	17 12	12 43	3 27	15 05	24 16	24 44
6 M	3 1 36	13 45 43	8 ♊ 27	20 10	0 ♐ 17	28 08	8 59	5 45	25 05	25 50	11 33	17 13	12 57	3 08	15 24	24 47	24 42
7 T	3 5 32	14 45 53	23 22	20 00	1 44	29 24	9 37	5 58	25 11	25 48	11 32	17 14	13 11	2 48	15 43	25 17	24 41
8 W	3 9 29	15 46 05	8 ♋ 07	19 54	3 10	0 ♏ 39	10 15	6 11	25 17	25 45	11 32	17 15	13 25	2 29	16 02	25 48	24 39
9 Th	3 13 26	16 46 19	22 36	19 50	4 36	1 54	10 53	6 24	25 23	25 43	11 31	17 16	13 38	2 10	16 21	26 19	24 38
10 F	3 17 22	17 46 35	6 ♌ 45	19 49	6 01	3 09	11 30	6 37	25 29	25 41	11 31	17 18	13 51	1 51	16 40	26 50	24 37
11 Sa	3 21 19	18 46 54	20 34	19 49	7 25	4 24	12 08	6 50	25 35	25 39	11 30	17 19	14 04	1 32	16 59	27 21	24 35
12 Su	3 25 15	19 47 14	4 ♍ 05	19 49	8 49	5 39	12 46	7 03	25 42	25 37	11 30	17 20	14 17	1 14	17 19	27 51	24 34
13 M	3 29 12	20 47 36	17 19	19 47	10 12	6 55	13 24	7 16	25 48	25 34	11 30	17 21	14 29	0 55	17 39	28 22	24 33
14 T	3 33 8	21 48 00	0 ♎ 18	19 43	11 33	8 10	14 02	7 29	25 54	25 32	11 29	17 23	14 41	0 37	17 59	28 53	24 32
15 W	3 37 5	22 48 26	13 05	19 35	12 54	9 25	14 40	7 42	26 00	25 30	11 29	17 24	14 53	0 19	18 19	29 24	24 31
16 Th	3 41 1	23 48 53	25 41	19 25	14 14	10 40	15 17	7 55	26 07	25 28	11 29	17 25	15 05	0 02	18 39	29 55	24 30
17 F	3 44 58	24 49 23	8 ♏ 07	19 12	15 32	11 56	15 55	8 08	26 13	25 26	11 28	17 27	15 16	29 ♍ 45	18 59	0 ♏ 25	24 29
18 Sa	3 48 54	25 49 54	20 18	18 58	16 48	13 11	16 33	8 20	26 19	25 24	11 28	17 28	15 27	29 29	19 20	0 56	24 27
19 Su	3 52 51	26 50 27	2 ♐ 32	18 43	18 04	14 26	17 11	8 33	26 26	25 22	11 28	17 29	15 37	29 12	19 40	1 27	24 26
20 M	3 56 48	27 51 01	14 32	18 30	19 17	15 42	17 49	8 46	26 32	25 20	11 28	17 31	15 48	28 56	20 01	1 58	24 26
21 T	4 0 44	28 51 36	26 26	18 18	20 28	16 57	18 27	8 59	26 39	25 18	11 28 D	17 32	15 58	28 40	20 22	2 28	24 25
22 W	4 4 41	29 52 14	8 ♑ 15	18 09	21 36	18 12	19 04	9 11	26 45	25 16	11 28	17 34	16 07	28 25	20 43	2 59	24 24
23 Th	4 8 37	0 ♐ 52 52	20 02	18 03	22 42	19 28	19 42	9 24	26 52	25 14	11 28	17 35	16 17	28 11	21 04	3 30	24 23
24 F	4 12 34	1 53 31	1 ♒ 51	17 59	23 44	20 43	20 20	9 37	26 59	25 13	11 28	17 37	16 26	27 57	21 25	4 00	24 23
25 Sa	4 16 30	2 54 12	13 46	17 58 D	24 44	21 59	20 58	9 49	27 05	25 11	11 28	17 38	16 34	27 43	21 46	4 31	24 22
26 Su	4 20 27	3 54 54	25 53	17 58 ℞	25 39	23 14	21 35	10 02	27 12	25 09	11 28	17 40	16 43	27 30	22 08	5 02	24 21
27 M	4 24 24	4 55 37	8 ♓ 15	17 58	26 30	24 29	22 13	10 14	27 19	25 07	11 28	17 42	16 51	27 17	22 29	5 32	24 21
28 T	4 28 20	5 56 20	20 59	17 57	27 15	25 45	22 51	10 27	27 25	25 06	11 28	17 43	16 58	27 05	22 51	6 03	24 21
29 W	4 32 17	6 57 05	4 ♈ 10	17 54	27 55	27 00	23 29	10 39	27 32	25 04	11 29	17 45	17 06	26 54	23 13	6 34	24 20
30 Th	4 36 13	7 57 51	17 50	17 49	28 27	28 16	24 06	10 52	27 39	25 02	11 29	17 47	17 13	26 43	23 35	7 04	24 20

EPHEMERIS CALCULATED FOR 12 MIDNIGHT GREENWICH MEAN TIME. ALL OTHER DATA AND FACING ASPECTARIAN PAGE IN **EASTERN TIME (BOLD)** AND PACIFIC TIME (REGULAR).

DECEMBER 2017

☽ Last Aspect day	ET / hr:mn / PT		asp	☽ Ingress sign	day	ET / hr:mn / PT	
1	**8:53 pm**	5:53 pm	△♇	♊	2	**4:21 pm**	1:21 pm
4	**2:13 pm**	11:13 am	☍♂	♋	4	**3:37 pm**	12:37 pm
6	**12:56 pm**	9:56 am	□♂	♌	6	**3:37 pm**	12:37 pm
8	**5:40 pm**	2:40 pm	⚹♂	♍	8	**6:09 pm**	3:09 pm
10	**10:02 pm**	7:02 pm	□♄	♎	10		9:01 pm
10	**10:02 pm**	7:02 pm	□♄	♎	11	**12:01 am**	
13	**7:27 am**	4:27 am	⚹♄	♏	13	**8:59 am**	5:59 am
14	**8:42 pm**	5:42 pm	⚹♇	♐	15	**8:07 pm**	5:07 pm
18	**8:10 am**	5:10 am	☌♄	♑	18	**8:33 am**	5:33 am
20	**10:37 am**	7:37 am	□♅	♒	20	**9:29 pm**	6:29 pm
23	**5:13 am**	2:13 am	⚹♀	♓	23	**9:42 am**	6:42 am
24	**9:48 pm**	6:48 pm	⚹♇	♈	25	**7:27 pm**	4:27 pm
27	**3:57 pm**	12:57 pm	☌♅	♉	27		10:23 pm
27	**3:57 pm**	12:57 pm	☌♅	♉	28	**1:23 am**	
29	**9:01 am**	6:01 am	△♇	♊	30	**3:31 am**	12:31 am
31	**6:38 pm**	3:38 pm	⚹♅	♋	1/1	**3:10 am**	12:10 am

☽ Phases & Eclipses phase	day	ET / hr:mn / PT	
Full Moon	3	**10:47 am**	7:47 am
4th Quarter	9		11:51 pm
4th Quarter	10	**2:51 am**	
New Moon	17		10:30 pm
New Moon	18	**1:30 am**	
2nd Quarter	26	**4:20 am**	1:20 am

Planet Ingress		day	ET / hr:mn / PT	
♀	♐	1	**4:14 am**	1:14 am
♂	♏	9	**3:59 am**	12:59 am
⚵	♒	16	**2:18 pm**	11:18 am
♄	♑	19	**11:49 pm**	8:49 pm
☉	♑	21	**11:28 am**	8:28 am
♀	♑	24		9:26 pm
♀	♑	25	**12:26 am**	

Planetary Motion		day	ET / hr:mn / PT	
☿	℞	2		11:34 pm
☿	℞	3	**2:34 am**	
⚷	D	5	**4:47 am**	1:47 am
⚳	℞	16	**5:28 pm**	2:28 pm
⚴	D	17	**6:36 pm**	3:36 pm
☿	D	22	**8:51 pm**	5:51 pm

1 FRIDAY
♂ ☍ ♅ **5:05 am** 2:05 am
☽ ⚻ ☉ **7:21 am** 4:21 am
☽ ☍ ♃ **10:07 am** 7:07 am
☽ ⚹ ♆ **10:36 am** 7:36 am
☽ △ ♇ **8:53 pm** 5:53 pm☽

2 SATURDAY
☽ ⚺ ♅ **8:21 am** 5:21 am
☽ ⚻ ♂ **9:35 am** 6:35 am
☽ ⚻ ♄ **1:07 pm** 10:07 am
☽ ⚻ ☿ **3:13 pm** 12:13 pm
☽ ☍ ♀ **7:37 pm** 4:37 pm
♃ △ ♆ **9:19 pm** 6:19 pm

3 SUNDAY
☉ □ ♆ **6:44 am** 3:44 am
☉ ⚺ ♃ **9:01 am** 6:01 am
☽ □ ♆ **10:31 am** 7:31 am
☽ ⚻ ♃ **10:41 am** 7:41 am
☽ ☍ ☉ **10:47 am** 7:47 am
☽ ⚻ ♇ **8:34 pm** 5:34 pm

4 MONDAY
☽ ⚹ ♅ **7:37 am** 4:37 am
☽ △ ♂ **10:57 am** 7:57 am
☽ ☍ ♄ **12:46 pm** 9:46 am
☽ ☍ ☿ **2:13 pm** 11:13 am☽
☽ ⚻ ♀ **11:08 pm** 8:08 pm

5 TUESDAY
☽ △ ♆ **9:50 am** 6:50 am
☽ △ ♃ **10:38 am** 7:38 am
☽ ⚻ ☉ **1:30 pm** 10:30 am
☽ ☍ ♇ **8:07 pm** 5:07 pm

6 WEDNESDAY
☿ ☌ ♄ **7:05 am** 4:05 am
☽ □ ♅ **7:17 am** 4:17 am
☿ ⚹ ♂ **10:58 am** 7:58 am
☽ ⚻ ☿ **12:46 pm** 9:46 am
☽ □ ♂ **12:56 pm** 9:56 am☽
☽ ⚻ ♄ **1:03 pm** 10:03 am
♂ ⚹ ♄ **4:21 pm** 1:21 pm

7 THURSDAY
☽ △ ♀ **4:01 am** 1:01 am
☽ ⚻ ♆ **10:40 am** 7:40 am
☽ □ ♃ **12:10 pm** 9:10 am
☽ △ ☉ **6:15 pm** 3:15 pm
☽ ⚻ ♇ **9:34 pm** 6:34 pm

8 FRIDAY
☽ △ ♅ **9:13 am** 6:13 am
☽ △ ☿ **12:21 pm** 9:21 am
☽ △ ♄ **3:50 pm** 12:50 pm
☽ ⚹ ♂ **5:40 pm** 2:40 pm☽

9 SATURDAY
☽ □ ♀ **12:37 pm** 9:37 am
☽ ☍ ♆ **2:29 pm** 11:29 am
☽ ⚹ ♃ **4:50 pm** 1:50 pm
☉ ⚺ ♇ **5:58 pm** 2:58 pm
☽ △ ♇ 11:12 pm
☽ □ ☉ 11:51 pm

10 SUNDAY
☽ △ ♇ **2:12 am**
☽ □ ☉ **2:51 am**
☿ △ ♅ **4:29 am** 1:29 am
♀ □ ♆ **8:47 am** 5:47 am
☽ □ ☿ **1:34 pm** 10:34 am
☽ ⚻ ♅ **2:25 pm** 11:25 am
☽ □ ♄ **10:02 pm** 7:02 pm☽
☽ ⚺ ♂ 11:16 pm

11 MONDAY
☽ ⚺ ♂ **2:16 am**
♀ ⚺ ♃ **5:16 pm** 2:16 pm
☽ ⚻ ♆ **9:40 pm** 6:40 pm
☽ ⚺ ♃ 9:59 pm
☽ ⚹ ♀ 10:42 pm

12 TUESDAY
☽ ⚺ ♃ **12:59 am**
☽ ⚹ ♀ **1:42 am**
☽ □ ♇ **10:09 am** 7:09 am
☽ ⚹ ☉ **3:39 pm** 12:39 pm
☽ ⚹ ☿ **4:32 pm** 1:32 pm
☉ ☌ ☿ **8:49 pm** 5:49 pm
☽ ☍ ♅ **10:49 pm** 7:49 pm

13 WEDNESDAY
☽ ⚹ ♄ **7:27 am** 4:27 am☽
☽ ☌ ♂ **2:23 pm** 11:23 am

14 THURSDAY
☽ △ ♆ **7:39 am** 4:39 am
☽ ☌ ♃ **11:58 am** 8:58 am
☽ ⚺ ♀ **6:29 pm** 3:29 pm
☽ ⚹ ♇ **8:42 pm** 5:42 pm☽
☽ ⚺ ☿ **9:15 pm** 6:15 pm
☿ ⚺ ♇ 11:16 pm

15 FRIDAY
☿ ⚺ ♇ **2:16 am**
☽ ⚺ ☉ **7:37 am** 4:37 am
☿ ☌ ♀ **9:09 am** 6:09 am
☽ ⚻ ♅ **9:34 am** 6:34 am
♀ ⚺ ♇ **4:23 pm** 1:23 pm
☽ ⚺ ♄ **7:08 pm** 4:08 pm

16 SATURDAY
☽ ⚺ ♂ **4:57 am** 1:57 am
☉ △ ♅ **6:28 am** 3:28 am
☽ □ ♆ **7:27 pm** 4:27 pm
☽ ⚺ ♃ 9:47 pm

17 SUNDAY
☽ ⚺ ♃ **12:47 am**
☽ ☌ ☿ **3:56 am** 12:56 am
☽ ⚺ ♇ **8:53 am** 5:53 am
☽ ☌ ♀ **1:34 pm** 10:34 am
☽ △ ♅ **9:46 pm** 6:46 pm
☽ ☌ ☉ 10:30 pm

18 MONDAY
☽ ☌ ☉ **1:30 am**
☽ ☌ ♄ **8:10 am** 5:10 am☽
☿ ⚺ ♃ **2:34 pm** 11:34 am
☽ ⚹ ♂ **8:55 pm** 5:55 pm

19 TUESDAY
☽ ⚹ ♆ **8:16 am** 5:16 am
☽ ⚺ ☿ **12:54 pm** 9:54 am
☽ ⚹ ♃ **2:33 pm** 11:33 am
☽ ☌ ♇ **9:54 pm** 6:54 pm

20 WEDNESDAY
☽ ⚺ ♀ **9:42 am** 6:42 am
☽ □ ♅ **10:37 am** 7:37 am☽
♀ △ ♅ **6:13 pm** 3:13 pm
☽ ⚺ ☉ **8:10 pm** 5:10 pm
☽ ⚺ ♄ **9:42 pm** 6:42 pm

21 THURSDAY
☽ □ ♂ **1:13 pm** 10:13 am
☉ ☌ ♄ **4:08 pm** 1:08 pm
☽ ⚺ ♆ **9:10 pm** 6:10 pm
☽ ⚹ ☿ **11:54 pm** 8:54 pm

22 FRIDAY
☽ □ ♃ **4:16 am** 1:16 am
☽ ⚺ ♇ **10:45 am** 7:45 am
☽ ⚹ ♅ **11:01 pm** 8:01 pm

23 SATURDAY
☽ ⚹ ♀ **5:13 am** 2:13 am☽
☽ ⚹ ♄ **10:30 am** 7:30 am
☽ ⚹ ☉ **1:55 pm** 10:55 am

24 SUNDAY
☽ △ ♂ **4:09 am** 1:09 am
☽ ☌ ♆ **8:43 am** 5:43 am
☽ □ ☿ **11:31 am** 8:31 am
☽ △ ♃ **4:20 pm** 1:20 pm
☽ ⚹ ♇ **9:48 pm** 6:48 pm☽

25 MONDAY
☽ ⚺ ♅ **9:18 am** 6:18 am
♀ ☌ ♄ **12:55 pm** 9:55 am
☽ □ ♄ **8:44 pm** 5:44 pm
☽ □ ♀ **9:30 pm** 6:30 pm

26 TUESDAY
☽ □ ☉ **4:20 am** 1:20 am
☽ ⚻ ♂ **3:37 pm** 12:37 pm
☽ ⚺ ♆ **5:09 pm** 2:09 pm
☽ △ ☿ **9:26 pm** 6:26 pm
☽ ⚻ ♃ 9:56 pm

27 WEDNESDAY
☽ ⚻ ♃ **12:56 am**
☽ □ ♇ **5:25 am** 2:25 am
☽ ☌ ♅ **3:57 pm** 12:57 pm☽
♂ △ ♆ 9:59 pm

28 THURSDAY
♂ △ ♆ **12:59 am**
☽ △ ♄ **3:03 am** 12:03 am
☽ △ ♀ **8:37 am** 5:37 am
☽ △ ☉ **1:47 pm** 10:47 am
☽ ⚹ ♆ **9:35 pm** 6:35 pm
☽ ☍ ♂ **10:29 pm** 7:29 pm

29 FRIDAY
☽ ⚻ ☿ **3:59 am** 12:59 am
☽ ☍ ♃ **5:22 am** 2:22 am
☽ △ ♇ **9:01 am** 6:01 am☽
☽ ⚺ ♅ **6:41 pm** 3:41 pm

30 SATURDAY
☽ ⚻ ♄ **5:28 am** 2:28 am
☿ ⚺ ♃ **10:09 am** 7:09 am
☽ ⚻ ♀ **2:52 pm** 11:52 am
☽ ⚻ ☉ **6:45 pm** 3:45 pm
☽ □ ♆ **10:35 pm** 7:35 pm
☽ ⚻ ♂ 10:29 pm

31 SUNDAY
☽ ⚻ ♂ **1:29 am**
☽ ⚻ ♃ **6:27 am** 3:27 am
☽ ☍ ☿ **7:29 am** 4:29 am
☽ ⚻ ♇ **9:29 am** 6:29 am
☽ ⚹ ♅ **6:38 pm** 3:38 pm☽

Eastern time in bold type
Pacific time in medium type

DECEMBER 2017

DATE	SID.TIME	SUN	MOON	NODE	MERCURY	VENUS	MARS	JUPITER	SATURN	URANUS	NEPTUNE	PLUTO	CERES	PALLAS	JUNO	VESTA	CHIRON
1 F	4 40 10	8 ♐ 58 38	2 ♉ 01	17 ♌ 41	28 ♐ 53	29 ♏, 31	24 ♎ 44	11 ♏ 04	27 ♐ 46	25 ♈ 01	11 ♓ 29	17 ♑ 48	17 ♌ 19	26 ♍ 32	23 ♑ 57	7 ♏, 35	24 ♓ 20
2 Sa	4 44 6	9 59 26	16 40	17 ♌ 31 ℞	29 10	0 ♐ 46	25 22	11 16	27 53	24 ♈ 59 ℞	11 29	17 50	17 25	26 ♍ 22 ℞	24 19	8 05	24 ♓ 19 ℞
3 Su	4 48 3	11 00 15	1 ♊ 40	17 20	29 ♐ 18 ℞	2 02	26 00	11 29	27 59	24 58	11 30	17 52	17 31	26 13	24 42	8 36	24 19
4 M	4 51 59	12 01 05	16 54	17 10	29 16	3 17	26 37	11 41	28 06	24 56	11 30	17 53	17 37	26 04	25 04	9 06	24 19
5 T	4 55 56	13 01 56	2 ♋ 09	17 01	29 03	4 33	27 15	11 53	28 13	24 55	11 31	17 55	17 42	25 56	25 26	9 37	24 19 D
6 W	4 59 53	14 02 48	17 15	16 56	28 40	5 48	27 53	12 05	28 20	24 53	11 31	17 57	17 47	25 49	25 49	10 07	24 19
7 Th	5 3 49	15 03 42	2 ♌ 04	16 53	28 05	7 04	28 30	12 17	28 27	24 52	11 32	17 59	17 51	25 42	26 12	10 38	24 19
8 F	5 7 46	16 04 36	16 29	16 52	27 19	8 19	29 08	12 29	28 34	24 51	11 32	18 00	17 55	25 36	26 35	11 08	24 19
9 Sa	5 11 42	17 05 32	0 ♍ 30	16 53	26 22	9 35	29 46	12 41	28 41	24 50	11 33	18 02	17 58	25 30	26 58	11 38	24 19
10 Su	5 15 39	18 06 30	14 05	16 53 ℞	25 16	10 50	0 ♏, 24	12 53	28 48	24 48	11 33	18 04	18 02	25 25	27 21	12 09	24 20
11 M	5 19 35	19 07 28	27 17	16 53	24 02	12 06	1 01	13 05	28 55	24 47	11 34	18 06	18 04	25 20	27 44	12 39	24 20
12 T	5 23 32	20 08 27	10 ♎ 01	16 51	22 43	13 21	1 39	13 17	29 02	24 46	11 34	18 08	18 07	25 16	28 07	13 10	24 20
13 W	5 27 28	21 09 28	22 46	16 48	21 30	14 37	2 17	13 28	29 09	24 45	11 35	18 09	18 08	25 13	28 30	13 40	24 21
14 Th	5 31 25	22 10 30	5 ♏ 12	16 39	19 58	15 52	2 54	13 40	29 16	24 44	11 36	18 11	18 10	25 10	28 54	14 10	24 21
15 F	5 35 22	23 11 32	17 22	16 30	18 37	17 08	3 32	13 51	29 23	24 43	11 37	18 13	18 11	25 08	29 17	14 40	24 21
16 Sa	5 39 18	24 12 36	29 26	16 20	17 22	18 23	4 10	14 03	29 30	24 42	11 37	18 15	18 ♌ 12 ℞	25 07	29 41	15 10	24 22
17 Su	5 43 15	25 13 40	11 ♐ 25	16 ♌ 09	16 14	19 39	4 47	14 14	29 37	24 41	11 38	18 17	18 12	25 06 D	0 ♒ 05	15 41	24 23
18 M	5 47 11	26 14 45	23 18	15 59	15 15	20 54	5 25	14 26	29 44	24 40	11 39	18 19	18 11	25 05	0 28	16 11	24 23
19 T	5 51 8	27 15 51	5 ♑ 08	15 51	14 27	22 10	6 02	14 37	29 51	24 40	11 40	18 21	18 11	25 06	0 52	16 41	24 24
20 W	5 55 4	28 16 57	16 57	15 44	13 49	23 25	6 40	14 48	29 59	24 39	11 41	18 23	18 10	25 07	1 16	17 11	24 25
21 Th	5 59 1	29 18 04	28 46	15 40	13 22	24 41	7 18	14 59	0 ♑ 06	24 38	11 42	18 25	18 08	25 08	1 40	17 41	24 25
22 F	6 2 57	0 ♑ 19 11	10 ♒ 38	15 38 D	13 06	25 56	7 55	15 10	0 13	24 38	11 43	18 27	18 06	25 10	2 05	18 11	24 26
23 Sa	6 6 54	1 20 19	22 36	15 39	13 00 D	27 12	8 33	15 21	0 20	24 37	11 44	18 29	18 04	25 13	2 29	18 41	24 27
24 Su	6 10 51	2 21 26	4 ♓ 44	15 40	13 04	28 27	9 10	15 32	0 27	24 37	11 45	18 31	18 01	25 16	2 53	19 11	24 28
25 M	6 14 47	3 22 34	17 05	15 41	13 17	29 43	9 48	15 43	0 34	24 36	11 46	18 33	17 58	25 20	3 18	19 40	24 29
26 T	6 18 44	4 23 42	29 46	15 42 ℞	13 38	0 ♑ 58	10 25	15 54	0 41	24 36	11 47	18 35	17 54	25 25	3 42	20 10	24 30
27 W	6 22 40	5 24 50	12 ♈ 49	15 42	14 07	2 14	11 03	16 04	0 48	24 35	11 48	18 37	17 50	25 29	4 07	20 40	24 31
28 Th	6 26 37	6 25 57	26 20	15 40	14 42	3 29	11 40	16 15	0 55	24 35	11 49	18 39	17 45	25 35	4 31	21 10	24 33
29 F	6 30 33	7 27 05	10 ♉ 19	15 37	15 24	4 45	12 18	16 25	1 02	24 35	11 50	18 41	17 40	25 41	4 56	21 39	24 34
30 Sa	6 34 30	8 28 13	24 46	15 32	16 10	6 00	12 55	16 36	1 09	24 35	11 52	18 43	17 35	25 47	5 21	22 09	24 34
31 Su	6 38 26	9 29 21	9 ♊ 38	15 26	17 02	7 16	13 33	16 46	1 16	24 34	11 53	18 45	17 29	25 54	5 46	22 38	24 37

EPHEMERIS CALCULATED FOR 12 MIDNIGHT GREENWICH MEAN TIME. ALL OTHER DATA AND FACING ASPECTARIAN PAGE IN **EASTERN TIME (BOLD)** AND PACIFIC TIME (REGULAR).

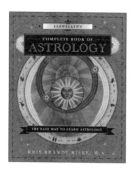

Notes

Notes

Notes